Mobile 3D Graphics
with OpenGL ES and M3G

Mobile 3D Graphics
with OpenGL ES and M3G

Kari Pulli

Tomi Aarnio

Ville Miettinen

Kimmo Roimela

Jani Vaarala

ELSEVIER

AMSTERDAM • BOSTON • HEIDELBERG • LONDON
NEW YORK • OXFORD • PARIS • SAN DIEGO
SAN FRANCISCO • SINGAPORE • SYDNEY • TOKYO

Morgan Kaufmann is an imprint of Elsevier

MORGAN KAUFMANN PUBLISHERS

Acquisitions Editor	Tiffany Gasbarrini
Publishing Services Manager	George Morrison
Senior Production Editor	Paul Gottehrer
Cover Design	Eric DeCicco
Composition	diacriTech
Interior printer	Maple-Vail Book Manufacturing Group
Cover printer	Phoenix Color Corp.

Morgan Kaufmann Publishers is an imprint of Elsevier.
30 Corporate Drive, Suite 400, Burlington, MA 01803, USA

This book is printed on acid-free paper.

Library of Congress Cataloging-in-Publication Data
Application submitted

ISBN: 978-0-12-373727-4

For information on all Morgan Kaufmann publications,
visit our Web site at *www.mkp.com* or *www.books.elsevier.com*

Printed in the United States of America
07 08 09 10 11   5 4 3 2 1

Contents

PART II   OPENGL ES AND EGL

Preface

The mobile phone is by far the most widely available device with rendering capabilities in the world, and it is very likely that this will continue to be the case. However, this ubiquitous tool may not continue to be centered around its phone function for much longer, as it evolves more and more into a multifaceted device, which you might want to call a *mobile Gizmo* (see Bruce Sterling's keynote at SIGGRAPH 2004). Inevitably, graphics is becoming a core part of such a Gizmo.

The pivotal role of graphics in the future of the Gizmo, and the fact that these devices are spread out (quite evenly, compared to other rendering platforms) over the entire globe, makes the mobile phone an incredibly exciting platform on which to develop graphics. Over the past few years, I have done quite a lot of research on mobile graphics and energy-efficient graphics hardware targeting these platforms. I believe that the authors of this book and I share the vision of omnipresent three-dimensional graphics on all mobile devices.

Compared to the contributions made through my research, the authors provide within these pages more than a small stepping stone. In my opinion, this book is an escalator, which takes the field to new levels. This is especially true because their text ensures that the topic is easily accessible to everyone with some background in computer science. Further, this book is unique in that it provides a single resource covering both OpenGL ES and M3G. These open APIs have been specifically developed for mobile devices, and many in the community, including myself, expect that these will be the most widely utilized APIs for the foreseeable future.

The foundations of this book are clear, and the authors are extremely knowledgeable about the subject, partly due to the enormous amounts of time and effort they have invested in standardization organizations, such as the Khronos Group and Java community, which are committed to making both the OpenGL ES and M3G standards faster, more robust, and easier to use. Undoubtedly, the authors of this book will continue to help develop even better versions of these APIs as the field progresses. I am certain that the future of mobile graphics will be more than bright, and with this book in your hand, you, the reader, will be able to create vibrant applications with three-dimensional graphics on mobile devices. Hopefully, your mobile graphics applications will be like nothing the world has ever seen before.

Please, do surprise me.
Tomas Akenine-Möller
Lund University
Sweden

About the Authors

Kari Pulli contributed to both OpenGL ES and M3G from the very beginning, and was among the most active technical contributors to each API. Kari, originally Principal Scientist and later Research Fellow, headed Nokia's graphics research, standardization, and technology strategy and implementation, and was Nokia's contact person for both standards.

Tomi Aarnio, Senior Research Engineer, mostly concentrated on the M3G standard. He was the specification editor of all versions of M3G, and headed the implementation project of both its Reference Implementation and the engine that is shipping on Nokia phones.

Ville Miettinen was active and influential on the definition of the first versions of both of these graphics standards. At the time he acted as the CTO of Hybrid Graphics, and later as a specialist of next-generation mobile graphics platforms at NVIDIA. Nowadays, he is a private consultant.

Kimmo Roimela, Senior Research Engineer at Nokia, also concentrated on the M3G standardization and implementation. He was the main architect of the M3G's animation model and an associate editor of the M3G specification. He was also the lead programmer of the Nokia M3G implementation.

Jani Vaarala, Graphics Architect at Nokia, was very active in the definition of OpenGL ES standard. He also headed the team that implemented and integrated Nokia's first OpenGL ES and EGL solution.

Acknowledgments

The creation and adoption of OpenGL ES and M3G was possible because of the hard work of many people and companies. When we use the term "we" in this book, we mean not just the authors but everybody who participated in the OpenGL ES working group or M3G expert group, and in some cases in both of them. Below we mention some of the most active contributors, the full list can be found from the API specifications.

Neil Trevett initiated the creation of OpenGL ES and chaired the OpenGL ES working group from the beginning until OpenGL ES 2.0. Tom Olson was an active contributor from the beginning and became the next chair of the OpenGL ES working group. David Blythe was the original specification editor for OpenGL ES. He also adapted the OpenGL sample implementation for OpenGL ES. Aaftab (Affie) Munshi became the editor after David left the Khronos Group to become the head architect of Direct 3D at Microsoft. Jon Leech, the OpenGL ARB secretary and EGL specification editor contributed a lot to all aspects of OpenGL ES. He is also the editor of the OpenGL ES 1.1 normative specification. Tom McReynolds, Robert Simpson, Petri Kero, Gary King, Graham Connor, and Remi Arnaud were important contributors for OpenGL ES, and Claude Knaus created the first OpenGL ES conformance tests.

Jyri Huopaniemi chaired the first M3G (JSR 184) expert group. Sean Ellis was one of the most active contributors to the M3G specification, and an associate specification editor, authoring the M3G file format. Mark Patel, Mark Tarlton, Doug Twilleager, Paul Beardow, Michael Steliaros, and Chris Grimm were among the most active members of the M3G expert group.

Mark Callow, Jacob Ström, and Ed Plowman have been very active contributors to both OpenGL ES and M3G APIs.

We would like to thank the following people who read at least parts of the book and provided many comments, making the book better than it would have otherwise been: Timo Aila, Tomas Akenine-Möller, Oliver Bimber, Suresh Chitturi, Sean Ellis, Michael Frydrych, Jiang Gao, Radek Grzeszczuk, Timo Haanpää, Kari Kangas, Laszlo Kishonti, Chris Knox, Sami Kyöstilä, Jon Leech, Mika Pesonen, Vidya Setlur, Robert Simpson, Dominic Symes, Yaki Tebeka, Juha Uola, Gareth Vaughan, and Yingen Xiong.

INTRODUCTION

Mobile phones are the new vehicle for bringing interactive graphics technologies to consumers. Graphics that in the 1980s was only seen in industrial flight simulators and at the turn of the millennium in desktop PCs and game consoles is now in the hands of billions of people. This book is about the technology underpinnings of *mobile three-dimensional graphics*, the newest and most rapidly advancing area of computer graphics.

Computer graphics has been around since the 1960s. Its application areas range from user interfaces to video gaming, scientific visualization, special effects in movies, and even full-length animated films. In the field of computer graphics, it is the subset of three-dimensional (3D) graphics that produces the most life-like visuals, the "wow" effects, and the eye-candy. Since the late 1990s, almost all computer games, and more recently even operating systems such as OS X and Windows Vista, have come to rely heavily on real-time 3D graphics. This has created an enormous drive for graphics hardware development. Dedicated graphics hardware is ubiquitous on desktop and laptop computers, and is rapidly becoming common on high-end mobile phones. Low-cost software-based implementations bring 3D graphics to mass-market consumer phones as well. Computer graphics is nowadays an integral part of the phone user experience: graphics is the face of the device.

Mobile phones, also known as cellular or cell phones, have recently become universal communication and computation devices. In countries such as the UK there are more mobile phone subscriptions than there are people. At the same time, the capabilities of the devices are improving. According to Moore's law [Moo65], the transistor density on integrated circuits roughly doubles every one or two years; today's high-end mobile phone has more computational power than a late 1990s home PC. The display resolutions of mobiles will soon reach and surpass that of conventional broadcast television, with much better color fidelity. Together, these advances have resulted in a truly *mobile* computer. As a side effect, real-time, interactive 3D graphics has become feasible and increasingly desirable for the masses.

1.1 ABOUT THIS BOOK

This book is about writing real-time 3D graphics applications for mobile devices. We assume the reader has some background in mathematics, programming, and computer graphics, but not necessarily in mobile devices.

The 3D graphics capabilities of mobile devices are exposed through two standardized application programming interfaces (APIs): OpenGL ES, typically accessed through C or C++, and M3G, for mobile Java. We introduce the latter standard in terms of the former. As OpenGL ES is utilized as the fundamental building block in many real-world M3G implementations, expressing this relationship explicitly is highly useful for describing the inner workings of M3G.

The two APIs are equally suited to programming embedded devices other than mobile phones, from car navigation systems to display screens of microwave ovens. However, most of such platforms are *closed*—parties other than the device manufacturer cannot develop and install new applications on them. By contrast, most mobile phones are *open*: third parties such as professional software developers, students, and individual enthusiasts can program, install, and distribute their own applications. Having a programmable mobile phone at hand to try out the techniques described in this book is actually a great idea. However, the details of mobile application development vary considerably across platforms, so we defer those details to each platform's developer documentation.

This book consists of three parts and several appendices. Part I gives an introduction to the 3D graphics concepts that are needed to understand OpenGL ES and M3G, which are then covered in Parts II and III, respectively. The use of each API is demonstrated with hands-on code examples. The appendices provide additional information and optimization tips for both C/C++ and Java developers as well as a glossary of acronyms and terms used in this book. There is also a companion web site, www.graphicsformasses.com, hosting code examples, errata, and links to other online resources.

A more comprehensive treatment of 3D graphics, such as Real-Time Rendering by Tomas Akenine-Möller and Eric Haines [AMH02], is recommended for readers new to computer graphics. The "OpenGL Red Book" [SWN05] is a traditional OpenGL beginner's guide, while a book by McReynolds and Blythe [MB05] collects more advanced OpenGL tips in one place. Those unfamiliar with programming in mobile Java may find Beginning J2ME: From Novice to Professional by Sing Li and Jonathan Knudsen [LK05] useful.

1.1.1 TYPOGRAPHIC CONVENTIONS

Alongside the basic text, there are specific tips for achieving good performance and avoiding common pitfalls. These hints are called *performance tips* and *pitfalls*, respectively. An example of each follows:

> **Performance tip:** Enabling the optimization flag in the compiler makes your application run faster.

> **Pitfall:** Premature optimization is the root of all evil.

Code snippets and class, token, and function names are shown in `typewriter` typeface like this:

```
glPointSize( 32 );
glEnable( GL_POINT_SPRITE_OES );
glTexEnvi( GL_POINT_SPRITE_OES, GL_COORD_REPLACE_OES, GL_TRUE );
glDrawArrays( GL_POINTS, 0, 1 );
```

When API functions are introduced, they are marked like this:

```
void function(int parameter).
```

Any later references to the `function` or *parameter* in the text are also similarly emphasized.

1.2 GRAPHICS ON HANDHELD DEVICES

The very first mobile phones were heavy bricks with separate handsets; a few examples can be seen in Figure 1.1. They were designed to be lugged around rather than carried in

Figure 1.1: The evolution of mobile phones from the early car phones on the left to the multimedia computer on the right spans roughly two decades. From the left: Mobira Talkman, Nokia R72, Mobira Cityman, Nokia 3410 (the first GSM phone with a 3D graphics engine), Nokia 6630 (the first phone to support both OpenGL ES and M3G), and Nokia N93 (the first phone with hardware acceleration for both APIs). Images Copyright © 2007 Nokia Corporation.

a pocket, and they operated using analog radio networks. Toward the late 1980s and early 1990s, mobile phones started to become truly portable rather than just movable. By then the phones were pocket-sized, but still only used for talking.

Eventually, features such as address books, alarm clocks, and text messaging started to appear. The early alphanumeric displays evolved into dot matrices, and simple games, such as the Snake available in many Nokia phones, arrived. Calendars and e-mail applications quickly followed. Since the late 1990s, the mobile phone feature palette has exploded with FM radios, color displays, cameras, music players, web browsers, and GPS receivers. The displays continue to improve with more colors and higher resolutions, memory is installed by the gigabyte for storing increasing amounts of data, and ever more processing power is available to run a plethora of applications.

1.2.1 DEVICE CATEGORIES

Mobile phones today can be grouped roughly into three categories (see Figure 1.2): *basic phones*, the more advanced *feature phones*, and the high-end *smart phones*. There is significant variance within each category, but the classification helps imagine what kind of graphics applications can be expected in each. The evolution of mobile phones is rapid— today's smart phones are tomorrow's feature phones. Features we now expect only in the most expensive high-end devices will be found in the mass market in just a few years' time.

The basic phone category is currently not very interesting from the point of view of graphics programming: basic phones have closed environments, usually with proprietary operating systems, and new applications can be developed only in close association with the maker of the device. Basic phones are very limited in terms of their processing power and both the physical screen size and the display resolution. This class of phones does not have graphics hardware, and while software-based 3D solutions can be implemented, the limited CPU performance allows only the simplest of 3D applications.

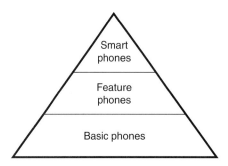

Figure 1.2:   Three phone categories. Smart phones are more powerful than feature phones or basic phones, but there are more basic phones than either feature phones or smart phones.

The second category, on the other hand, *is* very interesting for graphics applications. Feature phones represent the bulk of the market in developed countries, and most of them incorporate mobile Java. Hundreds of different Java-enabled phone models are manufactured, and every year hundreds of millions of handsets are sold. Mobile Java makes it possible to develop applications for that entire volume of devices through a fairly uniform programming platform. It offers sufficient programming interfaces for most multimedia needs, 3D graphics included; the Mobile 3D Graphics API for Java ME (M3G) is one of the main topics in this book. The Java phones also span the largest range in terms of performance and feature differences—while the theory is "write once, run anywhere," in practice a lot of time is spent managing tens or even hundreds of different application configurations for different devices, prompting some to re-express the theory as "write once, debug everywhere."

The Qualcomm BREW platform[1] can be seen as a subset of mid-range devices that allow installation of native applications, written in C or C++. The security concerns of native applications are addressed through mandatory certification of developers and applications. BREW provides 3D graphics through OpenGL ES. Many BREW devices also support Java and M3G.

The top category in our classification is the high-end smart phone. The logical conclusion to the current smart phone evolution seems to be that these devices evolve into true mobile computers. Already today, the key features of the category include large, sharp, and vivid color displays, powerful processors, plenty of memory, and full-blown multimedia capabilities, not to mention the inherent network connectivity. Some of the latest devices also incorporate dedicated 3D graphics hardware. The operating systems (OSes), such as Symbian, Linux, and Windows Mobile, support the installation of third-party native applications. Java is also featured on practically all smart phones, and both OpenGL ES and M3G are typically available for 3D content.

1.2.2 DISPLAY TECHNOLOGY

The evolution of mobile phones coincides with the evolution of digital photography. Digital cameras started the demand for small, cost-efficient, low-power, high-quality displays. Mobile phones were able to leverage that demand, and soon small-display technology was being driven by mobile phones—and, eventually, by mobile phones *incorporating* digital cameras. Suddenly the world's largest mobile phone manufacturer is also the world's largest camera manufacturer.

Apart from the extreme low end, all mobile phones today have color displays. In the mid-range, resolutions are around one or two hundred pixels per side, with 16 or 18 bits of color depth, yielding 65K or 262K unique colors. High-end devices pack screens from QVGA (320 × 240 pixels) upward with good contrast, rapid refresh rates, and

---

1   brew.qualcomm.com/brew/en/

24 bits becoming the norm in color depth. Although there is room for improvement in brightness, color gamut, and field of view, among other things, it is safe to assume that display quality will not be the main obstacle for interactive 3D graphics on any recent feature phone or smart phone.

The main limitation of mobile displays is clearly their small physical size. A 50mm screen will never provide a truly immersive experience, even though the short viewing distance compensates for the size to some extent. For high-end console type of gaming, the most promising new development is perhaps the TV-out interface, already included in some high-end devices. A phone connected to a high-definition display has the potential to deliver the same entertainment experience as a dedicated games console. Near-eye displays, also known as data goggles, may one day allow as wide a viewing angle as the human eye can handle, while embedded video projectors and foldable displays may become viable alternatives to TV-out. Finally, autostereoscopic displays that provide different images to both eyes may yield a more immersive 3D experience than is possible using only a single image.

As with most aspects of mobile phones, there is a lot of variation in display properties. Application developers will have to live with a variety of display technologies, sizes, orientations, and resolutions—much more so than in the desktop environment.

1.2.3 PROCESSING POWER

Mobile phones run on battery power. While the processing power of integrated circuits may continue to increase in line with Moore's law [Moo65], roughly 40–60% per year, this is certainly not true of battery capacity. Battery technology progresses at a much more modest rate, with the energy capacity of batteries increasing perhaps 10% per year at best. In ten years' time, processing power may well increase twenty times *more* than battery capacity.

Needless to say, mobile devices need to conserve battery power as much as possible in order to provide sufficient operating times. Another reason to keep the power consumption low is heat dissipation: mobile devices are small, so there is very little surface area available for transferring the heat generated in the circuits out of the device, and very few users appreciate their devices heating noticeably. There is a potential ray of hope, though, in the form of *Gene's law*. It states that the power usage, and therefore heat dissipation, of integrated circuits drops in half every 18 months. This effect has made it possible to build ever smaller and faster circuits.

As shown in Figure 1.3, mobile phones typically have one or two processors. Each processor incorporates an embedded CPU, a digital signal processor (DSP), and perhaps some dedicated hardware for audio, imaging, graphics, and other tasks. The *baseband processor* takes care of the fundamental real-time operations of the device, such as processing the speech and radio signals. In basic phones and feature phones, the baseband

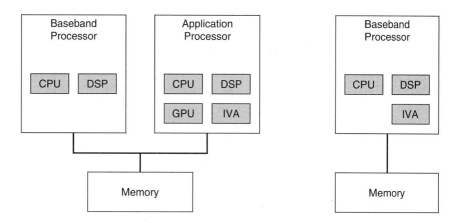

Figure 1.3: System architecture of a typical high-end smart phone (*left*) and a feature phone (*right*) in late 2007. Note that feature phones often include an Imaging and Video Accelerator (IVA), whereas a Graphics Processing Unit (GPU) is still relatively uncommon even in the smart phone segment.

processor also runs the operating system, applications, and the user interface—but of course at a lower priority. Smart phones usually have a separate *application processor* for these secondary purposes. To anyone coming from outside the mobile phone industry it may seem odd to call all this complex functionality "secondary." Indeed, the way forward is to make the application processor the core of the system with the modem becoming a peripheral.

The presence or absence of an application processor does not make much difference to the developer, though: exactly one CPU is available for programming in either case, and dedicated hardware accelerators may be present whether or not there is a separate application processor. The phone vendors also tend to be secretive about their hardware designs, so merely finding out what hardware is included in a particular device may be next to impossible. As a rule, the presence or absence of any hardware beyond the CPU that is running the application code can only be inferred through variation in performance. For example, a dual-chip device is likely to perform better for web browsing, multiplayer gaming, and other tasks that involve network access and heavy processing at the same time. In the rest of this book, we will not differentiate between baseband and application processors, but will simply refer to them collectively as "the processor" or "the CPU."

A mainstream mobile phone can be expected to have a 32-bit reduced instruction set (RISC) CPU, such as an ARM9. Some very high-end devices may also have a hardware floating-point unit (FPU). Clock speeds are reaching into half a gigahertz in the high end, whereas mid-range devices may still be clocked at barely 100MHz. There are also large variations in memory bus bandwidths, cache memories, and the presence or absence of hardware accelerators, creating a wide array of different performance profiles.

1.2.4 GRAPHICS HARDWARE

At the time of writing, the first generation of mobile phones with 3D graphics accelerators (GPUs) is available on the market. Currently, most of the devices incorporating graphics processors are high-end smart phones, but some feature phones with graphics hardware have also been released. It is reasonable to expect that graphics acceleration will become more common in that segment as well. One reason for this is that using a dedicated graphics processor is more power-efficient than doing the same effects on a general-purpose CPU: the CPU may require a clock speed up to 20 times higher than a dedicated chip to achieve the same rendering performance. For example, a typical hardware-accelerated mobile graphics unit can rasterize one or two bilinear texture fetches in one cycle, whereas a software implementation takes easily more than 20 cycles.

Figure 1.4 shows some of the first-generation mobile graphics hardware in its development stage. When designing mobile graphics hardware, the power consumption or *power efficiency* is the main driving factor. A well-designed chip does not use a lot of power internally, but power is also consumed when accessing external memory—such as the frame buffer—outside of the graphics core. For this reason, chip designs that cache graphics resources on the GPU, or store the frame buffer on the same chip and thus minimize traffic to and from external memory, are more interesting for mobile devices than for desktop graphics cards.

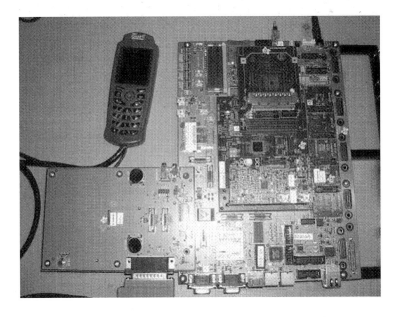

Figure 1.4: Early mobile graphics hardware prototype. Image copyright © Texas Instruments.

The graphics processor is only a small part of a multi-purpose consumer device which is sold as a complete package. Not all consumers take full advantage of the features made possible by the graphics hardware (e.g., high-end gaming, 3D navigation or fancy user interfaces), so they are not willing to pay a premium for it. In order to keep the cost of the device appealing to a variety of customers, the graphics core must be cheap to manufacture, i.e., it must have a small silicon area.

Graphics hardware for mobile devices cannot take the same approach as their desktop counterparts, sacrificing silicon area and power consumption for high performance. The design constraints are much tighter: the clock speeds and memory bandwidths are lower, and different levels of acceleration are required by different types of devices. For instance, many mobile GPUs only implement the rasterization stage of the rendering pipeline in hardware, leaving the transformation and lighting operations to be executed in software.

Rather than looking at raw performance, a much better metric is *performance per milliwatt*. High-end mobile GPUs in phones currently available in the market consume some hundreds of milliwatts of power at full speed, and can reach triangle throughputs of several million triangles per second, and pixel fill rates of hundreds of megapixels per second. Next-generation mobile GPUs are expected to have relative performance an order of magnitude higher.

1.2.5 EXECUTION ENVIRONMENTS

In the desktop arena, there are only three major families of operating systems: Windows, Linux, and Mac OS. Even though they have various differences in their design, and can seem very different from each other on the surface, the basic low-level idioms for writing programs are relatively similar. In the mobile space, there are dozens of different operating systems, and they each have their own quirks. As an example, some OSes do not support writable static data, i.e., static variables inside functions, global variables, or nonconstant global arrays. Other operating systems may lack a traditional file system. This means that things often taken for granted cannot be used in a portable fashion.

Open development environments

Traditionally all the embedded operating systems were closed, meaning that only the platform providers could write and install applications on them. The basic phones are appliances dedicated to a single purpose: making phone calls.

There are several reasons to keep platforms closed. If you allow third parties to install applications on your device after the purchase, the requirements for system stability are much higher. There are also significant costs related to software development, e.g., documentation, supporting libraries, and developer relations. Additionally, you have less freedom to change your implementations once other parties rely on your legacy features. Security is also a critical aspect. If applications cannot be installed, neither can malware, e.g., viruses that could erase or forward your private information such as the address book and calendar entries, or call on your behalf to a \$9.95-per-minute phone number.

However, modern smart phones are not any longer dedicated appliances, they are true multimedia computers. Providing all applications is a big and expensive engineering task for a single manufacturer. When a platform is opened, a much larger number of engineers, both professionals and hobbyists, can develop key applications that can both create additional revenue and make the device on the whole a more attractive offering. Opening up the platform also opens possibilities for innovating completely new types of applications. On the other hand, there may be financial reasons for the exact opposite behavior: if one party can control which applications and functionalities are available, and is able to charge for these, it may be tempted to keep an otherwise open platform closed.

Nevertheless, the majority of mobile phones sold today have an open development environment. In this book, we employ the term *open platform* rather loosely to cover all devices where it is possible to program and install your own applications. Our definition also includes devices that require additional certifications from the phone manufacturer or the operator. Examples of open platforms include Java, BREW/WIPI, Linux, Palm OS, Symbian OS, and Windows Mobile.

A *native* application is one that has been compiled into the machine code of the target processor. We use the designation *open native platform* for devices that allow installing and executing native applications. For example, S60 devices are considered native whereas Java-only phones are not. Some 10–15% of all phones sold worldwide in 2006 fall into this category, roughly half of them being S60 and the other half BREW/WIPI phones.

Native applications

In basic phones and feature phones, the only way to integrate native binary applications is to place them into the firmware when the phone is manufactured. Smart phones, by contrast, allow installing and executing native binary applications. A key advantage for such applications is that there are few or no layers of abstraction between the running code and the hardware. They also can have access to all device capabilities and the functionality provided by system libraries. Therefore these applications can get all the performance out of the hardware.

This comes at the cost of portability. Each platform has its own quirks that the programmers have to become familiar with. There are several initiatives underway that aim to standardize a common native programming environment across the various operating systems, e.g., the OpenKODE standard[2] from the Khronos Group.

With regards to the 3D graphics capability, most mobile operating system vendors have selected OpenGL ES as their native 3D programming API. There still exist a few

---

2   www.khronos.org/openkode

proprietary solutions, such as Direct3D Mobile on Windows Mobile, and the Mascot Capsule API in the Japanese market. Regardless, it seems highly unlikely that any new native 3D rendering APIs would emerge in the future—the graphics API wars waged in the desktop arena in the mid-1990s are not to be re-fought in the embedded world. This furthers the portability of the core graphics part of an application. Even if OpenGL ES is not integrated with the operating system out of the box, software-based OpenGL ES implementations are available which can be either directly linked to applications or installed afterward as a system-level library.

Mobile Java

Nearly all mobile phones sold in developed countries today are equipped with Java Micro Edition,[3] making it by far the most widely deployed application platform in the world. Java ME has earned its position because of its intrinsic security, fairly open and vendor-neutral status, and its familiarity to millions of developers. It also provides better productivity for programmers compared to C/C++, especially considering the many different flavors of C/C++ that are used on mobile devices. Finally, the fact that Java can abstract over substantially different hardware and software configurations is crucial in the mobile device market where no single vendor or operating system has a dominating position. Most manufacturers are hedging their bets between their proprietary software platforms and a number of commercial and open-source options, but Java developers can be blissfully unaware of which operating system each particular device is using. Practically all mobile Java platforms provide the same 3D graphics solution: the M3G API, described in this book.

The Java platform is a perfect match for an otherwise closed system. It gives security, stability, and portability almost for free, thanks to its virtual machine design, while documentation and support costs are effectively spread among all companies that are participating in Java standardization, i.e., the Java Community Process, or JCP, and shipping Java-enabled products.

Even for a platform that does allow native applications, it makes a lot of sense to make Java available as a complementary option. Java gives access to a vast pool of applications, developers, tools, and code that would otherwise not be available for that platform. Also, developers can then choose between the ease of development afforded by Java, and the more powerful native platform features available through C/C++.

Of course, the secure and robust virtual machine architecture of Java has its price: reduced application performance and limited access to platform capabilities. Isolating applications from the underlying software and hardware blocks access to native system libraries and rules out any low-level optimizations. It is not just a myth that Java code is slower than C/C++, particularly not on mobile devices. The Java performance issues are covered more thoroughly in Appendix B.

---

3   java.sun.com/javame

1.3 MOBILE GRAPHICS STANDARDS

The mobile graphics revolution started small. The first phones with an embedded 3D engine were shipped by J-Phone, a Japanese carrier, in 2001. The graphics engine was an early version of the Mascot Capsule engine from HI Corporation. Its main purpose at the time was to display simple animated characters. Therefore many common 3D graphics features such as perspective projection, smooth shading, and blending were omitted altogether.

The first mobile phone to support 3D graphics outside of Japan was the Nokia 3410, first shipped in Europe in 2002 (see Figure 1.1). Unlike the Japanese phones, it still had a monochrome screen—with a mere 96 by 65 pixels of resolution—but it did incorporate all the essential 3D rendering features; internally, the graphics engine in the 3410 was very close to OpenGL ES 1.0, despite preceding it by a few years. A lightweight animation engine was also built on top of it, with an authoring tool chain for Autodesk 3ds Max. The phone shipped with animated 3D text strings, downloadable screensaver animations, and a built-in Java game that used simple 3D graphics. The application that allowed the users to input a text string, such as their own name or their sweetheart's name, and select one of the predefined animations to spin the 3D extruded letters around proved quite popular. On the other hand, downloading of artist-created screensaver animations was less popular.

Other early 3D graphics engines included Swerve from Superscape, ExEn (Execution Engine) from InFusio, X-Forge from Fathammer, and mophun from Synergenix. Their common denominator was that they were not merely hardware abstraction layers. Instead, they were middleware and game engine solutions incorporating high-level features such as animation and binary file formats, and in many cases also input handling and sound. All the solutions were based on software rendering, so there was no need to standardize hardware functionality, and features outside of the traditional OpenGL rendering model could easily be incorporated. However, in the absence of a unified platform, gaining enough market share to sustain a business proved difficult for most contenders.

1.3.1 FIGHTING THE FRAGMENTATION

A multitude of different approaches to the same technical problem slows down the development of a software application market. For example, a large variety of proprietary content formats and tools increases the cost of content creation and distribution. To make creating interesting content sensible for content developers, the market needs to be sufficiently robust and large. This is not so much an issue with pre-installed content, such as built-in games on handsets, but it is crucial for third-party developers.

There are strong market forces that encourage fragmentation. For example, the mobile phone manufacturers want their phones to differentiate from their competition. Operators want to distinguish themselves from one another by offering differing services. And the dozens of companies that create the components that form a mobile phone, i.e., the hardware and software vendors, all want to compete by providing distinct features. In other words, there is a constant drive for new features. When you want the engineering problems related to a new feature solved, you will not normally wait for a standard to develop. As a result, any new functionality will usually be introduced as a number of proprietary solutions: similar, but developed from different angles, and more or less incompatible with each other.

After the first wave, a natural next step in evolution is a *de facto* standard—the fittest solution will rise above the others and begin to dominate the marketplace. Alternatively, lacking a single leader, the industry players may choose to unite and develop a joint standard. The required committee work may take a while longer, but, with sufficient support from the major players, has the potential to become a win-win scenario for everyone involved.

For the third-party application developer, the size—or market potential—of a platform is important, but equally important is the ease of developing for the platform. Portability of code is a major part of that. It can be achieved at the binary level, with the same application executable running on all devices; or at the source code level, where the same code can be compiled, perhaps with small changes, to all devices. Standard APIs also bring other benefits, such as better documentation and easier transfer of programming skills. Finally, they act as a concrete target for hardware manufacturers as to which features should be supported in their hardware.

In 2002, the Khronos Group, a standardization consortium for specifying and promoting mobile multimedia APIs, created a steering committee for defining a subset of OpenGL suitable for embedded devices. The following companies were represented in the first meeting: 3d4W, 3Dlabs, ARM, ATI, Imagination Technologies, Motorola, Nokia, Seaweed, SGI, and Texas Instruments. Concurrently with this, a Nokia-led effort to standardize a high-level 3D graphics API for Java ME was launched under the auspices of the Java Community Process (JCP). It was assigned the Java Specification Request number 184 (hence the moniker "JSR 184") but the standard has become better known as M3G. The Expert Group of JSR 184 was a mixture of key mobile industry players including Nokia, Motorola, Vodafone, and ARM, as well as smaller companies specializing in 3D graphics and games such as Hybrid Graphics, HI Corporation, Superscape, and Sumea. The two standards progressed side-by-side, influencing each other as there were several people actively contributing to both. In the fall of 2003 they were both ratified within a few months of each other, and OpenGL ES 1.0 and M3G 1.0 were born. The first implementations in real handheld devices began shipping about a year later.

Figure 1.5: Uses of OpenGL ES in the Nokia N95 multimedia computer. On the left the multimedia menu and the mapping application of Nokia N95; on the right, a mobile game. Images Copyright © 2007 Nokia Corporation. (See the color plate.)

Today, you can get an overview about the market status by looking at the result databases of the different mobile graphics benchmarks: JBenchmark[4] (Figure 1.12), GLBenchmark[5] (Figure 1.6), and the various Futuremark benchmarks[6] (Figure 1.9). Devices supporting M3G are available from all major handset vendors, and OpenGL ES 1.1 hardware is being supplied to them by several companies, e.g., AMD, ARM, NVIDIA, and Imagination Technologies (PowerVR). Practical implementations vary from software renderers on ARM7 processors to high-end GPUs. The initial focus of mobile 3D graphics has also broadened from games and screen savers; it is now finding its way to user interfaces (see Figures 1.5, 1.7, and 1.8), and is available for the visualization needs of all applications.

The emergence of open standards shows that healthy competition should occur over implementation—quality, performance, cost, and power consumption—but not functionality that causes fragmentation.

1.3.2 DESIGN PRINCIPLES

The planning for the mobile 3D graphics standards was based on the background outlined earlier in this chapter: the capabilities of mobile devices, the available software platforms, and the need to create an interesting, unified market for both content developers and hardware vendors. It was clear from the start that a unified solution that caters for both Java and native applications was needed. A number of design principles, outlined in the following, were needed to guide the work. For a more in-depth exposition, see the article by Pulli et al. [PARV05].

---

4   www.jbenchmark.com

5   www.glbenchmark.com

6   www.futuremark.com

Performance is crucial on devices with limited computation resources. To allow all of the processing power to be extracted, the APIs were designed with performance in mind. In practice, this means minimizing the overhead that an application would have to pay for using a standard API instead of a proprietary solution.

Figure 1.6: Screen shot from the GLBenchmark benchmarking suite for OpenGL ES. Image copyright © Kishonti Informatics LP. (See the color plate.)

Figure 1.7: More 3D user interface examples. Images copyright © Acrodea. (See the color plate.)

Figure 1.8: 3D user interface examples. Images copyright © TAT. (See the color plate.)

Figure 1.9: A VGA resolution screen shot from 3DMark Mobile 06, an OpenGL ES benchmark program. Image copyright © Futuremark. (See the color plate.)

COLOR PLATE 1: (Figure 1.5) Uses of OpenGL ES in the Nokia N95 multimedia computer. On the left the multimedia menu and the mapping application of Nokia N95; on the right, a mobile game. Images Copyright © 2007 Nokia Corporation.

COLOR PLATE 2: (Figure 1.6) Screen shot from the GLBenchmark benchmarking suite for OpenGL ES. Image copyright © Kishonti Informatics LP.

COLOR PLATE 3: (Figure 1.7) More 3D user interface examples. Images copyright © Acrodea.

COLOR PLATE 4: (Figure 1.8) 3D user interface examples. Images copyright © TAT.

COLOR PLATE 5: (Figure 1.9) A VGA resolution screen shot from 3DMark Mobile 06, and OpenGL ES benchmark program. Image copyright © Futuremark.

COLOR PLATE 6: (Figure 1.10) Demonstrating some of the advanced shading capabilities made possible by OpenGL ES 2.0. Images copyright © AMD.

COLOR PLATE 7: (Figure 1.11) Java games using M3G. Images copyright © Digital Chocolate.

COLOR PLATE 8: (Figure 1.12) Screen shot from the Jbenchmark performance benchmarking suite for M3G. Image copyright © Kishonti Informatics LP.

COLOR PLATE 9: (Figure 3.2) Illustrating the various stages of shading discussed in Chapters 3 and 8–10. *Top row, left to right:* wire frame model; filled model; diffuse lighting; diffuse and Phong specular lighting. *Bottom row:* texturing added; texturing with a separate specular pass; bump mapping added; and rendered with an intersecting translucent object to demonstrate Z-buffering and alpha blending.

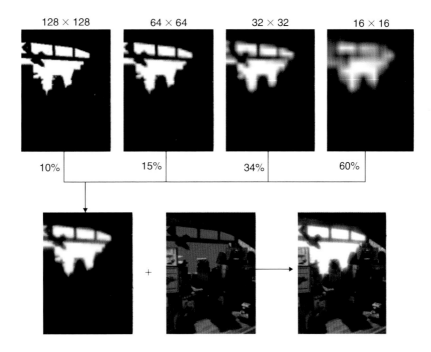

COLOR PLATE 10: (Figure 3.14) Rendering a light bloom effect by blurring the highlights and compositing on top of the normal scene. Images copyright © AMD.

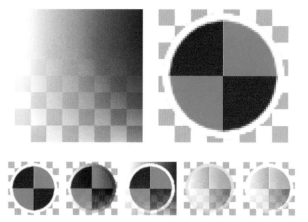

COLOR PLATE 11: (Figure 3.15) The effect of different texture functions. *Top*: incoming fragment colors (*left*) and texture (*right*); transparency is indicated with the checkerboard pattern behind the image. *Bottom*: resulting textures after each texture operation; left to right: REPLACE, MODULATE, DECAL, BLEND, ADD. For the BLEND mode, the user-defined blending color is pure yellow.

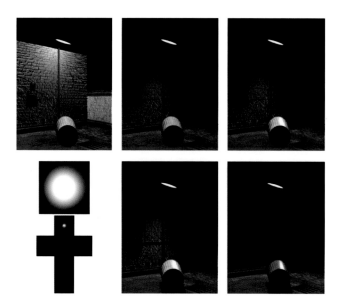

COLOR PLATE 12: (Figure 3.17) Several passes of a scene: bump mapping, projective lighting (using the circular light map on left middle), adding environment map reflection to the barrel (the cube map at left bottom), adding shadows, final image. Image copyright © AMD.

COLOR PLATE 13: (Figure 3.19) An environment cube map (*right*) and refraction map (*center*) used to render a well. Image copyright © AMD.

COLOR PLATE 14: (Figure 6.11) An example of automatically packing textures into a texture atlas (refer to Section 6.7.1). Image courtesy of Bruno Levy.

COLOR PLATE 15: (Figure 8.3) Screen shot of the texture matrix manipulation example code.

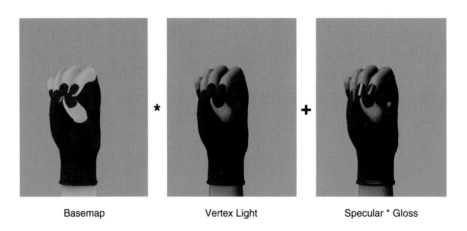

| Basemap | Vertex Light | Specular * Gloss |

COLOR PLATE 16: (Figure 14.2) Demonstrating a separate specular pass with controllable degree of glossiness. The per-pixel gloss factors can be stored in the alpha channel of the base texture map. Image copyright © AMD.

Low complexity as a requirement stems from the stringent silicon area and ROM footprint budgets of mobile phones. To satisfy this goal, the engines underlying the OpenGL ES and M3G APIs were required to be implementable, in software, in under 50kB and 150kB, respectively. The key tools for reaching these targets were removal of redundant and seldom-used features.

A rich feature set should not be compromised even when aiming for compact APIs. As a guideline, features that would be very difficult to replicate in application code—the latter parts of the graphics pipeline, such as blending and texture mapping, fall into this category—should be adopted as fully as feasible, whereas front-end features such as spline evaluation or texture coordinate generation can be left for the applications to implement.

Small applications are much more important on mobile devices than on the desktop. Applications are often delivered over relatively slow over-the-air connections, with the users paying by the kilobyte, and stored in small on-device memories. This means that the 3D content has to be delivered efficiently, preferably in a compressed binary format. Support of compact geometry formats (such as using bytes or shorts for coordinates, instead of floats) helps in reducing the RAM consumption. Finally, it makes sense for the API to incorporate functionality that is common to many applications, thus saving the code space that would otherwise be required to duplicate those features in each application.

Hardware-friendly features and a clear path for hardware evolution were among the most important design goals. Adopting the familiar OpenGL rendering model as the base technology enabled the design of dedicated mobile graphics hardware for mass markets.

Productivity is especially important for mobile developers, as the development times of mobile games are typically short compared to desktop. M3G is designed especially to have a good match to existing content creation tools and to support concurrent development of application code and art assets.

Orthogonal feature set means that individual rendering features are not tied to each other. Feature orthogonality makes the behavior of the graphics engine easier to predict, as complex interdependencies and side-effects are minimized. This was already one of the key design criteria for desktop OpenGL.

Extensibility is important for any API that is to be around for several years. The mobile graphics industry is proceeding rapidly, and there has to be a clearly defined path for evolution as new features need to be incorporated.

Minimal fragmentation lets content developers work on familiar ground. Therefore, both OpenGL ES and M3G attempt to strictly mandate features, keeping the number of optional features as small as possible.

Figure 1.10: Demonstrating some of the advanced shading capabilities made possible by OpenGL ES 2.0. Images copyright © AMD. (See the color plate.)

1.3.3 OPENGL ES

OpenGL ES is a compact version of the well-known OpenGL graphics standard. It is a low-level rendering API adapted for embedded systems. The first version, OpenGL ES 1.0, aimed to provide an extremely compact API without sacrificing features: it had to be implementable fully in software in under 50kB of code while being well-suited for hardware acceleration. The graphics effects familiar from desktop had to be available on mobile devices as well.

Later, OpenGL ES 1.1 included more features amenable to hardware acceleration, in line with the feature set of first-generation mobile 3D graphics chipsets. The latest version, OpenGL ES 2.0, provides a completely revamped API, and support for a high-level shading language (GLSL ES): it replaces several stages of the traditional fixed-function graphics pipeline with programmable vertex and fragment shaders, and is therefore not backward-compatible with the 1.x series. The 1.x and 2.x generations of OpenGL ES continue to coexist, together providing 3D graphics capabilities to the entire range of embedded devices from wristwatches to smart phones, modern games consoles, and beyond. All OpenGL ES 2.x devices are expected to ship with ES 1.1 drivers. Details of the 2.x standard are beyond the scope of this book. GLSL ES is closely related to the OpenGL Shading Language, well described by Rost [Ros04].

A companion API called EGL, described in Chapter 11, handles the integration of OpenGL ES into the native windowing system of the operating system, as well as managing rendering targets and contexts. Finally, there is a separately specified safety-critical profile called OpenGL SC, but its markets are mostly outside of consumer devices—for example, in avionics instrumentation. OpenGL ES bindings are also available for other languages, such as Java and Python.

Figure 1.11: Java games using M3G. Images copyright © Digital Chocolate. (See the color plate.)

1.3.4 M3G

As the first Java-enabled phones hit the market in 2000 or so, it became evident that the performance and memory overhead of Java was prohibitive for real-time 3D. Software rasterizers written in pure Java would run orders of magnitude slower compared to those implemented in native code, while the power of any graphics hardware would be wasted on not being able to feed it with triangles fast enough.

Since the overhead of mobile Java was not going to magically vanish, there was a need for a new standard API that would shift as much processing as possible into native code. Since the data used by the native code cannot reside in the Java heap, a *retained mode* API was deemed more suitable than a direct mapping of OpenGL ES to mobile Java.

M3G is a completely new high-level API that borrows ideas from previous APIs such as Java 3D and OpenInventor. It consists of nodes that encapsulate 3D graphics elements. The nodes can be connected to form a scene graph representing the graphics objects and their relationships. M3G is designed so that it can be efficiently implemented on top of an OpenGL ES renderer.

Standardized high-level APIs have never been as popular on desktop as low-level ones. The main reason is that a high-level API is always a compromise. The threshold of writing a dedicated engine, such as a game engine, on top of a hardware-accelerated low-level API has been relatively low. However, if developers want to create such an engine using mobile Java, it has to be implemented completely in Java, incurring a significant performance penalty compared to native applications. A standardized high-level API, on the

Figure 1.12: Screen shot from the JBenchmark performance benchmarking suite for M3G. Image copyright © Kishonti Informatics LP. (See the color plate.)

other hand, can be provided by the device manufacturers, and it can be implemented and optimized in C/C++ or even assembly language. The native core then only has a thin Java layer to make the functionality available to Java applications.

Additional features of M3G include extensive support for animation and binary content files. Any property of any object can be keyframe-animated, and there are special types of meshes that support *skinning* (e.g., for character animation), and *morphing* (e.g., for facial animation). There is also an associated standardized binary file format that has one-to-one mapping with the API. This greatly facilitates separation of artistic content from programmable application logic.

Version 1.1 of M3G was released in mid-2005, with the aim of tightening up the specification for better interoperability. As M3G 1.1 does not add any substantial functionality over the original version, device vendors have been able to upgrade to it pretty quickly. M3G 1.1 is in fact required by the Mobile Service Architecture standard (JSR 248).

As of this writing, M3G 2.0 is being developed under JSR 297. The new version will make programmable shaders available on high-end devices, while also expanding the feature set and improving performance on the mass-market devices that do not have programmable graphics hardware, or any graphics hardware at all.

1.3.5 RELATED STANDARDS

There are several mobile graphics and multimedia standards closely related to OpenGL ES and M3G. This book concentrates only on graphics APIs, but for sound and multimedia in general, you can refer to standards such as JSR 135 for Java applications, or the native standards OpenSL ES, OpenMAX, and OpenKODE from the Khronos Group.

OpenGL ES for Java (JSR 239)

JSR 239[7] is a Java Specification Request that aims to expose OpenGL ES and EGL to mobile Java as directly as possible. Its promise is to provide the full OpenGL ES functionality for maximum flexibility and performance. The different OpenGL ES versions are presented as a hierarchy of Java interfaces. The base `GL` interface is extended with new functions and tokens in `GL10` and `GL11`, for OpenGL ES versions 1.0 and 1.1, respectively. Several OpenGL ES extensions are also exposed in the API, so features beyond the core functionality can be accessed.

Being a Java API, JSR 239 extends the error handling from native OpenGL ES with additional exceptions to catch out-of-bounds array accesses and other potential risks to system security and stability. For example, each draw call is required to check for indices referring outside the currently enabled vertex arrays.

There are no devices available as of this writing that would include JSR 239. Sony Ericsson have announced support for it in their latest Java Platform release (JP-8), and the first conforming phone, the Z750i, is likely to be shipping by the time this book goes to press. There is also a reference implementation available in the Java Wireless Toolkit from Sun Microsystems. Finally, in Japan, the DoCoMo Java (DoJa) platform version 5.0 includes proprietary OpenGL ES bindings.

2D vector graphics

The variety of screen resolutions on mobile devices creates a problem for 2D content. If graphics are rendered and distributed as bitmaps, chances are that the resolution of the content is different from the screen resolution of the output device. Resampling the images to different resolutions often degrades the quality—text especially becomes blurry and difficult to read. Bitmap graphics also requires significant amounts of memory to store and a high bandwidth to transmit over a network, and this problem only gets worse as the display resolutions increase. Scalable 2D vector graphics can address both of these

---

7   www.jcp.org/en/jsr/detail?id=239

problems. If the content is represented as shapes such as curves and polygons instead of pixels, it can often be encoded more compactly. This way content can also be rendered to different display resolutions without any loss of quality, and can be displayed as the content author originally intended.

2D vector graphics has somewhat different requirements from 3D graphics. It is used for high-quality presentation graphics, and features such as smooth curves, precise rules for line caps, line joins, and line dashes are much more important than they are for 3D content. Indeed, these features are often only defined in 2D, and they may not have any meaning in 3D. It is also much easier to implement high-quality anti-aliasing for 2D shapes.

Scalable Vector Graphics (SVG) is a standard defined by the World Wide Web Consortium (W3C).[8] It is an XML-based format for describing 2D vector graphics content. SVG also includes a declarative animation model that can be used, for example, for cartoons and transition effects. In addition, the content can be represented as a Document Object Model (DOM), which facilitates dynamic manipulation of the content through native application code or scripting languages such as JavaScript. The DOM API also allows applications to register a set of event handlers such as `mouseover` and `click` that can be assigned to any SVG graphical object. As a result, SVG can be used to build dynamic web sites that behave somewhat like desktop applications.

W3C has also defined mobile subsets of the standard, SVG Tiny and SVG Basic.[9] The latter is targeted for Personal Digital Assistants (PDAs), while the smaller SVG Tiny is aimed for mobile phones. However, it seems that SVG Basic has not been widely adopted by the industry, while SVG Tiny is becoming commonplace and is being further developed.

The Khronos Group has defined the OpenVG API for efficient rendering of 2D vector graphics. OpenVG has similar low-level structure as OpenGL ES, and its main use cases include 2D user interfaces and implementations of 2D vector graphics engines such as SVG Tiny and Adobe's Flash. Whereas most 2D vector graphics engines traditionally execute on the CPU, OpenVG has been designed for off-loading the rasterization to dedicated graphics hardware (see Figure 1.13). This was necessary in the mobile space because most devices have limited CPU resources. The OpenVG rendering primitives were chosen so that all rendering features of SVG Tiny can be easily implemented using the API. The basic drawing primitive is a path which can contain both straight line segments as well as smoothly curving Bézier line segments. The paths can describe arbitrary polygons, which can be filled with solid colors, color gradients, bitmap images, or even patterns made of other 2D objects. Recent versions of EGL allow rendering with both OpenGL ES and OpenVG to the same image, and even allow sharing data such as texture maps across the different Khronos APIs.

---

8   www.w3.org/Graphics/SVG/

9   www.w3.org/TR/SVGMobile/

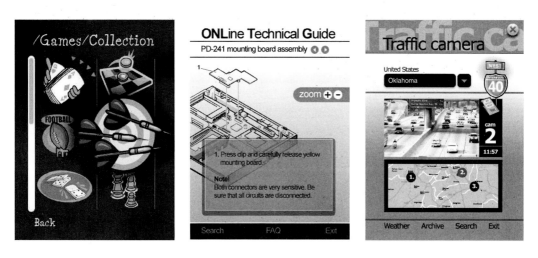

Figure 1.13: The use of vector graphics makes it possible to create scalable, antialiased user interfaces. Hardware-accelerated OpenVG demonstrations. Images copyright © AMD.

Various 2D graphics interfaces exist for Java ME. Mobile Information Device Profile (MIDP), the most common Java profile on mobile phones, offers basic 2D graphics functionality with primitives such as lines, circles, and polygons, as well as bitmap graphics. It is quite well suited for the needs of simple 2D games and applications.

JSR 226, the scalable 2D vector graphics API for Java,[10] was created for more challenging 2D vector graphics applications. It is compatible with SVG Tiny 1.1, and can render individual images and graphics elements under the control of a Java application, or simply used as an "SVG Tiny player." It also supports the XML/SVG Micro DOM (μDOM) for manipulating properties of the SVG content via accessor methods and event handlers. JSR 226 was completed in 2005, and can be found in several phone models from manufacturers such as Nokia and Sony Ericsson.

JSR 287[11] is a backward-compatible successor to JSR 226. The enhancements of this API include the new graphics and multimedia features from SVG Tiny 1.2, e.g., opacity, gradients, text wrapping, audio, and video. The new version also allows creating animations on the fly. The Micro DOM support is extended from the previous version. The API also includes the necessary framework for processing streamed SVG scenes, and there is an immediate-mode rendering API that is compatible with OpenVG and designed for high performance. The standard is expected to be completed by the end of 2007. Based on historical evidence, the first devices can then be expected in late 2008.

---

10 www.jcp.org/en/jsr/detail?id=226

11 www.jcp.org/en/jsr/detail?id=287

COLLADA

COLLADA, short for COLLAborative Design Activity,[12] started as an open-source project led by Sony, but is nowadays being developed and promoted by the Khronos Group. COLLADA is an interchange format for 3D content; it is the glue which binds together digital content creation (DCC) tools and various intermediate processing tools to form a production pipeline. In other words, COLLADA is a tool for content development, not for content delivery—the final applications are better served with more compact formats designed for their particular tasks.

COLLADA can represent pretty much everything in a 3D scene that the content authoring tools can, including geometry, material and shading properties, physics, and animation, just to name a few. It also has a mobile profile that corresponds to OpenGL ES 1.x and M3G 1.x, enabling an easy mapping to the M3G binary file format. One of the latest additions is COLLADA FX, which allows interchange of complex, multi-pass shader effects. COLLADA FX allows encapsulation of multiple descriptions of an effect, such as different levels of detail, or different shading for daytime and nighttime versions.

Exporters for COLLADA are currently available for all major 3D content creation tools, such as Lightwave, Blender, Maya, Softimage, and 3ds Max. A stand-alone viewer is also available from Feeling Software. Adobe uses COLLADA as an import format for editing 3D textures, and it has been adopted as a data format for Google Earth and Unreal Engine. For an in-depth coverage of COLLADA, see the book by Arnaud and Barnes [AB06].

---

12 www.khronos.org/collada

PART I
ANATOMY OF A GRAPHICS ENGINE

2

LINEAR ALGEBRA FOR 3D GRAPHICS

This chapter is about the coordinate systems and transformations that 3D objects undergo during their travel through the graphics pipeline, as illustrated in Figure 2.1. Understanding this subset of linear algebra is crucial for figuring out what goes on inside a 3D graphics engine, as well as for making effective use of such an engine. If you want to rush ahead into the graphics primitives instead, study Figure 2.1, skip to Chapter 3, and return here later.

2.1 COORDINATE SYSTEMS

To be able to define shapes and locations, we need to have a frame of reference: a *coordinate system*, also known as a *space*. A coordinate system has an origin and a set of axes. The origin is a point (or equivalently, a location), while the axes are directions.

As a mathematical construct, a coordinate system may have an arbitrary set of axes with arbitrary directions, but here we are only concerned about coordinate systems that are *three-dimensional*, *orthonormal*, and *right-handed*. Such coordinate systems have three axes, usually called x, y, and z. Each axis is *normalized* (unit length) and *orthogonal* (perpendicular) to the other two. Now, if we first place the x and y axes so that they meet at the origin at right angles (90°), we have two possibilities to orient the z axis so that it is perpendicular to both x and y. These choices make the coordinate system either right-handed or left-handed; Figure 2.2 shows two formulations of the right-handed choice.

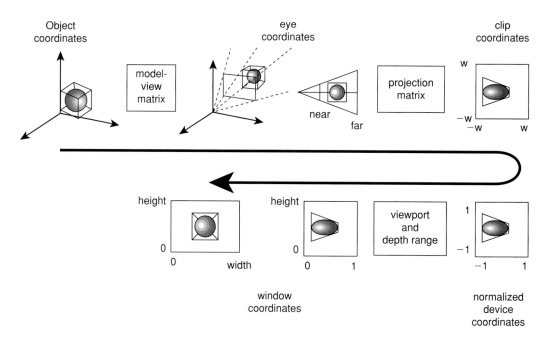

Figure 2.1: Summary of the coordinate system transformations from vertex definition all the way to the frame buffer.

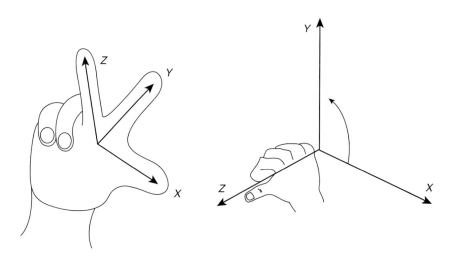

Figure 2.2: Two different ways to visualize a right-handed, orthogonal 3D coordinate system. *Left:* the thumb, index finger, and middle finger of the right hand are assigned the axes x, y, and z, in that order. The positive direction of each axis is pointed to by the corresponding finger. *Right:* we grab the z axis with the right hand so that the thumb extends toward the positive direction; the other fingers then indicate the direction of positive rotation angles on the xy-plane.

A coordinate system is always defined with respect to some other coordinate system, except for the global *world coordinate system*. For example, the coordinate system of a room might have its origin at the southwest corner, with the *x* axis pointing east, *y* pointing north, and *z* upward. A chair in the room might have its own coordinate system, its origin at its center of mass, and its axes aligned with the chair's axes of symmetry. When the chair is moved in the room, its coordinate system moves and may reorient with respect to the *parent* coordinate system (that of the room).

2.1.1 VECTORS AND POINTS

A 3D *point* is a location in space, in a 3D coordinate system. We can find a point $\boldsymbol{p}$ with coordinates $\begin{bmatrix} p_x & p_y & p_z \end{bmatrix}$ by starting from the origin (at $\begin{bmatrix} 0 & 0 & 0 \end{bmatrix}$) and moving the distance p_x along the *x* axis, from there the distance p_y along *y*, and finally the distance p_z along *z*.

Two points define a line segment between them, three points define a triangle with corners at those points, and several interconnected triangles can be used to define the surface of an object. By placing many such objects into a world coordinate system, we define a virtual world. Then we only need to position and orient an imaginary *camera* to define a viewpoint into the world, and finally let the graphics engine create an image. If we wish to animate the world, we have to move either the camera or some of the points, or both, before rendering the next frame.

When we use points to define geometric entities such as triangles, we often call those points *vertices*. We may also expand the definition of a vertex to include any other data that are associated with that surface point, such as a color.

Besides points, we also need *vectors* to represent surface normals, viewing directions, light directions, and so on. A vector $\boldsymbol{v}$ is a displacement, a difference of two points; it has no position, but does have a direction and a length. Similar to points, vectors can be represented by three coordinates. The vector $\boldsymbol{v_{ab}}$, which is a displacement from point $\boldsymbol{a}$ to point $\boldsymbol{b}$, has coordinates $\begin{bmatrix} b_x - a_x & b_y - a_y & b_z - a_z \end{bmatrix}$. It is also possible to treat a point as if it were a vector from the origin to the point itself.

The sum of two vectors is another vector: $\boldsymbol{a} + \boldsymbol{b} = \begin{bmatrix} a_x + b_x & a_y + b_y & a_z + b_z \end{bmatrix}$. If you add a vector to a point, the result is a new point that has been displaced by the vector. Vectors can also be multiplied by a scalar: $s\boldsymbol{a} = \begin{bmatrix} sa_x & sa_y & sa_z \end{bmatrix}$. Subtraction is simply an addition where one of the vectors has been multiplied by -1.

2.1.2 VECTOR PRODUCTS

There are two ways to multiply two 3D vectors. The *dot product* or *scalar product* of vectors $\boldsymbol{a}$ and $\boldsymbol{b}$ can be defined in two different but equivalent ways:

$$\boldsymbol{a} \cdot \boldsymbol{b} = a_x b_x + a_y b_y + a_z b_z \tag{2.1}$$

$$\boldsymbol{a} \cdot \boldsymbol{b} = \cos(\theta) \|\boldsymbol{a}\| \, \|\boldsymbol{b}\| \tag{2.2}$$

The first definition is algebraic, using the vector coordinates. The latter definition is geometric, and is based on the lengths of the two vectors ($||\boldsymbol{a}||$ and $||\boldsymbol{b}||$), and the smallest angle between them (θ). An important property related to the angle is that when the vectors are orthogonal, the cosine term and therefore the whole expression goes to zero. This is illustrated in Figure 2.3.

The dot product allows us to compute the length, or *norm*, of a vector. We first compute the dot product of the vector with itself using the algebraic formula: $\boldsymbol{a} \cdot \boldsymbol{a}$. We then note that $\theta = 0$ and therefore $\cos(\theta) = 1$. Now, taking the square root of Equation (2.2) yields the norm:

$$||\boldsymbol{a}|| = \sqrt{\boldsymbol{a} \cdot \boldsymbol{a}}. \tag{2.3}$$

We can then normalize the vector so that it becomes unit length:

$$\hat{\boldsymbol{a}} = \boldsymbol{a}/||\boldsymbol{a}||. \tag{2.4}$$

The other way to multiply two vectors in 3D is called the *cross product*. While the dot product can be done in any coordinate system, the cross product only exists in 3D. The cross product creates a new vector,

$$\boldsymbol{a} \times \boldsymbol{b} = \begin{bmatrix} a_y b_z - a_z b_y & a_z b_x - a_x b_z & a_x b_y - a_y b_x \end{bmatrix}, \tag{2.5}$$

which is perpendicular to both $\boldsymbol{a}$ and $\boldsymbol{b}$; see Figure 2.3. The new vector is also right-handed with respect to $\boldsymbol{a}$ and $\boldsymbol{b}$ in the same way as shown in Figure 2.2. The length of the new vector is $\sin(\theta)||\boldsymbol{a}||\,||\boldsymbol{b}||$. If $\boldsymbol{a}$ and $\boldsymbol{b}$ are parallel ($\theta = 0°$ or $\theta = 180°$), the result is zero. Finally, reversing the order of multiplication flips the sign of the result:

$$\boldsymbol{a} \times \boldsymbol{b} = -\boldsymbol{b} \times \boldsymbol{a}. \tag{2.6}$$

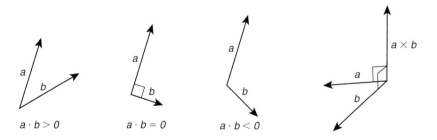

Figure 2.3: The dot product produces a positive number when the vectors form an acute angle (less than 90°), zero when they are perpendicular (exactly 90°), and negative when the angle is obtuse (greater than 90°). The cross product defines a third vector that is in a right-hand orientation and perpendicular to both vectors.

2.1.3 HOMOGENEOUS COORDINATES

Representing both points and direction vectors with three coordinates can be confusing. *Homogeneous coordinates* are a useful tool to make the distinction explicit. We simply add a fourth coordinate (w): if $w = 0$, we have a direction, otherwise a location.

If we have a homogeneous point $[h_x\ h_y\ h_z\ h_w]$, we get the corresponding 3D point by dividing the components by h_w. If $h_w = 0$ we would get a point infinitely far away, which we interpret as a direction toward the point $\begin{bmatrix} h_x & h_y & h_z \end{bmatrix}$. Conversely, we can homogenize the point $\begin{bmatrix} p_x & p_y & p_z \end{bmatrix}$ by adding a fourth component: $\begin{bmatrix} p_x & p_y & p_z & 1 \end{bmatrix}$. In fact, we can use any non-zero w, and all such $\begin{bmatrix} wp_x & wp_y & wp_z & w \end{bmatrix}$ correspond to the same 3D point.

We can also see that with normalized homogeneous coordinates—for which w is either 1 or 0—taking a difference of two points creates a direction vector (w becomes $1 - 1 = 0$), and adding a direction vector to a point displaces the point by the vector and yields a new point (w becomes $1 + 0 = 1$).

There is another, even more important, reason for adopting homogeneous 4D coordinates instead of the more familiar 3D coordinates. They allow us to express all linear 3D transformations using a 4×4 matrix that operates on 4×1 homogeneous vectors. This representation is powerful enough to express translations, rotations, scalings, shearings, and even perspective and parallel projections.

2.2 MATRICES

A 4×4 matrix M has components m_{ij} where i stands for the row and j stands for the column:

$$M = \begin{bmatrix} m_{00} & m_{01} & m_{02} & m_{03} \\ m_{10} & m_{11} & m_{12} & m_{13} \\ m_{20} & m_{21} & m_{22} & m_{23} \\ m_{30} & m_{31} & m_{32} & m_{33} \end{bmatrix}, \tag{2.7}$$

while a column vector v has components v_i:

$$v = \begin{bmatrix} v_0 \\ v_1 \\ v_2 \\ v_3 \end{bmatrix} = [\, v_0 \quad v_1 \quad v_2 \quad v_3 \,]^T. \tag{2.8}$$

The *transpose* operation above converts a row vector to column vector, and vice versa. We will generally use column vectors in the rest of this book, but will write them in transposed form: $v = [\, v_0 \quad v_1 \quad v_2 \quad v_3 \,]^T$. On a matrix $M = [m_{ij}]$, transposition produces a matrix that is mirrored with respect to the diagonal: $M^T = [m_{ji}]$, that is, columns are switched with rows.

2.2.1 MATRIX PRODUCTS

A matrix times a vector produces a new vector. Directions and positions are both transformed by multiplying the corresponding homogeneous vector v with a transformation matrix M as $v' = Mv$. Each component of this column vector v' is obtained by taking a dot product of a row of M with v; the first row ($M_{0\bullet}$) producing the first component, the second row ($M_{1\bullet}$) producing the second component, and so on:

$$v' = Mv = \begin{bmatrix} [\, m_{00} & m_{01} & m_{02} & m_{03} \,] \cdot v \\ [\, m_{10} & m_{11} & m_{12} & m_{13} \,] \cdot v \\ [\, m_{20} & m_{21} & m_{22} & m_{23} \,] \cdot v \\ [\, m_{30} & m_{31} & m_{32} & m_{33} \,] \cdot v \end{bmatrix}. \tag{2.9}$$

Note that for this to work, M needs to have as many columns as v has rows.

An alternative, and often more useful way when trying to understand the geometric meaning of the matrix product, is to think of M being composed of four column vectors $M_{\bullet 0}, \ldots, M_{\bullet 3}$, each being multiplied by the corresponding component of v, and finally being added up:

$$v' = Mv = v_0 \begin{bmatrix} m_{00} \\ m_{10} \\ m_{20} \\ m_{30} \end{bmatrix} + v_1 \begin{bmatrix} m_{01} \\ m_{11} \\ m_{21} \\ m_{31} \end{bmatrix} + v_2 \begin{bmatrix} m_{02} \\ m_{12} \\ m_{22} \\ m_{32} \end{bmatrix} + v_3 \begin{bmatrix} m_{03} \\ m_{13} \\ m_{23} \\ m_{33} \end{bmatrix}. \tag{2.10}$$

The product of two matrices, on the other hand, produces another matrix, which can be obtained from several products of a matrix and a vector. Simply break the columns of the rightmost matrix apart into several column vectors, multiply each of them by the matrix on the left, and join the results into columns of the resulting matrix:

$$AB = \begin{bmatrix} A(B_{\bullet 0}) & A(B_{\bullet 1}) & A(B_{\bullet 2}) & A(B_{\bullet 3}) \end{bmatrix}. \tag{2.11}$$

Note that in general matrix multiplication does not commute, that is, the order of multiplication is important ($AB \neq BA$). The transpose of a product is the product of transposes, but in the reverse order:

$$(AB)^T = B^T A^T. \tag{2.12}$$

Now we are ready to express the dot product as a matrix multiplication:

$$\boldsymbol{a} \cdot \boldsymbol{b} = \boldsymbol{a}^T \boldsymbol{b} = \begin{bmatrix} a_0 & a_1 & a_2 \end{bmatrix} \begin{bmatrix} b_0 \\ b_1 \\ b_2 \end{bmatrix}, \tag{2.13}$$

that is, transpose $\boldsymbol{a}$ into a row vector and multiply it with a column vector $\boldsymbol{b}$.

2.2.2 IDENTITY AND INVERSE

The number one is special in the sense that when any number is multiplied with it, that number remains unchanged ($1 \cdot a = a$), and for any number other than zero there is an inverse that produces one ($a\frac{1}{a} = aa^{-1} = 1$). For matrices, we have an *identity* matrix:

$$\boldsymbol{I} = \begin{bmatrix} 1 & 0 & 0 & 0 \\ 0 & 1 & 0 & 0 \\ 0 & 0 & 1 & 0 \\ 0 & 0 & 0 & 1 \end{bmatrix} \tag{2.14}$$

A matrix multiplied by the identity matrix remains unchanged ($\boldsymbol{M} = \boldsymbol{IM} = \boldsymbol{MI}$). If a matrix $\boldsymbol{M}$ has an *inverse* we denote it by $\boldsymbol{M}^{-1}$, and the matrix multiplied with its inverse yields identity: $\boldsymbol{MM}^{-1} = \boldsymbol{M}^{-1}\boldsymbol{M} = \boldsymbol{I}$. Only *square* matrices, for which the number of rows equals the number of columns, can have an inverse, and only the matrices where all columns are linearly independent have inverses.

The inverse of a product of matrices is the product of inverses, in reverse order:

$$(\boldsymbol{AB})^{-1} = \boldsymbol{B}^{-1}\boldsymbol{A}^{-1}. \tag{2.15}$$

Let us check: $\boldsymbol{AB}(\boldsymbol{AB})^{-1} = \boldsymbol{ABB}^{-1}\boldsymbol{A}^{-1} = \boldsymbol{AIA}^{-1} = \boldsymbol{AA}^{-1} = \boldsymbol{I}$. We will give the inverses of most transformations that we introduce, but in a general case you may need to use a numerical method such as Gauss-Jordan elimination to calculate the inverse [Str03].

As discussed earlier, we can use 4 × 4 matrices to represent various transformations. In particular, you can interpret every matrix as transforming a vertex to a new coordinate system. If $\boldsymbol{M}_{ow}$ transforms a vertex from its local coordinate system, the *object coordinates*, to world coordinates ($\boldsymbol{v}' = \boldsymbol{M}_{ow}\boldsymbol{v}$), its inverse performs the transformation from world coordinates to object coordinates ($\boldsymbol{v} = \boldsymbol{M}_{ow}^{-1}\boldsymbol{v}' = \boldsymbol{M}_{wo}\boldsymbol{v}'$), that is, $\boldsymbol{M}_{ow}^{-1} = \boldsymbol{M}_{wo}$.

2.2.3 COMPOUND TRANSFORMATIONS

Transformation matrices can be compounded. If $\boldsymbol{M}_{ow}$ transforms a vertex from object coordinates to world coordinates, and $\boldsymbol{M}_{we}$ transforms from world coordinates to eye coordinates (see Section 2.4), $M_{we}M_{ow}$ takes a vertex from object coordinates to eye coordinates. Notice the order of application: $v' = M_{ow}v$ is applied first, followed by $v'' = M_{we}v' = M_{we}M_{ow}v$.

A compound transformation can in principle be evaluated in two orders. You can do it from right to left ($M_{we}(M_{ow}v)$), that is, transform the vertex through each of the coordinate systems one at a time, or from left to right (($M_{we}M_{ow})v$), that is, collapse the transformations into one before applying them to the vertex. Let us now analyze which order is more efficient.

If you take the first approach, repeatedly transforming each vertex, you will need $16mn$ multiplications, where m is the number of transformations and n the number of vertices. If you take the second approach, you need $64(m - 1)$ multiplications to collapse the matrices, and $16n$ multiplications to apply the transformation to each vertex. Therefore, if $64(m - 1) + 16n < 16mn$, it makes sense to compound the matrices before applying the result to the vertices. For example, if you have 20 points and 3 transformations, the approach of transforming each point 3 times would require $16 \cdot 3 \cdot 20 = 960$ multiplications, while first combining the transformations and then applying them would only require $64 \cdot (3 - 1) + 16 \cdot 20 = 448$ multiplications. You can see that it almost always makes more sense to collapse the transformations before applying them to the vertices.

Repeating this analysis for the number of additions rather than multiplications only changes the constant factors in the above inequality (from 64 to 48, and from 16 to 12), thus not changing the outcome in a significant way.

2.2.4 TRANSFORMING NORMAL VECTORS

Even though vectors in general are transformed the same way as points, *normal vectors* must be transformed differently. Normal vectors are not just any direction vectors, they are defined by the surface so that a normal vector is perpendicular to the surface. If M is used to transform the surface, then normals must be transformed by the *transpose of the inverse* of M, that is, $(M^{-1})^T$, or M^{-T} for short.

Figure 2.4 illustrates why simply using M does not work: on the left, we have a line and a vector that is perpendicular to it. On the right, both the line and the vector have been scaled by two in y. Obviously the vector is not perpendicular to the line any longer. The correctly transformed vector, shown by the dotted line, remains normal to the surface.

The key observation is that normal vectors are not really independent directions; instead, they are *defined* to be perpendicular to the underlying surface. That is, assume v_1 and v_2 are points on a surface and that they are close enough that $t = v_1 - v_2$ is a tangent vector on the surface, while n is the normal vector. The normal is perpendicular to the tangent, so the dot product $n^T t$ must remain zero.

Now, if we transform the surface points v_1 and v_2 by M, the tangent vector becomes Mt, and the dot product $n^T(Mt)$ is not necessarily zero any longer. Then how should

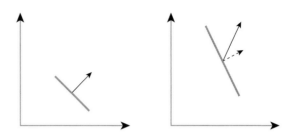

Figure 2.4: On the left we have a line and a normal vector that is perpendicular to it. On the right both have been scaled by 2 in *y*, and the normal is obviously not perpendicular to the line any more. The correctly transformed normal is shown dashed.

we transform the normal to keep it perpendicular to the tangent? All we need to do is to eliminate M from the equation by inserting M^{-1}:

$$n^T M^{-1} M t = n^T t. \tag{2.16}$$

Recalling from Equation (2.12) that $(AB)^T = B^T A^T$, we can rewrite $(n^T M^{-1})^T$ as $(M^{-1})^T n$, and see that the normals need to be transformed by the inverse transpose of M.

There is a very common special case where Mn is parallel to $M^{-T}n$, namely when M consists only of rotations, translations, and uniform scalings (these transformations are introduced in Section 2.3.1). In such a case transforming the normals does not require inverting and transposing M. However, if nonuniform scaling or shearing is involved, the transposed inverse formula must be used. In this case, the normal vectors will generally not be unit length after the transformation, and will have to be renormalized; see Equation (2.4).

2.3 AFFINE TRANSFORMATIONS

Affine transformations are the most widely used modeling operations, and they are simpler than the full 4 × 4 matrices that also encode projections: their bottom row is always [0 0 0 1]. This section covers the different types of affine transformations: translation, rotation, scaling, and shearing. We also give examples how to use transformations for hierarchical modeling.

2.3.1 TYPES OF AFFINE TRANSFORMATIONS

There are four basic component transformations that are affine, and all their combinations are affine as well. They are translation, rotation, scaling, and shearing, and are illustrated in Figure 2.5. They are commonly used to position and orient objects in a scene, or change their size or shape.

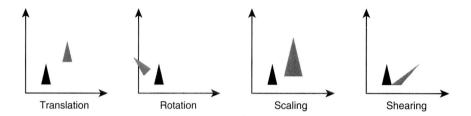

Figure 2.5: The four types of affine transformations: translation, rotation, scaling, shearing. The black shape is the original, the gray after it has been transformed. Note that all transformations take place with respect to the origin.

Translation by a constant offset $\begin{bmatrix} t_x & t_y & t_z \end{bmatrix}^T$ moves a vertex $\boldsymbol{a}$ to $\begin{bmatrix} a_x + t_x & a_y + t_y & a_z + t_z \end{bmatrix}^T$, and is expressed by the matrix

$$T(t_x, t_y, t_z) = \begin{bmatrix} 1 & 0 & 0 & t_x \\ 0 & 1 & 0 & t_y \\ 0 & 0 & 1 & t_z \\ 0 & 0 & 0 & 1 \end{bmatrix}. \tag{2.17}$$

As seen in Figure 2.5 the shape is not changed, it is simply relocated. A translation does not affect a direction vector: directions have $w = 0$ and the only components that differ from the identity matrix are in the last column which corresponds to the w. The inverse of translation is simply another translation to the opposite direction:

$$T^{-1}(t_x, t_y, t_z) = T(-t_x, -t_y, -t_z). \tag{2.18}$$

A *rotation* matrix rotates a point around an axis that passes through the origin. Here is the rotation matrix around the x axis by angle θ:

$$R_x(\theta) = \begin{bmatrix} 1 & 0 & 0 & 0 \\ 0 & \cos(\theta) & -\sin(\theta) & 0 \\ 0 & \sin(\theta) & \cos(\theta) & 0 \\ 0 & 0 & 0 & 1 \end{bmatrix}. \tag{2.19}$$

Similar matrices can be created for rotations around the y and z axes. The rotation axis always goes through the origin, and the positive direction of rotation is chosen using the right-hand rule, as shown in Figure 2.2. Thus, if you look along the axis toward the origin, positive rotation of the other axes is counterclockwise.

Rotations around the main axes are easiest to write down. By combining three main axis rotations, an arbitrary rotation around an arbitrary axis can be created. This technique is called the *Euler angles* after Leonhard Euler who developed the method in the eighteenth century. People have used several axis orders, for example by first rotating around x axis, followed by z axis, then again x axis. Euler rotations can get stuck in a singularity known as *gimbal lock*, where the value of the third rotation becomes irrelevant.

An alternative to Euler angles is to use *quaternions* [Sho85] that can be obtained from an arbitrary rotation axis and rotation angle. Quaternions do not suffer from gimbal lock, and since quaternions are generally quicker to calculate and simpler to interpolate, they are usually preferred over Euler angles for rotations in computer graphics.

A quaternion is a 4D imaginary number with three *imaginary* components and one *real* component

$$q = x\boldsymbol{i} + y\boldsymbol{j} + z\boldsymbol{k} + w, \tag{2.20}$$

but we usually represent a quaternion as a four-vector $\begin{bmatrix} x & y & z & w \end{bmatrix}$. Every 3D rotation can be expressed by a unit rotation axis $\hat{\boldsymbol{a}}$ and a rotation angle θ, and using them we can construct a matching unit quaternion as

$$\hat{q}(\hat{\boldsymbol{a}}, \theta) = \begin{bmatrix} \sin(\theta/2)a_x & \sin(\theta/2)a_y & \sin(\theta/2)a_z & \cos(\theta/2) \end{bmatrix}. \tag{2.21}$$

From the normalized unit quaternion $\hat{q}$ we obtain the following rotation matrix:

$$\boldsymbol{R}(\hat{q}) = \begin{bmatrix} w^2 + x^2 - y^2 - z^2 & 2xy - 2wz & 2xz + 2wy & 0 \\ 2xy + 2wz & w^2 - x^2 + y^2 - z^2 & 2yz - 2wx & 0 \\ 2xz - 2wy & 2yz + 2wx & w^2 - x^2 - y^2 + z^2 & 0 \\ 0 & 0 & 0 & 1 \end{bmatrix}. \tag{2.22}$$

Note, however, that quaternions do not have a one-to-one mapping to 3D rotations: both $\hat{q}$ and $-\hat{q}$ (all components are negated) represent the same rotation. You can check this from the Equation (2.22): all the entries consist of a quadratic combination of quaternion components, so negating them all at the same time yields the same rotation matrix. However, when we later interpolate quaternions in Section 4.1.2 it is very important not to flip the quaternion signs, since the interpolation path from a rotation $\hat{p}$ to $\hat{q}$ is different than the path from $\hat{p}$ to $-\hat{q}$.

Rotations are a member of a special class of matrices, *orthogonal* matrices: all the columns are unit vectors, and they are perpendicular to each other (this also holds for the rows). Let us see what happens when we multiply $\boldsymbol{R}^T\boldsymbol{R}$. The first row of $\boldsymbol{R}^T$ is the same as the first column of $\boldsymbol{R}$, and since it is a unit vector, dotted with itself it produces 1. Further, since it is perpendicular to the rest of the columns, the first row of $\boldsymbol{R}^T\boldsymbol{R}$ yields [1 0 0 0]. Similarly, the other rows consist of a 1 at the diagonal and 0 elsewhere. From this we see that the inverse of a rotation equals its transpose, that is,

$$\boldsymbol{R}^{-1} = \boldsymbol{R}^T. \tag{2.23}$$

Whereas translation and rotation are so-called *rigid* transformations, that is, they do not change the shape or size of objects, *scaling* does change the size and potentially also shape. The scaling matrix is

$$S(s_x, s_y, s_z) = \begin{bmatrix} s_x & 0 & 0 & 0 \\ 0 & s_y & 0 & 0 \\ 0 & 0 & s_z & 0 \\ 0 & 0 & 0 & 1 \end{bmatrix}, \tag{2.24}$$

which scales the x component of a vector by s_x, the y component by s_y, and the z component by s_z. If $s_x = s_y = s_z$, S is a *uniform* scaling which changes the size but not the shape, as in Figure 2.5. If the factors are not the same, then the shape is also changed. The inverse of scaling is equivalent to scaling down by the same factor:

$$S^{-1}(s_x, s_y, s_z) = S(1/s_x, 1/s_y, 1/s_z). \tag{2.25}$$

Shearing is the last type of affine transformations, and also the least frequently used in computer graphics. A shearing matrix is obtained by changing one of the zeros in the upper-left 3×3 corner of the identity matrix to a non-zero value. An example is the matrix

$$H_{01}(h) = \begin{bmatrix} 1 & h & 0 & 0 \\ 0 & 1 & 0 & 0 \\ 0 & 0 & 1 & 0 \\ 0 & 0 & 0 & 1 \end{bmatrix}, \tag{2.26}$$

where the term in the first row and second column is set to $h = 1$ to create the shear in the last image of Figure 2.5. In this case, the greater the y component of the input, the more the x component is sheared to the right. Shearing always distorts the shape. The inverse of shearing is obtained by negating the same shear:

$$H_{ab}^{-1}(h) = H_{ab}(-h). \tag{2.27}$$

One of the most common compound modeling transformations is *rigid motion*, which changes the location and orientation of an object, but retains its shape and size. Rigid motion consists of an arbitrary sequence of rotations and translations, and has the form

$$M = \begin{bmatrix} R & t \\ 0 & 1 \end{bmatrix}, \tag{2.28}$$

where R is a 3×3 matrix, t is a 3×1 column vector, and $0 = [0 \ \ 0 \ \ 0]$. M is equivalent to a rotation by R followed by a translation t. It has a simple inverse, obtained from the inverse of compound transformations (see Equation (2.15)) and the inverses of rotation and translation: start with a translation by $-t$ followed by a rotation by $R^{-1} = R^T$, yielding

$$\begin{bmatrix} R & t \\ 0 & 1 \end{bmatrix}^{-1} = \begin{bmatrix} R^T & -R^T t \\ 0 & 1 \end{bmatrix}. \tag{2.29}$$

2.3.2 TRANSFORMATION AROUND A PIVOT

As shown in Figure 2.5, all these operations are done using the origin as the pivot, the center of rotation. In the second image the triangle rotates around the origin, so it is both re-oriented and moved to a different location. In the third image the triangle grows and every point moves away from the origin. In the last image the vertical position is unchanged, but each point is sheared along the x axis and moved away toward the positive direction of the x axis. Of course, if the scaling would shrink the shape it would move toward the origin, or if the sign of the shearing was flipped the movement would be to the opposite direction.

However, often a transformation should be applied with respect to a *pivot point*, such as the center or one of the corners of the shape. By default, the origin is the only point that does not move in rotation, scaling, or shearing. The trick is to move the pivot first to the origin, apply the transformation, and move the pivot back to where it was. For rotation, for example, the sequence would be $T(p)\,R\,T(-p)$, where p is the pivot. A more complicated example would scale the shape not only around a pivot, but also along a coordinate system that has been rotated by 30° about the z axis. Here the correct sequence would be $T(p)\,R_z(30°)\,S\,R_z(-30°)\,T(-p)$. Reading from right to left, it first moves the pivot to the origin, then applies an inverse rotation to align the desired direction of the scaling with the coordinate axes, performs the scaling, then rotates back and moves the pivot back.

2.3.3 EXAMPLE: HIERARCHICAL MODELING

The basic transformations can be nested to model objects in a hierarchical fashion. Figure 2.6 gives a simple example, a crane, which has been constructed from three boxes and two disks that hide the cracks that the boxes would make at the joints.

The following pseudocode shows how an immediate mode API such as OpenGL would call the modeling operations to draw the crane of Figure 2.6. For simplicity we stay in 2D. The methods `translate`, `rotate`, and `scale` modify the current transformation matrix M by multiplying it *from the right* by a new matrix T, R, or S, respectively for each method. For example, the new matrix after `rotate` is obtained by $M' = MR$.

We have two functions available, `draw_box()` and `draw_unit_disk()`, which draw a box and a disk, respectively, extending from −1 to 1 in both x and y. Note that the sides of the box and the diameter of the disk have length 2, not 1.

Here we also introduce the concept of a *matrix stack*. `push_matrix()` stores the current transformation matrix into a stack, from which it can be recovered by a matching `pop_matrix()`. At first we save the current transformation. We are going to modify the current coordinate system, so we want to be able to restore the original for drawing the rest of the scene:

```
push_matrix()              # save the current matrix
```

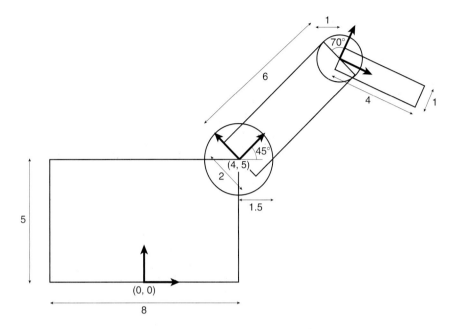

Figure 2.6: A simple crane made of three boxes and two disks (to hide the seams at the joints). The origins of the coordinate systems of the base, upper arm, and the lower arm are indicated with the bold arrows that make a right angle.

We start with a translation that places the crane:

```
translate( x, y )        # move the whole crane
```

Next we draw the base:

```
push_matrix()
  scale( 4, 5/2 )        # scale the box to be 8 x 5
  translate( 0, 1 )      # move the box up so its bottom is at origin
  draw_box()             # draw a box from −1 to 1 in x and y
pop_matrix()             # restore the matrix at the time of last push
```

The call to `draw_box()` is the last one before restoring the current transformation using `pop_matrix()`. Reading backward, we draw a box that would extend from −1 to 1 in x and −1 to 1 in y. However, before that we call `translate` which moves the box up by one so it extends from 0 to 2 in y. In other words, it now sits on top of the origin. This origin is now a good pivot for scaling the box to extend it from −4 to 4 in x and from 0 to 5 in y. Note that if we did not have the matrix stack available, we should manually undo the modeling transformations by issuing `translate( 0, −1 )` and scale(1/4, 2/5) at the end. Also note that even though we write in the code first scale, then translate, and finally draw, the primitives that are drawn are translated first, and scaled second, that is, the order of writing and evaluating is reversed.

Now we translate the coordinate system to the upper right corner of the base so we can place the first disk there:

```
translate( 4, 5 )        # move the origin to the upper right corner
                         # first disk
push_matrix()
  scale( 3/2 )           # scale the disk to have radius 3/2==1.5
  draw_unit_disk()       # draw a disk with radius 1
pop_matrix()
```

Next we use the current origin as the rotation pivot for the upper arm. We rotate the upper arm by angle_1 degrees, which in this example is +45 degrees:

```
rotate( angle_1 )        # rotate upper arm (45 degrees)
```

The upper arm is then modified so that its origin is at the left end of a 6 by 2 box, and the box is drawn:

```
push_matrix()
  scale( 3, 1 )          # scale the box to be 6 x 2
  translate( 1, 0 )      # move left center of the box to the origin
  draw_box()             # draw a box from −1 to 1 in x and y
pop_matrix()
```

Next we translate to the end of the upper arm. It is important to notice that we are currently in the coordinate system of the upper arm, so we simply move the origin 6 units to the right along the *x* axis:

```
translate( 6, 0 )        # move the origin to the end of upper arm
```

There we draw the second disk that is already just the right size:

```
draw_unit_disk()         # draw a disk with radius 1
```

Finally, we rotate the coordinate system for the lower arm, draw the lower arm, clean up the transformations, and exit:

```
rotate( angle_2 )      # rotate lower arm (−70 degrees)

push_matrix()
  scale( 2, 1/2 )      # scale the box to be 4 x 1
  translate( 1, 0 )    # move left center of the box to the origin
  draw_box()           # draw a box from −1 to 1 in x and y
pop_matrix()

pop_matrix()             # final pop to restore coordinate axes as they
                         # were
```

By calling this routine with different values of (x,y), angle_1 and angle_2 it is possible to move and animate the crane. (x,y) moves everything, angle_1 rotates both the upper arm and the lower arm attached to it, while angle_2 only rotates the lower arm.

2.4 EYE COORDINATE SYSTEM

Objects in world coordinates or object coordinates must be transformed into the *eye coordinate system*, also known as *camera coordinates*, for rendering. By definition, the camera in OpenGL ES and M3G lies at the origin of the eye coordinate system, views down along the negative *z* axis, with the positive *x* axis pointing to the right and the positive *y* pointing up.

Rather than modeling directly in the eye coordinates, it is easier to model objects in world coordinates, and start with a world-to-eye coordinate transformation. To calculate this transformation, we first study the structure of affine transformations and how they transform homogeneous points v. We exploit that structure to directly write down the eye-to-world transformation M_{ew}, which we finally invert to obtain the world-to-eye transformation M_{we}.

We begin by asserting that M_{ew} is an affine transformation and therefore has the last row [0 0 0 1]:

$$M_{ew} = \begin{bmatrix} a & b & c & d \\ e & f & g & h \\ i & j & k & l \\ 0 & 0 & 0 & 1 \end{bmatrix}. \tag{2.30}$$

The first three columns of M_{ew} are direction vectors, since their *w* components are zero, while the last column is a point as its $w = 1$. Looking at Figure 2.7 (and ignoring t and u for now), we want to choose values for M_{ew} so that it transforms any point in the eye coordinate system xyz to the world coordinate system XYZ. Let us start from the origin o; its coordinates in xyz are $[0 \ 0 \ 0 \ 1]^T$ by definition. This extracts the last column of M_{ew}: $M_{ew}[0 \ 0 \ 0 \ 1]^T = \begin{bmatrix} d & h & l & 1 \end{bmatrix}^T = \begin{bmatrix} o_x & o_y & o_z & 1 \end{bmatrix}^T$. Hence the last column of M_{ew} is the location of o expressed in XYZ coordinates.

Similarly, the first column is the directional vector x, again in XYZ coordinates: $M_{ew}[1 \ 0 \ 0 \ 0]^T = [a \ e \ i \ 0]^T = \begin{bmatrix} x_x & x_y & x_z & 0 \end{bmatrix}^T$, and the second and third columns are y and z, respectively, expressed in XYZ coordinates.

Now we can take an arbitrary point $v = \begin{bmatrix} v_x & v_y & v_z & 1 \end{bmatrix}^T$ in eye coordinates xyz, and M_{ew} produces the world coordinates XYZ for the same point. Let us see how this works. The last component $w = 1$ takes us to the origin o. From the origin, we move a distance v_x to the direction of x, from there v_y times y, and finally v_z times z. To summarize, with the matrix from Equation (2.30) we get the 3D point $o + v_x x + v_y y + v_z z$.

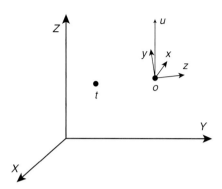

Figure 2.7: Defining an eye coordinate system (lowercase *xyz*) using the camera origin *o*, target *t*, and view-up vector *u*, all defined in the world coordinate system (uppercase *XYZ*).

We can now write down the whole eye-to-world transformation as

$$
M_{ew} = \begin{bmatrix} x_x & y_x & z_x & o_x \\ x_y & y_y & z_y & o_y \\ x_z & y_z & z_z & o_z \\ 0 & 0 & 0 & 1 \end{bmatrix}
\tag{2.31}
$$

from which we obtain the world-to-eye matrix using the inversion formula of Equation (2.29):

$$
M_{we} = \begin{bmatrix} x_x & x_y & x_z & -x^T o \\ y_x & y_y & y_z & -y^T o \\ z_x & z_y & z_z & -z^T o \\ 0 & 0 & 0 & 1 \end{bmatrix}.
\tag{2.32}
$$

You can place this in the beginning of the rendering loop, and model the rest of the scene in world coordinates. The compound transformation moves the objects into the eye coordinates, ready for projection into the frame buffer.

What remains is to calculate the coordinate axes *xyz* in the world coordinate system. In Figure 2.7 the camera is located at *o*, is looking toward the target point *t*, and is oriented so that the view-up vector *u* is aligned with the up direction on the image plane. Note that the view-up vector must point at some other direction than the viewing direction *t*−*o* for the following to work.

Since the camera is viewing along the negative *z* axis, *z* must be the direction vector that extends from *t* to *o*, and we assign $z = \frac{o-t}{\|o-t\|}$. We know that *y* must be on the same plane as *z* and the view-up vector *u*, while *x* must be perpendicular to that plane. We also know that x, y, z must form a right-handed coordinate system. Therefore, we can obtain x from $u \times z$, also normalized as z was. Finally, we get $y = z \times x$. In this case we know that z and x are already perpendicular unit vectors, so y will also be a unit vector, and there is no need to normalize it (except to perhaps make sure no numerical error has crept in). Note the order of the cross products: they must follow a circular order so that $x \times y$ produces z, $y \times z$ produces x, and $z \times x$ produces y.

2.5 PROJECTIONS

After the scene has been transformed to the eye coordinates, we need to *project* the scene to the image plane of our camera. Figure 2.8 shows the principle of *perspective projection*. We have placed the eye at the origin so that it looks along the negative z axis, with the image plane at $z = -1$. A point (Y, Z) is projected along the *projector*, a line connecting the point to the *center of projection* (the origin), intersecting the image plane at $(Y', -1)$. From similar triangles we see that $Y' = -Y/Z$. We can also see that this model incorporates the familiar *perspective foreshortening* effect: an object with the same height but being located further away appears smaller (as illustrated by the second, narrower projector). The projection matrix

$$P = \begin{bmatrix} 1 & 0 & 0 & 0 \\ 0 & 1 & 0 & 0 \\ 0 & 0 & 1 & 0 \\ 0 & 0 & -1 & 0 \end{bmatrix} \tag{2.33}$$

performs this projection. Let us check: with $x = [\, X \ \ Y \ \ Z \ \ 1 \,]^T$, $Px = [\, X \ \ Y \ \ Z \ \ -Z \,]^T$, which, after the homogeneous division by the last component, becomes $(-X/Z, -Y/Z, -1)$. This is the projected point on the plane $z = -1$.

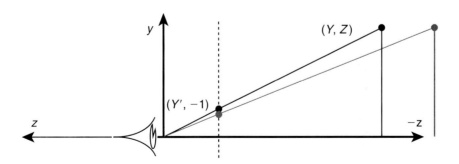

Figure 2.8: Perspective camera projection. Objects that are farther away appear smaller.

2.5.1 NEAR AND FAR PLANES AND THE DEPTH BUFFER

Equation (2.33) loses information, namely the depth, as all objects are projected to the same $z = -1$ plane. We could try to retain the depth order by sorting objects based on their depths, and drawing them in a back-to-front order (this is called the Painter's Algorithm). However, it may not be possible to sort the objects, especially if there is a cyclic overlap so that A hides B which hides C which hides A, or some objects intersect each other. One possibility is to leave the z component unmodified and use it directly to sort each pixel using a *depth buffer*, also known as the *z-buffer* [Cat974].

A depth buffer must be of finite size, and therefore cannot store all depths between zero and infinity. Instead, we define two planes, the *near* and *far* camera planes, and quantize the depths between the planes. Any objects between these two planes are rendered, and any others ignored. The depths of these objects are stored and compared on a per-pixel basis, leaving only the topmost object visible at each pixel.

Similarly, we cannot display the infinite image plane, but only a finite window of it. If we define that window on the near plane, we end up with a *view frustum*, displayed on the left side of Figure 2.9. The word "frustum" means a truncated pyramid, and that pyramid is formed from the *view cone* starting from the origin and passing through the window in the near plane, and cut off by the near and far planes. Only objects or parts of objects that lie within the view frustum will be displayed.

We now modify our projection matrix so that objects at $z = -n$ project to -1 and at $z = -f$ project to 1:

$$P = \begin{bmatrix} 1 & 0 & 0 & 0 \\ 0 & 1 & 0 & 0 \\ 0 & 0 & -\dfrac{f+n}{f-n} & -\dfrac{2fn}{f-n} \\ 0 & 0 & -1 & 0 \end{bmatrix}. \tag{2.34}$$

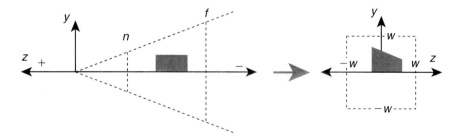

Figure 2.9: The viewing frustum of the eye coordinate system is transformed to the clip coordinates, yielding a cube from $-w$ to w in x, y, and z. Observe how objects closer to the camera become larger.

Let us check: a point $\begin{bmatrix} x & y & -n & 1 \end{bmatrix}^T$ on the near plane moves to

$$
\begin{bmatrix} x \\ y \\ (fn + nn - 2fn)/(f - n) \\ n \end{bmatrix} = \begin{bmatrix} x \\ y \\ -n \\ n \end{bmatrix} = \begin{bmatrix} x/n \\ y/n \\ -1 \\ 1 \end{bmatrix}.
$$

Similarly, a point $\begin{bmatrix} x & y & -f & 1 \end{bmatrix}^T$ on the far plane moves to $\begin{bmatrix} x & y & f & f \end{bmatrix}^T = \begin{bmatrix} x/f & y/f & 1 & 1 \end{bmatrix}^T$.

Multiplying a point in eye coordinates with **P** takes it to the *clip coordinates*. The viewing frustum is transformed into a box where the x, y, and z components are between $-w$ and w. *Clipping*, described in Section 3.3, takes place in this coordinate system. Briefly, clipping is the process of removing any parts of a geometric primitive, such as a triangle, that extend outside the view frustum.

After clipping, the points are transformed into *normalized device coordinates* (NDC) by dividing the clip coordinates by w. As a result, all remaining points have x, y, and z coordinates that are between -1 and 1. This is illustrated on the right side of Figure 2.9. Notice how the near end of the box is much bigger than the far end, as each side of the cube is transformed to the size that it is going to appear in the final image.

The homogeneous division by w causes a nonlinearity in how the z or depth values are transformed, as illustrated in Figure 2.10.

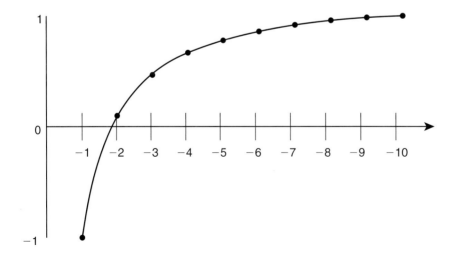

Figure 2.10: Nonlinear transformation of z with **near** $= 1$ and **far** $= 10$. With camera at $z = 0$ and looking down to negative z, values in $[-1, -10]$ (horizontal axis) map to $[-1, 1]$ (vertical axis).

> **Pitfall:** Whereas it would be easy for the programmer to set n to a very small and f to large number (to see everything that is in front of the camera), that is not a good strategy. Depth buffers have only a finite accuracy (sometimes as low as 16 bits). As Figure 2.10 shows, the first 10% of the range between the near and far planes consumes over half of the transformed z accuracy. You should always try to get the near and far planes as close to the objects in the scene as feasible. Of these two it is more important to get the near plane away from the camera, getting tight bounds on the far plane is less crucial.

If we do not have enough useful resolution in the depth buffer, different depths may get mapped to the same value, and the graphics engine cannot reliably separate which surface should be behind and which in front, leading to visual artifacts called *z-fighting*, as illustrated in Figure 2.11.

The likelihood of z-fighting grows with the far/near ratio, with coarser display and depth buffer resolution, with increasing field of view and distance from the camera, and with increasing distance from the z axis (that is, screen corners do worse than the center) [AS06]. Some tricks that relate to depth buffer resolution are described in Section 2.6.

2.5.2 A GENERAL VIEW FRUSTUM

The previous section defined a *canonical* frustum, with an opening angle of 90° both vertically and horizontally, and with the window centered on the z axis. More precisely, it contains points with $-n > z > -f$, $|z| > |x|$, and $|z| > |y|$.

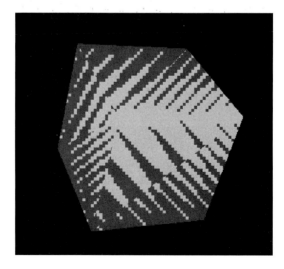

Figure 2.11: Z-fighting caused by two nearly coplanar surfaces. In this case, two instances of the same cube are rendered with slightly different transformations.

However, we often want a window that is not square, and sometimes not even centered with respect to the viewing direction. It is possible to define the projection matrix P directly from the near distance n, far distance f, and the extent of the window on the near plane with left and right edges at l and r and bottom and top edges at b and t, as shown in Figure 2.12.

The trick is to transform the irregular viewing cone to the canonical one and then use Equation (2.34). First, we shear the asymmetric frustum as a function of the z coordinate so the frustum becomes symmetric around the z axis. The window center has coordinates $((r + l)/2, (t + b)/2, -n)$, and we want to map that to $(0, 0, -n)$. This is illustrated as the first transition at the bottom row of Figure 2.12, and contained in the third matrix in Equation (2.35). Next, the window is scaled so it becomes square and opens with a 90° angle both horizontally and vertically. That is, we need to map both the width $r - l$ and the height $t - b$ to $2n$. We achieve this with the second matrix in Equation (2.35), illustrated by the second transition at the bottom row of Figure 2.12. What remains to be done is to use Equation (2.34) to map the view frustum to a unit box for depth comparisons and eventual image display.

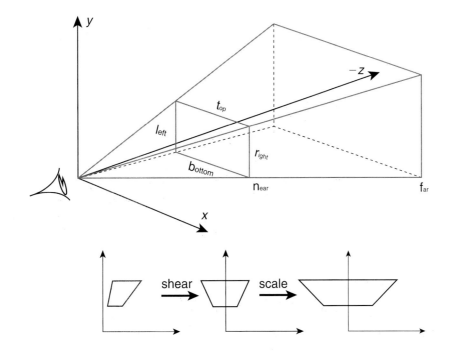

Figure 2.12: A general view frustum is defined by the near and far distances, and a window on the near plane defined by the window top, bottom, left, and right edges. The bottom row illustrates the operations needed to transform a general view frustum to the canonical one.

$$
\mathbf{P} =
\begin{bmatrix}
1 & 0 & 0 & 0 \\
0 & 1 & 0 & 0 \\
0 & 0 & -\dfrac{f+n}{f-n} & -\dfrac{2fn}{f-n} \\
0 & 0 & -1 & 0
\end{bmatrix}
\begin{bmatrix}
\dfrac{2n}{r-l} & 0 & 0 & 0 \\
0 & \dfrac{2n}{t-b} & 0 & 0 \\
0 & 0 & 1 & 0 \\
0 & 0 & 0 & 1
\end{bmatrix}
\begin{bmatrix}
1 & 0 & \dfrac{r+l}{2n} & 0 \\
0 & 1 & \dfrac{t+b}{2n} & 0 \\
0 & 0 & 1 & 0 \\
0 & 0 & 0 & 1
\end{bmatrix}
\quad (2.35)
$$

$$
=
\begin{bmatrix}
\dfrac{2n}{r-l} & 0 & \dfrac{r+l}{r-l} & 0 \\
0 & \dfrac{2n}{t-b} & \dfrac{t+b}{t-b} & 0 \\
0 & 0 & -\dfrac{f+n}{f-n} & -\dfrac{2fn}{f-n} \\
0 & 0 & -1 & 0
\end{bmatrix}.
\quad (2.36)
$$

Its inverse is

$$
\mathbf{P}^{-1} =
\begin{bmatrix}
\dfrac{r-l}{2n} & 0 & 0 & \dfrac{r+l}{2n} \\
0 & \dfrac{t-b}{2n} & 0 & \dfrac{t+b}{2n} \\
0 & 0 & 0 & -1 \\
0 & 0 & -\dfrac{f-n}{2fn} & \dfrac{f+n}{2fn}
\end{bmatrix}.
\quad (2.37)
$$

However, in most cases you do not need to use this generic version. It is often easier to define a straight projection (one that is aligned with z) with a given aspect ratio a ($a = w/h$, where w and h are window width and height, respectively), and a vertical opening angle θ. Now the projection simplifies to

$$
\mathbf{P} =
\begin{bmatrix}
\dfrac{1}{a\tan(\theta/2)} & 0 & 0 & 0 \\
0 & \dfrac{1}{\tan(\theta/2)} & 0 & 0 \\
0 & 0 & -\dfrac{f+n}{f-n} & -\dfrac{2fn}{f-n} \\
0 & 0 & -1 & 0
\end{bmatrix}.
\quad (2.38)
$$

Now we can fully appreciate the usefulness of homogeneous coordinates. Earlier we saw that they unify directions and locations into a single, unambiguous representation. They also allow representing all affine transformations using 4 × 4 matrices. Using only three-vectors, rotations would require a matrix multiplication, while translations would require vector addition. Finally, perspective projection requires a division by z, which is not a linear operation and cannot therefore be expressed with matrices. However, the conversion of homogeneous coordinates to 3D by dividing by the *w* component allows us to express the division, which is a nonlinear operation in 3D, as a linear operation in 4D homogeneous coordinates.

2.5.3 PARALLEL PROJECTION

An advantage of the perspective projection is the foreshortening: objects that are far away seem smaller. However, making accurate measurements from such images becomes difficult. This is illustrated in Figure 2.13, where the top row shows a cube drawn using perspective projection. The diagram on the right shows the projector from each cube corner connecting to the center of projection. The image of the front face is larger than that of the rear face, even though the faces in reality are equally large. *Parallel projection* is useful when you want to place an object onto the display in 2D image coordinates rather than 3D world coordinates, or when you want to see axis-aligned projections as in engineering drawings or CAD programs. This is illustrated on the bottom row of Figure 2.13. Now the projectors are parallel, and the images of the front and rear face are of equal size.

We only cover the simplest parallel projection, the *orthographic* projection, where the projectors are perpendicular to the image plane. Directions parallel to the image plane retain

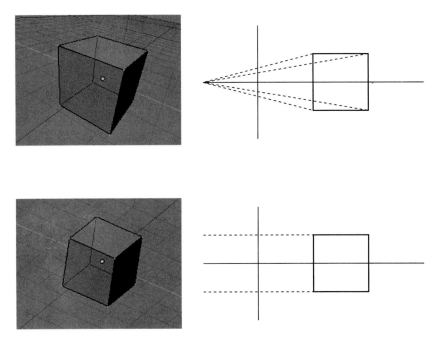

Figure 2.13: Perspective and parallel projection views of a cube.

their size, and it is easy to make measurements along those directions. The direction along the projection vanishes, however. As no perspective division is required, we simply need to define a box in camera coordinates that is first centered around the origin and then scaled so all sides extend from -1 to 1. Therefore, if we define the viewing volume with l, r, t, b, n, f as before, the projection matrix becomes

$$P = \begin{bmatrix} \dfrac{2}{r-l} & 0 & 0 & -\dfrac{r+l}{r-l} \\ 0 & \dfrac{2}{t-b} & 0 & -\dfrac{t+b}{t-b} \\ 0 & 0 & \dfrac{-2}{f-n} & -\dfrac{f+n}{f-n} \\ 0 & 0 & 0 & 1 \end{bmatrix}. \tag{2.39}$$

Its inverse is

$$P^{-1} = \begin{bmatrix} \dfrac{r-l}{2} & 0 & 0 & \dfrac{r+l}{2} \\ 0 & \dfrac{t-b}{2} & 0 & \dfrac{t+b}{2} \\ 0 & 0 & \dfrac{f-n}{-2} & \dfrac{f+n}{2} \\ 0 & 0 & 0 & 1 \end{bmatrix}. \tag{2.40}$$

Parallel projections require fewer computations than perspective projections because when you transform a regular 3D point $\begin{bmatrix} x & y & z & 1 \end{bmatrix}^T$, the w component of the result remains 1, and the homogeneous division is not needed.

2.6 VIEWPORT AND 2D COORDINATE SYSTEMS

In the normalized device coordinate system (NDC), each coordinate of the vertex $\begin{bmatrix} x & y & z \end{bmatrix}$ can only have values between -1 and 1, assuming that the vertex lies within the view frustum. The x and y coordinates are mapped into a *viewport* that starts at pixel (v_x, v_y), is w pixels wide and h pixels high, and is centered at $(c_x, c_y) = (v_x + w/2, v_y + h/2)$.

The z coordinate is mapped to the range $[0, 1]$ by default, but it is possible to restrict it between a smaller *depth range* interval $[d_n, d_f]$. The "width" of the depth range is then $d = d_f - d_n$, and its "center" is $c_z = (d_n + d_f)/2$. Now the viewport transformation from NDC (x_d, y_d, z_d) to window coordinates (x_w, y_w, z_w) is

$$\begin{bmatrix} x_w \\ y_w \\ z_w \end{bmatrix} = \begin{bmatrix} (w/2)x_d + c_x \\ (h/2)y_d + c_y \\ (d/2)z_d + c_z \end{bmatrix}. \tag{2.41}$$

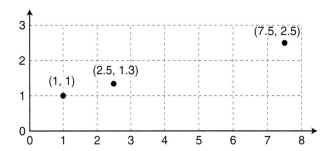

Figure 2.14: The pixel coordinate system of OpenGL. Integer values fall *between* pixels; pixels are the squares of the integer grid.

The 2D coordinate system used in OpenGL (ES) has its origin at the lower left corner such that x grows to the right and y upward, as illustrated in Figure 2.14. In many windowing systems, as well as in M3G, the y axis is flipped: the origin is at the upper left corner and y grows down.

Regardless of the orientation of y, integer values fall between the pixels. Looking at the pixel at the bottom left in OpenGL, its lower left corner has coordinates $(0, 0)$, the center of that pixel is at $(0.5, 0.5)$, and its top right corner is at $(1, 1)$. For the top right corner pixel the corresponding coordinates would be $(w - 1, h - 1)$, $(w - 0.5, h - 0.5)$, and (w, h).

If you want to place vertices accurately to the center of a pixel, and use integer coordinates for the pixels, you can define a parallel projection with $(l, r, b, t) = (-0.5, w - 0.5, -0.5, h - 0.5)$, and use identity for the camera transformation. Now $(0, 0)$ lands at the center of the lower left corner pixel, and $(w - 1, h - 1)$ at the center of the top right corner pixel.

The possibility to set the depth range seems a bit curious at first glance, as the use cases are not very obvious; here we mention two. Many applications render a background image or "sky box" behind the rest of the scene, so as to give a sense of depth without actually drawing any distant objects. For best performance, the background should only be drawn where it will not be covered by foreground objects. An easy way to accomplish that is to render the background last, after all opaque objects, and set its depth range to $[1.0, 1.0]$. This ensures that the background always lies at the maximum depth.

Another use case relates to the nonlinear distribution of the resolution of the depth buffer, where most of the accuracy is spent on the near field by default. If you have some objects very close to the camera (such as the controls in a cockpit of an airplane), and other objects faraway, e.g., other planes, or buildings on the ground, the nonlinearity of the depth buffer means that there is hardly any depth resolution left for the faraway objects. Now, if you give the range $[0.0, 0.1]$ for the nearby objects, render them with the far view frustum plane pulled just beyond them, and then render the other objects with depth range $[0.1, 1.0]$ such that the near plane is pushed relatively far from the camera, you have a much better chance of having sufficient depth buffer resolution so the distant objects render correctly without z-fighting. The generalization of the above technique is to divide the scene into *n* slices, and render each of them with the near and far planes matching the start and end of the slice. This distributes the depth buffer resolution more evenly to all depths.

LOW-LEVEL RENDERING

This chapter describes the traditional low-level 3D pipeline as it has been defined in OpenGL. A diagram of the OpenGL ES pipeline in Figure 3.1 shows how various pipeline components relate to each other, and how the data flows from an application to the frame buffer. Figure 3.2 visualizes some of the processing in these various pipeline stages. Note that the diagram, and the whole pipeline specification, is only conceptual; implementations may vary the processing order, but they must produce the same result as the conceptual specification.

We start by describing the primitives that define the shapes and patterns that are displayed, including both the 3D geometric primitives such as points, lines, and triangles, as well as the 2D image primitives. The geometric primitives can have materials that interact with light, and they can be affected by fog. The primitives are projected into a coordinate system that allows simple determination of what is visible: a primitive is visible if it is not occluded by other primitives, and it lies in the viewing frustum of the camera. Continuous 3D shapes are then rasterized into discrete fragments, and the fragment colors can be modulated by one or more texture maps. The fragments can still be rejected by various tests, and their colors can be blended with the pixels that already exist in the frame buffer.

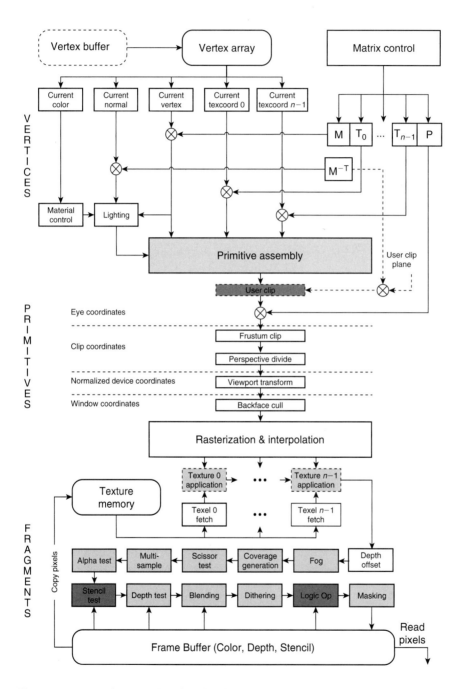

Figure 3.1: A simplified view of the OpenGL ES 1.1 pipeline. Shapes with dashed outlines indicate features that are new or significantly expanded in version 1.1. Dark gray and light gray shapes indicate features that are not included in M3G, or are included in simplified form, respectively. M is the modelview matrix, the T_i are texture matrices, and P is the projection matrix.

Figure 3.2: Illustrating the various stages of shading discussed in Chapters 3 and 8–10. *Top row, left to right:* wire frame model; filled model; diffuse lighting; diffuse and Phong specular lighting. *Bottom row:* texturing added; texturing with a separate specular pass; bump mapping added; and rendered with an intersecting translucent object to demonstrate Z-buffering and alpha blending. (See the color plate.)

3.1 RENDERING PRIMITIVES

In this section we describe the rendering primitives of a 3D engine. We begin with the geometric primitives such as points, lines, and triangles, and then continue to raster primitives using texture map data.

3.1.1 GEOMETRIC PRIMITIVES

The basic geometric primitives defined in OpenGL are points, lines, triangles, quads, and polygons. However, in many hardware-accelerated 3D engines triangles are the only truly native rendering primitive. They are in a sense the easiest and best-behaved of the primitives. Three points always lie on a common plane, and if they are not collinear, they uniquely define that plane. The projection of a triangle into the image plane is well defined and changes continuously as we zoom in or zoom out.

Points and lines are mathematically even simpler than triangles. The problem is that a mathematical point does not have any extent, nor does a line have any width. Instead of turning a point into a sphere and a line into a cylinder—which would still be real 3D entities—OpenGL defines points and lines as mixed 2D/3D entities, where the location of a point or line end points are true 3D entities, but after they are projected into the image plane they have a *point size* or *line width* defined in pixels, making them partially 2D entities. When you zoom into them, the distance between the points or line end points grows, but the point size or line width remains constant. However, it is possible to attenuate the size of a point based on its distance from the camera, so as to approximate the effect of true perspective.

Quads or quadrilaterals, i.e., polygons with four corners, and other polygons are problematic, because unlike triangles, they are not guaranteed to be planar. If the vertices of a polygon do not lie on the same plane, the edges between the vertices are still well defined, but the surface between them is not. In the worst case, when viewed from the side, the viewer would see both the front and back side at the same time. An obvious solution, which most OpenGL drivers perform internally, is to split the polygon into triangles. The OpenGL ES standardization group decided to sidestep the whole issue and only support triangles.

Figure 3.3 shows the primitives supported by OpenGL ES. All of them can be expressed as an array of vertices with implicit connectivity. In the upper row we have four vertices, and depending on the primitive type, the four vertices are interpreted either as four points, two disjoint line segments, a strip of three lines, or a loop of four lines. Similarly, in the bottom row six vertices define either two disjoint triangles, a four-triangle strip where the first three vertices define the first triangle and then every new vertex is connected with the two previous vertices, or a four-triangle fan where the first vertex is the center of the fan, and all the other vertices connect to it. The use of the basic primitives to define a more complex object is illustrated in the first image in Figure 3.2.

Figure 3.4 shows a small segment of a regular triangle mesh. You can see that all the internal vertices are adjacent to six triangles, that is, every vertex is responsible for two triangles (see the grayed out triangles on the right upper corner), giving 0.5 vertices per triangle. This, however, works only in the limit with a large enough closed mesh. For smaller and irregular meshes, possibly with boundaries, there are usually 0.5–1.0 vertices

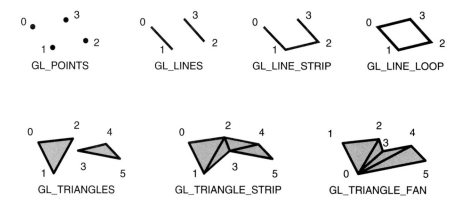

Figure 3.3: The geometric primitives in OpenGL ES include points, three ways of defining line segments, and three ways of defining triangles.

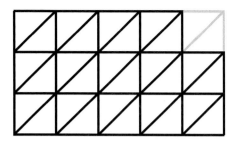

Figure 3.4: A piece of a regular triangle mesh. In this case every nonboundary vertex is shared by six triangles. In other words, most vertices define two new triangles.

per triangle. The ratios become important as we study how much data must be passed from the program to the graphics hardware, and possibly replicated.

The most straightforward way uses *implicit indexing*, and simply lists the triangles of a mesh, three vertices of a triangle at a time. This is clearly wasteful, as each vertex is expressed and transformed six times, on the average. Triangle strips and fans are much more efficient, as after the first triangle every new vertex produces a new triangle. But as you can see in Figure 3.4, if you make each row of triangles a strip, the vertices in the internal rows have to be processed twice, once when they are the "lower" vertices of a strip, and the second time as the "upper" vertices of the next strip.

If you want to do better, you have to use *explicit indexing*. That is, instead of giving the vertices in a particular order from which the primitive connectivity is deduced, you first just give the vertices in an array, and then have another array which indexes into the first array and gives the triangle connectivity using the same methods as with the implicit ordering, e.g., triangles, triangle strips, and so on. A key advantage is that now it is possible to avoid transforming vertices more than once. Many engines use a *vertex cache*, which buffers transformed vertices on the GPU. If the same vertex is indexed again, the system may avoid retransforming the same vertex. A naive implementation would require a large vertex cache, but a careful ordering of the triangles so that the vertices are accessed again soon after the first use, instead of much later, can provide almost the same savings using only a small vertex cache [Hop99].

Similar primitives should be *batched* as much as possible, i.e., they should be put into the same array. It is much faster to draw one array of a hundred triangles than fifty arrays of two triangles each. This becomes even more important if parts of the scene use different materials and textures—combining primitives that share the same state, e.g., texture maps, can produce considerable savings as the state changes are often quite costly. See Section 6.4 for more information.

Most modeling programs support higher-order smooth surfaces and curves such as subdivision surfaces [ZSD+00], Bézier patches [Boo01], or nonuniform rational b-splines

(NURBS) [PT96]. Smooth primitives encode smooth surfaces much more compactly than a dense triangle mesh can. Additionally, when you zoom close enough, the triangle mesh becomes visibly polygonal, while a smooth surface remains smooth no matter how closely inspected. This makes smooth surfaces good candidates for a storage format. However, smooth surfaces are much more complicated to rasterize into pixels than triangles are. Furthermore, there are many choices for the representation of smooth surfaces, and there is no general consensus of a type that would be optimal for all uses. Therefore modern 3D engines do not usually provide direct support for smooth surfaces, but require the application to tessellate them into a set of triangles, which may be cached for repeated rendering.

3.1.2 RASTER PRIMITIVES

Raster primitives consist of image data, blocks of pixels, and do not scale as naturally as geometric primitives. If you scale a raster image down, several input pixels map to each output pixel, and they need to be first low-pass filtered, averaged, so that the right amount of blurring in the output takes place. This can be done, and it only requires some additional computation. However, when scaling a raster image up, no new information is introduced. Instead, the pixels grow to become large visible squares, and the image quality suffers.

An advantage of raster images over geometric primitives is that arbitrarily complicated imagery can be rendered very quickly. In its simplest form, a raster image is just copied into the frame buffer without any scaling or blending operations. Another advantage is that obtaining raster images can be easy. One can draw the images with an image-editing program, or one can take photos with a digital camera. Applications of raster images include using them to draw a background, e.g., the faraway landscape and sky in a rally game, or the foreground, e.g., the dashboard of the rally car, while the moving objects such as the road, other cars, and trees that are close enough are drawn using geometric primitives. 2D games are often designed and implemented using *sprites*, small raster images that are directly placed on the 2D window. In 3D, sprites are often called *impostors*, especially if they are used in place of an object with complicated geometry, such as a tree or a bush.

Unless the sprite or impostor is a rectangular block, some of the pixels need to be marked as transparent, while the rest are fully or partially opaque. The opacity information is stored in an additional *alpha* channel value associated with each pixel. With bitmaps one can take this approach to the extreme, storing only a single bit per pixel for opacity. Such bitmaps can be used for drawing non-antialiased text, for example.

The concept of *texture mapping* complements geometric primitives with raster images. In texture mapping one "pastes" a raster image on the geometric primitives such as triangles, before drawing the scene from the vantage point of the camera. We will cover texture mapping in more detail later. Whereas OpenGL supports direct drawing of both raster images and bitmaps, OpenGL ES simplifies the API by supporting only texture mapping, with the idea that the omitted functionality can be simply emulated by drawing a rectangle formed of two texture-mapped triangles. While M3G supports background images and sprites, those are often implemented using textured triangles.

3.2 LIGHTING

The earlier sections have covered the 3D primitives and transformations needed to model objects, place a camera, and project a scene to the camera's frame buffer. That is sufficient for line drawings, or silhouettes of shapes in uniform colors. However, that is not enough to get an impression of the 3D shape of an object. For this we need to estimate how light sources illuminate the surfaces of the objects. As Figure 3.1 shows, the user may specify vertex colors that are used either as is, or as surface material properties used in the lighting equation.

Properly determining the correct color of a surface illuminated by various light sources is a difficult problem, and a series of simplifications is required to come up with a computationally reasonable approximation of the true interaction of light, matter, participating media (such as the air with fog and airborne dust), and finally the eye observing the scene. A light source, such as the sun or an electric bulb, emits countless photons to every direction; These photons then travel, usually along a straight path, and can be absorbed or filtered by the medium through which they travel. When a photon hits a surface it can be reflected to various directions; it can be refracted and transmitted through a transparent or translucent material, it can be scattered inside the material and exit in a different location from where it entered, it can be absorbed by the matter, and the absorbed energy may be later released as fluorescence or phosphorescence. Raytracing algorithms mimic this complicated behavior of rays, but traditional real-time graphics architectures use local, simpler approximations.

In this section we first describe the color representation. Then we explain normal vectors and what they are used for. We continue with the OpenGL reflectance model consisting of ambient, diffuse, specular, and emissive components of material properties, cover the supported light sources, and finish with the complete lighting equation. The second through fourth images in Figure 3.2 illustrate the effects of ambient, diffuse, and specular shading, respectively.

3.2.1 COLOR

Light is electromagnetic radiation of any wavelength, but the visible range of a typical human eye is between 400 and 700 nm. *Color*, on the other hand, is more of a perception in people's minds than a part of objective reality. The eye contains three types of sensors called cones. Each type is sensitive to different wavelengths. There is also a fourth sensor type, rod, but its signals are only perceived when it is dark. From this fact two interesting observations follow. First, even though all the colors of a rainbow correspond to a single wavelength, many colors that people can see, e.g., pink, brown, purple, or white, can only be created by a combination of at least two or even three different wavelengths. Second, one can use three "primary" colors (in computer graphics **Red**, **Green**, and **Blue**), the combinations of which create most colors that people are capable of seeing. The absence of R, G, and B is black, adding red and green together produces yellow, green and blue produce cyan, and red and blue produce magenta. Adding equal amounts of R, G, and B produces a shade of gray ranging from black to white.

In OpenGL light is represented as a triplet of arbitrary numbers denoting the amount of red, green, and blue light, each of which is clamped to the range [0, 1] before being stored into the frame buffer. 1.0 means the maximum amount of light that can be displayed on a traditional display, and the RGB triplet (1.0, 1.0, 1.0) indicates white light, (1.0, 0.0, 0.0) provides bright red, and (0.0, 0.0, 0.3) corresponds to dark blue. Larger values are simply clamped to 1.0, so (11.0, 22.0, 0.5) will become (1.0, 1.0, 0.5) at the time of display. If 8-bit integers are used to encode the color components, 0 maps to 0.0 and 255 maps to 1.0.

The stored light values do not really correspond to the amount of light *energy*. The human eye responds to the amount of light very nonlinearly, and the number rather encodes a roughly linear color *perception*. For example, (0.5, 0.5, 0.5) produces a gray color, roughly halfway between black and white. This is useful as it makes it easy to assign colors, but it does not correspond to true light intensities. A more physically correct representation would store floating-point numbers that correspond to the amount of light energy at each channel of a pixel, and finally map the result into color values between 0.0 and 1.0 by taking into account the eye's nonlinear response to light. Such *high dynamic range* (HDR) light and color representations are possible on desktop hardware with the support of floating-point frame buffers and textures, and there are even HDR displays that can emit brighter lights than traditional displays. The mobile APIs only support the traditional low-dynamic range representation of 4–8 bits per color channel.

In addition to the color channels, OpenGL defines an additional alpha channel. The alpha channel does not have any inherent meaning or interpretation, but is usually used to encode the level of transparency of a material or surface. Alpha is crucial for compositing, such as merging of nonrectangular images so that the boundaries blend in smoothly with the background. Many systems save in storage by omitting the *destination* alpha, that is, the frame buffer only stores the RGB value, and the stored alpha is implicitly 1.0. However, it is always possible to define an arbitrary (between 0.0 and 1.0) value as the *source* alpha, for example, in the definition of a surface material.

The amount of storage used in the frame buffer can be denoted by the names of the channels and the number of bits in each channel. Some first-generation mobile graphics engines use 16-bit frame buffers. For example, an RGB565 frame buffer has a total of 16 bits for the red, green, and blue channels, and does not store any alpha. Here the red and blue channels have only 5 bits each (31 maps to 1.0) while the green channel has 6 bits (63 maps to 1.0). RGBA4444 and RGBA5551 also use 16 bits per pixel, the former allocates four and the latter one bit for alpha. Desktop engines have for long used frame buffers with 8 bits per channel, i.e., RGB888 and RGBA8888, and those are becoming increasingly common also on handhelds. The desktop and console world is already moving to 16-bit floating-point frame buffers (a total of 64 bits for RGBA), but those are not yet available for mobile devices.

3.2.2 NORMAL VECTORS

The intensity of the light reflected back from a surface element to the camera depends strongly on the orientation of the element. An orientation can be represented with a unit normal vector, i.e., a vector that is perpendicular to the surface and has a length of one. As three vertices a, b, c define a triangle uniquely, we can calculate the orientation by

$$n = (b - c) \times (a - c),\qquad\qquad(3.1)$$

and then normalizing n using Equation (2.4). A triangle is planar, therefore the whole triangle has the same orientation and reflects a constant amount of light (assuming a small triangle, of the same material at every vertex, far away from the light source). When a smooth surface is approximated by a triangle mesh, the polygonal nature of the approximation is readily observed as the human eye is very good at seeing color discontinuities.

The color discontinuity corresponds to normal vector discontinuity, as each vertex has several normals, as many as there are adjoining triangles. A better solution is to define a unique normal vector at each vertex, and then let either the normal vector or the shading vary smoothly between the vertices. These two cases are illustrated in Figure 3.5. As the shading is then continuously interpolated both within and across triangles, the illusion of a smooth surface is retained much better, at least inside the silhouette boundaries (a coarsely triangulated mesh still betrays its polygonal nature at the piecewise straight silhouette). For this reason OpenGL requires each vertex to be associated with its own normal vector.

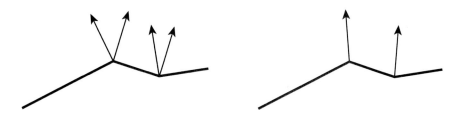

Figure 3.5: *Left:* the vertices of a polygonal mesh are replicated so that each polygon has its own copy of the shared vertex, and the vertices are assigned the surface normals of the polygons. This yields shading discontinuity at vertices. *Right:* each shared vertex exists only once, with a normal that is the average of the normals of the neighboring faces, resulting in smooth shading.

You can approximate a smooth unique vertex normal by averaging the normals of the adjacent triangles, possibly weighted by the triangle areas:

$$n = \sum_i a_i n_i, \tag{3.2}$$

where a_i is the area of the triangle associated with n_i, and n again needs to be normalized. This gives a smooth look to the surface. A more involved approach would be to fit a smooth surface to the neighborhood of a vertex and to evaluate the surface normal at the vertex.

A unique normal vector for each mesh vertex is useful for smooth objects, but fails if we actually want to represent a sharp crease. The solution is to define the vertex as many times as there are different orientations around it. Similarly vertices need to be replicated if other properties, such as material attributes, should change abruptly between triangles.

The simplest approach for determining the color of a primitive is to choose the coloring at one vertex and use it for the whole triangle; this is called *flat* shading. More pleasing results can be obtained by interpolation, however. There are two key approaches for such interpolation: one could either first interpolate the normal vectors and then separately shade each pixel within a triangle (*Phong* shading [Pho75]), or alternatively calculate the shading at the vertices and interpolate colors across the triangle (*Gouraud* shading [Gou71]). Phong shading produces visually better results than Gouraud shading. However, Gouraud shading is much cheaper to calculate, for two reasons. First, linear interpolation of colors is less expensive than interpolation of orientations. Second, assuming triangles typically cover several pixels, the lighting equations have to be evaluated less often: only at the vertices. For this reason OpenGL only supports Gouraud shading, and all lighting happens at vertices. However, we will see in Section 3.4.1 that one can modulate both the colors and the apparent orientations within the triangles using texture and bump mapping.

If the surface is transformed by matrix M, each vector that is normal to the original surface must be transformed by M^{-T}, the inverse transpose of M, so that it remains perpendicular to the transformed surface (see Section 2.2.4 for proof). If M only consists of rotations and translations, the length of the normal vectors does not change. By default OpenGL does not rescale the normals after the transformation; therefore, if more complex transformations are used, the user needs to ask the system to renormalize the normals. Too long normals will make the surface appear too bright, and too short normals make it too dark.

3.2.3 REFLECTION MODELS AND MATERIALS

Lighting and reflection models can be classified into global and local ones. A *global* lighting model accounts for shadows caused by other objects or self-shadowing due to other parts of the same object, as well as light reflected from other surfaces, requiring complicated analysis of spatial relationships and perhaps access to all of the scene description. Real-time graphics engines such as OpenGL have traditionally used much simpler *local* lighting models. Local models ignore the effects of other surfaces of the scene, and only require that you know the position and normal vector at a single surface point, various local material properties, and the light sources that potentially illuminate the surface point.

However, even a local lighting model can have a complicated *reflection* model to determine how much and what kind of light is reflected toward the camera. Some materials, such as hair, silk, velvet, or brushed metal, reflect different amounts and colors of light to different directions, defying simple analytic reflection models and requiring sampling and tabulating the reflectance function into a *bidirectional reflectance distribution function* (BRDF). For some other materials it is possible to define a function that approximates the actual reflectance behavior quite closely.

OpenGL uses a combination of several simple reflectance models that for the most part are not very accurate models of true materials, but are a reasonable approximation for some materials such as plastics or paper. Off-line photorealistic rendering systems used for special effects, advertisements, and even feature-length movies use much more realistic, but computationally more involved lighting and reflectance models. The main components of the OpenGL lighting model, *ambient*, *diffuse*, and *specular* reflectance models are illustrated in Figure 3.6 and described in the following text. We also discuss materials that emit light, e.g., neon signs.

Ambient reflectance

Ambient reflectance is the simplest reflectance model. The idea is that the ambient light has been reflected and scattered around the scene so many times that it permeates the whole scene without any directional preference. Assuming we have ambient light I_a with red, green, blue, and alpha components, and a surface material k_a with the same components, the light projecting to the camera is simply $I = k_a I_a$, where the matching components are multiplied (red of I is the red of k_a times red of I_a, and so forth).

This simple equation uses very little information, just the color of the ambient light and the ambient material reflectance coefficient. In particular it does not use any information

Figure 3.6: A densely triangulated sphere with ambient, diffuse, and diffuse + specular shading.

that relates to the direction of the light, the surface normal vector, or the viewing direction. Therefore it does not encode any information about surface shape, and the image of a sphere on the left in Figure 3.6 appears as a flat disk. Since ambient lighting loses all shape information, it should be used as little as possible. However, the other reflectance models typically do not illuminate the side of the object opposing the light, and using ambient lighting allows at least the object outlines to be drawn in their own colors, instead of being just black.

Diffuse reflectance

Diffuse reflectance takes into account the direction of the incoming light with respect to the surface normal to calculate the amount of light reflected toward the camera. Since it assumes that the material reflects all the incoming light uniformly into every direction away from the surface, we do not need the direction to the camera. With this assumption, the diffuse reflectance rule follows from geometry. In Figure 3.7 we have two bundles of rays coming to the surface, one bundle perpendicular to the surface (dark) and one in an angle θ (gray). Denoting a unit area by the width of the ray bundle in the image, the dark bundle illuminates the unit area, reflecting then all the light out to every direction that can actually see the surface point (the dark arc). However, the gray bundle comes in at an angle, and thus illuminates a larger surface area (larger by factor $\dfrac{1}{\cos\theta}$), and therefore reflects out only a factor $\cos\theta$ of the incoming light per unit area (the gray arc). Therefore, for diffuse reflectance we get $I = k_d I_d \cos\theta$. By denoting the surface unit normal by $\boldsymbol{n}$ and the unit direction vector to the light source by $\boldsymbol{l}$, we see that $\cos\theta = \boldsymbol{n} \cdot \boldsymbol{l}$. Finally, only

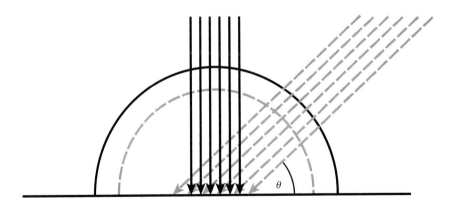

Figure 3.7: Geometry of diffuse reflectance. Rays coming perpendicular (dark) to the surface illuminate the surface more and also reflect more light away (dark arc). Rays coming in an angle θ (gray) illuminate an area larger by factor $\dfrac{1}{\cos\theta}$, thus a unit area reflects only $\cos\theta$ times less light (gray arc).

light directions that can see the surface point are considered, so the negative values are clamped to zero, which we denote by parentheses with a plus sign as a subscript $(\cdot)_+$, yielding $I = k_d I_d \left(\boldsymbol{n} \cdot \boldsymbol{l} \right)_+$.

No real surface material is completely diffuse, but many materials such as dust, chalk, or rough paper can be approximated fairly well with the diffuse reflectance model. Even then the approximation breaks down at grazing angles, i.e., when θ is small. You can test this by taking a piece of paper and looking at a bright light source almost along the surface of the paper; the paper reflects the light like a very dull mirror.

Specular reflectance

The specular reflection accounts for the highlights that you see on shiny objects, like the rightmost sphere in Figure 3.6. Whereas in ambient or diffuse reflectance the direction to the viewer does not matter, that direction is important in specular reflectance. In Figure 3.8, most of the light coming from $\boldsymbol{l}$ is reflected to the mirror reflection direction $\boldsymbol{r}$, that is, to the direction of the light source reflected about the normal vector $\boldsymbol{n}$. The larger the angle θ between the viewer direction $\boldsymbol{v}$ and $\boldsymbol{r}$, the less light is reflected toward the viewer.

One way to approximate this drop-off is using $\cos \theta$. The half-vector $\boldsymbol{h}$ (half way between $\boldsymbol{l}$ and $\boldsymbol{v}$) is slightly less expensive to calculate than the reflection vector $\boldsymbol{r}$, and since $\boldsymbol{h}$ makes the angle $\theta/2$ with the normal $\boldsymbol{n}$, OpenGL uses $\boldsymbol{h} \cdot \boldsymbol{n}$ to calculate the specular drop-off term. Notice that as opposed to the diffuse reflectance, the cosine term has no physical or

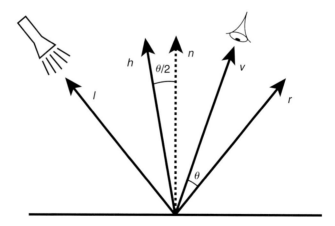

Figure 3.8: Geometry of specular reflectance. Light coming from a light source $\boldsymbol{l}$ hits a surface with normal vector $\boldsymbol{n}$, and most of the light is reflected to the direction $\boldsymbol{r}$. The larger the angle θ between the viewer direction $\boldsymbol{v}$ and the mirror reflection direction $\boldsymbol{r}$, the less light is reflected toward the viewer. Note that the angle between the half-vector $\boldsymbol{h}$ (splits evenly $\boldsymbol{l}$ and $\boldsymbol{v}$) and the normal $\boldsymbol{n}$ is $\theta/2$.

geometrical significance; it is simply a heuristic model to reduce reflectance to directions other than r. Since lighting is done in camera coordinates, and the camera looks toward the negative z axis, the viewing direction v can be approximated by $(0, 0, 1)$. Finally, the cosine term is raised to a *shininess* power n_{spec}. A large n_{spec}, e.g., 128, attenuates the reflectance very quickly, and produces a small and sharp highlight, while a small n_{spec}, e.g., 2, produces a fairly wide highlight. Putting it all together, we get the specular component from $I = k_s I_s \left(n \cdot h \right)_+^{n_{spec}}$.

Emission

The simplest material property is the emissive coefficient. Emission simply adds light to the material without requiring any external light sources. An emissive material does not illuminate any other surfaces. You could use this to model the surface of a light source such as a light bulb or a television screen, or to model fluorescent and phosphorescent materials.

3.2.4 LIGHTS

OpenGL defines several simple light sources: the *global ambient* light, *point* lights, *directional* lights, and *spot* lights. These lights work for sources that are very far away or have a small surface area. Accurate modeling of area light sources is much more expensive, but is sometimes done by discretizing the area source into a set of point light sources.

Lights have RGBA colors where the channels can have "overbright" values exceeding 1.0. The global ambient light only has the ambient color component, but the other lights have a separate color for each of ambient, diffuse, and specular components. In this section we cover those light types, as well as the light attenuation function.

Global ambient light

The simplest of the lights is the global ambient light. There can only be one of those and it is simply defined by an RGBA value, it is not associated with a position, and it affects all surfaces.

Point lights

Even a large area light source can be accurately modeled as a point light if the objects illuminated by the source are sufficiently far away from the source. A point light is located at a given $(x, y, z, 1)$ position, and emits light to every direction, as shown on the left in Figure 3.9. Like the rest of the light types, it contains a separate color for each of the ambient, diffuse, and specular components. If a light attenuation function is defined, it affects the intensity of the light reaching the surface. The light direction is calculated as the vector difference from the light position to the vertex being illuminated.

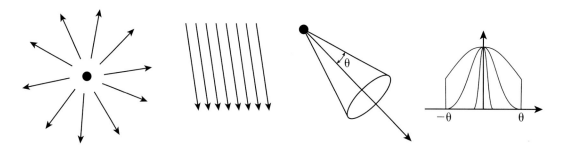

Figure 3.9: Various light sources: point light, directional light, spot light, and directional attenuation of spot lights.

Directional lights

A directional light can be thought of as a point light infinitely far away. For most practical purposes sunlight on earth can be modeled as a directional light. To define the direction, place the light source into direction $(x, y, z, 0)$. The light will then shine toward the opposite direction, $(-x, -y, -z, 0)$. Directional light is cheaper to evaluate than point light as the light direction is constant for all the vertices (see the second image in Figure 3.9), and the intensity of the light is never attenuated.

Spot lights

A spot light is a mixture between a point light and a directional light, and aims to model the behavior of a typical desk lamp. Like the point light, a spot light has a position, and its intensity can be attenuated as a function of distance. However, it also has a preferred direction toward which it shines brightest. No light escapes to directions farther than the cut-off angle θ from the preferred direction (third image in Figure 3.9), and the light that is not cut off is attenuated for directions other than the spot light direction using a similar exponentiated cosine function as already familiar from specular reflectance. That is, if $\boldsymbol{l}$ is the direction from the light to the surface, $\boldsymbol{s}$ is the spot light direction, and n_{spot} is the spot direction fall-off exponent, the directional fall-off becomes $spot = (\boldsymbol{l} \cdot \boldsymbol{s})^{n_{spot}}$, unless the angle between $\boldsymbol{l}$ and $\boldsymbol{s}$ is greater than the cut-off angle, in which case $spot = 0$. The last image in Figure 3.9 illustrates the directional attenuation function, which cuts to zero for angles larger than θ, and gets more concentrated toward the spot light direction $\boldsymbol{s}$ as the exponent n_{spot} grows.

Light attenuation

A faraway light source casts fewer photons of light to a given surface area than if the same light source were nearby. OpenGL models attenuation of light due to distance with $att = 1/(k_c + k_l d + k_q d^2)$, where k_c stands for the constant coefficient, and k_l and k_q are the linear and quadratic coefficients, while d is the distance from the light source to the surface.

Real point light source energy is attenuated by the square of the distance from the light source. However, OpenGL does not typically represent the true light energy, but a compressed representation of light, and quadratic attenuation typically produces too harsh changes in illumination. Also, most indoor lights are area lights, not point lights, and have a more complicated and softer attenuation behavior that can be better matched by adding the linear and constant terms into the equation. The main outdoor light source, the sun, is so far away that all the visible points in practice get the same amount of light and therefore the relative light attenuation can be ignored. Purely quadratic attenuation may make sense in a situation where the only light source really is a relatively weak point light source, such as a single candle, and a very dramatic attenuation is desired.

3.2.5 FULL LIGHTING EQUATION

Combining Sections 3.2.1–3.2.4, the full OpenGL lighting equation can be formulated as Equation (3.3). The resulting light intensity (I) consists of the emissive term of the material (k_e), ambient term of the material (k_a) illuminated by the global ambient light (I_a), and then the contributions due to each active light source are summed up. For each light i, the ambient term ($k_a I_{ai}$) is added, and the distance attenuation att_i and spot light fall-off ($spot_i$) are combined with the diffuse ($k_d I_{di}(\bm{n} \cdot \bm{l_i})_+$) and specular ($k_s I_{si} f_i (\bm{n} \cdot \bm{h})_+^{n_{spec}}$) components. For a directional light $att_i = 1$, and for directional and point lights $spot_i = 1$. Finally, $f_i = 0$ turns off the calculation of the specular term if the direction to the light is perpendicular to the surface normal ($\bm{n} \cdot \bm{l_i} = 0$), otherwise $f_i = 1$.

$$I = k_e + k_a I_a + \sum_i \left[k_a I_{ai} + att_i \; spot_i \left(k_d I_{di}(\bm{n} \cdot \bm{l_i})_+ + k_s I_{si} f_i (\bm{n} \cdot \bm{h})_+^{n_{spec}} \right) \right] \qquad (3.3)$$

It is also possible to compute *double-sided* lighting, in which case the lighting equations are evaluated both for the outside normal $\bm{n}$ and the inside normal $-\bm{n}$. This can be useful if you want to draw a thin object, such as a sheet of paper, without having to separately model both the front and the back side. On desktop OpenGL one can even give different materials to the different sides, but mobile APIs simplify this and use the same material on both sides.

3.3 CULLING AND CLIPPING

Not all primitives end up being visible. For example, almost half of the triangles of typical scenes face away from the camera and may thus be discarded in the rendering pipeline. Others fall outside of the view frustum, or overlap it only partially. In this section we cover back-face culling and clipping of primitives.

3.3.1 BACK-FACE CULLING

With real solid objects it is impossible to directly see the back side of an object: by definition it faces away from the observer, and it is always occluded by another part of the same object. Since rendering back-facing triangles would not contribute to the final image, it makes sense to save time by not rendering them. On average half of the triangles are back-facing, and the time savings due to skipping them can be substantial. With back-face culling, the system may be able to avoid the cost of lighting the vertices, and in any case it avoids rasterizing the triangle.

There are several ways to cull back-facing triangles. One possibility is to calculate the true normal vector to the triangle, and compare that to the direction to the camera. Another approach, often faster and more stable, is to project the vertices to the image plane, calculate the signed area of the projected triangle, and cull the triangle if the area turns out to be negative. One can even try back-projecting the camera into object space and doing the check there.

In order to determine which is the front and which the back side of a triangle, a *winding* convention has to be used. By default, triangles are defined so that when viewed from outside, the vertices are given in a counterclockwise order. Similarly, by default, it is the back faces that are culled. However, the user may override both of these conventions, that is, explicitly set the front face to have clockwise or counterclockwise vertex ordering, or specify that the front face should be culled instead of the back face. One reason to do so is if the user first models one-half of a symmetrical object, and then obtains the other half by mirroring the first half. In such a case the user should toggle the winding direction for the second half to ensure correct culling and shading of the triangles on the mirrored half.

Back-facing triangles are not culled by default in OpenGL, so the culling has to be explicitly enabled. A reason for not using back-face culling would be if one would like to model thin objects with double-sided triangles.

3.3.2 CLIPPING AND VIEW-FRUSTUM CULLING

The camera sees only a finite region of space—the view frustum. The sides of the viewing cone are defined by the extent of the window in the image plane through which the camera views the scene, and the cone is capped at the near and far distances, making it a truncated pyramid, a frustum. Primitives that fully fall outside of the frustum will not affect the scene and can therefore be ignored. Determining that complete objects lie outside of the viewing frustum and skipping them completely may be done sometimes with an easy check within the application. Some engines may also perform an automatic conservative viewport culling by calculating a bounding box of a vertex array and testing for an intersection with the view frustum, and rejecting the whole array if the bounding box is fully outside the frustum. For example, most M3G implementations include this optimization (see Section 5.3).

Clipping to the view frustum

If a primitive intersects the view frustum it may need to be clipped. Here we describe clipping as specified in OpenGL. There are always six clipping planes, corresponding to the left, right, top, and bottom of the viewport, and the near (front) and far (back) clipping planes. As described before, in clip coordinates (after the multiplication by the projection matrix but before homogeneous division by w) the clipping planes correspond to one of the x, y, or z coordinates being either $-w$ or w.

When a triangle is clipped by a plane, there are several possible outcomes. If the triangle does not intersect the plane, the triangle is either completely accepted or completely rejected, depending on which side of the plane it is. If it does intersect the plane, the clipping may shave off two vertices and an edge, resulting in a smaller triangle, or shave off just one vertex and yield a smaller quadrangle. Thus each clip may grow the number of vertices by one, and clipping a triangle against six planes may lead up to a nine-vertex polygon (see Figure 3.10). Some systems may be able to just evaluate the parts of the primitives within the viewport without doing real clipping. Clipping lines and points is simpler. Clipping a line may shorten the line but the result is still a line. Clipping a point either erases or keeps the point, and the clipping is done based on the point center, even for wide points.

Artifacts caused by clipping

Real clipping may cause some artifacts. Ideally, if you render an image in four pieces, one quarter at a time, into smaller images, not forgetting to set up the projection matrix appropriately, you should get the same pixels as when you render the whole image in one go. However, if clipping the primitives introduces new vertices at image boundaries, and unless the colors and possibly other properties are interpolated using exactly the same algorithm as used in rasterization, some pixels at the screen boundaries will appear different in the smaller images.

The middle image in Figure 3.10 illustrates some problems when clipping wide lines and points. Clipping a wide line may omit a part of the line; in this case the areas that are gray

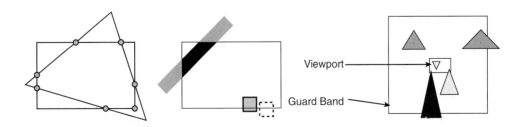

Figure 3.10: *Left:* Each clip plane may grow the number of vertices by one. *Middle:* For wide points and lines clipping may produce artifacts. *Right:* Guard band clipping combines clipping and scissoring.

but inside the viewport. Since points are clipped based on their center, an animated wide point approaching the viewport boundary may suddenly vanish once the center exits the viewport, instead of gracefully sliding off the screen.

Guard band clipping

Some implementations may avoid some of these problems by implementing clipping implicitly as part of the rasterization, for example by using *guard bands* [BSD+89], or by evaluating only those pixels of the primitives that fall on the screen using 2D homogeneous coordinates [OG97]. The rightmost image in Figure 3.10 illustrates guard band clipping, which can both avoid some clipping artifacts and accelerate clipping. There the medium gray triangles can be trivially rejected as they are completely outside of the viewport. The light triangles are completely within the guard band, and they are simply rasterized and the pixels outside of the viewport are ignored. Only the dark triangle which enters the viewport and exits the guard band needs to be clipped.

Clipping to an arbitrary plane

Finally, the user can define arbitrary *clip planes* (supported in OpenGL ES 1.1). Each plane is defined by the coefficients $[a\ b\ c\ d]^T$ of the equation $ax + by + cz + d = 0$, defined in object coordinates. If you have a plane with a normal vector $[N_x\ N_y\ N_z]^T$ toward the half-space you want to keep, going through the point $[p_x\ p_y\ p_z]^T$, the coefficients become

$$\begin{bmatrix} a \\ b \\ c \\ d \end{bmatrix} = \begin{bmatrix} N_x \\ N_y \\ N_z \\ -(N_x p_x + N_y p_y + N_z p_z) \end{bmatrix}. \tag{3.4}$$

Since the user clip plane is defined in object coordinates, the system transforms the coefficients into eye coordinates by $M^{-T}\begin{bmatrix} a & b & c & d \end{bmatrix}^T$, as also shown in Figure 3.1.

User clip planes have been used for a variety of visual effects, such as reflections from water—here the algorithm is to mirror the world geometry to be below the water, and use the clip plane to only render the parts that are below the waterline.

3.4 RASTERIZATION

Before rasterization, vertices are collected into primitives in a stage called *primitive assembly*. Rasterization then decides which pixels of the frame buffer the primitives cover, and which colors and depth values those pixels are assigned. This is done by interpolating various values associated with the vertices, such as the colors due to illumination, the depth values, and the texture coordinates.

For each pixel within the primitive, one or more *fragments*, or samples of the geometry within the pixel, are generated. The fragment contains the interpolated values, which are used to texture map the fragment, to blend it with previous values in the frame buffer, and to subject it to various tests, such as the depth test to determine visibility. If the fragment passes the tests, it is finally stored into the frame buffer.

Determining which pixels a primitive should cover is not trivial. For example, when rasterizing the area covered by two adjacent triangles, each pixel needs to be rasterized exactly once, that is, no gaps may appear, nor may the neighboring triangles draw twice any of the edge pixels.

After the rasterization has been prepared, traditional 3D pipelines that do not support floating-point values in the frame buffer may perform all the remaining steps of rasterization and pixel processing using fixed-point, i.e., integer arithmetic. Color values, for example, can be expressed in a few bits, for example 8 bits per channel. How many bits are needed to express and interpolate screen coordinates depends on the size of the display. For example, if the width and height of the display are at most 512 pixels, 9 bits are enough to store the x and y pixel coordinates. Some additional decimal bits are needed to maintain sub-pixel accuracy, as otherwise slowly moving objects would produce jerky motion.

Being able to convert floating-point values to fixed point means that software rasterization on devices without floating-point hardware remains feasible, and even if the rasterization uses specialized hardware, that hardware is simpler, using less silicon and also less power.

Below we will first describe texture mapping; then we study the ways to interpolate the vertex values across the primitive, we deal with fog, and finally take a look at antialiasing. The images on the bottom row of Figure 3.2 illustrate basic texture mapping on a sphere, and multitexturing using a *bump map* as the second texture map.

3.4.1 TEXTURE MAPPING

Coarse models where geometry and colors change only at vertices are fast to model and draw, but do not appear realistic. For example, one could model a brick wall simply with two orange triangles. An alternative is to have a very detailed model of the wall, inserting vertices anywhere the geometry or colors change. The results can be highly realistic, but modeling becomes difficult and rendering terribly slow. Texture mapping combines the best aspects of these two approaches. The base geometric model can be coarse, but a detailed image is mapped over that geometry, producing more detailed and realistic apparent geometry and detailed varying colors. The texture map can be created, for example, by taking digital photographs of real objects.

The typical case is a 2D texture map, where the texture is a single image. A 1D texture map is a special case of a 2D texture that has only one row of texture pixels, or *texels* for short. A 3D texture consists of a stack of 2D images; one can think of them filling

Figure 3.11: Texture mapping. Portions of a bitmap image on the left are mapped on two triangles on the right. If the triangles do not have the same shape as their preimages in the texture map, the image appears somewhat distorted.

a volume. However, 3D texture data requires a lot of memory at runtime, more than is usually available on mobile devices, and thus the mobile 3D APIs only support 2D texture maps.

Images are often stored in compressed formats such as JPEG or PNG. Usually the developer first has to read the file into memory as an uncompressed array, and then pass the texture image data to the 3D API. Some implementations may also support hardware texture compression [BAC96, Fen03, SAM05], but those compression formats are proprietary and are not guaranteed to be supported by different phones.

Texture coordinates

The way texture data is mapped to the geometry is determined using texture coordinates. For a textured surface every vertex needs to have an associated texture coordinate. The texture coordinates are also 4D homogeneous coordinates, similar as covered before for geometry, but they are called (s, t, r, q). If only some of them are given, say s and t, r is set to 0 and q to 1. The texture coordinates can be transformed using a 4×4 texture matrix, and for 2D texture mapping s and t of the result are divided by q, while the output r is ignored. The transformed texture coordinates map to the texture map image so that the lower left image corner has coordinates (0.0, 0.0) and the top right image corner has coordinates (1.0, 1.0).

During rasterization, the texture coordinates are interpolated. If the values of q are different on different vertices, we are doing *projective texture mapping*. In that case also the

q component needs to be interpolated, and the division of r and s by q should happen at each fragment, not only at the vertices. For each fragment the interpolated coordinates are used to fetch the actual texture data, and the texture data is used to adjust or replace the fragment color. If multiple texture maps are assigned for a surface, there needs to be a separate set of texture coordinates for each map, and the textures are applied in succession.

It is much easier to build hardware to access texture data if the texture image sizes are powers of two, that is, 1, 2, 4, …, 64, 128, and so on. Therefore the texture image dimensions are by default restricted to be powers of two, though the width can differ from height, e.g., 32×64 is a valid texture size, while 24×24 is not. As shown in Figure 3.12(a), the origin $(s, t) = (0, 0)$ of the texture coordinates is in the lower left corner of the texture data, and for all texture sizes, even if the width differs from the height, the right end is at $s = 1$, the top at $t = 1$, and the top right corner at $(s, t) = (1, 1)$. Some implementations provide an extension that lifts the requirement that the texture sizes must be powers of two.

Texture coordinates that have a value less than zero or greater than one have to be wrapped so that they access valid texture data. The two basic wrapping modes are *clamp-to-edge*, that is, projecting the texture coordinate to the closest texel on the edge of the texture map, and *repeat*, which repeats the image by ignoring the integer part of the texture coordinate and only using the fractional part. These are illustrated in Figure 3.12(b) and (c) respectively. Note that it is possible to use a different wrapping mode for the s (horizontal) and t (vertical) directions.

Texture fetch and filtering

For each fragment, the rasterizer interpolates a texture coordinate, with which we then need to sample the texture image. The simplest approach is to use *point sampling*: convert the texture coordinate to the address of the texel that matches the coordinate, and fetch that value. Although returning just one of the values stored in the texture map is sometimes just what is needed, for better quality more processing is required. On the left side of Figure 3.13 the diagram shows the area of the texture map that corresponds to

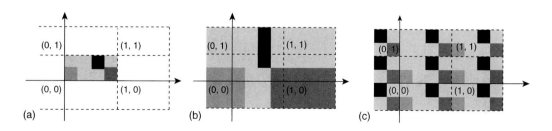

Figure 3.12: (a) The (s, t) coordinate system of a texture image of 4×2 texels. (b) Wrapping with clamp to edge. (c) Wrapping with repeat.

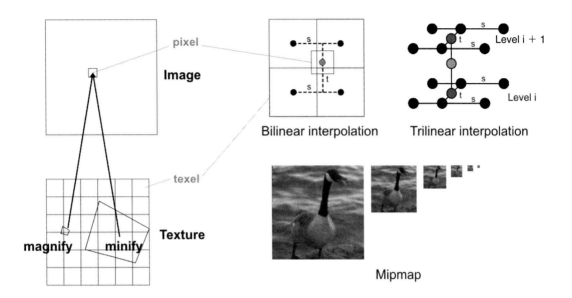

Figure 3.13: Texture filtering. If a screen pixel corresponds to an area in the texture map smaller than a texel, the texture map needs to be magnified, otherwise it needs to be minified for the pixel. In bilinear interpolation texel colors are first interpolated based on the *s*-coordinate value, then on the *t*-coordinate. Trilinear interpolation additionally interpolates across mipmap levels. A mipmap image sequence consists of smaller filtered versions of the detailed base level texture map.

a particular image pixel. In one case a smaller area than one texel is *magnified* to fill the pixel; in the other the area of almost eight texels needs to be *minified* into a single pixel.

In magnification, if the texel area matching the pixel comes fully from a single texel, point sampling would give a correct solution. However, in Figure 3.13 at the center of the top row, the pixel happens to project roughly to the corner of four texels. A smoother filtered result is obtained by *bilinear* interpolation as illustrated at top middle. In the illustration, the pixel projects to the gray point in the middle of the small square among the four texels. The values of the two top row texels are interpolated based on the *s*-coordinate, and the same is done on the lower row. Then these interpolated values are interpolated again using the *t*-coordinate value. The closer the gray point is to the black centers of texels, the closer the interpolated value is to that of the texel.

Minification is more demanding than magnification, as more texels influence the outcome. Minification can be made faster by prefiltering, usually done by *mipmapping* [Wil83]. The term mip comes from the Latin phrase *multum in parvo*, "much in little," summarizing or compressing much into little space. A mipmap is a sequence of prefiltered images. The most detailed image is at the zeroth level; at the first level the image is only a quarter of the size of the original, and its pixels are often obtained by averaging four pixels from the finer level. That map is then filtered in turn, until we end up with a 1 × 1 texture map which is the average of the whole image. The complete mipmap pyramid takes only $\frac{1}{3}$ more space than the original texture map. Now if roughly seven texels would be needed to cover the pixel in Figure 3.13, we can perform a bilinear interpolation at the levels 1 (1 texel covers 4 original texels) and 2 (1 texel covers 16 original texels), and linearly interpolate between those bilinearly filtered levels, producing *trilinear* filtering.

Mipmapping improves performance for two reasons. First, the number of texels required is bound, even if the whole object is so far away that it projects to a single pixel. Second, even if we did only point sampling for minification, neighboring image pixels would need to fetch texels that are widely scattered across the texture map. At a suitable mipmap level the texels needed for neighboring image pixels are also adjacent to each other, and it is often cheaper to fetch adjacent items from memory than scattered items. Nevertheless, trilinear filtering requires accessing and blending eight texels, which is quite a lot for software engines without dedicated texture units, so the mobile 3D APIs allow approximating full trilinear filtering with a bilinear filtering at the closest mipmap level.

In general, point sampling is faster than bilinear filtering, whereas bilinear filtering gives higher-quality results. However, if you want to map texels directly to pixels so they have the same size (so that neither minification nor magnification is used) and the *s*-direction aligns with screen *x* and *t* with *y*, point sampling yields both faster and better results.

Bilinear filtering can also be leveraged for post-processing effects. Figure 3.14 demonstrates a light bloom effect, where the highlights of a scene are rendered into a separate image. This image is then repeatedly downsampled by using bilinear filtering, averaging four pixels into one in each pass. Finally, a weighted blend of the downsampled versions is composited on top of the normal image, achieving the appearance of bright light outside of the window.

In desktop OpenGL there are some additional filtering features that are not available in the current versions of the mobile APIs. They include *level of detail* (LOD) parameters for better control of the use and memory allocation of mipmap levels, and *anisotropic* filtering for surfaces that are slanted with respect to the camera viewing direction.

Texture borders and linear interpolation

The original OpenGL clamps texture coordinates to [0, 1], which gives problems for texture filtering. Let us see what happens at $(s, t) = (0, 0)$. It lies at the lower left corner of the lower leftmost texel, and bilinear interpolation should return the average of that texel and its west, south, and southwest neighbors. The problem is that those neighbors do not exist.

To overcome this problem, one could add a one-texel-wide boundary or *border* around the texture map image to provide the required neighbors for correct filtering. However, the introduction of the clamp-to-edge mode mostly removes the need of such neighbors. This mode clamps the texture coordinates to [*min, max*] where $min = 1/(2N)$ and $max = 1 - min$, and N is either the width or height of the texture map. As a result, borders were dropped from OpenGL ES.

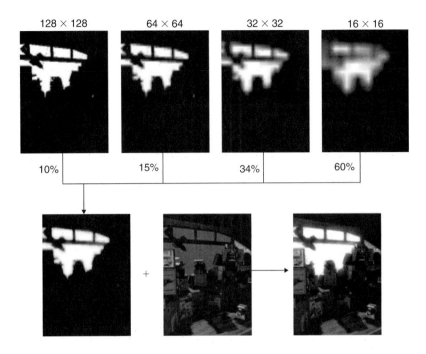

Figure 3.14: Rendering a light bloom effect by blurring the highlights and compositing on top of the normal scene. Images copyright AMD. (See the color plate.)

There is one case where the border would be useful, however: if a larger texture map should be created from several smaller ones, and filtering across them should work correctly. The triangle corners would have texture coordinate values of 0 or 1, and the borders would be copied from the neighboring texture maps. However, you can emulate that even without borders. First, create texture maps so that they overlap by one texel. Then set the texture coordinates of the neighboring triangles to $1/N$ or $1 - 1/N$ instead of 0 or 1. Now the texture maps filter correctly and blend to each other seamlessly.

Note that borders are never needed with the repeat mode, since if a neighboring texel that would be outside of the texture image is needed, it is fetched from the other side of the same image. If you do not intend to repeat your textures, enabling the repeat mode may create artifacts on the boundary pixels as the colors may bleed from the other side of the texture at the boundaries. Therefore you should not use the repeat mode if clamp-to-edge is sufficient.

Texture formats and functions

Depending on the texture pixel format and blending function, the fragment's base color, that is interpolated from the vertices, is replaced with, modulated by, or otherwise combined with the filtered texel.

The most versatile of the *texture formats* is RGBA, a four-channel texture image. The RGB format stores only the color but no alpha value. If all the color channels have the same value, we can save space and use only a single luminance channel L. Finally, we can have one-channel alpha A, or combine luminance and alpha into LA.

Now as we describe the *texture functions*, also known as texture blending functions or modes, we define the interpolated fragment color and alpha as C_f and A_f, the texture source color and alpha as C_s and A_s, and the user-given constant color as C_c and A_c. See Figure 3.15 for an example of using each mode. The texture function and the constant color together comprise the *texture environment*. Note that these attributes are set separately for each texture unit.

With the REPLACE function, the texture source data replaces the fragment color and/or alpha. RGBA and LA formats produce (C_s, A_s), L and RGB formats give (C_s, A_f), and A format yields (C_f, A_s).

With the MODULATE function, the source data modulates the fragment data through multiplication. RGBA and LA formats produce $(C_f C_s, A_f A_s)$, L and RGB formats give $(C_f C_s, A_f)$, and A format yields $(C_f, A_f A_s)$.

The DECAL function can be only used with RGB and RGBA formats. The color of the underlying surface is changed, but its transparency (alpha) is not affected. With RGB the color is simply replaced (C_s, A_f), but RGBA blends the fragment and texture colors using the texture alpha as the blending factor $(C_f(1 - A_s) + C_s A_s, A_f)$.

The BLEND function modulates alpha through multiplication, and uses the texture color to blend between the fragment color and user-given constant color. RGBA and LA formats produce $(C_f(1 - C_s) + C_c C_s, A_f A_s)$, L and RGB formats give $(C_f(1 - C_s) + C_c C_s, A_f)$, and A format yields $(C_f, A_f A_s)$.

Finally, the ADD function modulates alpha and adds together the fragment and texture source colors. RGBA and LA formats produce $(C_f + C_s, A_f A_s)$, L and RGB formats give $(C_f + C_s, A_f)$, and A format yields $(C_f, A_f A_s)$.

Multitexturing

A 3D engine may have several texturing units, each with its own texture data format, function, matrix, and so on. By default, the input fragment color is successively combined with each texture according to the state of the corresponding unit, and the resulting color is passed as input to the next unit, until the final output goes to the next stage of 3D pipeline, i.e., tests and blending.

On OpenGL ES 1.1, it is possible to use more powerful *texture combiner* functions. A separate function can be defined for the RGB and alpha components. The inputs to the function can come either from the texture map of the current unit, from the original fragment color, from the output of the previous unit, or it can be the constant user-defined color (C_c, A_c). The functions allow you to add, subtract, multiply, or interpolate

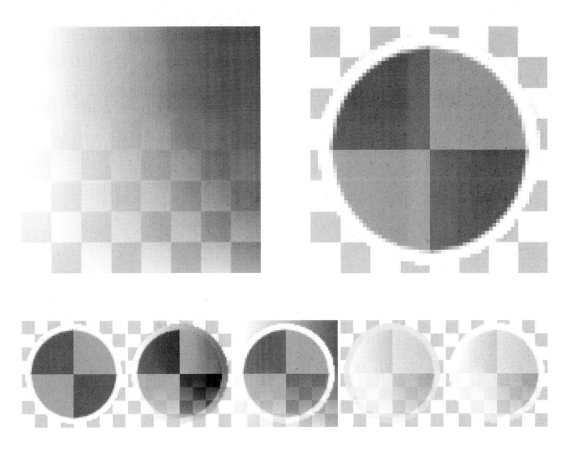

Figure 3.15: The effect of different texture functions. At the top, incoming fragment colors (*left*) and texture (*right*); transparency is indicated with the checkerboard pattern behind the image. *Bottom:* resulting textures after each texture operation; left to right: REPLACE, MODULATE, DECAL, BLEND, ADD. For the BLEND mode, the user-defined blending color is pure yellow. (See the color plate.)

the inputs, and even take a texel-wise dot product, which can be used for per-pixel lighting effects.

With multiple texture units it is useful to separate which part of the texture mapping state belongs to each texturing unit, and which part belongs to each texture object. A texture *object* contains the texture image data, the format that the data is in, and the filtering parameter (such as clamp-to-edge or repeat). Each texturing *unit*, on the other hand, includes a currently bound texture object, a texture blending function, a user-given constant color (C_c, A_c), a texture matrix that is applied to texture coordinates, and a pointer to texture coordinates of the unit.

3.4.2 INTERPOLATING GRADIENTS

The simplest way to spread the values at vertices across triangles is to choose the values at one of the vertices and assign the same value to every fragment within the triangle. In OpenGL this is called *flat shading*, since the triangle will then have a constant color, the color calculated when shading the first vertex of the triangle. Although fast to compute, this results in a faceted look. Much better results can be obtained when the vertex values are interpolated.

Screen linear interpolation

Screen linear interpolation projects the vertices to the frame buffer, finds the target pixels, and linearly interpolates the associated values such as colors and texture coordinates to the pixels between the vertices. We can express this using so-called *barycentric* coordinates. If we take any a, b, and c such that they sum up to one, the point $p = ap_a + bp_b + cp_c$ will lie on the plane defined by the three points p_a, p_b, and p_c, and if none of a, b, c are negative, then p lies within the triangle formed by the three points. We can use the same weights to blend the values at triangle corners to get a linearly interpolated value for any pixel within the triangle:

$$f = af_a + bf_b + cf_c \qquad (3.5)$$

where f_a, f_b, and f_c are the values at triangle corners, and f is the interpolated value.

Many graphics systems interpolate vertex colors this way as it produces smoothly varying shading where the triangulated nature of the underlying surface is far less obvious than with flat shading. However, linear interpolation on the screen space ignores perspective effects such as foreshortening. While vertices are projected correctly, the values on the pixels between them are not. Figure 3.16 shows two squares (pairs of triangles) that

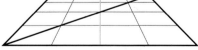

Figure 3.16: A square made of two triangles, with a grid pattern, seen in perspective. For the first square the grid pattern is interpolated in screen space. The center vertical bar on the upper triangle goes from the center of the upper edge to the center of the diagonal, and continues to the center of the lower edge of the lower triangle. For the second square the interpolation is perspective-correct, and the center vertical bar remains straight.

are tilted with respect to the camera, and the errors caused by screen linear interpolation. The grid pattern on the squares makes the effect obvious. The vertical lines, which appear straight on the right image, are broken in the left one. The center of the square interpolates to the middle of the diagonal, and when that is connected to the middle of the top edge and of the bottom edge, the bar does not make a straight line.

Perspective-correct interpolation

The fragments on the square on the right have been interpolated in a *perspective-correct* manner. The key to do this is to delay the perspective division of homogeneous coordinates until after the interpolation. That is, linearly interpolate both f/w and $1/w$, where f is the value and w is the last component of the homogeneous coordinate, then recover the perspective-correct value by dividing the interpolated f/w by the interpolated $1/w$, yielding

$$f = \frac{af_a/w_a + bf_b/w_b + cf_c/w_c}{a/w_a + b/w_b + c/w_c}. \tag{3.6}$$

If we add another projection to the system—that is, projective texture mapping—we also need to bring q into the equation:

$$f = \frac{af_a/w_a + bf_b/w_b + cf_c/w_c}{aq_a/w_a + bq_b/w_b + cq_c/w_c}. \tag{3.7}$$

Perspective-correct interpolation is clearly quite expensive: it implies more interpolation (also the $1/w$ term), but even worse, it implies a division at each fragment. These operations require either extra processing cycles or more silicon.

Because of its impact to performance, some software-based engines only do perspective-correct interpolation for texture coordinates; other values are interpolated linearly in screen space. Another approach is based on the fact that if the triangles are very small— only a few pixels in image space—the error due to screen linear interpolation becomes negligible. Reasonably good results can be achieved by doing the perspective-correct interpolation only every few screen pixels, and by linearly interpolating between those samples. Many software implementations achieve this by recursively subdividing triangles. If done at the application level, this is likely to be slow, but can be made reasonably fast if implemented inside the graphics engine.

3.4.3 TEXTURE-BASED LIGHTING

There are several ways to do high-quality lighting effects using texture maps. The basic OpenGL lighting is performed only at vertices, and using a relatively simple lighting model. Using texture mapping it is possible to get per-pixel illumination using arbitrary lighting models.

The simplest situation is if the lighting of the environment is static and view-independent, that is, if the lighting is fixed and we only have diffuse lighting. Then one can *bake in* the illumination either to vertex colors or to texture maps. This is done so that the environment and the light sources are modeled, and then rendered using a high-quality but perhaps non–real-time method such as raytracing or radiosity calculations. One could even take photographs of real environments or model environments with real lighting and use those as texture maps. The illuminated surfaces are then copied to the texture maps which are used in the real-time application.

Below we describe various approaches of using texture maps to provide advanced lighting effects. Figure 3.17 illustrates several of them. From top left, the first image shows dot3 bump mapping that gives an illusion of higher geometric detail on the barrel and walls that are affected by the main light source. The next image shows a projective spot light,

Figure 3.17: Several passes of a scene: bump mapping, projective lighting (using the circular light map on left middle), adding environment map reflection to the barrel (the cube map at left bottom), adding shadows, final image. Image copyright AMD. (See the color plate.)

using the light map on the left middle. Top right adds an environment map that reflects the light from the lamp from the surface of the barrel; the environment map is shown at bottom left. The bottom middle image adds shadows, and the last image shows the final image with all lighting effects combined.

Light mapping

Often you might want to reuse the same texture maps, e.g., a generic floor, a wall panel, or ceiling, for different parts of your scene, but those different areas have different lighting. Then you can use *light maps* that can usually be in a much lower resolution than the texture map. The light maps are used to attenuate the texture maps (for white light) or modulate them (for colored light) using multitexturing. The advantage over baking in is the potential savings in storage space, and the possibility of having more dynamic lighting effects. However, you need to have at least two texturing units, or you have to render the object in two passes and suffer a significant speed penalty.

For moving lights, the light maps have to be generated on the fly. For simple scenes you may be able to just project the polygons into the same space as the light, and calculate the lighting equation directly into a corresponding texture map.

Projective lighting

It is possible to use projective texture mapping to project a light pattern such as using a slide projector [SKv+92]. The texture map is usually an intensity map that looks like a cross section of a spot light's beam, often a bright circle that falls off to the boundaries. Since projecting light out is the inverse of a camera projection where light projects into the camera from the scene, it should be no surprise that the mathematics are quite similar. Whereas with a camera you project the scene vertices into the frame buffer, you now project them into a texture map so you find which part of the texture projects to which vertex. This is done by first copying the object-space vertex locations into texture coordinates, and then accumulating a transformation into the texture matrix, as follows.

First, the texture coordinates need to be transformed from object space into the world coordinate system. Then you need to use a similar transformation as with the camera to transform the vertices into the "eye coordinates" of the spot light. This is followed by an application of a similar perspective projection matrix as with the camera. The last step is to apply a bias matrix that maps the (s, t) coordinates from the $[-1, 1]$ range to $[0, 1]$, which covers the spot light texture. These transformations happen at vertices, and the final division by q is done, as discussed before, during the rasterization for each fragment.

Let us check how the bias step works. Assume that after projection, we have an input texture coordinate $\begin{bmatrix} -q & q & 0 & q \end{bmatrix}^T$. Without applying the bias, this would yield $\begin{bmatrix} -1 & 1 & 0 & 1 \end{bmatrix}^T$, that is, $s = -1$ and $t = 1$. To turn that into $s = 0$ and $t = 1$, we need to scale and translate the coordinates by $\frac{1}{2}$:

$$
\begin{bmatrix}
\frac{1}{2} & 0 & 0 & \frac{1}{2} \\
0 & \frac{1}{2} & 0 & \frac{1}{2} \\
0 & 0 & 0 & 0 \\
0 & 0 & 0 & 1
\end{bmatrix}
\begin{bmatrix}
-q \\ q \\ 0 \\ q
\end{bmatrix}
=
\begin{bmatrix}
0 \\ q \\ 0 \\ q
\end{bmatrix}.
\tag{3.8}
$$

This matrix ensures that (s, t) will always span the range $[0, 1]$ after the homogeneous division. The third row can be zero as the third texture coordinate is ignored. To summarize, the complete texture matrix T is as follows:

$$
T = B P M_{we} M_{ow},
\tag{3.9}
$$

where M_{ow} is the transformation from object coordinates to world coordinates, M_{we} is the transformation from world space to the eye space of the spot light, P is the spot light projection matrix, and B is the the bias matrix with a scale and offset shown in Equation (3.8).

Ambient occlusion

Another technique that improves the quality of shading is *ambient occlusion* [Lan02], derived from *accessibility shading* [Mil94]. Uniform ambient lighting, as discussed previously, is not very useful as it strips away all the shape hints. However, a very useful hint of the local shape and shadowing can be obtained by estimating the fraction of the light each surface point is likely to receive. One way to estimate that is to place a relatively large sphere around a point, render the scene from the surface point, and store the fraction of the surrounding sphere that is not occluded by other objects. These results are then stored into an ambient occlusion map which, at rendering time, is used to modulate the amount of light arriving to the surface. Figure 3.18 shows an ambient occlusion map on a polygon mesh. The effect is that locations under other objects get darker, as do indentations in the surface. Note that the creation of this map is typically done off-line and is likely to take too long to be used interactively for animated objects.

Environment mapping

Environment mapping is a technique that produces reflections of the scene on very shiny objects. The basic idea involves creating an image of the scene from the point of view of the reflecting object. For *spherical* environment mapping one image is sufficient; for *parabolic* mapping two images are needed; and for *cube maps* six images need to be created. Then, for each point, the direction to the camera is reflected about the local normal vector, and the reflected ray is used to map the texture to the surface.

Figure 3.18: A mesh rendered using just an ambient occlusion map without any other shading. The areas that are generally less exposed to light from the environment are darker. Image courtesy of Janne Kontkanen.

Spherical environment maps are view-dependent and have to be re-created for each new eye position. Dual paraboloid mapping [HS98] is view-independent but requires two texturing units or two passes. Cube mapping (Figure 3.19) is the easiest to use, and the easiest to generate the texture maps for: just render six images from the center of the object (up, down, and to the four sides). However, cube mapping is not included in the first generation of mobile 3D APIs.

Besides reflections, you can also do diffuse lighting via environment mapping [BN76]. If you filter your environment map with a hemispherical filter kernel, you can use the surface normal directly to index into the environment map and get cheap per-pixel diffuse lighting. This saves you from having to compute the reflection vector—you just need to transform the surface normals into world space, which is easily achieved with the texture matrix.

Texture lighting does not end with environment mapping. Using multiple textures as lookup tables, it is possible to approximate many kinds of complex reflectance functions at interactive rates [HS99]. The details are beyond the scope of this book, but these

Figure 3.19: An environment cube map (*right*) and refraction map (*center*) used to render a well. (Image copyright ©
AMD.) (See the color plate.)

techniques achieve much more realistic shading than is possible using the built-in lighting
model.

3.4.4 FOG

In the real world, the air filters the colors of a scene. Faraway mountains tend to seem
bluish or grayish, and if there is fog or haze, objects get mixed with gray before disappear-
ing completely. OpenGL has support for a simple atmospheric effect called fog. Given
a fog color, objects close to the camera have their own color, a bit farther away they get
mixed with the fog color, and yet farther away they are fully covered by the fog.

There are three functions for determining the intensity of the fog: linear, exponential, and
square exponential. *Linear fog* is easy to use: you just give a starting distance before which
there is no fog, and an ending distance after which all objects are covered by fog. The
fraction of the fragment color that is blended with the fog color is

$$f = \frac{end - z}{end - start};$$

(3.10)

where z is the distance to the fragment along the z axis in eye coordinates, *start* is the
fog start distance, and *end* is the fog end distance. The result is clamped to [0, 1]. Linear

fog is often used for simple distance cueing, but it does not correspond to real-life fog attenuation. A real homogeneous fog absorbs, say, 10% of the light for every 10 meters. This continuous fractional attenuation corresponds to the *exponential* function, which OpenGL supports in the form of

$$f = e^{-dz},$$ (3.11)

where d is a user-given density, a nonnegative number. Real fog is not truly homogeneous but its density varies, so even the exponential function is an approximation. OpenGL also supports a *squared exponential* version of fog:

$$f = e^{-(dz)^2}.$$ (3.12)

This function has no physical meaning; it simply has an attenuation curve with a different shape that can be used for artistic effect. In particular, it does not correspond to double attenuation due to light traversing first to a reflective surface and then reflecting back to the observer, as some sources suggest. With large values of d both the exponential (EXP) and the squared exponential (EXP2) fog behave fairly similarly; both functions approach zero quite rapidly. However, at near distances, or with small density values, as shown in Figure 3.20, the functions have different shapes. Whereas EXP begins to attenuate much more sharply, EXP2 first attenuates more gradually, followed by a sharper fall-off before flattening out, and often produces a better-looking blend of the fog color.

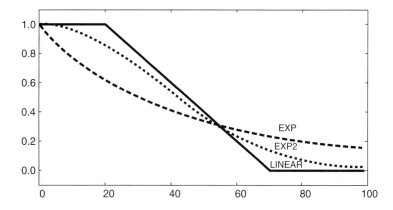

Figure 3.20: Fog functions. In this example, LINEAR fog starts from 20 and ends at 70, EXP and EXP2 fogs both have $d = 1/50$. LINEAR is the easiest to control, but produces sharp transitions. EXP corresponds to the attenuation by a uniformly distributed absorbing material, such as real fog, but gives less control as the attenuation in the beginning is always so severe. EXP2 can sometimes give the esthetically most pleasing results.

Performance tip: A common use of fog is really a speed trick to avoid having to draw too many objects in a scene. If you use fog that obscures the faraway objects, you can skip drawing them entirely, which brings frame rates up. The distance to the complete fog and to the far viewing plane should be aligned: if you use linear fog, place the far viewing plane slightly beyond the fog end distance, or with exponentials to a distance where the fog contributes over 99% or so.

Pitfall: Implementations are allowed to perform the fog calculations at the vertices, even though fog really should be calculated at every pixel. This may yield artifacts with large triangles. For example, even if you select a nonlinear (exponential or double exponential) fog mode, it may be interpolated linearly across the triangle. Additionally, if the triangle extends beyond the far plane and is clipped, the vertex introduced by clipping may have a completely incorrect fog intensity.

3.4.5 ANTIALIASING

The frame buffer consists of pixels that are often thought of as small squares.[1] When a polygon edge is rasterized in any angle other than horizontal or vertical, the pixels can only approximate the smooth edge by a staircase of pixels. In fact, there is a range of slopes that all produce, or *alias* to, the same staircase pattern. To make the jagged pixel pattern less obvious, and to disambiguate those different slopes, one can blend the foreground and background colors of the pixels that are only partially covered by the polygon. This is called *antialiasing*, and is illustrated in Figure 3.21.

Since optimal antialiasing needs to take into account human visual perception, characteristics of the monitor on which the final image is displayed, as well as the illumination surrounding the monitor, most 3D graphics APIs do not precisely define an antialiasing algorithm. In our graphics pipeline diagram (Figure 3.1), antialiasing relates to the "coverage generation" and "multisampling" boxes.

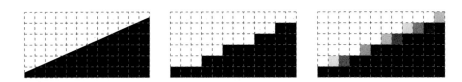

Figure 3.21: A square grid cannot accurately represent slanted edges; they can only be approximated with a staircase pattern. However, blending the foreground and the background at the partially covered pixels makes the staircase pattern far less obvious.

---

1 Although there are good arguments why that is not the right view [Smi95].

Edge antialiasing

When rasterizing straight edges, it is fairly trivial to calculate the *coverage* of the polygon over a pixel. One could then store the coverage value [0, 1] to the alpha component of the fragment, and use a later blending stage to mix the polygon color with the background color. This *edge antialiasing* approach can do an acceptable job when rendering line drawings, but it has several drawbacks. Think about the case where two adjacent polygons jointly fully cover a pixel such that each individually covers only half of it. As the first polygon is drawn, the pixel gets 50% of the polygon color, and 50% of the background color. Then the second polygon is drawn, obtaining 75% of the polygon's color, but still 25% background at the seam. There are tricks that mark the outer edges of a continuous surface so this particular problem can be avoided, but this is not always possible. For example, if a polygon penetrates through another, the penetration boundary is inside the two polygons, not at their edges, edge antialiasing does not work, and the jaggies are fully visible.

Full-scene antialiasing

Edge antialiasing only works at the edges of primitives, but jaggies can happen also at intersections of polygons. The depth buffer is resolved at a pixel level, and if a blue triangle pokes through a white one, the jagged intersection boundary is clearly visible. *Full-scene antialiasing* (FSAA) can correctly handle object silhouettes, adjacent polygons, and even intersecting polygons. Whereas edge antialiasing can be turned on or off per primitive, FSAA information is accumulated for the duration of the whole frame, and the samples are filtered in the end.

There are two main approaches for FSAA, supersampling and multisampling. The basic idea of *supersampling* is simply to first rasterize the scene at higher resolution using point sampling, that is, each primitive affects the pixel if one point such as the center of a pixel is covered by the object. Once the frame is complete, the higher resolution image is filtered down, perhaps using a box filter (simple averaging) or Gaussian or sinc filters that tend to give better results but require more samples and work [GW02]. This is a very brute force approach, and the processing and memory requirements increase linearly by the number of samples per pixel.

Multisampling approximates supersampling with a more judicious use of resources. At each pixel, the objects are sampled several times, and various information such as color and depth may be stored at each sample. The samples coming from the same primitive often sample the textured color only once, and store the same value at each sample. The depth values of the samples, on the other hand, are typically computed and stored separately. The OpenGL specification leaves lots of room to different antialiasing approaches; some implementations may even share samples with their neighboring pixels, sometimes gaining better filtering at the cost of image sharpness.

Other types of aliasing

There are other sources of aliasing in 3D graphics beyond polygon rasterization. They can also usually be remedied by denser sampling followed by filtering, as is done with pixels in FSAA. Examples of other aliasing artifacts include approximating *area light sources* with point lights, where using only a few may create artifacts.

Sampling a moving object at discrete times may produce *temporal aliasing*—the familiar effect where the spokes of a wheel appear to rotate backward. The eye would integrate such motion into a blur; this can be simulated by rendering the animation at a higher frame rate and averaging the results into *motion blur*.

3.5 PER-FRAGMENT OPERATIONS

Each pixel, from the point of view of memory and graphics hardware, is a collection of bits. If the corresponding bits are viewed as a collection over the frame buffer, they are called *bitplanes*, and some of those bitplanes are in turn combined into *logical buffers* such as the back color buffer (usually RGB with or without alpha), depth buffer, and stencil buffer.

After the fragments have been generated by the rasterization stage, there are still several operations that can be applied to them. First, there is a sequence of tests that a fragment is subjected to, using either the fragment location, values generated during rasterization, or a value stored in one of the logical buffers.

A blending stage then takes the incoming color and blends it with the color that already exists at the corresponding pixel. Dithering may change the color values to give an illusion of a greater color depth than what the frame buffer really has. Finally, a logical operation may be applied between the incoming fragment's color and the existing color in the frame buffer.

3.5.1 FRAGMENT TESTS

There are four different tests that a fragment can be subjected to before blending and storing into frame buffer. One of them (scissor) is based on the location of the fragment, while the rest (alpha, stencil, depth) compare two values using a comparison function such as LESS ($<$), LEQUAL ($\leq$), EQUAL ($=$), GEQUAL ($\geq$), GREATER ($>$), NOTEQUAL ($\neq$), or accept (ALWAYS) or reject (NEVER) the fragment regardless of the outcome of the comparison.

Scissor test

The scissor test simply determines whether the fragment lies within a rectangular scissor rectangle, and discards fragments outside that rectangle. With scissoring you can draw the screen in several stages, using different projection matrices. For example, you could first draw a three-dimensional view of your world using a perspective projection matrix, and then render a map of the world on the side or corner of the screen, controlling the drawing area with a scissor rectangle.

Alpha test

The alpha test compares the alpha component of the incoming fragment with a user-given reference or threshold value, and based on the outcome and the selected comparison function either passes or rejects the fragment. For example, with LESS the fragment is accepted if the fragment's alpha is less than the reference value.

One use case for alpha test is rendering transparent objects. In the first pass you can draw the fully opaque objects by setting the test to EQUAL 1 and rendering the whole scene, and then in the second pass draw the scene again with blending enabled and setting the test to NOTEQUAL 1.

Another use is to make real holes to textured objects. If you use a texture map that modifies the fragment alpha and sets it to zero, the pixel may be transparent, but the depth value is still written to the frame buffer. With alpha test LESS 0.1 fragments with alpha smaller than 0.1 will be completely skipped, creating a hole.

Stencil test

The stencil test can only be performed if there is a stencil buffer, and since every additional buffer uses a lot of memory, not all systems provide one. The stencil test conditionally discards a fragment based on the outcome of a comparison between the pixel's stencil buffer value and a reference value. At its simplest, one can initialize the stencil buffer with zeros, paint an arbitrary pattern with ones, and then with NOTEQUAL 0 draw only within the stencil pattern. However, if the stencil pattern is a simple rectangle, you should use scissor test instead and disable stencil test since scissoring is much faster to execute.

Before using the stencil test some values must be drawn into the stencil buffer. The buffer can be initialized to a given value (between zero and $2^s - 1$ for an s bit stencil buffer), and one can draw into the stencil buffer using a stencil operator. One can either KEEP the current value, set it to ZERO, REPLACE it with the reference value, increment (INCR) or decrement (DECR) with saturation or without saturation (INCR_WRAP, DECR_WRAP), or bitwise INVERT the current stencil buffer value. The drawing to the stencil buffer can be triggered by a failed stencil test, a failed depth test, or a passed depth test.

Some more advanced uses of stencil test include guaranteeing that each pixel is drawn only once. If you are drawing a partially transparent object with overlapping parts, the overlapping sections will appear different from areas with no overlap. This can be fixed by clearing the stencil buffer to zeros, drawing only to pixels where the stencil is zero, and replacing the value to one when you draw (KEEP operation for stencil fail, REPLACE for both depth fail and pass). A very advanced use case for stenciling is volumetric shadow casting [Hei91].

Depth test

Depth testing is used for hidden surface removal: the depth value of the incoming fragment is compared against the one already stored at the pixel, and if the comparison fails, the fragment is discarded. If the comparison function is LESS only fragments with smaller depth value than already in the depth buffer pass; other fragments are discarded. This can be seen in Figure 3.2, where the translucent object is clipped to the depth values written by the opaque object. The passed fragments continue along the pipeline and are eventually committed to the frame buffer.

There are other ways of determining the visibility. Conceptually the simplest approach is the *painter's algorithm*, which sorts the objects into a back-to-front order from the camera, and renders them so that a closer object always draws over the previous, farther objects. There are several drawbacks to this. The sorting may require significant extra time and space, particularly if there are a lot of objects in the scene. Moreover, sorting the primitives simply does not work when the primitives interpenetrate, that is, a triangle pokes through another. If you instead sort on a per-pixel basis using the depth buffer, visibility is always resolved correctly, the storage requirements are fixed, and the running time is proportional to the screen resolution rather than the number of objects.

With depth buffering it may make sense to have at least a partial front-to-back rendering order, the opposite that is needed without a depth buffer. This way most fragments that are behind other objects will be discarded by the depth test, avoiding a lot of useless frame buffer updates. At least blending and writing to the frame buffer can be avoided, but some engines even perform texture mapping and fogging only after they detect that the fragment survives the depth test.

Depth offset

As already discussed in Section 2.5.1, the depth buffer has only a finite resolution. Determining the correct depth ordering for objects that are close to each other but not close to the near frustum plane may not always be easy, and may result in *z-fighting*, as shown in Figure 2.11. Let us examine why this happens.

Figure 3.22 shows a situation where two surfaces are close to each other, and how the distance between them *along the viewing direction* increases with the slope or slant of the surfaces. Let us interpret the small squares as pixel extents (in the horizontal direction as one unit of screen x, in the vertical direction as one unit of depth buffer z), and study the image more carefully. On the left, no matter where on the pixel we sample the surfaces, the lower surface always has a higher depth value, but at this z-resolution and at this particular depth, both will have the same quantized depth value. In the middle image, if the lower surface is sampled at the left end of the pixel and the higher surface at the right end, they

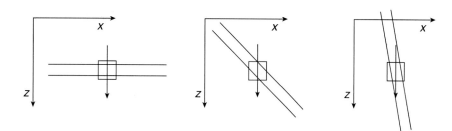

Figure 3.22: The slope needs to be taken into account with polygon offset. The two lines are two surfaces close to each other, the arrow shows the viewing direction, and the coordinate axes illustrate *x* and *z* axis orientations. On the left, the slope of the surfaces with respect to the viewing direction is zero. The slope grows to 1 in the middle, and to about 5 on the right. The distance between the surfaces along the viewing direction also grows as the slope increases.

will have the same depth. On the rightmost image, the depth order might be inverted depending on where the surfaces are evaluated. In general, due to limited precisions in the depth buffer and transformation arithmetic, if two surfaces are near each other, but have different vertex values and different transformations, it is almost random which surface appears in the front at any given pixel.

The situation in Figure 2.11 is contrived, but z-fighting can easily occur in real applications, too. For example, in a shooter game, after you spray a wall with bullets, you may want to paint bullet marks on top of the wall. You would try to align the patches with the wall, but want to guarantee that the bullet marks will resolve to be on top. By adding a *polygon offset*, also known as *depth offset*, to the bullet marks, you can help the rendering engine to determine the correct order. The depth offset is computed as

$$d = m \cdot factor + units, \tag{3.13}$$

where m is the maximum depth slope of the polygon, computed by the rendering engine for each polygon, while *factor* and *units* are user-given constants.

3.5.2 BLENDING

Blending takes the incoming fragment color (the *source color*) and the current value in the color buffer (the *destination color*) and mixes them. Typically the value in the alpha channel determines how the blending is done.

Some systems do not reserve storage for alpha in the color buffer, and do not therefore support a destination alpha. In such a case, all computations assume the destination alpha to be 1, allowing all operations to produce meaningful results. If destination alpha is supported, many advanced compositing effects become possible [PD84].

Two interpretations of alpha

The transparency, or really *opacity* (alpha = 1 typically means opaque, alpha = 0, transparent) described by alpha has two different interpretations, as illustrated in Figure 3.23. One interpretation is that the pixel is partially covered by the fragment, and the alpha denotes that coverage value. Both in the leftmost image and in the middle image two triangles each cover about one-half of the pixel. On the left the triangle orientations are independent from each other, and we get the expected coverage value of $0.5 + 0.5 \cdot 0.5 = 0.75$, as the first fragment covers one-half, and the second is expected to cover also one-half of what was left uncovered. However, if the triangles are correlated, the total coverage can be anything between 0.5 (the two polygons overlap each other) and 1.0 (the two triangles abut, as in the middle image).

The other interpretation of alpha is that a pixel is fully covered by a transparent film that adds a factor of alpha of its own color and lets the rest (one minus alpha) of the existing color to show through, as illustrated on the right of Figure 3.23. In this case, the total opacity is also $1 - 0.5 \cdot 0.5 = 0.75$.

These two interpretations can also be combined. For example, when drawing transparent, edge-antialiased lines, the alpha is less than one due to transparency, and may be further reduced by partial coverage of a pixel.

Blend equations and factors

The basic *blend equation* adds the source and destination colors using blending factors, producing $C = C_s S + C_d D$. The basic blending uses factors $(S, D) = $ (SRC_ALPHA, ONE_MINUS_SRC_ALPHA). That is, the alpha component of the incoming fragment determines how much of the new surface color is used, e.g., 0.25, and the remaining

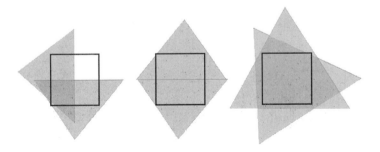

Figure 3.23: *Left:* Two opaque polygons each cover half of a pixel, and if their orientations are random, the chances are that 0.75 of the pixel will be covered. *Center:* If it is the same polygon drawn twice, only half of the pixel should be covered, whereas if the polygons abut as in the image, the whole pixel should be covered. *Right:* Two polygons with 50% opacity fully cover the pixel, creating a compound film with 75% opacity.

portion comes from the destination color already in the color buffer, e.g., $1.0 - 0.25 = 0.75$. This kind of blending is used in the last image in Figure 3.2.

There are several additional blending factors that may be used. The simplest ones are ZERO and ONE where all the color components are multiplied with 0 or 1, that is, either ignored or taken as is. One can use either the destination or source alpha, or one minus alpha as the blending factor (SRC_ALPHA, ONE_MINUS_SRC_ALPHA, DST_ALPHA, ONE_MINUS_DST_ALPHA). Using the ONE_MINUS version flips the meaning of opacity to transparency and vice versa.

With all the factors described so far, the factors for each of the R, G, B, and A channels are the same, and they can be applied to both source or destination colors. However, it is also possible to use the complete 4-component color as the blending factor, so that each channel gets a unique factor. For example, using SRC_COLOR as the blending factor for destination color produces $(R_sR_d, G_sG_d, B_sB_d, A_sA_d)$. In OpenGL ES, SRC_COLOR and ONE_MINUS_SRC_COLOR are legal blending factors only for destination color, while DST_COLOR and ONE_MINUS_DST_COLOR can only be used with the source color. Finally, SRC_ALPHA_SATURATE can be used with the source color, producing a blending factor $(f, f, f, 1)$ where $f = \min(A_s, 1 - A_d)$.

Here are some examples of using the blending factors. The default rendering that does not use blending is equivalent to using (ONE, ZERO) as the (*src*, *dst*) blending factors. To add a layer with 75% transparency, use 0.25 as the source alpha and select the (SRC_ALPHA, ONE_MINUS_SRC_ALPHA) blending factors. To equally mix *n* layers, set the factors to (SRC_ALPHA, ONE) and render each layer with alpha = $1/n$. To draw a colored filter on top of the frame, use (ZERO, SRC_COLOR).

A later addition to OpenGL, which is also available in some OpenGL ES implementations through an extension,[2] allows you to subtract C_sS from C_dD and vice versa. Another extension[3] allows you to define separate blending factors for the color (RGB) and alpha components.

Rendering transparent objects

OpenGL renders primitives in the same order as they are sent to the engine. With depth buffering, one can use an arbitrary rendering order, as the closest surface will always remain visible. However, for correct results in the presence of transparent surfaces in the scene, the objects should be rendered in a back-to-front order. On the other hand, this is usually the slowest approach, since pixels that will be hidden by opaque objects are unnecessarily rendered. The best results, in terms of both performance and quality, are obtained if you sort the objects, render the opaque objects front-to-back with depth

---

2 OES_blend_subtract
3 OES_blend_func_separate

testing and depth writing turned on, then turn depth write off and enable blending, and finally draw the transparent objects in a back-to-front order.

To see why transparent surfaces need to be sorted, think of a white object behind blue glass, both of which are behind red glass, both glass layers being 50% transparent. If you draw the blue glass first (as you should) and then the red glass, you end up with more red than blue: (0.75, 0.25, 0.5), whereas if you draw the layers in opposite order you get more blue: (0.5, 0.25, 0.75).

As described earlier, if it is not feasible to separate transparent objects from opaque objects otherwise, you can use the alpha test to render them in two passes.

Multi-pass rendering

The uses of blending are not limited to rendering translucent objects and compositing images on top of the background. *Multi-pass rendering* refers to techniques where objects and materials are synthesized by combining multiple rendering passes, typically of the same geometry, to achieve the final appearance. Blending is a fundamental requirement for all hardware-accelerated multi-pass rendering approaches, though in some cases the blending machinery of texture mapping units can be used instead of the later blending stage.

An historical example of multi-pass rendering is light mapping, discussed in Section 3.4.3: back in the days of old, when graphics hardware only used to have a single texture unit, light mapping could be implemented by rendering the color texture and light map texture as separate passes with (DST_COLOR, ZERO) or (ZERO, SRC_COLOR) blending in between. However, this is the exact same operation as combining the two using a MODULATE texture function, so you will normally just use that if you have multi-texturing capability.

While multi-texturing and multi-pass rendering can substitute for each other in simple cases, they are more powerful combined. Light mapping involves the single operation AB, which is equally doable with either multi-texturing or multi-pass rendering. Basically, any series of operations that can be evaluated in a straightforward left-to-right order, such as $AB + C$, can be decomposed into either texturing stages or rendering passes. More complex operations, requiring one or more intermediate results, can be decomposed into a combination of multi-texturing and multi-pass rendering: $AB + CD$ can be satisfied with two multi-textured rendering passes, AB additively blended with CD.

While you can render an arbitrary number of passes, the number of texture units quickly becomes the limiting factor when proceeding toward more complex shading equations. This can be solved by storing intermediate results in textures, either by copying the frame buffer contents after rendering an intermediate result or by using direct render-to-texture capability.

Multi-pass rendering, at least in theory, makes it possible to construct arbitrarily complex rendering equations from the set of basic blending and texturing operations. This has been demonstrated by systems that translate a high-level shading language into OpenGL rendering passes [POAU00, PMTH01]. In practice, the computation is limited by the numeric accuracy of the individual operations and the intermediate results: with 8 bits per channel in the frame buffer, rounding errors accumulate fast enough that great care is needed to maximize the number of useful bits in the result.

3.5.3 DITHERING, LOGICAL OPERATIONS, AND MASKING

Before the calculated color at a pixel is committed to the frame buffer, there are two more processing steps that can be taken: dithering and logical operations. Finally, writing to each of the different buffers can also be *masked*, that is, disabled.

Dithering

The human eye can accommodate to great changes in illumination: the ratio of the light on a bright day to the light on a moonless overcast night can be a billion to one. With a fixed lighting situation, the eye can distinguish a much smaller range of contrast, perhaps 10000 : 1. However, in scenes that do not have very bright lights, 8 bits, or 256 levels, are sufficient to produce color transitions that appear continuous and seamless. Since 8 bits also matches pretty well the limits of current displays, and is a convenient unit of storage and computation on binary computers, using 8 bits per color channel on a display is a typical choice on a desktop.

Some displays cannot even display all those 256 levels of intensity, and some frame buffers save in memory costs by storing fewer than 8 bits per channel. Having too few bits available can lead to *banding*. Let us say you calculate a color channel at 8 bits where values range from 0 to 255, but can only store 4 bits with a range from 0 to 15. Now all values between 64 and 80 (0100000 and 0101000 in binary) map to either 4 or 5 (0100 or 0101). If you simply quantize the values in an image where the colors vary smoothly, so that values from 56 to 71 map to 4 and from 72 to 87 map to 5, the flat areas and the sudden jumps between them become obvious to the viewer. However, if you mix pixels of values 4 and 5 at roughly equal amounts where the original image values are around 71 or 72, the eye fuses them together and interprets them as a color between 4 and 5. This is called *dithering*, and is illustrated in Figure 3.24.

Figure 3.24: A smooth ramp (*left*) is quantized (*middle*) causing banding. Dithering (*right*) produces smoother transitions even though individual pixels are quantized.

OpenGL allows turning dithering on and off per drawing command. This way, internal computations can be calculated at a higher precision, but color ramps are dithered just after blending and before committing to the frame buffer.

Another approach to dithering is to have the internal frame buffer at a higher resolution than the display color depth. In this case, dithering takes place only when the frame is complete and is sent to the display. This allows allows reasonable results even on displays that only have a single bit per pixel, such as the monochrome displays of some low-end mobile devices, or newspapers printed with only black ink. In such situations, dithering is absolutely required so that any impression of continuous intensity variations can be conveyed.

Logical operations

Logical operations, or *logic ops* for short, are the last processing stage of the OpenGL graphics pipeline. They are mutually exclusive with blending. With logic ops, the source and destination pixel data are considered bit patterns, rather than color values, and a logical operation such as AND, OR, XOR, etc., is applied between the source and the destination before the values are stored in the color buffer.

In the past, logical operations were used, for example, to draw a cursor without having to store the background behind the cursor. If one draws the cursor shape with XOR, then another XOR will erase it, reinstating the original background. OpenGL ES 1.0 and 1.1 support logical operations as they are fast to implement in software renderers and allow some special effects, but both M3G and OpenGL ES 2.0 omit this functionality.

Masking

Before the fragment values are actually stored in the frame buffer, the different data fields can be masked. Writing into the color buffer can be turned off for each of red, green, blue, or alpha channels. The same can be done for the depth channel. For the stencil buffer, even individual bits may be masked before writing to the buffer.

3.6 LIFE CYCLE OF A FRAME

Now that we have covered the whole low-level 3D graphics pipeline, let us take a look at the full life cycle of an application and a frame.

In the beginning of an application, resources have to be obtained. The most important resource is the frame buffer. This includes the color buffer, how many bits there are for each color channel, existence and bit depth of the alpha channel, depth buffer, stencil buffer, and multisample buffers. The geometry data and texture maps also require memory, but those resources can be allocated later.

The viewport transformation and projection matrices describe the type of camera that is being used, and are usually set up only once for the whole application. The modelview matrix, however, changes whenever something moves, whether they are objects in the scene or the camera viewing the scene.

After the resources have been obtained and the fixed parameters set up, new frames are rendered one after another. In the beginning of a new frame, the color, depth, and other buffers are usually cleared. We then render the objects one by one. Before rendering each object, we set up its rendering state, including the lights, texture maps, blending modes, and so on. Once the frame is complete, the system is told to display the image. If the rendering was quick, it may make sense to wait for a while before starting the next frame, instead of rendering as many frames as possible and using too much power. This cycle is repeated until the application is finished. It is also possible to read the contents of the frame buffer into user memory, for example to grab screen shots.

3.6.1 SINGLE VERSUS DOUBLE BUFFERING

In a simple graphics system there may be only a single color buffer, into which new graphics is drawn at the same time as the display is refreshed from it. This *single buffering* has the benefits of simplicity and lesser use of graphics memory. However, even if the graphics drawing happens very fast, the rendering and the display refresh are usually not synchronized with each other, which leads to annoying tearing and flickering.

Double buffering avoids tearing by rendering into a *back buffer* and notifying the system when the frame is completed. The system can then synchronize the copying of the rendered image to the display with the display refresh cycle. Double buffering is the recommended way of rendering to the screen, but single-buffering is still useful for off-screen surfaces.

3.6.2 COMPLETE GRAPHICS SYSTEM

Figure 3.25 presents a conceptual high-level model of a graphics system. Applications run on a CPU, which is connected to a GPU with a first-in-first-out (FIFO) buffer. The GPU feeds pixels into various frame buffers of different APIs, from which the display subsystem composites the final displayed image, or which can be fed back to graphics processing through the texture-mapping unit. The Graphics Device Interface (GDI) block implements functionality that is typically present in 2D graphics APIs of the operating systems. The Compositor block handles the mixing of different types of content surfaces in the system, such as 3D rendering surfaces and native OS graphics.

Inside the GPU a command processor processes the commands coming from the CPU to the 2D or 3D graphics subsystems, which may again be buffered. A typical 3D subsystem consists of two executing units: a vertex unit for transformations and lighting, and a fragment unit for the rear end of the 3D pipeline. Real systems may omit some of the components; for example, the CPU may do more (even all) of the graphics processing,

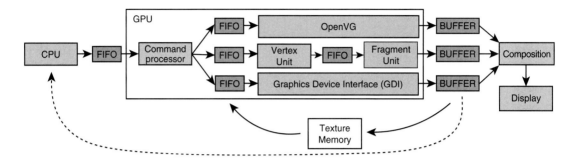

Figure 3.25: A conceptual model of a graphics system.

some of the FIFO buffers may be direct unbuffered bus connections, or the compositor is not needed if the 3D subsystem executes in a full-screen mode. Nevertheless, looking at the 3D pipeline, we can separate roughly four main execution stages: the CPU, the vertex unit that handles transformations and lighting (also known as the geometry unit), the rasterization and fragment-processing unit (pixel pipeline), and the display composition unit.

Figure 3.26 shows an ideal case when all four units can work in parallel. While the CPU is processing a new frame, the vertex unit performs geometry processing for the previous frame, the rasterization unit works on the frame before that, and the display subunit displays a frame that was begun three frames earlier. If the system is completely balanced, and the FIFOs are large enough to mask temporary imbalances, this pipelined system can produce images four times faster than a fully sequential system such as the one in Figure 3.27. Here, one opportunity for parallelism vanishes from the lack of double buffering, and all the stages in general wait until the others have completed their frame before proceeding with the next frame.

3.6.3 SYNCHRONIZATION POINTS

We call the situation where one unit of the graphics system has to wait for the input of a previous unit to complete, or even the whole pipeline to flush, a *synchronization point*.

Even if the graphics system has been designed to be able to execute fully in parallel, use of certain API features may create a synchronization point. For example, if the application asks to read back the current frame buffer contents, the CPU has to stall and wait until all the previous commands have fully executed and have been committed into the frame buffer. Only then can the contents be delivered to the application.

Another synchronization point is caused by binding the rendering output to a texture map. Also, creating a new texture map and using it for the first time may create a bottleneck for transferring the data from the CPU to the GPU and organizing it into a format

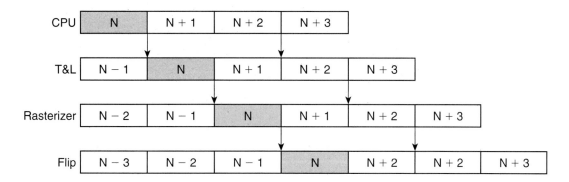

Figure 3.26: Parallelism of asynchronous multibuffered rendering.

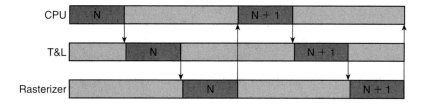

Figure 3.27: Nonparallel nature of single-buffered or synchronized rendering.

that is native to the texturing unit. A similar synchronization point can result from the modification of an existing texture map.

In general, the best performance is obtained if each hardware unit in the system executes in parallel. The first rule of thumb is to keep most of the traffic flowing in the same direction, and to query as little data as possible back from the graphics subsystem. If you must read the results back, e.g., if you render into a texture map, delaying the use of that data until a few frames later may help the system avoid stalling. You should also use server-side objects wherever possible, as they allow the data to be cached on the GPU. For best performance, such cached data should not be changed after it has been loaded. Finally, you can try to increase parallelism, for example, by executing application-dependent CPU processing immediately after GPU-intensive calls such as clearing the buffers, drawing a large textured mesh, or swapping buffers. Another way to improve parallelism is to move non-graphics–related processing into another thread altogether.

4

ANIMATION

Animation is what ultimately breathes life into 3D graphics. While still images can be nice as such, most applications involve objects moving and interacting with each other and the user, or scenes in some other way changing over time. This chapter introduces basic, commonly used animation concepts that we will encounter when we discuss the M3G animation functionality later in the book.

4.1 KEYFRAME ANIMATION

Keyframe animation is perhaps the most common way of describing predefined motions in computer graphics. The term originates from cartoons, where the senior animator would first draw the most important "key" frames describing the main poses within an animation sequence. The in-between frames or "tweens" could then be filled in to complete the animation, based on those defining features. This allowed the valuable time of the senior animator to be focused on the important parts, whereas the work of drawing the intermediate frames could be divided among the junior colleagues.

In computer animation today, a human animator still defines the keyframes, but the data in between is *interpolated* by the computer. An example of keyframe interpolation is shown in Figure 4.1. The keyframes are values that the animated property has at specific points in time, and the computer applies an interpolation function to these data points to produce the intermediate values. The data itself can be anything from

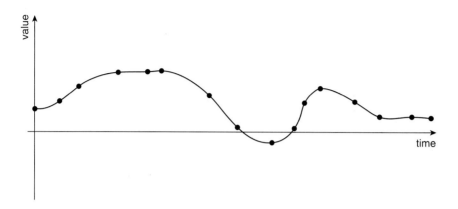

Figure 4.1: Keyframe values (points) and interpolated data (curve).

positions and orientations to color and lighting parameters, as long as it can be represented numerically to the computer.

Expressing this mathematically, we have the set of N keyframes $K = (\mathbf{k}_0, \mathbf{k}_1, \ldots, \mathbf{k}_{N-1})$ and an interpolation function f. The value of the animated property can then be evaluated at any time t by evaluating $f(K, t)$; we can also say that we *sample* the animated value at different times t. Using different functions f, we can vary the characteristics of the interpolated data, as well as the computational complexity of evaluating the function.

The main benefit of keyframe animation today is perhaps not the time saved in producing the animation, but the memory saved by the keyframe representation. Data need only be stored at the keyframe locations, and since much of the animation data required can be produced from fairly sparse keyframes, keyframe animation is much more space-efficient than storing the data for each frame. A related benefit is that the keyframe rate need not be tied to the display rate; once you have your keyframe sequence, you can play it back at any rate, speeding up or slowing down as necessary.

4.1.1 INTERPOLATION

In practice, interpolation is usually implemented in a *piecewise* manner: each interpolated segment, separated by two adjacent keyframes, is computed on its own, and the slope or curvature of the adjacent segments has no effect on the result. In some schemes, the interpolation parameters depend on the keyframes of the adjacent segments as well, but once those parameters are known, each segment is still interpolated as a separate entity.

Interpolating an entire keyframe sequence amounts to identifying the segment we are interested in, by finding the keyframes surrounding our sampling time t, and computing the interpolated value for that segment only. Let us call the values of our chosen keyframes simply $\mathbf{a}$ and $\mathbf{b}$. Those will be the desired values at the beginning and end of the segment, respectively. Let us also define a new interpolation parameter s, derived from time t, to give our position within the segment: the value of s shall be 0 at keyframe $\boldsymbol{a}$ and increase linearly to 1 at keyframe $\boldsymbol{b}$. Armed with this information, we can begin looking for different ways to move from $\boldsymbol{a}$ to $\boldsymbol{b}$.

The simplest way to interpolate keyframes is the step function, which does not interpolate at all:

$$f_{step}(s) = \boldsymbol{a}. \tag{4.1}$$

Instead, as shown in Figure 4.2, the interpolated value always remains at that of the previous keyframe. This is very easy from a computational perspective, but as seen in the figure, it produces a discontinuous result that is ill-suited to animating most aspects of a visual scene—for example, a character jumping from one place to another is not what we typically expect of animation. The step function can still have its uses: switching light sources on and off at preprogrammed times is one intuitive application.

Going toward smoother motion, we need to take into account more than one keyframe. Using both keyframes, we can linearly interpolate, or *lerp*, between them:

$$f_{lerp}(s) = (1 - s)\boldsymbol{a} + s\boldsymbol{b} \tag{4.2}$$
$$= \boldsymbol{a} + s(\boldsymbol{b} - \boldsymbol{a}). \tag{4.3}$$

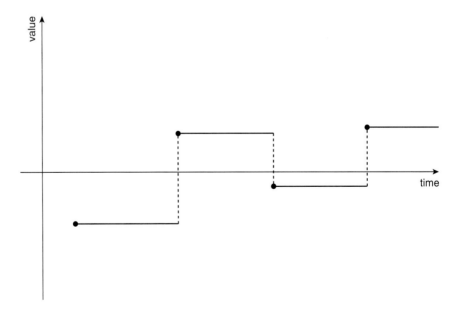

Figure 4.2: Step interpolation.

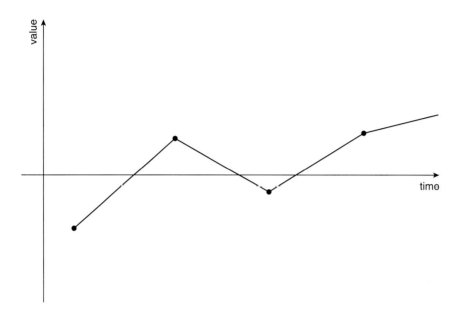

Figure 4.3: Linear interpolation, or *lerp*.

As we can see in Figure 4.3, lerp actually connects the keyframes without sudden jumps. However, it is immediately obvious that the result is not smooth: the direction of our interpolated line changes abruptly at each keyframe, and the visual effect is very similar. This, again, defies any expectations of physically based motion, where some manner of inertia is to be expected. Lerping is still computationally very cheap, which makes it well suited to ramping things such as light levels up and down at various speeds, and it can be used to approximate nonlinear motion by adding more keyframes. Of course, any purely linear motion at constant speed is a natural application, but such motions are quite uncommon in practice—consider, for example, city traffic during rush hour, or the individual limbs and joints of a walking human.

For more life-like animation, we need a function that can provide some degree of *ease-in* and *ease-out*: instead of jumping into and out of motion, short periods of acceleration and deceleration make the animation appear much more natural. Also, since much of the animation in computer graphics is not linear, being able to represent curved motion is another feature in the wish list. It would seem that changing the linear segments of Figure 4.3 into curved ones would solve both problems, and indeed it does—in a number of different flavors. There are many different formulations for producing curves, each with its individual characteristics that make it better suited for some particular tasks and less well for others. In the following, we will only cover what is relevant to using and understanding M3G in the later chapters of this book.

The curves commonly used in computer graphics are *parametric cubic curves*, which offer a good balance between the amount of control, computational efficiency, and ease of use [FvFH90]. Each interpolated curve segment is a separate polynomial function of s that connects the two keyframes a and b. Depending on the type of curve, the actual polynomial coefficients are usually defined through more intuitive parameters, such as additional control points or explicit tangent vectors. In this discussion, we will use a *Hermite* curve [FvFH90, AMH02] to construct a *Catmull-Rom spline* [CR74] that smoothly interpolates our keyframe sequence similarly to Figure 4.4.

As illustrated in Figure 4.5, each Hermite curve segment is controlled by tangent vectors at both ends in addition to the actual keyframes. If you think of interpolating the position of an object using a Hermite curve, the tangent vectors are essentially the velocity—speed and direction—of the object at the endpoints of the curve.

When discussing lerp, we mentioned that natural objects do not jump from one position to another, and neither do they change velocity abruptly. For natural-looking motion, we therefore want not only the position, but also the velocity to be continuous. Therefore, when interpolating across multiple segments, we want to align the tangent vectors between neighboring segments such that the velocity remains constant. Since our keyframes are not necessarily spaced uniformly in time, we cannot trivially use the same tangent vector for both segments connected to a keyframe; instead, the tangents

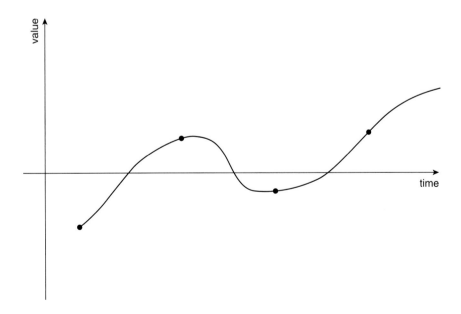

Figure 4.4: Curve interpolation.

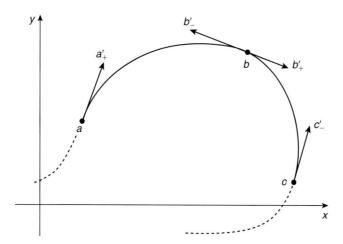

Figure 4.5: Two Hermite curve segments and their tangent vectors; the end tangent of each segment is reversed for clarity. In order to illustrate the tangent vectors, the coordinate system is different from Figures 4.2 to 4.4, and time is not plotted at all. Note that the relative magnitude of tangents b_- and b_+ depends on keyframe timing and need not be the same; see text.

may have to be scaled to different magnitudes in order to maintain smooth velocity [KB84, AMH02].

In order to compute the tangent vectors b'_- and b'_+ using the three-keyframe sequence (a, b, c) in Figure 4.5 so that they maintain smooth motion over keyframe b, we need to take into account the durations of the adjacent interpolation segments. Let us denote the time differences between b and its adjacent keyframes by Δt_{ab} and Δt_{bc}. Our tangent values will then be [KB84, AMH02]

$$b'_- = \frac{\Delta t_{ab}}{\Delta t_{ab} + \Delta t_{bc}} b' \tag{4.4}$$

and

$$b'_+ = \frac{\Delta t_{bc}}{\Delta t_{ab} + \Delta t_{bc}} b', \tag{4.5}$$

where b' is a finite central difference over keyframe b:

$$b' = \frac{c - a}{2}. \tag{4.6}$$

The tangents for keyframes a and c are computed in a similar manner from their adjacent keyframes.

Based on the equations for Hermite curve interpolation [AMH02, FvFH90, WW92] and the tangent vectors we defined above, we can, again, express the segment between keyframes a and b as a function of our interpolation parameter s:

$$f_{spline}(s) = [a \quad b \quad a'_+ \quad b'_-] \, M^T \, [s^3 \quad s^2 \quad s \quad 1]^T, \qquad (4.7)$$

where M is a *basis matrix* of coefficients specific to a Hermite curve:

$$M = \begin{bmatrix} 2 & -2 & 1 & 1 \\ -3 & 3 & -2 & -1 \\ 0 & 0 & 1 & 0 \\ 1 & 0 & 0 & 0 \end{bmatrix}. \qquad (4.8)$$

As we have mentioned, there are numerous other classes of curves and splines used in computer graphics. One type of spline commonly used in animation and modeling tools is an extension of Catmull-Rom splines called Kochanek-Bartels splines [KB84]. They are also known as TCB splines after the *tension, continuity,* and *bias* parameters they add to control the shape of the curve at each keyframe. However, for the purposes of this book, it is sufficient to know that it is possible to approximate the shape of any other curve using Catmull-Rom curves, to an arbitrary degree, by adding more keyframes. For further reading on other kinds of curves, again, refer to more comprehensive computer graphics textbooks [FvFH90, AMH02, WW92].

4.1.2 QUATERNIONS

Interpolating positions and most other parameters is easy to understand: you can plot the keyframe values on paper, draw a line or curve in between, and pick any point on the line for an intuitive interpolated position. You can interpolate each of the x, y, and z coordinates independently and get the correct result. Interpolating orientations, however, is not quite as intuitive.

Most computer animation today, M3G included, uses *unit quaternions* to represent orientation, as described in Section 2.3.1. As a quick recap, a unit quaternion is a four-vector $[x \quad y \quad z \quad w]$ of length one where the first three imaginary components relate to an axis of rotation and the last, real, component relates to a rotation angle.

Each and every quaternion that we are interested in will always rest on a four-dimensional sphere that has a radius of one. Imagine that the unit sphere of quaternions has a North pole (at $[0 \quad 0 \quad 0 \quad 1]$) and a South pole (at $[0 \quad 0 \quad 0 \quad -1]$). The quaternion on the North pole stands for the initial position of your object, before any rotation has been applied to it. Each quaternion elsewhere on the surface of the sphere represents a rotation away from the initial position. The farther you go from the North pole, the more you rotate. Walking along the shortest path possible along the surface will rotate along the shortest path (and about a single axis) between two orientations. However, moving by any number of degrees on the 4D sphere will rotate *twice* that number in 3D space—refer to Equation 2.21 for the proof. Therefore, if you reach the South pole, your 3D object will have rotated a full 360 degrees, back to where it started from; but it is important to realize that in quaternion space, we could not be farther away from the initial position!

To interpolate along the surface of the 4D sphere, spherical linear interpolation or *slerp* can be used. Assuming two unit quaternion keyframes $\hat{a}$ and $\hat{b}$, with the interpolation arc angle θ defined such that $\cos \theta = \hat{a} \cdot \hat{b}$, slerp is defined as:

$$f_{slerp}(s) = slerp(s \cdot \hat{a}, \hat{b}) = \frac{\hat{a} \sin((1-s)\theta) + \hat{b} \sin(s\theta)}{\sin(\theta)} \qquad (4.9)$$

Each quaternion $\hat{q}$ has a counterpart $-\hat{q}$, on exactly the opposite side of the unit sphere, which results in exactly the same orientation. As long as you are dealing with rotations of 180 degrees or less, you can optimize your slerp routine a bit by explicitly flipping the signs on one of the quaternions so that they land on the same hemisphere of the 4D unit sphere. This is what many code examples on quaternion interpolation do, and it will work as long as all you want is to interpolate along the shortest path between two 3D orientations. However, sometimes you may want to interpolate along the longer path, in the opposite direction, or blend between more than two orientations, and in such a case using the whole 4D unit sphere is required.

Also, using the proper slerp without any sign mangling, you can actually rotate by up to 360 degrees between two keyframes, so there is more power available to you that way. In any case, be warned that unless you know very well what you are doing, you will be better off using the full-blown slerp for interpolation. On the other hand, you will also need to take greater care when exporting the animations from your tools; some of these only return the orientation keyframes as matrices, requiring a conversion back to quaternions, and you will need to decide between the quaternions $\hat{q}$ and $-\hat{q}$ for each matrix. However, this small headache will enable the rest of the animation pipeline to work correctly also when more advanced features than simple two-keyframe interpolation are introduced.

Slerp for quaternions has the same problem as lerp for positions: you get instant changes in angular velocity at keyframes. The solution is also similar: use curved interpolation. The equivalent of splines for quaternions is often dubbed *squad*. We omit the associated hairy math here, but for more details, refer to the paper by Shoemake [Sho87] or a graphics book that treats the subject [WW92, AMH02]. Suffice it to say that squad will interpolate rotations like spline interpolates positions, albeit with increased computational intensity. In practice, slerp or even lerp followed by renormalization (Equation (2.4)) is often sufficient for purposes such as character animation, and regular spline interpolation can be leveraged for most use cases. Squad can still be useful for achieving perfectly smooth camera interpolation, for example.

4.2 DEFORMING MESHES

Keyframe animation is good for controlling animated objects, for example moving the limbs of an articulated character. If we are modeling robots, rigid-body animation suffices, and we can just render the pieces individually. To affect the motion on a more soft-bodied character, however, we want the mesh to deform without seams or cracks. This calls for some form of per-vertex deformation.

4.2.1 MORPHING

A straightforward way to animate a mesh is to do as the cartoonists do: define keyframes that comprise the essential poses of an animation, then interpolate or *morph* between those. A simple example is shown in Figure 4.6. The way we can do this is to define a set of alternative vertex array definitions $M_0, M_1, M_2, \ldots, M_{N-1}$ so that each M_i represents the vertex coordinates (and other related data, such as normals and texture coordinates) for one keyframe. The mesh topology or list of primitives is only specified once.

To interpolate between the mesh keyframes, we can just lerp between any two of them if the keyframes represent poses on a timeline. Better yet, we can think of our keyframes as alternative shapes, or *morph targets*, that we can arbitrarily blend between:

$$M = \sum w_i M_i, \tag{4.10}$$

where the w_i are weights we can freely assign to each of the morph targets. Note that using weights outside of the [0, 1] range, it is also possible to extrapolate the predefined shapes. An alternative formulation is to add the weighted morph targets to a base shape:

$$M = B + \sum w_i M_i \tag{4.11}$$

This emphasizes the role of some base shape that is being modified through morphing, but mathematically, both formulations express the same thing.

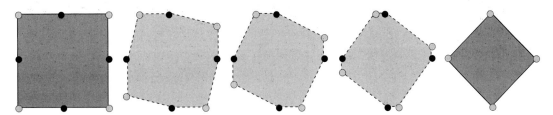

Figure 4.6: Morphing some of the vertex positions between the two base shapes on the left and the right. Note that the number of vertices remains the same.

Morphing is a good technique for producing complex deformations, such as facial expressions, that are not easily reproduced by simple transformations. The downside of morphing is that it takes a lot of memory per keyframe, so the number of base shapes should be kept relatively small for complex meshes. Alternatively, morphing can be used to define lots of keyframes for very simple meshes to get fairly complex animation that is still computationally cheap to render in real time.

4.2.2 SKINNING

For complex characters with lots of vertices and more or less arbitrary numbers of possible poses, morphing quickly becomes inefficient. Another way to deform meshes is to assign vertices to the joints of an articulated skeleton, animate them, and connect the vertices with a skin of polygons [Cat72]. However, that still leads to sharp changes at joints. During the 1990s the gaming and 3D modeling industry generalized this approach and started calling it *skinning* [Lan98]. The idea is that each vertex can be associated with several joints or bones, weighted by linear weights. This technique is sometimes referred to as subspace surface deformation, or linear blend skinning; we simply call it skinning. It is so commonly used today that we can call it the *de facto* standard of character animation.

The general idea behind skinning is that instead of transforming the whole mesh with a single transformation matrix, each vertex is individually transformed by a weighted blend of several matrices as shown in Figure 4.7. By assigning different weights to different vertices, we can simulate articulated characters with soft flesh around rigid bones.

The skeleton used in skinning stands for a hierarchy of transformations. An example hierarchy can be seen in Figure 4.7. The pelvis is the root node, and the rest of the body parts are connected to each other so that the limbs extend deeper into the hierarchy. Each bone has a transformation relative to the parent node—usually at least translation and rotation, but scaling can be used, for example, for cartoon-like animation. The hierarchy also has a *rest pose* (also known as *bind pose*) in which the bone transformations are such that the skeleton is aligned with the untransformed mesh.

Having the skeleton hierarchy, we can compute transformations from the bones to the common root node. This gives us a transformation matrix T_i for each bone i. The matrices for the rest pose are important, and we denote those B_i.

The relative transformation that takes a rest pose B to a target pose T is TB^{-1}. From this, and allowing a vertex v to have weighted influence w_i from several bones, we get the skinning equation for a transformed vertex

$$v' = \sum_i w_i T_i B_i^{-1} v. \tag{4.12}$$

Note that we can either transform the vertex with each matrix, then compute a blend of the transformed vertices, or compute a blend of the matrices and transform the vertex just once using the blended matrix. The latter can in some cases be more efficient if the inverse

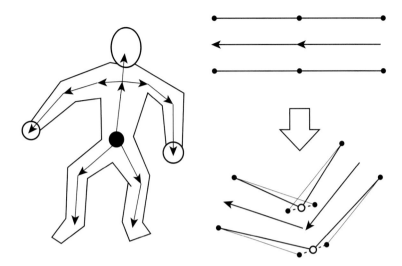

Figure 4.7: *Left:* A skeletally animated, or skinned, character. Each arrow ends in a joint, and each joint has a bone transformation, usually involving at least translation and rotation. *Right:* A close-up of one animated joint, demonstrating vertex blending. The vertices around the joint are conceptually transformed with both bone transformations, resulting in the positions denoted by the thin lines and black dots. The transformed results are then interpolated (dotted line, white dots) to obtain the final skins (thick lines).

transpose matrix is needed for transforming vertex normals. Also, the modelview matrix can be premultiplied into each matrix T_i to avoid doing the camera transformation as a separate step after the vertex blending.

With hardware-accelerated skinning, using either vertex shaders or the OpenGL matrix palette extension (Section 10.4.3), the vertices will be transformed each time the mesh is rendered. With multi-pass rendering in particular, the mesh will therefore be transformed multiple times. A software implementation can easily perform the calculations only when necessary and cache the results, but this will still place a considerable burden on the CPU. As an animated mesh typically changes for each frame, there is usually no gain from using software skinning if hardware acceleration is available, but it is worth keeping the option in mind for special cases.

The animation for skinning can come from a number of sources. It is possible to use keyframe animation to animate the bones of the skeleton, with the keyframes modeled by hand or extracted from motion capture data. Another possibility is to use physics-based animation. Rigid body dynamics [Len04] are often used to produce "ragdoll" effects, for example when a foe is gunned down and does a spectacular fall from height in a shooter game. Inverse kinematics (IK) [FvFH90, WW92] can also be used to make hands touch scene objects, align feet with the ground, and so forth. Often a combination of these techniques is used with keyframe animation driving the normal motion, rigid body dynamics stepping in for falling and other special effects, and IK making small corrections to avoid penetrating scene geometry.

4.2.3 OTHER DYNAMIC DEFORMATIONS

Naturally, dynamic deformation of meshes need not be limited to morphing and skinning. As we can apply arbitrary processing to the vertices, either in the application code or, more commonly, in graphics hardware, almost unlimited effects are possible.

One common example of per-vertex animation is water simulation. By applying displacements to each vertex based on a fluid simulation model, a convincing effect can be created. Different kinds of physics-based deformation effects include soft body modeling, whereby the mesh deforms upon contact based on, for example, a mass-and-spring simulation. A variation of this is cloth modeling, where air density plays a more important role. The details of creating these and other effects are beyond the scope of this book. For further information, refer to the bibliography ([WW92, EMP+02]).

Once the vertex data is dynamically modified by the application, it needs to be fed to the rendering stage. Most graphics engines prefer static vertex data, which allows for optimizations such as precomputing bounding volumes or optimizing the storage format and location of the data. Vertex data that is dynamically uploaded from the application prohibits most such optimizations, and it also requires additional memory bandwidth to transfer the data between application and graphics memory. Therefore, there is almost always some performance reduction associated with dynamically modifying vertices. The magnitude of this performance hit can vary greatly by system and application—for example, vertex shaders in modern GPUs can perform vertex computations more efficiently than application code because there is no need to move the data around in memory, and it has an instruction set optimized for that particular task. This is also the reason that modern rendering APIs, including both OpenGL ES and M3G, have built-in support for the basic vertex deformation cases—to enable the most efficient implementation for the underlying hardware.

SCENE MANAGEMENT

By dealing with individual triangles, matrices, and disparate pieces of rendering state, you are in full control of the rendering engine and will get exactly what you ask for. However, creating and managing 3D content at that level of detail quickly becomes a burden; this typically happens when cubes and spheres no longer cut it, and graphic artists need to get involved. Getting their animated object hierarchies and fancy materials out of 3ds Max or Maya and into your real-time application can be a big challenge. The task is not made any easier if your runtime API cannot handle complete objects, materials, characters, and scenes, together with their associated animations. The artists and their tools deal with higher-level concepts than triangle strips and blending functions, and your runtime engine should accommodate to that.

Raising the abstraction level of the runtime API closer to that of the modeling tools facilitates a content-driven approach to development, where designers can work independently of programmers, but it has other benefits as well. It flattens the learning curve, reduces the amount of boilerplate code, eliminates many common sources of error, and in general increases the productivity of both novice and expert programmers. A high-level API can also result in better performance, particularly if you are not already a 3D guru with in-depth knowledge of all the software and hardware configurations that your application is supposed to be running on.

In this chapter, we take a look at how 3D objects are composed, how the objects can be organized into a scene graph, and how the scene graph can be efficiently rendered and updated. Our focus is on how these concepts are expressed in M3G, so we do not cover the whole spectrum of data structures that have been used in other systems or that you could use in your own game engine. For the most part, we will use terminology from M3G.

5.1 TRIANGLE MESHES

A *3D object* combines geometric primitives and rendering state into a self-contained visual entity that is easier to animate and interact with than the low-level bits and pieces are. 3D objects can be defined in many ways, e.g., with polygons, lines, points, Bézier patches, NURBS, subdivision surfaces, implicit surfaces, or voxels, but in this chapter we concentrate on simple triangle meshes, as they are the only type of geometric primitive supported by M3G.

A *triangle mesh* consists of vertices in 3D space, connected into triangles to define a surface, plus associated rendering state to specify how the surface is to be shaded. The structure of a triangle mesh in M3G is as shown in Figure 5.1: vertex coordinates, other per-vertex attributes, and triangle indices are stored in their respective buffers, while rendering state is aggregated into what we call the *appearance* of the mesh. Although this exact organization is specific to M3G, other scene graphs are usually similar. We will explain the function of each of the mesh components below.

VertexBuffers are used to store per-vertex attributes, which, in the case of M3G, include vertex coordinates (x, y, z), texture coordinates (s, t, r, q), normal vectors (n_x, n_y, n_z), and colors (R, G, B, A). Note that the two first texture coordinates (s, t) are

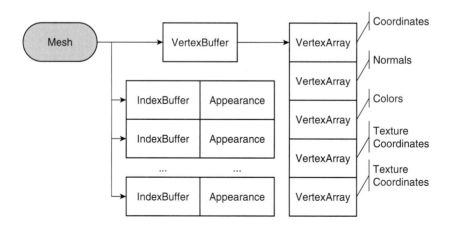

Figure 5.1: The components of a triangle mesh in M3G.

enough for typical use cases, but three or four can be used for projective texture mapping and other tricks.

The coordinates and normals of a triangle mesh are given in its local coordinate system—*object coordinates*—and are transformed into *eye coordinates* by the modelview matrix. The mesh can be animated and instantiated by changing the modelview matrix between frames (for animation) or between draw calls (for instantiation). Texture coordinates are also subject to a 4×4 projective transformation. This allows you to scroll or otherwise animate the texture, or to project it onto the mesh; see Section 3.4.1 for details.

`IndexBuffers` define the surface of the mesh by connecting vertices into triangles, as shown in Figure 5.2. OpenGL ES defines three ways to form triangles from consecutive indices—triangle strips, lists, and fans—but M3G only supports triangle strips. There may be multiple index buffers per mesh; each buffer then defines a *submesh*, which is the basic unit of rendering in M3G. Splitting a mesh into submeshes is necessary if different parts of the mesh have different rendering state; for example, if one part is translucent while others are opaque, or if the parts have different texture maps.

The `Appearance` defines how a mesh or submesh is to be shaded, textured, blended, and so on. The appearance is typically divided into components that encapsulate coherent subsets of the low-level rendering state: Figure 5.3 shows how this was done for M3G. The appearance components have fairly self-explanatory names: the `Texture2D` object, for instance, contains the texture blending, filtering, and wrapping modes, as well as the 4×4 texture coordinate transformation matrix. The texture image is included by reference, and stored in an `Image2D` object. Appearances and their component objects can

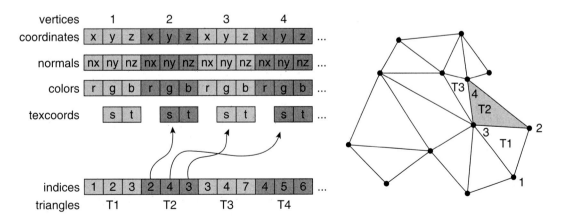

Figure 5.2: Triangle meshes are formed by indexing a set of vertex arrays. Here the triangles are organized into a triangle list, i.e., every three indices define a new triangle. For example, triangle T2 is formed by the vertices 2, 4, and 3.

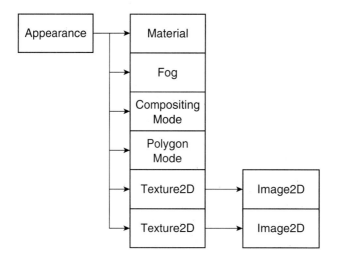

Figure 5.3: The appearance components in M3G. Implementations may support an arbitrary number of texturing units, but the most common choice (two units) is shown in this diagram.

be shared between an arbitrary number of meshes and submeshes in the scene graph. The appearance components of M3G are discussed in detail in Chapter 14.

5.2 SCENE GRAPHS

Rendering a single 3D object may be useful in a demo or a tutorial, but to create something more exciting you will need a number of 3D objects in a particular spatial and logical arrangement—a *3D scene*.

3D scenes can be organized into many different data structures that are collectively referred to as *scene graphs*. The term is decidedly vague, covering everything from simple lists of objects up to very sophisticated spatial databases. In this section we aim to characterize the design space of scene graphs, progressively narrowing down our scope to the small subset of that space that is relevant for M3G.

5.2.1 APPLICATION AREA

When setting out to design a scene graph system, the first thing to decide is what it is for. Is it for graphics, physics, artificial intelligence, spatial audio, or a combination of these? Is it designed for real-time or offline use, or both? Is it for a specific game genre, such as first-person shooters or flight simulators, or maybe just one title? A unified scene representation serving all conceivable applications would certainly be ideal, but in practice we have to specialize to avoid creating a huge monolithic system that runs slowly and is difficult to use.

Typical scene graphs strike a balance by specializing in real-time animation and rendering, but not in any particular application or game genre. This is also the case with M3G. Physics, artificial intelligence, audio, user interaction, and everything else is left for the user, although facilitated to some extent by the ability to store metadata and invisible objects into the main scene graph. Adjunct features such as collision detection are included in some systems to serve as building blocks for physics simulation, path finding, and so on. M3G does not support collision detection, but it does provide for simple *picking*—that is, shooting a ray into the scene to see which object and triangle it first intersects. This can be used as a replacement to proper collision detection in some cases.

5.2.2 SPATIAL DATA STRUCTURE

Having decided to go for a rendering-oriented scene graph, the next step is to pick the right spatial data structure for our system. The application areas or game genres that we have in mind play a big role in that decision, because there is no single data structure that would be a perfect fit for all types of 3D scenes.

The main purpose of a spatial data structure in this context is *visibility processing*, that is, quickly determining which parts of the scene will not contribute to the final rendered image. Objects may be too far away from the viewer, occluded by a wall, or outside the field of view, and can thus be eliminated from further processing. This is called *visibility culling*. In large scenes that do not fit into memory at once, visibility processing includes *paging*, i.e., figuring out when to load each part of the scene from the mass storage device, and which parts to remove to make room for the new things.

Depending on the type of scene, the data structure of choice may be a hierarchical space partitioning scheme such as a quadtree, octree, BSP tree, or *kd*-tree. Quadtrees, for example, are a good match with terrain rendering. Some scenes might be best handled with portals or precomputed potentially visible sets (PVS). Specialized data structures are available for massive terrain scenes, such as those in Google Earth. See Chapter 9 of *Real-Time Rendering* [AMH02] for an overview of these and other visibility processing techniques.

Even though this is only scratching the surface, it becomes clear that having built-in support for all potentially useful data structures in the runtime engine is impossible. Their sheer number is overwhelming, not to mention the complexity of implementing them. Besides, researchers around the world are constantly coming up with new and improved data structures.

The easy way out, taken by M3G and most other scene graphs, is to not incorporate any spatial data structures beyond a *transformation hierarchy*, in which scene graph nodes are positioned, oriented, and otherwise transformed with respect to their scene graph parents. This is a convenient way to organize a 3D scene, as it mirrors the way that things are often laid out in the real world—and more important, in 3D modeling tools.

The solar system is a classic example of hierarchical transformations: the moons orbit the planets, the planets orbit the sun, and everything revolves around its own axis. The solar system is almost trivial to set up and animate with hierarchical transformations, but extremely difficult without them. The human skeleton is another typical example.

Visibility processing in M3G is limited to view frustum culling that is based on a *bounding volume hierarchy*; see Figure 5.4. While the standard does not actually say anything about bounding volumes or visibility processing, it appears that all widely deployed implementations have independently adopted similar means of hierarchical view frustum culling. We will discuss this in more detail in Section 5.3.

Implementing more specialized or more advanced visibility processing is left for the user. Luckily, this does not mean that you would have to ditch the whole scene graph and start from scratch if you wanted to use a quadtree, for instance. You can leverage the built-in scene tree as a basis for any of the tree structures mentioned above. Also, the same triangle meshes and materials can often be used regardless of the higher-level data structure.

The fact that typical scene graphs are geared toward hierarchical view frustum culling and transformations is also their weakness. There is an underlying assumption that the scene graph structure is a close match to the spatial layout of the scene. To put it another way, nodes are assumed to lie close to their siblings, parents, and descendants in world space. Violating this assumption may degrade performance. If this were not the case, you might want to arrange your scene such that all nonplayer characters are in the same branch of the graph, for instance.

The implicit assumption of physical proximity may also cause you trouble when nodes need to be moved with respect to each other. For instance, characters in a game world

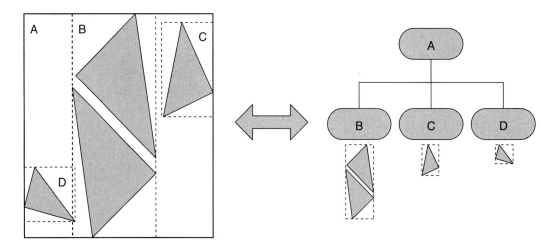

Figure 5.4: A bounding volume hierarchy (BVH) consisting of axis-aligned bounding boxes, illustrated in two dimensions for clarity. The bounding volume of node A encloses the bounding volumes of its children.

may be wandering freely from one area to another. The seemingly obvious solution is to relocate the moving objects to the branches that most closely match their physical locations. However, sometimes it may be difficult to determine where each object should go. Structural changes to the scene graph may not come for free, either.

5.2.3 CONTENT CREATION

Creating any nontrivial scene by manually typing in vertices, indices and rendering state bits is doomed to failure. Ideally, objects and entire scenes would be authored in commercial or proprietary tools, and exported into a format that can be imported by the runtime engine. M3G defines its own file format to bridge the gap between the runtime engine and DCC tools such as 3ds Max, Maya, or Softimage; see Figure 5.5. The file format is a precise match with the capabilities of the runtime API, and supports a reasonable subset of popular modeling tool features.

From the runtime engine's point of view, the main problem with DCC tools is that they are so flexible. The scene graph designer is faced with an abundance of animation and rendering techniques that the graphics artists would love to use, but only a fraction of which can be realistically supported in the runtime engine. See Figure 5.6 to get an idea of the variety of features that are available in a modern authoring tool.

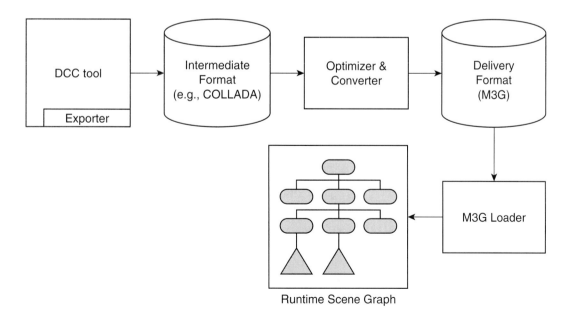

Runtime Scene Graph

Figure 5.5: A typical M3G content production pipeline. None of the publicly available exporters that we are aware of actually use COLLADA as their intermediate format, but we expect that to change in the future.

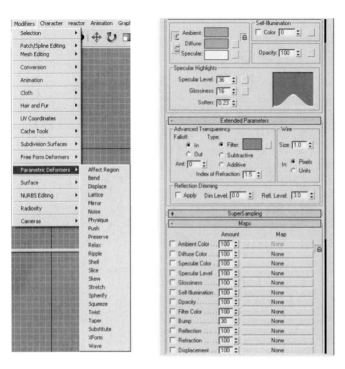

Figure 5.6: Some of the features that are available in 3ds Max for meshes (*left*), materials (*middle*), and animations (*right*). Only a fraction of these can be supported in real-time systems, particularly on mobile devices that have no programmable graphics hardware. (Images copyright © Autodesk.)

Many exciting authoring tool features are ruled out by technical limitations alone, especially when targeting mobile devices. For example, it is hardly feasible to animate a subdivision-surface model by free-form deformations and render it with refractions, displacement mapping, and soft shadows. Technical constraints notwithstanding, the mere effort to define and implement such a huge array of techniques is formidable. The definition effort becomes even more difficult if the features need to be standardized so that independent implementations will work the same way. Finally, including everything that is "nice to have" will lead to a bloated system with lots of little-used functionality that mostly just obscures the essential parts.

The M3G standardization group settled for relatively few built-in animation and rendering techniques. Beyond what is directly provided by OpenGL ES 1.0, the key features are hierarchical transformations, layered (multipass) rendering, two mesh modifiers (vertex morphing and skinning), and keyframe animation. These allow surprisingly complex animated scenes to be exported from authoring tools, and reproduced at runtime with very little application code. Many sophisticated mesh deformations, for example, can be exported as suitably keyframed morph targets. Of course, almost any technique can be written in Java, using M3G only for rasterization, but then performance might become an issue.

5.2.4 EXTENSIBILITY

Now that we have a fairly generic, rendering-oriented scene graph design, we need to decide whether to make it *extensible*, that is, to open up the rendering traversal and expose the underlying rendering engine so that the user can plug in completely new types of objects, write rendering methods for them, and have them blend in seamlessly and behave just like built-in objects. The M3G scene graph was not made extensible, for the reasons outlined below.

A key issue affecting the extensibility of a scene graph is whether the underlying rendering engine can be dictated at the time of design, or whether the implementations need to be able to use different low-level APIs. M3G is based on the latter approach. Although conceptually based on OpenGL ES 1.0, it does not expose the low-level rendering context that it uses internally. This design allows practical implementations to use later versions of OpenGL ES, proprietary extensions, customized software rasterizers, or perhaps even Direct3D Mobile. Similarly, emulators and development tools on the PC may well be based on desktop OpenGL.

For a scene graph to be considered extensible, it would also have to support user-defined callbacks. However, if user-defined callbacks are allowed to modify the scene graph right in the middle of the rendering traversal, it becomes an implementation nightmare to maintain the security and stability of the system. What happens if one of the callbacks removes a scene graph branch that the engine was just processing, for example? On the other hand, if the callbacks are not given write access to the scene graph, they become much less useful.

Even providing read-only access to the scene graph during callbacks may be problematic. For example, a callback should ideally have access to global data about light sources, bounding boxes, modelview matrices, nearby objects, and so on, but to arrange the internal operations and data structures of the engine so that this information is readily available may not be easy or cheap.

For M3G, the final straw that settled the extensibility issue was the environment that the engine is running on. Interrupting a relatively tight piece of code, such as the rendering traversal, is inefficient even in pure native code, let alone if it involves transitioning from native code to Java and vice versa. As a result, M3G was made a "black box" that never interrupts the execution of any API methods by calling back to user code.

5.2.5 CLASS HIERARCHY

Having nailed down the key features of our scene graph, the final step is to come up with an object-oriented class hierarchy to support those features in a logical and efficient way.

We need to decide what kind of nodes are available, what components and properties do they have, which of those may be shared or inherited, and so on.

M3G has a very simple hierarchy of nodes: as shown in Figure 5.7, it only has eight concrete node types and an abstract base class. Although the node hierarchy in M3G is small, it is representative of scene graphs in general. In the following, we go through the M3G node hierarchy from top to bottom, discussing alternative designs along the way.

All nodes in a typical object-oriented scene graph are derived from an abstract base class, which in M3G is called `Node`. Attributes that are deemed applicable to just any type of node are defined in the base class, along with corresponding functions that operate on those attributes. There are no hard-and-fast rules on what the attributes should be, but anything that needs to be inherited or accumulated in the scene graph is a good candidate. In M3G, the most important thing that is present in every node is the *node transformation*. The node transformation specifies the position, orientation, and scale of a node relative to its parent, with an optional 3×4 matrix to cover the whole spectrum of affine transformations (see Section 2.3). Other properties of M3G nodes include various on/off toggles and masks.

Some scene graph systems also allow low-level rendering state, such as blending modes, to be inherited from parent nodes to their children. This capability is more trouble than it is worth, though, and so was left out of M3G. Resolving the complete rendering state for an object is slow and error-prone if each individual state bit is a function of arbitrarily many nodes encountered along the way from the root to the leaf. Also, it makes little sense for rendering attributes to be inheritable in a system that is

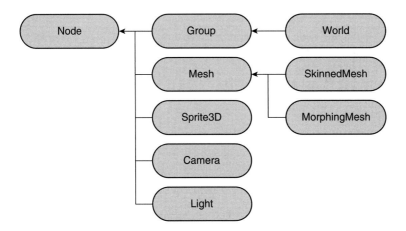

Figure 5.7: The class hierarchy of scene graph nodes in M3G. The arrows denote inheritance: `World` is derived from `Group`, `SkinnedMesh` and `MorphingMesh` are derived from `Mesh`, and everything is ultimately derived from `Node`.

optimized for spatial organization: objects should be grouped according to their physical proximity, not because of their texture map or shininess.

Group nodes are the basic building blocks of a scene graph, and they come in many flavors; some examples are shown in Figure 5.8. The basic `Group` node in M3G stores an unordered and unlimited set of child nodes. The only other type of group in M3G is the designated root node, `World`. Other scene graph designs may support groups that store an ordered set of nodes, groups that select only one of their children for rendering, groups that store a transformation, and so on.

The structure of the basic rigid-body `Mesh` of M3G was already described in Section 5.1; see Figure 5.1 for a quick recap. The `MorphingMesh` is otherwise the same, but includes multiple `VertexBuffers`—the morph targets—and a weighting factor for each. The `SkinnedMesh` is a hierarchical construct that forms an entire branch in the main scene graph; it is essentially a very specialized kind of group node. See Figure 12.5 for how a `SkinnedMesh` is structured. Note that regardless of the type of mesh, the vertex buffers and other mesh components in M3G can be shared between multiple meshes. This allows, for example, a variety of car objects to share a single base mesh while only the texture maps are different.

`Sprite3D` is a screen-aligned quadrilateral having a position and optionally a size in 3D space. It can be used for billboards, text labels, UI widgets, and others. `Sprite3D` also

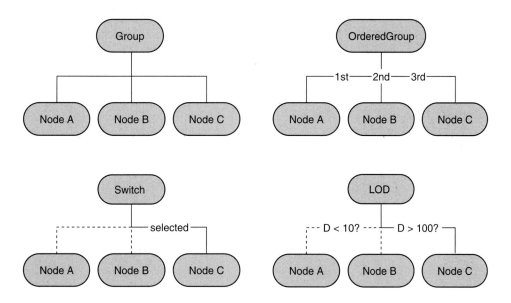

Figure 5.8: Different kinds of group nodes that have been used in earlier scene graphs. M3G only supports the basic, unordered groups, but has other means to implement the `OrderedGroup` and `Switch` behaviors. There is no direct substitute for the level-of-detail node `LOD`; to get the same effect, you will need to manually enable and disable nodes based on their distance (*D*) from the camera.

illustrates the notion of having different kinds of renderable objects in a scene graph, not only triangle meshes. Some scene graphs support a wide variety of renderables that are not ordinary triangle meshes, at least not from the user's point of view. Such renderables include spheres, cylinders, terrains, particles, impostors, skyboxes, and so on.

The `Camera` node defines from where and how the scene is viewed. The camera node has a position and orientation in the scene, together constituting the transformation from world coordinates to eye coordinates. The camera also defines a projective transformation that maps the eye coordinates into clip coordinates. The projective transformation may be given explicitly in the form of a 4 × 4 matrix, or implicitly by defining the extents of the view frustum. There are often several camera nodes in the scene to facilitate easy switching from one viewpoint to another. For example, a racing game might feature the driver's view, rear view, and a view from behind.

Finally, the `Light` node defines a light source. The types of lights supported by M3G include ambient, directional, point, and spot lights. They are modeled after the OpenGL lighting equation.

5.3 RETAINED MODE RENDERING

Retained mode refers to a programming paradigm for 3D graphics where a persistent representation of graphical content is stored in memory and managed by a library layer. The persistent representation is often called a scene graph. Compared to *immediate mode*, where fine-grained rendering commands are submitted to the graphics API and immediately executed, the retained-mode programmer performs less low-level work in loading, managing, culling, and rendering the scene. Also, giving more control over the content to the graphics library gives the library an opportunity to optimize the data for the underlying hardware.

Early scene graphs, such as Performer by SGI [RH94], were designed to work around the performance problems of the original OpenGL, which had a very immediate-mode API indeed: several function calls had to be made to draw each triangle, yielding a lot of overhead. Also, vertices, indices, textures, and all other graphics resources were held in application memory and controlled by the application. This made it difficult for OpenGL to internally cache or optimize any of the source data. The only retained-mode concept available were *display lists*, i.e., compiled sequences of OpenGL function calls, but they turned out to be inflexible from the application point of view, and difficult to optimize from the OpenGL driver point of view.[1]

Later versions of OpenGL, and OpenGL ES even more so, have departed from their pure immediate-mode roots. Vertex arrays and texture objects were introduced first,

---

1   As a result, display lists were not included in OpenGL ES.

followed by Vertex Buffer Objects (VBOs), and most recently Frame Buffer Objects (FBOs). This trend of moving more and more data into graphics memory—the "server side" in OpenGL parlance—is still ongoing with, e.g., Direct3D 10 adding State Objects [Bly06].

M3G was designed to be a retained-mode system from the ground up. Although it does have a concept of immediate mode, all data are still held in Java objects that are fully managed by M3G. The difference is the "full" retained mode is just that: those objects are rendered individually, as opposed to collecting them into a complete scene graph.

Retained-mode rendering in a typical M3G implementation is, at least on a conceptual level, done as shown in Figure 5.9. Note that this is all happening in native code, without having to fetch any data from the Java side. We will now describe each step in more detail.

5.3.1 SETTING UP THE CAMERA AND LIGHTS

The first step is to set up global parameters, such as the camera and lights. Finding the active camera is easy, as there is a direct link to it from the `World`. To find the light sources, we have to scan through the entire scene graph, but in practice this only needs to be done once. The set of lights in a scene is unlikely to change on a regular basis, so we can easily cache direct pointers to them for later use.

Once we have the lights collected into a list, we transform them into eye coordinates by multiplying the position and/or direction of each light by its modelview matrix. To compute the modelview matrices, we trace the scene graph path from each light node to the camera node, concatenating the node transformations along the way into a 3 × 4 matrix. Note that many of these paths will typically overlap, particularly the closer we get to the camera node, so it makes a lot of sense to cache the transformations in some form. A simple but effective scheme is to cache the world-to-camera transformation; this will be

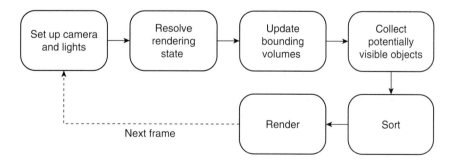

Figure 5.9: Scene graph rendering in a typical M3G implementation. No Java code is involved in this process, as the scene graph is retained in native data structures.

needed a lot as we go forward. Caching the local-to-world transformation for each node may be a good idea, as well.

5.3.2 RESOLVING RENDERING STATE

After setting up global state, we move on to individual objects. Traversing the scene graph, we first eliminate any nodes and their descendants that have the *rendering enable flag* turned off. For each mesh that remains, we check whether its *scope mask* (see Section 15.6.2) matches with that of the camera, culling the mesh if not. As the final quick check, we drop any submeshes that have no associated `Appearance`.

We then resolve the rendering state for each remaining object. The state includes numerous transformations, appearance components, vertex and index buffers, and so on. At this stage we also quickly validate each object, checking that its vertex coordinates are present, that triangle indices do not point beyond vertex array boundaries, that a `SkinnedMesh` has all the necessary bones in place, and so on.

To compute the modelview matrix for a mesh, we again trace the path from the mesh node upward in the scene graph until we hit the root node, compounding any node transformations along the way into one matrix. This matrix is then concatenated with the world-to-camera transformation, which we cached earlier, to obtain the final modelview matrix.

Compared to ordinary meshes, skinned meshes (see Section 4.2.2) need some special treatment. For each bone in the skeleton, we need to compute a compound transformation to the coordinate system where the actual skinning is to be done. This may be the eye space, the world space, or the coordinate system of the `SkinnedMesh` node itself. In principle, the choice of coordinate system makes no difference to the end result, but in practice, the impact of low-precision arithmetic gets more severe the more transformations we compound into the bone matrices. Thus, using the `SkinnedMesh` coordinate system may be a good idea on an integer-only CPU.

Once we are done with the transformations, we associate each mesh with the lights that potentially affect it; this is again determined using the scope masks. If there are more lights associated with an object than the underlying rendering engine can handle, we simply select the N most relevant lights and ignore the rest.

5.3.3 FINDING POTENTIALLY VISIBLE OBJECTS

The next stage in retained-mode rendering is to determine which objects are inside or intersecting the view frustum, and are therefore *potentially visible*. Note that any number of the potentially visible objects may be entirely occluded by other objects, but in the absence of occlusion culling, we need to render all of them anyway.

Before the actual view frustum culling, we need to update the bounding volumes that are stored in each node. In a bounding volume hierarchy (BVH), such as the one shown in

Figure 5.4, the bounding volume of a group node encloses the bounding volumes of its children. We start updating the volumes from the meshes at the leaf nodes, proceeding upward in the tree until we reach the root node. *Dirty flags*, propagated upward in the hierarchy, may be used to speed up the traversal: only those branches need to be processed where some node transformations or vertex coordinates have changed since the last frame.

The bounding volume of a node may be a sphere, an *axis-aligned bounding box* (AABB), an *oriented bounding box* (OBB), or any arbitrary shape as long as it encloses all vertices contained in that node and its descendants. The most common types of bounding volumes are shown in Figure 5.10. Practical M3G implementations are likely to be using AABBs and bounding spheres only. The more complex volumes are too slow to generate automatically, and there is no way in the M3G API for the developer to provide the bounding volumes. Bounding spheres and AABBs are also the fastest to check against the view frustum for intersections.

Ideally, different kinds of bounding volumes would be used on different types of objects and scenes. For example, bounding spheres are not a good fit with architectural models, but may be the best choice for skinned meshes. Bounding spheres are the fastest type of bounding volume to update, which is an important property for deformable meshes, and they also provide a fairly tight fit to human-like characters (recall the famous "Vitruvian Man" by Leonardo da Vinci).

With the bounding volume hierarchy updated and the rendering state resolved, we traverse the scene graph one final time; this time to cull the objects that are outside the view frustum. Starting from the `World`, we check whether the bounding volume of the current node is inside, outside, or intersecting the view frustum. If it is inside, the objects in that branch are potentially visible, and are inserted to the list of objects that will ultimately be sent to the rendering engine. If the bounding volume is outside the view frustum, the branch is not visible and gets culled. If the bounding volume and view frustum intersect, we recurse into the children of that node, and repeat from the beginning.

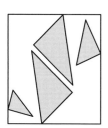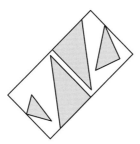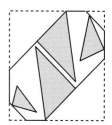

Figure 5.10: Different kinds of bounding volumes, illustrated in two dimensions for clarity. *From the left:* axis-aligned bounding box (AABB), oriented bounding box (OBB), bounding sphere, and convex polytope. The convex polytope in this example is constructed from an AABB, shown in dashed line, by beveling its horizontal and vertical edges at 45° angles.

5.3.4 SORTING AND RENDERING

As the final step before rendering, we sort the list of potentially visible objects by two or more criteria. The primary criterion is the *rendering layer*, which is a user-specified global ordering of submeshes; see Section 15.4. The secondary sorting key is transparency—opaque objects must be rendered first so that translucent objects can be properly blended with them. Ideally, the transparent objects would be further sorted into a back-to-front order (see Section 3.5.2), but this is not required by M3G due to the potential impact to performance.

Any further sorting keys exist merely to optimize the rendering order for the underlying rendering engine, and are thus specific to each implementation and device. A good rule of thumb is to sort into buckets by rendering state, then front-to-back within each bucket to minimize overdraw. See Chapter 6 for more information on rendering optimizations.

State sorting is made easier and faster by the fact that rendering state is grouped into appearance components to begin with. There are usually just a few different instances of each type of component in a scene, so they are easily enumerated or hashed into a fixed number of bits, and used as part of the sorting key. The sorting key can therefore be made very compact, for instance a 32-bit or 64-bit integer.

Finally, we iterate through the sorted queue of objects and dispatch them to the low-level rendering engine. To start off, we set the low-level rendering state to that of the first object in the queue. We render that object and any subsequent objects having the same state, and repeat from the start when we hit the first object with differing state.

When all objects have been sent to the renderer, we return control back to the application, letting it draw some more graphics or just flush the frame buffer to the screen. The application is then expected to animate and otherwise update the scene graph in preparation for the next frame.

CHAPTER

PERFORMANCE AND SCALABILITY

The fundamental challenge anyone programming for mobile phones faces is that to be successful in the marketplace, an application needs to be deployed on dozens of different phone models. Although the existence of programming standards such as OpenGL ES and M3G has reduced the fragmentation in the market, one still has to deal with a broad and diverse range of devices.

The performance characteristics, available memory, potential display configurations, programming tool chains, Java stack implementations, control devices, available libraries, operating systems, and underlying CPU architectures vary from one phone model to another. The problem of writing applications that port and scale to all these devices is such a hard and complex one that several industry-wide standardization efforts have emerged to tackle it, e.g., OpenKODE from the Khronos Group, and the Java platform and related JSR libraries defined by the Java Community Process.

For the purposes of this discussion, we will ignore most of the portability and scalability issues and concentrate on those that are related to 3D graphics. Even so, dealing with the variety in the devices out there is a formidable challenge. The performance difference in raw rendering power between a software and a hardware-based renderer can be hundredfold—whether this can be utilized and measured in real-life scenarios is an entirely different matter. The lowest-end devices with a 3D engine use 96 × 65 monochrome displays, and have a 20MHz ARM7 processor. The high end at the time of writing boasts VGA true color displays, powered by dedicated GPUs and 600MHz multicore ARM11 processors with vector floating-point units. Currently only the expensive smart phones have dedicated graphics processors, but the situation is changing rapidly with ever-cheaper GPU designs entering the feature phone market.

Programming standards such as OpenGL ES attempt to unify the variety of devices by providing a common interface for accessing the underlying graphics architecture: they act as hardware abstraction layers. This is important, as now the set of available graphics features is reasonably constant from the programmer's point of view. Apart from the API and feature set these standards unify a third important factor: the underlying rendering model. Both OpenGL ES and M3G build on the shoulders of desktop OpenGL by adopting its rendering paradigms as well as its well-specified and documented pipeline. So, even though a programmer can assume to have more or less the same feature set on a low-end and a high-end device, use the same APIs to program both, and have some expectations about the rendering quality, one thing cannot be guaranteed: performance.

6.1 SCALABILITY

When building a scalable 3D application two major factors need to be taken into account. First of all, the application should have maximum graphics performance; no major bottlenecks or loss of performance should exist. This is extremely important as the lowest-end mobile phones being targeted have very limited capabilities. The second thing to consider is identifying all aspects of the rendering process that can be scaled. Scaling in this context means that once an application runs adequately on the lowest-end device being targeted, the application can be made more interesting on devices that have better rendering performance by adding geometric detail, using higher-quality textures, more complex special effects, better screen resolution, more accurate physics, more complex game logic, and so forth. In other words, you should always scale applications upward by adding eye candy, because the opposite—that is downscaling a complex application—is much more difficult to accomplish.

3D content is reasonably easy to scale using either automated or manually controlled offline tools. For example, most modeling packages support automatic generation of low-polygon-count models. This allows exporting the same scene using different triangle budgets. Methods such as texture-based illumination, detail textures, and bump mapping make it possible to use fewer triangles to express complex shapes; these were covered earlier in Section 3.4.3. Texture maps are highly scalable, and creating smaller textures is a trivial operation supported by all image-editing programs. The use of compressed texture formats [BAC96, Fen03, SAM05] reduces the memory requirements even further. Figure 6.1 illustrates how few triangles are needed for creating a compelling 3D game.

 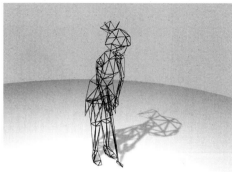

Figure 6.1: Low-polygon models from a golf game by Digital Chocolate.

6.1.1 SPECIAL EFFECTS

Most game applications contain highly scalable visual elements that do not have any impact on the game play. For example, bullet holes on walls, skid marks left by a race car, and drifting clouds in the sky are typical examples of eye candy that could be reduced or dropped altogether without altering the fundamentals of the game. Whether a special effect is a game play element depends on the context. As an example, fog is often used to mask the popping rendering artifacts caused by geometric level-of-detail optimizations and culling of distant objects. It is also a visual effect that makes scenes moodier and more atmospheric. On the other hand, fog may make enemies more difficult to spot in a shooter game—removing the fog would clearly affect the game play. Ensuring that the game play is not disturbed is especially important in multiplayer games as players should not need to suffer from unfair disadvantages due to scaling of special effects.

If you want to expose performance controls to the user, special effects are one of the prime candidates for this. Most users can understand the difference between rendering bullet holes and not rendering them, whereas having to make a choice between bilinear and trilinear filtering is not for the uninitiated.

One family of effects that can be made fully scalable are *particle systems* such as explosions, water effects, flying leaves, or fire, as shown in Figure 6.2. The number of particles, the complexity of the particle simulation, and the associated visuals can all be scaled based on the graphics capabilities of the device. Furthermore, one can allocate a shared budget for all particle systems: this ensures that the load on the graphics system is controlled dynamically, and that the maximum load can be bounded. A similar approach is often used for sounds, e.g., during an intense firefight the more subtle sound effects are skipped, as they would get drowned by the gunshots anyway.

Figure 6.2: Particle effects can be used to simulate natural phenomena, such as fire, that are not easily represented as polygonal surfaces. (Image copyright © AMD.)

6.1.2 TUNING DOWN THE DETAILS

Other scalable elements include noncritical detail objects and background elements. In many 3D environments the most distant elements are rendered using 2D backdrops instead of true 3D objects. In this technique faraway objects are collapsed into a single panoramic sky cube at the expense of losing parallax effects between and within those objects. Similarly, multi-pass detail textures can be omitted on low-end devices.

The method selected for rendering shadows is another aspect that can be scaled. On a high-performance device it may be visually pleasing to use stencil shadows [Cro77, EK02] for some or all of the game objects. This is a costly approach, and less photorealistic methods, such as rendering shaded blobs under the main characters, should be utilized on less capable systems. Again, one should be careful to make sure that shadows are truly just a visual detail as in some games they can affect the game play.

6.2 PERFORMANCE OPTIMIZATION

The most important thing to do when attempting to optimize the performance of an application is profiling. Modern graphics processors are complex devices, and the interaction between them and other hardware and software components of the system is not trivial. This makes predicting the impact of program optimizations difficult. The only effective way for finding out how changes in the program code affect application performance is measuring it.

The tips and tricks provided in this chapter are good rules of thumb but by no means gospel. Following these rules is likely to increase overall rendering performance on most devices, but the task of identifying device-specific bottlenecks is always left to the application programmer. Problems in performance particular to a phone model often arise from system integration issues rather than deficiencies in the rendering hardware. This means that the profiling code must be run on the actual target device; it is not sufficient just to obtain similar hardware. Publicly available benchmark programs such as those from FutureMark[1] or JBenchmark[2] are useful for assessing approximate graphics processing performance of a device. However, they may not pinpoint individual bottlenecks that may ruin the performance of a particular application.

Performance problems of a 3D graphics application can be classified into three groups: pixel pipeline, vertex pipeline, and application bottlenecks. These groups can be then further partitioned into different pipeline stages. The overall pipeline runs only as fast as its slowest stage, which forms a bottleneck. However, regardless of the source of the bottleneck, the strategy for dealing with one is straightforward (see Figure 6.3). First, you should locate the bottleneck. Then, you should try to eliminate it and move to the next one. Locating bottlenecks for a single rendering task is simple. You should go through each pipeline stage and reduce its workload. If the performance changes significantly, you have found the bottleneck. Otherwise, you should move to the next pipeline stage. However, it is good to understand that the bottleneck often changes within a single frame that contains multiple different primitives. For example, if the application first renders a group of lines and afterward a group of lit and shaded triangles, we can expect the bottleneck to change. In the following we study the main pipeline groups in more detail.

6.2.1 PIXEL PIPELINE

Whether an application's performance is bound by the pixel pipeline can be found out by changing the rendering resolution—this is easiest done by scaling the viewport. If the performance scales directly with the screen resolution, the bottleneck is in the pixel pipeline. After this, further testing is needed for identifying the exact pipeline stage (Figure 6.4). To determine if memory bandwidth is the limiting factor, you should try using smaller pixel formats for the different buffers and textures, or disable texturing altogether. If a performance difference is observed, you are likely to be bandwidth-bound. Other factors contributing to the memory bandwidth include blending operations and depth buffering. Try disabling these features to see if there is a difference. Another culprit for slow fragment processing may be the texture filtering used. Test the application with nonfiltered textures to find out if the performance increases.

---

1 www.futuremark.com
2 www.jbenchmark.com

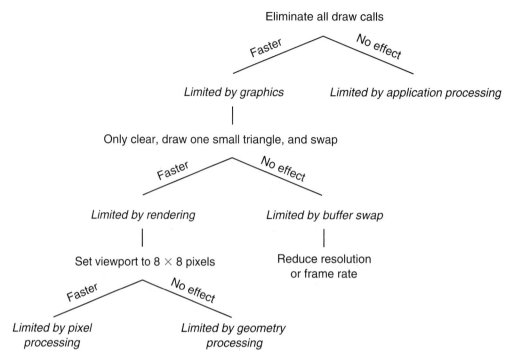

Figure 6.3: Determining whether the bottleneck is in application processing, buffer swapping, geometry processing, or fragment processing.

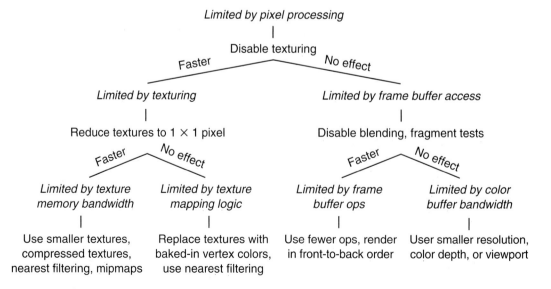

Figure 6.4: Finding the performance bottleneck in fill rate limited rendering.

To summarize: in order to speed up an application where the pixel pipeline is the bottleneck, you have to either use a smaller screen resolution, render fewer objects, use simpler data formats, utilize smaller texture maps, or perform less complex fragment and texture processing. Many of these optimizations are covered in more detail later in this chapter.

6.2.2 VERTEX PIPELINE

Bottlenecks in the vertex pipeline can be found by making two tests (Figure 6.5). First, you should try rendering only every other triangle but keeping the vertex arrays used intact. Second, you should try to reduce the complexity of the transformation and lighting pipeline. If both of these changes show performance improvements, the application is bound by vertex processing. If only the reduced triangle count shows a difference, we have a *submission bottleneck*, i.e., we are bound by how fast the vertex and primitive data can be transferred from the application.

When analyzing the vertex pipeline, you should always scale the viewport to make the rendering resolution small in order to keep the cost of pixel processing to a minimum. A good size for the current mobile phone display resolutions would be 8 × 8 pixels or

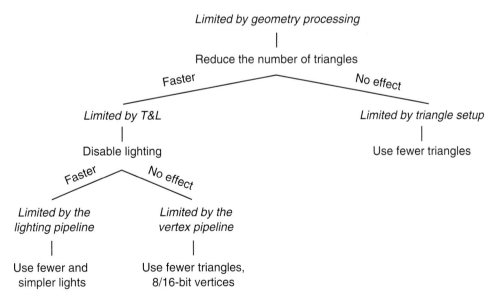

Figure 6.5: Finding the performance bottleneck in geometry-limited rendering.

so. A resolution smaller than this might cause too many triangles to become subpixel-sized; optimized drivers would cull them and skip their vertex processing, complicating the analysis.

Submission bottlenecks can be addressed by using smaller data formats, by organizing the vertices and primitives in a more cache-friendly manner, by storing the data on the server rather than in the client, and of course by using simplified meshes that have fewer triangles. On the other hand, if vertex processing is the cause for the slowdown, the remedy is to reduce complexity in the transformation and lighting pipeline. This is best done by using fewer and simpler light sources, or avoiding dynamic lighting altogether. Also, disabling fog, providing prenormalized vertex normals, and avoiding the use of texture matrices and floating-point vertex data formats are likely to reduce the geometry workload.

6.2.3 APPLICATION CODE

Finally, it may be that the bottleneck is not in the rendering part at all. Instead, the application code itself may be slow. To determine if this is the case, you should turn off all application logic, i.e., just execute the code that performs the per-frame rendering. If significant performance differences can be observed, you have an application bottleneck. Alternatively, you could just comment out all rendering calls, e.g., `glDrawElements` in OpenGL ES. If the frame rate does not change much, the application is not rendering-bound.

A more fine-grained analysis is needed for pinpointing the slow parts in an application. The best tool for this analysis is a profiler that shows how much time is spent in each function or line of code. Unfortunately hardware profilers for real mobile phones are both very expensive and difficult to obtain. This means that applications need to be either executed on other similar hardware, e.g., Lauterbach boards[3] are commonly used, or they may be compiled and executed on a desktop computer where software-based profilers are readily available. When profiling an application on anything except the real target device, the data you get is only indicative. However, it may give you valuable insights into where time is potentially spent in the application, the complexities of the algorithms used, and it may even reveal some otherwise hard-to-find bugs.

As floating-point code tends to be emulated on many embedded devices, slowdowns are often caused by innocent-looking routines that perform math processing for physics simulation or game logic. Re-writing these sections using integer arithmetic may yield significant gains in performance. Appendix A provides an introduction to fixed-point programming. Java programs have their own performance-related pitfalls. These are covered in more detail in Appendix B.

---

3 www.lauterbach.com

6.2.4 PROFILING OPENGL ES APPLICATIONS

Before optimizing your code you should always clean it up. This means that you should first fix all graphics-related errors, i.e., make sure no OpenGL ES errors are raised. Then you should take a look at the OpenGL ES call logs generated by your application. You will need a separate tool for this: we will introduce one below. From the logs you will get the list of OpenGL ES API calls made by your application. You should verify that they are what you expect, and remove any redundant ones. At this stage you should trap typical programming mistakes such as clearing the buffers multiple times, or enabling unnecessary rendering states.

One potentially useful commercial tool for profiling your application is gDEBugger ES from Graphic Remedy. [4] It is an OpenGL ES debugger and profiler that traces application activity on top of the OpenGL ES APIs to provide the application behavior information you need to find bugs and to optimize application performance (see Figure 6.6). gDEBugger ES essentially transforms the debugging task of graphics applications from a "black box" into a "white box" model; it lets you peer inside the OpenGL ES usage to see how individual commands affect the graphic pipeline implementation. The profiler enables viewing context state variables (Figure 6.7), texture data and properties, performance counters, and OpenGL ES function call history. It allows adding breakpoints on OpenGL ES commands, forcing the application's raster mode and render target, and breaking on OpenGL ES errors.

Another useful tool for profiling the application code is Carbide IDE From Nokia for S60 and UIQ Symbian devices. With commercial versions of Carbide you can do on-target debugging, performance profiling, and power consumption analysis. See Figure 6.8 for an example view of the performance investigator.

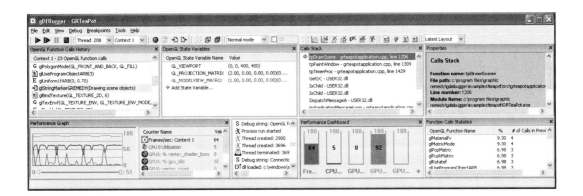

Figure 6.6: gDEBugger ES is a tool for debugging and profiling the OpenGL ES graphics driver.

---

4   www.gremedy.com

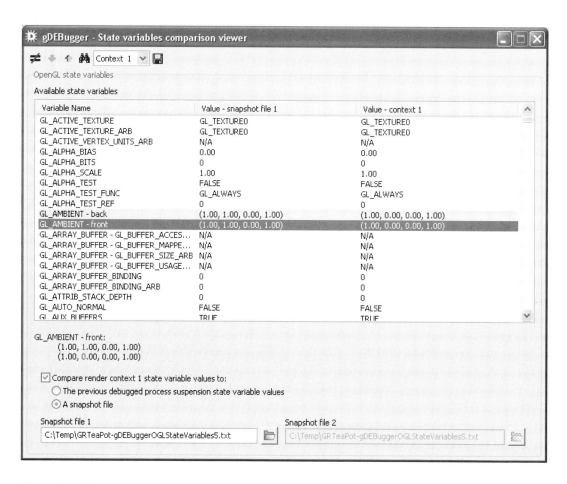

Figure 6.7: gDEBugger ES showing the state variables of the OpenGL ES context.

6.2.5 CHECKLISTS

This section provides checklists for reviewing a graphics application for high performance, quality, portability, and lower power usage. Tables 6.1–6.4 contain questions that should be asked in a review, and the "correct" answers to those questions. The applicability of each issue is characterized as ALL, MOST, or SOME to indicate whether the question applies to practically all implementations and platforms, or just some of them. For example, on some platforms enabling perspective, correction does not reduce performance while on others you will have to pay a performance penalty. Note that even though we are using OpenGL ES and EGL terminology and function names in the tables, most of the issues also apply to M3G.

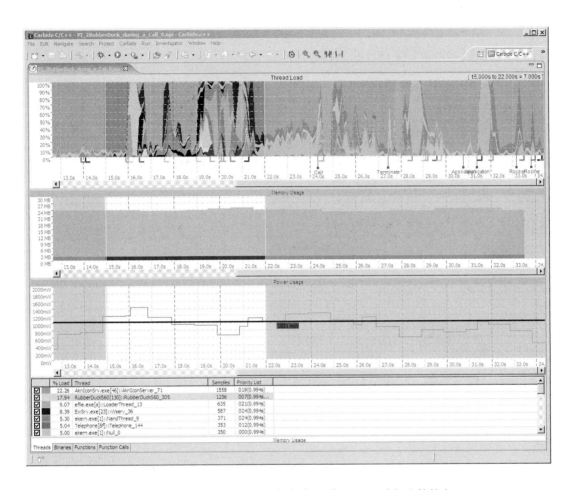

Figure 6.8: Carbide showing one of the performance analysis views. (Image copyright © Nokia.)

Table 6.1 contains a list of basic questions to go through for a quick performance analysis. The list is by no means exhaustive, but it contains the most common pitfalls that cause performance issues.

A checklist of features affecting rendering quality can be found in Table 6.2. Questions in the table highlight quality settings that improve quality but do not have any negative performance impact on typical graphics hardware. However, the impact on software implementations may be severe.

In a similar fashion, Table 6.3 provides checks for efficient power usage, and finally, Table 6.4 covers programming practices and features that may cause portability problems.

Table 6.1: Performance checklist.

Check item	OK Answer	Applicability
Do you use full-screen window surfaces?	Yes	ALL
Do you use glReadPixels?	No	ALL
Do you use eglCopyBuffers?	No	MOST
Do you use glCopyTex(Sub)Image2D?	No	MOST
Do you change texture data of existing texture?	No	ALL
Do you load textures during the rendering pass?	No	MOST
Do you use render-to-texture results during the same frame?	No	SOME
Do you clear the whole depth buffer at the start of a frame?	Yes	SOME
Do you use mipmapping?	Yes	ALL
Do you use vertex buffer objects?	Yes	ALL
Do you use texture compression?	Yes	SOME
Is any unnecessary state enabled?	No	ALL
Do you use auto mipmap generation or change filter modes?	No	SOME
Do you use perspective correction?	No	SOME (SW)
Do you use bilinear or trilinear filtering?	No	SOME (SW)
Do you use floating-point vertex data?	No	SOME

Table 6.2: Quality checklist.

Check item	OK Answer	Applicability
Do you use multisampling?	Yes	MOST (HW)
Do you use LINEAR_MIPMAP_NEAREST?	Yes	MOST (HW)
Do you have enough depth buffer bits?	Yes	ALL
Do you have enough color buffer bits?	Yes	ALL
Have you enabled perspective correction?	Yes	ALL

Table 6.3: Power usage checklist.

Check item	OK Answer	Applicability
Do you terminate EGL when application is idling?	Yes	MOST (HW)
Do you track the focus and halt rendering if focus is lost?	Yes	ALL
Do you limit your frame rate?	Yes	ALL

Table 6.4: Portability checklist.

Check item	OK Answer	Applicability
Do you use writable static data?	No	SOME (OS)
Do you handle display layout changes?	Yes	SOME (OS)
Do you depend on pixmap surface support?	No	SOME
Do you use EGL from another thread than main?	No	SOME
Do you specify surface type when asking for a config?	Yes	MOST
Do you require exact number of samples for multi-sampling?	No	SOME

6.3 CHANGING AND QUERYING THE STATE

Modern rendering pipelines are one-way streets: data keeps flowing in, it gets buffered, number-crunching occurs, and eventually some pixels come out. State changes and dynamic state queries are operations that disturb this flow. In the worst case a client-server roundtrip is required. For example, if the application wants to read back the contents of the color buffer, the application (the "client") has to stall until the graphics hardware (the "server") has processed all of the buffered primitives—and the buffers in modern hardware, especially tile-based devices, can be very long. An example of an extreme state change is modifying the contents of a texture map mid-frame as this may lead to internal duplication of the image data by the underlying driver.

While having some state changes is unavoidable in any realistic applications, you should steer clear of dynamic state queries, if possible. Applications should shadow the relevant state in their own code rather than query it from the graphics driver, e.g., the application should know whether a particular light source is enabled or not. Dynamic queries should only be utilized when keeping an up-to-date copy of the graphics driver's state is cumbersome, for example when combining application code with third-party middleware libraries that communicate directly with the underlying OpenGL ES or M3G layers. If for some reason dynamic state queries are absolutely needed, they should all be executed together once per frame, so that only a single pipeline stall is generated.

Smaller state changes, such as operations that alter the transformation and lighting pipeline or the fragment processing, affect the performance in various ways. Changing state that is typically set only during initialization, such as the size of the viewport or scissor rectangle, may cause a pipeline flush and may therefore be costly. State changes and under-the-hood synchronization may also happen when an application uses different APIs to access the same graphics resources. For example, you may be tempted to mix 2D and 3D functionality provided by different APIs. This is more than likely to be extremely slow, as the entire 3D pipeline may have to be completely flushed before the 2D operations can take place and vice versa. The implementations of the graphics libraries may well come from different vendors, and their interaction can therefore be nonoptimal. This is a significant problem in the Java world, as the whole philosophy of Java programming is to be able to mix and match different libraries.

6.3.1 OPTIMIZING STATE CHANGES

The rule of thumb for all state changes is to minimize the number of stalls created by them. This means that changes should be grouped and executed together. An easy way to do this is to group related state changes into "shaders" (we use the term here to indicate a collection of distinct pieces of the rendering state, corresponding roughly with the `Appearance` class of M3G), and to organize the rendering so that all objects sharing a shader are rendered together. It is a good idea to expose this shader-based approach in the artists' modeling tools as well. If one lets the artists tweak attributes that can create state changes, the end result is likely to be a scene where each object has slightly different materials and fragment pipelines, and the application needs to do a large number of stage changes to render the objects. It is therefore better to just let the artist pick shaders from a predefined list.

Also, it is important to be aware that the more complex a shader is, the slower it is likely to be. Even though graphics hardware may perform some operations "for free" due to its highly parallel nature, in a software implementation everything has an associated cost: enabling texture mapping is going to take dozens of CPU cycles for every pixel rendered, bilinear filtering of textures is considerably more expensive than point sampling, and using blending or fog will definitely slow down a software renderer. For this reason, it is crucial that the application disables all operations that are not going to have an impact on the final rendered image. As an example, it is typical that applications draw overlay images after the 3D scene has been rendered. People often forget to disable the fog operation when drawing the overlays as the fog usually does not affect objects placed at the near clipping plane. However, the underlying rendering engine does not know this, and has to perform the expensive fog computations for every pixel rendered. Disabling the fog for the overlays in this case may have a significant performance impact.

In general, simplifying shaders is more important for software implementations of the rendering pipeline, whereas keeping the number of state changes low is more important for GPUs.

6.4 MODEL DATA

The way the vertex and triangle data of the 3D models is organized has a significant impact on the rendering performance. Although the internal caching rules vary from one rendering pipeline implementation to another, straightforward rules of thumb for presentation of data exist: *keep vertex and triangle data short and simple, and make as few rendering calls as possible.*

In addition to the layout and format of the vertex and triangle data used, *where* the data is stored plays an important role. If it is stored in the client's memory, the application has more flexibility to modify the data dynamically. However, since the data is now transferred from the client to the server during every render call, the server loses its opportunity for optimizing and analyzing the data. On the other hand, when the mesh data is stored by the server, it is possible to perform even expensive analysis of the data, as the cost is amortized over multiple rendering operations. In general, one should always use such server-stored *buffer objects* whenever provided by the rendering API. OpenGL ES supports buffer objects from version 1.1 onward, and M3G implementations may support them in a completely transparent fashion.

6.4.1 VERTEX DATA

Optimization of model data is an offline process that is best performed in the exporting pipeline of a modeling tool. The most important optimization that should be done is *vertex welding*, that is, finding shared vertices and removing all but one of them. In a finely tessellated grid each vertex is shared by six triangles. This means an effective vertices-per-triangle ratio of 0.5. For many real-life meshes, ratios between 0.6 and 1.0 are obtained. This is a major improvement over the naive approach of using three individual vertices for each triangle, i.e., a ratio of 3.0. The fastest and easiest way for implementing welding is to utilize a hash table where vertices are hashed based on their attributes, i.e., position, normal, texture coordinates, and color.

Any reasonably complex 3D scene will use large amounts of memory for storing its vertex data. To reduce the consumption, one should always try to use the smallest data formats possible, i.e., bytes and shorts instead of integers. Because quantization of floating-point vertex coordinates into a smaller fixed-point representation may introduce artifacts and gaps between objects, controlling the quantization should be made explicit in the modeling and exporting pipeline. All interconnecting "scene" geometry could be represented with a higher accuracy (16-bit coordinates), and all smaller and moving objects could be expressed with lower accuracy (8-bit coordinates). For vertex positions this quantization is typically done by scanning the axis-aligned bounding box of an object, re-scaling the bounding [min,max] range for each axis into [−1, +1], and converting the resulting values into signed fixed-point values. Vertex normals usually survive quantization into 8 bits per component rather well, whereas texture coordinates often require 16 bits per component.

In general, one should always prefer integer formats over floating-point ones, as they are likely to be processed faster by the transformation and lighting pipeline. Favoring small formats has another advantage: when vertex data needs to be copied over to the rendering hardware, less memory bandwidth is needed to transfer smaller data elements. This improves the performance of applications running on top of both hardware and software renderers. Also, in order to increase cache-coherency, one should interleave vertex data if possible. This means that all data of a single vertex is stored together in memory, followed by all of the data of the next vertex, and so forth.

6.4.2 TRIANGLE DATA

An important offline optimization is ordering the triangle data in a coherent way so that subsequent triangles share as many vertices as possible. Since we cannot know the exact rules of the vertex caching algorithm used by the graphics driver, we need to come up with a generally good ordering. This can be achieved by sorting the triangles so that they refer to vertices that have been encountered recently. Once the triangles have been sorted in a coherent fashion, the vertex indices are remapped and the vertex arrays are re-indexed to match the order of referral. In other words, the first triangle should have the indices 0, 1, and 2. Assuming the second triangle shares an edge with the first one, it will introduce one new vertex, which in this scheme gets the index 3. The subsequent triangles then refer to these vertices and introduce new vertices 4, 5, 6, and so forth.

The triangle index array can be expressed in several different formats: triangle lists, strips, and fans. Strips and fans have the advantage that they use fewer indices per triangle than triangle lists. However, you need to watch out that you do not create too many rendering calls. You can "stitch" two disjoint strips together by replicating the last vertex of the first strip and the first vertex of the second strip, which creates two degenerate triangles in the middle. In general, using indexed rendering allows you to take full advantage of vertex caching, and you should sort the triangles as described above. Whether triangle lists or strips perform better depends on the implementation, and you should measure your platform to find out the winner.

6.5 TRANSFORMATION PIPELINE

Because many embedded devices lack floating-point units, the transformation pipeline can easily become the bottleneck as matrix manipulation operations need to be performed using emulated floating-point operations. For this reason it is important to minimize the number of times the matrix stack is modified. Also, expressing all object vertex data in fixed point rather than floating point can produce savings, as a much simpler transformation pipeline can then be utilized.

6.5.1 OBJECT HIERARCHIES

When an artist models a 3D scene she typically expresses the world as a complex hierarchy of nodes. Objects are not just collections of triangles. Instead, they have internal structure, and often consist of multiple subobjects, each with its own materials, transformation matrices and other attributes. This flexible approach makes a lot of sense when modeling a world, but it is not an optimal presentation for the rendering pipeline, as unnecessary matrix processing is likely to happen.

A better approach is to create a small piece of code that is executed when the data is exported from the modeling tool. This code should find objects in the same hierarchy sharing the same transformation matrices and shaders, and combine them together. The code should also "flatten" static transformation hierarchies, i.e., premultiply hierarchical transformations together. Also, if the scene contains a large number of replicated static objects such as low-polygon count trees forming a forest or the kinds of props shown in Figure 6.9, it makes sense to combine the objects into a single larger one by transforming all of the objects into the same coordinate space.

6.5.2 RENDERING ORDER

The rendering order of objects has implications to the rendering performance. In general, objects should be rendered in an approximate front-to-back order. The reason for this is that the z-buffering algorithm used for hidden surface removal can quickly discard covered fragments. If the occluding objects are rasterized first, many of the hidden fragments require less processing. Modern GPUs often perform the depth buffering in a hierarchical fashion, discarding hidden blocks of 4×4 or 8×8 pixels at a time. The best practical way to exploit this early culling is to sort the objects of a scene in a coarse fashion. Tile-based rendering architectures such as MBX of Imagination Technologies and Mali of ARM buffer the scene geometry before the rasterization stage and are thus able to perform the hidden surface removal efficiently regardless of the object ordering. However, other GPU architectures can benefit greatly if the objects are in a rough front-to-back order.

Depth ordering is not the only important sorting criterion—the state changes should be kept to a minimum as well. This suggests that one should first group objects based on their materials and shaders, then render the groups in depth order.

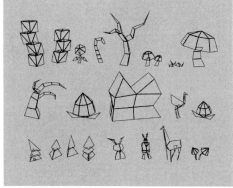

Figure 6.9: Low-polygon in-game objects. (Images copyright © Digital Chocolate.)

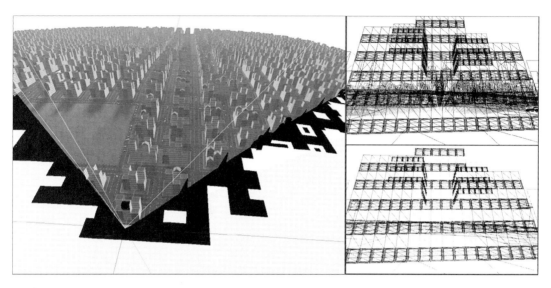

Figure 6.10: Occlusion culling applied to a complex urban environment consisting of thousands of buildings. *Left:* view frustum intersecting a city as seen from a third person view. *Right:* wireframe images of the camera's view without (*top*) and with (*bottom*) occlusion culling. Here culling reduces the number of objects rendered by a factor of one hundred. (Image copyright © NVidia.)

6.5.3 CULLING

Conservative culling strategies are ones that reduce the number of rendered objects without introducing any artifacts. *Frustum culling* is used to remove objects falling outside the view frustum, and *occlusion culling* to discard objects hidden completely by others. Frustum culling is best performed using conservatively computed bounding volumes for objects. This can be further optimized by organizing the scene graph into a bounding volume hierarchy and performing the culling using the hierarchy. Frustum culling is a trivial optimization to implement, and should be used by any rendering application— practically all scene graph engines support this, including all real-world M3G implementations. Occlusion culling algorithms, on the other hand, are complex, and often difficult to implement (see Figure 6.10). Of the various different algorithms, two are particularly suited for handheld 3D applications: pre-computed: Potentially Visible Sets (PVSs) and *portal rendering*. Both have modest run-time CPU requirements [Air90, LG95].

When an application just has too much geometry to render, *aggressive culling* strategies need to be employed. There are several different options for choosing which objects are not rendered. Commonly used methods include *distance-based culling* where faraway objects are discarded, and *detail culling*, where objects having small screen footprints after projection are removed. Distance-based culling creates annoying popping artifacts which are often reduced either by bringing the far clipping plane closer, by using fog effects to mask the transition, or by using distance-based alpha blending to fade faraway objects into full transparency. The popping can also be reduced by *level-of-detail rendering*, i.e., by switching to simplified versions of an object as its screen area shrinks.

6.6 LIGHTING

The fixed-functionality lighting pipeline of OpenGL ES and M3G is fairly limited in its capabilities and it inherits the basic problems inherent in the original OpenGL lighting model. The fundamental problem is that it is vertex-based, and thus fine tessellation of meshes is required for reducing the artifacts due to sparse lighting sampling. Also, the lighting model used in the mobile APIs is somewhat simplified; some important aspects such as properly modeled specular illumination have been omitted.

Driver implementations of the lighting pipeline are notoriously poor, and often very slow except for a few hand-optimized fast paths. In practice a good bet is that a single directional light will be properly accelerated, and more complex illumination has a good chance of utilizing slower code paths. In any case the cost will increase at least linearly with the number of lights, and the more complex lighting features you use, the slower your application runs.

When the vertex lighting pipeline is utilized, you should always attempt to simplify its workload. For example, prenormalizing vertex normals is likely to speed up the lighting computations. In a similar fashion, you should avoid using truly homogeneous vertex positions, i.e., those that have *w* components other than zero or one, as these require a more complex lighting pipeline. Specular illumination computations of any kind are rather expensive, so disabling them may increase the performance. The same advice applies to distance attenuation: disabling it is likely to result in performance gains. However, if attenuating light sources are used, a potential optimization is completely disabling faraway lights that contribute little or nothing to the illumination of an object. This can be done using trivial bounding sphere overlap tests between the objects and the light sources.

6.6.1 PRECOMPUTED ILLUMINATION

The quality problems of the limited OpenGL lighting model will disappear once programmable shaders are supported, though even then you will pay the execution time penalty of complex lighting models and of multiple light sources. However, with fixed-functionality pipelines of OpenGL ES 1.x and M3G 1.x one should primarily utilize texture-based and precomputed illumination, and try to minimize the application's reliance on the vertex-based lighting pipeline.

For static lighting, precomputed vertex-based illumination is a cheap and good option. The lighting is computed only once as a part of the modeling phase, and the vertex illumination is exported along with the mesh. This may also reduce the memory consumption of the meshes, as vertex normals do not need to be exported if dynamic lighting is omitted. OpenGL ES supports a concept called *color material tracking* which allows changing a material's diffuse or ambient component separately for each vertex of a mesh. This allows combining precomputed illumination with dynamic vertex-based lighting.

6.7 TEXTURES

Texturing plays an especially important role in mobile graphics, as it makes it possible to push lighting computations from the vertex pipeline to the fragment pipeline. This reduces the pressure to tessellate geometry. Also, it is more likely that the fragment pipeline is accelerated; several commonly deployed hardware accelerators such as MBX Lite perform the entire transformation and lighting pipeline on the CPU but have fast pixel-processing hardware.

Software and hardware implementations of texture mapping have rather different performance characteristics. A software implementation will take a serious performance hit whenever linear blending between mipmap levels or texels is used. Also, disabling perspective correct texture interpolation may result in considerable speed-ups when a software rasterizer is used. Mipmapping, on the other hand, is almost always a good idea, as it makes texture caching more efficient for both software and hardware implementations.

It should be kept in mind that modifying texture data has almost always a significant negative performance impact. Because rendering pipelines are generally deeply buffered, there are two things that a driver may do when a texture is modified by the application. Either the entire pipeline is flushed—this means that the client and the server cannot execute in parallel, or the texture image and associated mipmap levels need to be duplicated. In either case, the performance is degraded. The latter case also temporarily increases the driver's memory usage.

Multi-texturing should be always preferred over multi-pass rendering. There are several good reasons for this. Z-fighting artifacts can be avoided this way, as the textures are combined before the color buffer write is performed. Also, the number of render state changes is reduced, and an expensive alpha blending pass is avoided altogether. Finally, the number of draw calls is reduced by half.

6.7.1 TEXTURE STORAGE

Both OpenGL ES and M3G abstract out completely how the driver caches textures internally. However, the application has still some control over the data layout, and this may have a huge impact on performance. Deciding the correct sizes for texture maps, and combining smaller maps used together into a single larger texture can be significant optimizations. The "correct size" is the one where the texture map looks good under typical viewing conditions—in other words, one where the ratio between the texture's texels and the screen's pixels approaches 1.0. Using a larger texture map is a waste of memory. A smaller one just deteriorates the quality.

The idea of combining multiple textures into a single texture map is an important one, and is often used when rendering fonts, animations, or light maps. Such *texture atlases* are also commonly used for storing the different texture maps used by a complex object (see Figure 6.11). This technique allows switching between texture maps without actually performing a state change—only the texture coordinates of the object need to vary. Long strings of text or complex objects using multiple textures can thus be rendered using a single rendering call.

Texture image data is probably the most significant consumer of memory in a graphics-intensive application. As the memory capacity of a mobile device is still often rather limited, it is important to pay attention to the texture formats and layouts used. Both OpenGL ES and M3G provide support for compressed texture formats—although only via palettes and vendor-specific extensions.

Nevertheless, compressed formats should be utilized whenever possible. Only in cases where artifacts generated by the compression are visually disturbing, or when the texture is often modified manually, should noncompressed formats be used. Even then, 16-bit texture formats should be favored over 32-bit ones. Also, one should take advantage of the intensity-only and alpha-only formats in cases where the texture data is monochrome. In addition to saving valuable RAM, the use of compressed textures reduces the internal memory bandwidth, which in turn is likely to improve the rendering performance.

Figure 6.11: An example of automatically packing textures into a *texture atlas* (refer to Section 6.7.1). Image courtesy of Bruno Levy. (See the color plate.)

Transferring a mobile application and associated data over the network is often both slow and expensive, and in many cases the network operators pose strict limits for the sizes of the applications. For these reasons it is important to ensure that the graphics assets do not consume any more space than necessary. Texture maps usually consume a lion's share of all the graphics data, so special attention should be paid to them. In general, textures should either be procedurally generated, or an efficient lossy compression scheme such as DCT or wavelet compression (as utilized by the JPEG and JPEG 2000 formats, respectively) should be applied to them.

PART II
OPENGL ES AND EGL

INTRODUCING OPENGL ES

This chapter covers the fundamentals of the OpenGL ES 1.x standard. First we take a brief look at its history and design principles, followed by an introduction to the resources available online. Then we examine the different profiles and versions of the API, give an overview of the different versions, and take a look at the main OpenGL ES conventions.

7.1 KHRONOS GROUP AND OPENGL ES

The Khronos Group was formed in 2000 to create the specification of OpenML, an open standard media authoring API. The consortium later expanded to include new working groups for several mobile media standards. The OpenGL ES working group was the first such group. Over time it has created several versions of a compact 3D graphics API (OpenGL ES stands for OpenGL for Embedded Systems). Nowadays, working groups exist for defining interfaces for 2D vector graphics (OpenVG), sound processing (OpenSL ES), video playback (OpenMAX), and application portability (OpenKODE). 3D content file formats are covered by the COLLADA working group, and other new groups are formed on a regular basis to meet the demands of the industry. OpenGL ARB (Architecture Review Board) joined Khronos in September 2006. This makes it easier for both the desktop and embedded versions of OpenGL to develop in aligned directions. The goal of Khronos is the timely creation of royalty-free open multimedia standards. The first versions of the APIs were created at quite a brisk pace; now the updates will be created when there is a real market need for them.

Khronos is a consortium of more than 120 member companies, including, e.g., graphics technology providers, phone manufacturers, operating system vendors, content creators, and operators. There are two levels of membership. The Promoter-level members, some 15 companies, act as the board of directors and decide which standards are created, and ratify the results of the different working groups. Contributor companies participate in the working groups to define the standards. Additionally, adopters may create implementations of the APIs.

The OpenGL ES working group was formed in May 2002 to create an API for rendering 3D graphics on embedded devices. The desktop OpenGL standard was chosen as a starting point since it is widely available, well known, and has extremely well-specified, solid architecture. However, the desktop version has been evolving since the early 1990s, and has bloated over the years with redundant and legacy features. Removing old features is not a problem for applications that are written once, such as most games, whereas the development life cycle of large CAD systems and other professional applications may be decades, and removing old features would greatly increase maintenance costs.

The goal of the OpenGL ES working group was to create a cleaned-up and trimmed-down version of OpenGL. Innovation in the marketplace would still be enabled through an extension mechanism, and new versions of the specification would be rolled out as the market evolves. The first version, OpenGL ES 1.0, was introduced at the SIGGRAPH conference in July 2003. Version 1.1 followed at SIGGRAPH 2004. A draft version 2.0 and the ES 1.x Extension Pack came out a year later. The final 2.0 specification was completed in late 2006.

The OpenGL ES working group consists of some 20 to 30 individuals representing different member companies. The group has weekly teleconferences, an active mailing list, and a few multi-day face-to-face meetings each year. In addition to the specification itself, the group also produces manual pages and the official conformance tests. These tests are used to raise the quality of OpenGL ES implementations in the market, as any implementation wanting to use the OpenGL ES trademark needs to pass them. Also, before the Promoters ratify any specification, at least one, and preferably two, working implementations have to be created. This ensures that the specifications also work in practice.

After its first introduction, OpenGL ES has been widely adopted by the mobile industry. It is an integral part of a number of operating systems, and implementations have been shipped on tens of millions of devices. For example, all new Symbian and BREW devices support OpenGL ES, and outside the mobile phone world Sony is using it as the graphics API of PlayStation 3.

7.2 DESIGN PRINCIPLES

When the OpenGL ES working group began its work of designing the API, several principles were laid out. One of the goals was to keep the API as compact as possible. This would allow software implementations of OpenGL ES to fit into a very small amount of code. Indeed, there exist implementations of OpenGL ES 1.0 with footprints of less than 50kB of binary code.

The working group chose OpenGL 1.3 as the starting point and engaged in the long process of removing redundant functionality. In the world of graphics technology, OpenGL is a well-established standard, created in 1992 and originally based on SGI's IrisGL. Due to the policy of maintaining backward-compatibility between versions, OpenGL has collected a lot of excess baggage over the years. Newer and better techniques have replaced older approaches and new hardware designs have made old ones obsolete. As a result, multiple different ways exist to accomplish the same goal. For example, there are half a dozen distinct ways for rendering a set of triangles! When creating the OpenGL ES specification, the goal was to identify only the most current and relevant variants and expose them.

Apart from removing unnecessary functionality, there are other ways to make OpenGL slimmer. Almost all OpenGL API calls accept parameters in a variety of data formats. The working group decided to trim the number down considerably. In most cases, only a single integer format and a single floating-point variant is supported. Rarely used and outdated operations, such as support for indexed colors, or selection and feedback modes, were removed. Several features whose implementation burden was found to be excessive (for example, display lists) were dropped. The rule-of-thumb was that features hard to emulate in the application code were mostly retained, whereas convenience functions were considerably trimmed. Therefore high-level operations such as evaluators were dropped, but the fragment processing pipeline was kept almost in its entirety.

Some features were also added to the API to support lower-end devices. All double-precision floating-point data types were replaced by single-precision, and a variant accepting fixed-point integer input was provided for all functions taking in floats.

There is one fundamental difference between the OpenGL ES and its desktop variant. To prevent OpenGL ES from becoming bloated, the working group decided that backward-compatibility between versions is retained only between minor versions of the API. In other words, OpenGL ES 1.1 is backward-compatible with OpenGL ES 1.0, while 2.0 is not compatible with any of the 1.x versions (though OpenGL ES 2.0 is still similar enough that 1.x drivers should be implementable for 2.0 hardware). Although this creates several "families" of OpenGL ES, it allows new major versions to start from a clean slate, and to come up with more elegant designs.

7.3 RESOURCES

Several free resources are available for those interested in using OpenGL ES. Additional resources are available for Khronos members. We list some of them below.

7.3.1 DOCUMENTATION

All of the official OpenGL ES documentation is hosted at Khronos Group's web site.[1] You will find there the most up-to-date versions of OpenGL ES and EGL specifications, reference manuals, and official header files. The original OpenGL ES specification described the differences with respect to the desktop OpenGL (1.0 was based on desktop 1.3; 1.1 was based on desktop 1.5), but in 2007 a complete stand-alone specification was created. Another good source of general OpenGL material is at `www.opengl.org`.

The `www.khronos.org` site offers a number of additional resources, such as presentations from conferences and trade shows about OpenGL ES programming and optimization. The site also contains tutorials and example source code for sample OpenGL ES programs.

If you are planning to implement OpenGL ES yourself, you should become a Khronos member. The members gain access to the OpenGL ES Conformance Test source code. This is needed in order to claim official conformance to the specification. Members also get the source code of the OpenGL ES 1.0 sample implementation, and get to participate on the internal technical mailing list dedicated for members.

7.3.2 TECHNICAL SUPPORT

If the various specifications, reference manuals, and tutorials cannot answer all of your questions, do not despair: the Internet is full of people willing to help you. There are several web forums where OpenGL ES experts can answer your trickiest questions. The official one is hosted by Khronos.[2] Also, different handset vendors and chip manufacturers have their own forums; we list them in this book's companion web site.

7.3.3 IMPLEMENTATIONS

There are several free implementations of OpenGL ES available; links to them can be found from the book's companion web site. *Vincent* is an open source implementation of OpenGL ES 1.1, and it runs on several handheld operating systems. Hybrid's *Rasteroid* package contains free implementations of both OpenGL ES 1.1 and OpenVG 1.0, and runs on desktop Windows and many Windows Mobile and S60 devices.

Other implementations include an OpenGL ES 1.0 Linux sample reference implementation that runs on top of desktop OpenGL 1.3, and PowerVR's implementation. Several handset vendors also provide SDKs that include OpenGL ES: Nokia's S60, SonyEricsson's Symbian UIQ 3 SDK, and Qualcomm's BREW.

---

1   www.khronos.org/opengles/
2   www.khronos.org/message_boards/

Additionally, OpenGL ES libraries come pre-installed on many newer PDAs and smartphones. The high-end ones, such as Nokia's N93 and N95, have even full hardware acceleration. All devices that are based on S60 2nd edition FP2, or later, have at least a software-based OpenGL ES implementation.

7.4 API OVERVIEW

OpenGL ES comes in several flavors. Various profiles have been defined to cater to the needs of different market segments. Later versions introduce additional features, and different vendors provide various extensions.

7.4.1 PROFILES AND VERSIONS

Two important concepts to understand about OpenGL ES are *profiles* and *versions*. Profiles are used to create different subsets to target very distinct use cases. Currently there are three major profiles of OpenGL ES: the Common profile (also known as CM), the Common Lite (CL) profile, and the Safety-Critical (SC) profile. The first two are similar; the main difference is the omission of all floating-point entry points from the Common Lite profile.

The Safety-Critical profile differs significantly from the other two profiles and is targeted primarily for the aviation market. It uses OpenGL 1.3 as its starting point and removes functionality not needed in cockpit displays while retaining functionality needed by legacy applications in this specialized market, e.g., display lists. We will not cover the Safety-Critical profile in this book, instead we focus on the Common and Common Lite profiles.

Each profile has versions indicated by two numbers, the major and minor version numbers. For example, in OpenGL ES 1.0 the major version number is 1 and the minor one 0. The specifications sharing the same major number are backward-compatible. This means that an application written with the OpenGL ES 1.0 specification will compile, link, and run unmodified using an OpenGL ES 1.1 implementation. However, the same application will not run on an OpenGL ES 2.0 implementation.

7.4.2 OPENGL ES 1.0 IN A NUTSHELL

The most compact way to cover OpenGL ES is to examine where it differs from its desktop cousin, although this approach assumes familiarity with the desktop version. While OpenGL ES misses a number of function entry points and even major parts of the desktop OpenGL functionality, the underlying rendering model, terminology, and key concepts are the same.

Floating-point and fixed-point values

OpenGL is at its core a floating-point API. However, most mobile devices do not support a hardware floating-point unit. Two changes were made to keep the API simple and efficient.

First, the double data type (a 64-bit high-precision floating-point number) is not supported. Many functions that take doubles as arguments already had a variant accepting floats, and for the rest (e.g., glFrustum) a new variant accepting float arguments (e.g., glFrustumf) was created.

Second, a new fixed-point data type was created: type GLfixed, with a correspoding enum GL_FIXED. GLfixed is a number stored in a 32-bit integer, but interpreted so that the first 16 bits describe a signed two's complement integer value, and the last 16 bits describe the fractional component. In other words, you can convert between GLfixed and GLfloat by multiplying a GLfloat by 2^{16} or by dividing a GLfixed by 2^{16}. Finally, for each function that takes in floats, a variant was created that takes in fixed-point arguments (e.g., glFrustumx). For details on fixed-point programming, refer to Appendix A.

As in OpenGL, the GLfloat type for passing arguments to the engine is an IEEE float, but inside the engine the representation can be different and only needs to keep the accuracy of 1 part in 10^5. The positional and normal coordinates must store magnitudes up to 2^{32}, while the colors and texture coordinates must only store magnitudes up to 2^{10}. Note that these requirements also apply when using the fixed-point functions.

In practice, in a well-implemented software engine the performance savings of using the fixed-point versions of the functions are not significant. The major exception is with vertex data, which should never be given in floating point, unless you *know* that both your CPU and GPU have hardware support for floating-point data.

Vertex data

Originally, the rendering primitives in OpenGL were described by issuing a *begin* command for a set of primitives, and then updating the current vertex positions, normal vectors, colors, or texture coordinates in an arbitrary order, and finally *end*ing the primitive. This creates a very complicated state machine that does not run at an optimal speed. In current OpenGL versions, the vertex data is provided through vertex arrays and is rendered using calls to glDrawElements or glDrawArrays. OpenGL ES adopted only these simpler and more efficient approaches.

Vertex data can be specified using byte, short, float, or fixed, whereas int and double are not supported. Note that unlike on desktop OpenGL, the vertices can also be specified in bytes. Fog coordinates and secondary colors have been dropped from the specification.

Primitives

Triangles, lines, and points are supported as lists, strips, or fans. Quads and polygons are not supported, as they are too trivial to implement inside an application, and their specification is ambiguous if the vertices are not all on the same plane. `glPolygonMode`, which allows the same geometry to be drawn either as triangles, lines, or points, is not supported; hence the concept of edge flags, denoting which edges to draw in the line drawing mode, does not exist either. Also, 2D primitives such as rectangles are not provided as they can be emulated with a pair of triangles. Line and polygon stippling are not supported; if needed, they can be emulated using texture mapping.

Transformation and lighting

The most significant changes to the matrix stacks of desktop OpenGL are dropping of the color matrix stack and reducing the minimum depth of the modelview stack from 32 to 16. OpenGL ES does not support transposed matrices. Texture coordinate generation has been omitted as it can be emulated in the applications. Only RGBA colors (or their subsets) are provided; there is no support for indexed colors.

The lighting pipeline has been left largely intact with a few exceptions. There is no support for secondary colors, local viewer lighting model, or color material tracking except for `GL_AMBIENT_AND_DIFFUSE`. Two-sided lighting has been retained, but separate front and back materials cannot be specified.

Texturing

OpenGL ES supports only 2D texture mapping since 1D maps are trivial to emulate using 2D maps, and 3D maps are too resource intensive to include at this stage. The implementation burden of cube mapping was deemed too high both for software and hardware implementations. Texture borders, proxies, priorities, and LOD clamping are not included. Texture formats must match internal formats, and only the five most important formats are supported. Texture addressing modes are limited to `GL_CLAMP_TO_EDGE` and `GL_REPEAT`.

OpenGL ES adds support for paletted textures, an efficient way of compressing texture data. This extension introduces a number of new internal texture formats.

Reading back texture data, i.e., support for `glGetTexImage`, is not allowed. Multitexturing is supported, but an implementation does not have to provide more than one texturing unit. OpenGL ES 1.1 raises this to a minimum of two units.

Fragment pipeline

OpenGL ES does not make major changes to the fragment pipeline. Both stencil and depth buffering are supported, although stencil buffering is left optional, and not many implementations currently support it. The stencil operations GL_INCR_WRAP and GL_DECR_WRAP have been omitted.

OpenGL ES blending functionality conforms to OpenGL 1.1, rather than version 1.3 like the rest of the API. This eliminates functions such as glBlendFuncSeparate, glBlendEquation, and glBlendColor that were introduced in OpenGL 1.2.

Frame buffer operations

The most significant changes relate to the frame buffer operations. There is only a single drawing buffer, and accumulation buffering is not supported. The entire imaging subset has been removed. 2D rendering through glDrawPixels or glBitmap is not supported, as it can be emulated with a texture-mapped pair of triangles. The depth and stencil buffers cannot be read back, as glReadBuffer and glCopyPixels have been omitted. glReadPixels is supported, although with a very limited number of pixel formats.

Miscellaneous

Evaluators, feedback, selection, and display lists have been omitted since they have a high implementation burden and can be reasonably easily emulated in the application. With the exception of display lists these features are not widely used even in desktop OpenGL.

OpenGL ES 1.0 supports only queries for static state whose values are defined when an OpenGL context is created, and will not change during execution. This means that an application must track its own state as it cannot be queried back from GL. An optional extension glQueryMatrixxOES was created to enable reading back the current matrix values. The convenience routines for saving and restoring the state via the attribute stacks are not supported.

7.4.3 NEW FEATURES IN OPENGL ES 1.1

OpenGL ES 1.1 was first introduced at SIGGRAPH 2004. This version is clearly more hardware-oriented than its predecessor, with features targeted at gaming applications and for higher-level APIs such as M3G. Nevertheless, software implementations of OpenGL ES 1.1 remain feasible.

Vertex buffer objects

Vertex buffer objects that allow encapsulating and storing vertex data on the server side are supported. However, to simplify efficient implementations, reading back the buffered vertex and index data is not allowed.

Point sprites

OpenGL ES 1.1 introduces *point sprites* for 2D billboards and particle effects. A *point size array* allows specifying an array of point sizes for efficient rendering of point sprites with differing sizes. The point sizes can also be *attenuated* as a function of distance from the camera.

User clip planes and matrix palette

User clip planes are supported, although the implementation is required to support only one.

OpenGL ES 1.1 provides also an optional *matrix palette* extension for accelerating character animation and vertex skinning.

Texturing enhancements

While the first version only requires one texturing unit, OpenGL ES 1.1 requires at least *two texturing units*. *Automatic mipmap generation* is supported. Also *texture combiners* are introduced (including bump mapping), only the crossbar functionality of combiners is not included.

Draw texture

An optional extension `glDrawTex{sifx}[v]OES` was created to support fast 2D rendering. The image data is given in a texture object, so that the data can be cached on the server. The `glDrawPixels` of OpenGL does not allow such caching.

Dynamic state queries

OpenGL ES 1.1 introduced *dynamic state queries*. The ability to query back the GL state makes the use of middleware libraries easier, as state does not have to be tracked externally.

7.4.4 EXTENSION MECHANISM

The extensibility of OpenGL has always been one of its key strengths. It enables individual hardware vendors to add new features reflecting advances in hardware design. If these features prove successful in the marketplace, they are introduced as core features in future versions of the GL specification. OpenGL ES continues this tradition and the extension mechanism is an integral part of its design.

There are several different kinds of extensions. The *core extensions* are mandatory components of the OpenGL ES specification that are not part of the desktop GL. The *optional extensions* are not strictly required. They are often the features that the working group expects to become a part of the core specification in the future, but does not yet feel comfortable mandating. Both the core and the optional extensions have the suffix *OES* added to their function names.

The *Vendor-specific extensions* are introduced by individual hardware vendors to provide access to their hardware-specific features. These functions get their postfixes from the names of the companies providing them. *Multi-vendor extensions* (with postfix *EXT*) are used when multiple companies want to expose the same feature.

Extensions often provide a faster and more efficient way of accomplishing a given task. Since the optional or the vendor-specific extensions are not particularly portable, we recommend that you first write a portable version of an algorithm using the core functionality, and then switch to using an extension if it is available on a given platform.

7.4.5 OPENGL ES EXTENSION PACK

The OpenGL ES extension pack was introduced in August 2005. It is a collection of extensions found in some existing and upcoming devices. Features introduced in the extension pack include several improvements to the texturing system, e.g., texture crossbar, cube mapping, and the mirrored repeat mode. New blending modes as well as stencil buffering modes are introduced. The minimum requirements for the size of the matrix palettes are made more rigorous. Finally, the concept of frame buffer objects (FBOs) is introduced into OpenGL ES.

7.4.6 UTILITY APIS

OpenGL ES does not contain any APIs for creating the windows and surfaces used as render targets. The portable way of doing this is using EGL, a companion API that acts as a glue between OpenGL ES and the operating system. EGL is similar to the WGL on Windows and GLX on X Windows, but designed to be portable across a number of embedded platforms. EGL is covered in more depth in Chapter 11.

GLU and GLUT are other utility libraries used on the desktop. Khronos has not specified embedded variants for these. Instead, the libraries have been ported directly as an open source effort.[3] The GLU library sits on top of OpenGL ES and contains functionality for creating various meshes, computing mipmaps, defining NURBS objects, and various helper functions for manipulating matrices. GLUT, on the other hand, is a cross-platform library for handling system-level input and output. This includes mouse event

---

3 glutes.sourceforge.net/

handling, keyboard input, timer events, and support for more exotic devices. The library also provides some UI components such as pop-up menus.

7.4.7 CONVENTIONS

OpenGL ES follows a number of conventions established by OpenGL. Some of the most important ones are briefly reviewed here.

Prefixes and suffixes

All GL functions are prefixed with the symbol *gl* (`glViewport`). Data types use the *GL* prefix (`GLbyte`) whereas macros and enumerants use the prefix *GL_* (`GL_LIGHT0`). Functions specific to OpenGL ES use the suffix *OES*.

Function names contain suffixes for indicating the types of their arguments. For example, `glClearDepthf` and `glClearDepthx` are two variants of the same function where the first takes its input parameters as floating-point and the latter as fixed-point numbers. The following data types are supported by OpenGL ES:

b	8-bit integer	GLbyte
s	16-bit integer	GLshort
i	32-bit integer	GLint, GLsizei, GLintptr, GLsizeiptr
x	32-bit fixed point	GLfixed, GLclampx
f	32-bit floating point	GLfloat, GLclampf
ub	8-bit unsigned integer	GLubyte, GLboolean
us	16-bit unsigned integer	GLushort
ui	32-bit unsigned integer	GLuint, GLenum, GLbitfield

In the following text, if several argument types are possible, the type is denoted by T. For example,

```
void glColor4{fx ub}(T red, T green, T blue, T alpha)
```

is a shorthand for three function definitions

```
void glColor4f(GLfloat red, GLfloat green, GLfloat blue, GLfloat alpha)
void glColor4x(GLfixed red, GLfixed green, GLfixed blue, GLfixed alpha)
void glColor4ub(GLubyte red, GLubyte green, GLubyte blue, GLubyte alpha).
```

A suffix v is added to variants that take in a pointer to a parameter array as an argument, for example

```
void glLight{fx}v(GLenum light, GLenum pname, const T * params)
```

passes parameters in *params* while

```
void glGetPointerv(GLenum pname, void ** params)
```

returns parameters in *params*.

State machine model

OpenGL ES operates as a state machine. The state consists of various features being either turned on or off, and most capabilities are turned off by default. On the server, or the graphics engine side, the following calls are used to set the state:

```
void glEnable(GLenum cap)
void glDisable(GLenum cap)
```

For example, to turn lighting on, one needs to enable both lighting itself and at least one light:

```
glEnable( GL_LIGHTING );
glEnable( GL_LIGHT0 );
```

Starting from OpenGL ES 1.1, the function glIsEnabled can be used for querying whether a given server-side capability is enabled.

The client-side, i.e., application or CPU-side, functions to enable and disable the use of various vertex arrays are:

```
void glEnableClientState(GLenum array)
void glDisableClientState(GLenum array)
```

Error handling

Instead of individual functions providing error codes as their return values, OpenGL ES uses a global error flag that is set whenever an error occurs in any of the API functions. Most GL functions validate their input parameters before modifying the internal GL state. If an invalid parameter is encountered, the global error flag is set, and the function returns without modifying the state.

```
GLenum glGetError(void)
```

returns the current error code and resets it to GL_NO_ERROR. The error codes are listed in Table 7.1. OpenGL allows distributed implementations to have a separate error flag for each replicated graphics unit, and in such a case you should call glGetError repeatedly until it returns GL_NO_ERROR. However, OpenGL ES implementations typically have only one graphics unit.

It is a good programming practice, at least in debug builds, to call glGetError every now and then to check that no GL errors have occurred. Some debugging libraries even

Table 7.1: GL error codes.

Error	Meaning	Command ignored?
GL_NO_ERROR	No errors	No
GL_INVALID_ENUM	Enum argument is out of range	Yes
GL_INVALID_VALUE	Numeric value is out of range	Yes
GL_INVALID_OPERATION	Operation illegal in current state	Yes
GL_STACK_OVERFLOW	Command would cause a stack overflow	Yes
GL_STACK_UNDERFLOW	Command would cause a stack underflow	Yes
GL_OUT_OF_MEMORY	Not enough memory to execute command	Unknown

wrap every GL call with a `glGetError` and then raise an assertion immediately when an error occurs.

Packaging

The main header file is called `GLES/gl.h`, and it always has to be included. Additionally, most applications need to include `EGL/egl.h`. The `gl.h` header also includes following version definitions:

```
#define GL_VERSION_ES_CL_1_x    1
```

or

```
#define GL_VERSION_ES_CM_1_x    1
```

depending on which profile is supported. *x* denotes the supported minor API version number.

> **Pitfall:** Even though the official OpenGL ES 1.0 specification states exactly how the version number definitions should be presented in the header file, many current GL header files define instead erroneously `GL_OES_VERSION_1_x`. For maximal portability one should use a construct such as this in the source code:
>
> ```
> #if (defined(GL_OES_VERSION_1_0) || defined(GL_VERSION_ES_CM_1_0)
> ```

When OpenGL ES and EGL were originally specified it was recommended that both APIs should be exposed from the same DLL. As new companion APIs that can be used with EGL emerged, such as OpenVG and OpenGL ES 2.0, this arrangement became burdensome as using EGL with OpenVG would require linking also to the OpenGL ES library which might not even be present on the device.

For this reason a new linkage was specified where the EGL API is exposed from a separate link library and the client APIs from their separate libraries. Note that the actual linkage may vary as it is actually controlled typically by the operating system vendor or the device

Table 7.2: Library naming scheme.

Library content	Name of the link library
OpenGL ES 1.x with EGL (Common Profile)	libGLES_CM.{lib,dll,a,so}
OpenGL ES 1.x with EGL (Lite Profile)	libGLES_CL.{lib,dll,a,so}
OpenGL ES 1.x without EGL (Common Profile)	libGLESv1_CM.{lib,dll,a,so}
OpenGL ES 1.x without EGL (Lite Profile)	libGLESv1_CL.{lib,dll,a,so}
EGL	libEGL.{lib,dll,a,so}

vendor. For documentation on how the linkage is done for your particular device, see the SDK documentation for the platform.

A recommended library naming scheme is presented in Table 7.2.

7.5 HELLO, OPENGL ES!

Here is a simple OpenGL ES example that renders one smoothly shaded triangle on the display. Before any OpenGL ES calls can be executed, some resources need to be created with the EGL API. See Chapter 11 for more information on EGL.

First we include some necessary headers, and define the vertex data:

```
#include <GLES/gl.h>

/* vertex data (3 vertices for single triangle) */
static const GLbyte vertices[3 * 3] =
{
  -1,    1,    0,
   1,   -1,    0,
   1,    1,    0
};

static const GLubyte colors[3 * 4] =
{
  255,      0,     0,    255,
    0,    255,     0,    255,
    0,      0,   255,    255
};
```

Let us set the basic state. Here we assume a clean OpenGL ES context with the default state settings. If the initial state were totally unknown, much more initialization code would be required.

```
glDisable( GL_DEPTH_TEST );
glShadeModel( GL_SMOOTH );
glClearColor( 0.f, 0.f, 0.1f, 1.f );
```

Next, we set the array pointers for vertex and color arrays, and enable the corresponding arrays:

```
glVertexPointer( 3, GL_BYTE, 0, vertices );
glColorPointer( 4, GL_UNSIGNED_BYTE, 0, colors );
glEnableClientState( GL_VERTEX_ARRAY );
glEnableClientState( GL_COLOR_ARRAY );
```

Then we set the view parameters:

```
glViewport( 0, 0, width, height );
glMatrixMode( GL_PROJECTION );
glFrustumf( -1.f, 1.f, -1.f, 1.f, 3.f, 1000.f );
glMatrixMode( GL_MODELVIEW );
```

Next we have the main function that gets called in each render cycle. Here the code typically clears the buffers and renders the frame.

At first, we clear the color buffer, then set the camera, and finally draw the triangle.

```
void render_frame( void )
{
  glClear( GL_COLOR_BUFFER_BIT );
  glLoadIdentity();
  glTranslatef( 0, 0, -5.f );
  glDrawArrays( GL_TRIANGLES, 0, 3 );
}
```

A buffer swap is required at the end of the frame. How to do that will be introduced later in Chapter 11.

OPENGL ES TRANSFORMATION AND LIGHTING

This chapter covers the geometry pipeline of OpenGL ES. This includes primitive and vertex specification, matrix processing, and the interaction between light sources and materials.

8.1 DRAWING PRIMITIVES

In this section we describe the geometric primitives supported by OpenGL ES. While there is also some support for raster primitives, we defer that discussion until we have introduced texture mapping.

The geometric primitives are made of vertices, and each vertex can have properties such as position, color, surface normal, texture coordinate, and point size. We briefly describe the original OpenGL model for specifying vertex data, and then the newer way of specifying vertex arrays, which was adopted by OpenGL ES. We continue by explaining how the primitives are actually drawn using the vertex data. Finally we describe an alternative to vertex arrays that was introduced in OpenGL ES 1.1: vertex buffer objects (see Section 8.1.4).

8.1.1 PRIMITIVE TYPES

OpenGL ES 1.0 supports the geometric primitives shown in Figure 3.3: points, lines, and triangles. OpenGL ES 1.1 amends this list with point sprites.

Points

The point is the simplest OpenGL primitive, and it requires only one vertex. Its primary property is its size, which is set by the function

```
void glPointSize{fx}(type size).
```

The point size corresponds to its diameter (the total width), defined in pixels, and it defaults to 1. Points can be drawn either with or without antialiasing (enabled and disabled with GL_POINT_SMOOTH). With antialiasing off, the points are drawn as squares and the point size is rounded to the closest integer. With antialiasing enabled, the points are drawn as circles, and the alpha values of the pixels on the boundary are affected by how much the point covers those pixels.

Even though points can be drawn quite efficiently, in practice many graphics engines are optimized for rendering of triangles. This may mean that non-antialiased points are drawn as two triangles, and the maximum point size for smooth points may be just one pixel. Similar optimizations may be used for line drawing.

Point sprites and size attenuation

OpenGL ES 1.1 provides features for points that are especially useful for particle effects: *point sprites*, *point size arrays*, and *point size attenuation*. Many natural phenomena such as rain, smoke, or fire, can be modeled by replicating several small pictures representing raindrops, puffs of smoke, or individual flames. The idea is that a set of points describes the positions of point sprites, and their appearance comes from the current texture map. Section 9.2.8 describes how to apply a texture to points.

When points are defined by an array, in OpenGL ES 1.0 they all have the same size, defined by glPointSize{fx}. In OpenGL ES 1.1 it is possible to give each point its own size (see Section 8.1.2), and the point sizes may be attenuated by the distance between each point and the camera. The derived point size comes from the formula:

$$derived\_size = impl\_clamp\left(user\_clamp\left(size * \sqrt{\frac{1}{a + bd + cd^2}}\right)\right) \quad (8.1)$$

where d is the eye-coordinate distance from the camera, the attenuated point *size* is affected by the distance attenuation coefficients a, b, c, it is clamped by user-specified min-max range of GL_POINT_SIZE_MIN and GL_POINT_SIZE_MAX, and finally clamped to implementation-dependent point size range. If multisampling is disabled, this is the size used for rasterizing the point. With multisampling, the point size is clamped to have a minimum threshold, and the alpha value of the point is modulated by

$$alpha\_fade = \left(\frac{derived\_size}{threshold} \right)^2. \tag{8.2}$$

The point attenuation components are set using

```
void glPointParameter{fx}(GLenum pname, T param)
void glPointParameter{fx}v(GLenum pname, T * params)
```

where *pname* GL_POINT_SIZE_MIN and GL_POINT_SIZE_MAX are used to change the clamping values for the point size calculation. GL_POINT_DISTANCE_ ATTENUATION is used to pass in *params* an array containing the distance attenuation coefficients *a*, *b*, and *c*, in that order. GL_POINT_FADE_THRESHOLD_SIZE specifies the point alpha fade threshold.

Keeping the attenuation components in their default values (1, 0, 0) in practice disables point size attenuation.

Point sprites are enabled by calling glEnable with the token GL_POINT_SPRITE_ OES. When the global point sprite mode is enabled and the texture environment for the given texture unit is set to GL_COORD_REPLACE_OES (see Section 9.2.8), all points submitted for drawing are handled as point sprites. A point sprite can be thought of as a textured quad whose center lies at the transformed screen-space position of the vertex representing the point and whose screen dimensions are equivalent to the derived size of the point.

Here is a simple code that draws a 32 × 32 point sprite. We use a single point size, but we could have varied it using glPointSizePointerOES.

```
glPointSize( 32 );
glEnable( GL_POINT_SPRITE_OES );
glTexEnvi( GL_POINT_SPRITE_OES, GL_COORD_REPLACE_OES, GL_TRUE );
glDrawArrays( GL_POINTS, 0, 1 );
```

The entry point definition for glTexEnv is

```
void glTexEnv{ifx}(GLenum target, GLenum pname,T param),
```

and its other uses for specifying how texture mapping is done are described in Section 9.2.5 and Section 9.2.7.

Pitfall: Point clipping in OpenGL ES works so that if the transformed vertex of the point is outside the view frustum, the whole primitive is considered to be outside the frustum and is thus discarded. This way a very simple clipping formula can be applied already at the geometry stage to cull away the point geometry. As a side effect, points or point sprites wider than one pixel vanish before all of the pixels of the primitive move outside of the view frustum. If this is a problem the application can set the viewport to be larger than the display and set the scissor to match the size of the display.

Although this should work as specified in the API, in practice most implementations of OpenGL ES in the market have some issues with either the point clipping when the viewport has been extended, or with point sprites in general.

Lines

There are three ways for defining a set of lines in OpenGL ES. The first is a collection of separate *lines*, with a line segment connecting the first and the second vertices, then the third and the fourth, and so on. The second type is a *line strip*, which simply connects each vertex in a list to the next one with a line segment. The third type is the *line loop*, which closes a line strip by adding a segment between the last and first vertex.

The *line width*, in pixels, can be set with

```
void glLineWidth{fx}(GLfloat width),
```

and the lines can be drawn either with or without antialiasing (enabled and disabled with `GL_LINE_SMOOTH`).

The desktop OpenGL also supports *stippling*, that is, dotting and dashing the lines. Since this can be emulated by texture mapping the lines, stippling is not supported in OpenGL ES.

Polygons

The only Polygon type supported by OpenGL ES is a triangle. Desktop OpenGL also supports quadrilaterals, *n*-sided polygons, and screen-aligned rectangles, but these were left out of OpenGL ES for the reasons described in Section 3.1.1.

There are three methods for defining triangles in OpenGL ES. The first way is as a collection of separate *triangles*, where the first three vertices of a vertex array form the first triangle, the next three form the second triangle, and so forth. The second way is a *triangle strip*. There the first three vertices create a triangle, and after that, every new vertex creates a new triangle by connecting to the two previous vertices. The third way is a *triangle fan*. Again, the first triangle is made of the first three vertices. After that, every new vertex creates a new triangle using the new vertex, the previous vertex, and the first vertex. Thus the triangles create a fan around the first vertex.

8.1.2 SPECIFYING VERTEX DATA

The original model for specifying vertex data in OpenGL used the `glBegin - glEnd` model. For example, a triangle strip of two triangles, with two red and two green vertices, could be specified by

```
/* glBegin - glEnd NOT SUPPORTED BY OpenGL ES!! */
glBegin   ( GL_TRIANGLE_STRIP );
glColor4f ( 1.0f, 0.0f, 0.0f, 1.0f );
glVertex3f( 0.0f, 1.0f, 0.0f );
glVertex3f( 0.0f, 0.0f, 0.0f );
glColor4f ( 0.0f, 1.0f, 0.0f, 1.0f );
glVertex3f( 1.0f, 1.0f, 0.0f );
glVertex3f( 1.0f, 0.0f, 0.0f );
glEnd();
```

The function `glBegin` indicates the primitive type. The current values of vertex properties such as color, the normal vector, and texture coordinates are specified in an arbitrary order. A call to `glVertex` specifies the vertex location and completes the vertex definition using the current property values. This approach creates a very complicated state machine, and requires a large number of function calls to render the geometry, slowing graphics hardware down. *Display lists* are a way to deal with this issue by collecting all the GL calls and their arguments into a list which can be cached by the graphics engine, and later drawn using a single function call.

Desktop OpenGL 1.1 introduced *vertex arrays*, which greatly simplified specification of the vertex data, and made both the `glBegin - glEnd` model and the display lists largely redundant. In this approach, the vertex properties are placed in arrays, which are then passed to OpenGL using the following calls:

```
void glColorPointer(GLint size, GLenum type, GLsizei stride, GLvoid * pointer)
void glTexCoordPointer(GLint size, GLenum type, GLsizei stride, GLvoid * pointer)
void glVertexPointer(GLint size, GLenum type, GLsizei stride, GLvoid * pointer)
void glNormalPointer(GLenum type, GLsizei stride, GLvoid * pointer)
void glPointSizePointerOES(GLenum type, GLsizei stride, GLvoid * pointer)
```

All of the functions above have similar syntax. The parameter *size* describes the dimensionality of the data, e.g., *size* = 2 for `glVertexPointer` indicates that the x and y coordinates are specified, while z is left to the default value of 0. Note that for `glNormalPointer` and `glPointSizePointerOES` the *size* parameter is omitted, as normals always have three components and points only one. The *type* parameter is used to denote the basic type for storing the array data. See Table 8.1 for the allowed combinations of *size* and *type* for each array. Also note that `glPointSizePointerOES` is only supported in OpenGL ES 1.1.

The *stride* parameter gives the distance in bytes between consecutive array elements. Finally, the *pointer* parameter points to the actual vertex attribute data.

Table 8.1: Vertex array sizes (values per vertex) and data types.

Command	Sizes	Types
glVertexPointer	2,3,4	GL_BYTE, GL_SHORT, GL_FIXED, GL_FLOAT
glNormalPointer	3	GL_BYTE, GL_SHORT, GL_FIXED, GL_FLOAT
glColorPointer	4	GL_UNSIGNED_BYTE, GL_FIXED, GL_FLOAT
glPointSizePointerOES	1	GL_FIXED, GL_FLOAT
glTexCoordPointer	2,3,4	GL_BYTE, GL_SHORT, GL_FIXED, GL_FLOAT

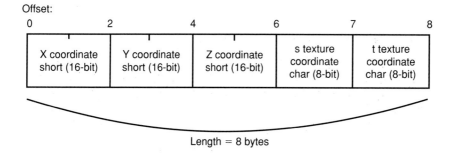

Figure 8.1: Example of packed vertex array data.

The stride can be used to skip data if the vertex array is in an interleaved format. Figure 8.1 shows an example of packed vertex data that stores vertex coordinates and texture coordinates in an interleaved format. The vertex pointer in this case would point to the beginning of the array and have a stride value of 8 (equaling the size of the packed vertex). The texture coordinate pointer in this case would point to the beginning of the array plus 6 bytes, and the stride value would be 8 bytes.

Specifying a *stride* of zero always matches the stride that would be used for tightly packed vertex data. For example, if the vertex array has three GL_SHORT coordinates and a stride of zero, the implementation interprets the actual stride as being 6 bytes.

> **Performance tip:** Depending on the implementation, the vertex data format may have a great impact on performance. For example, the amount of bandwidth required for transmitting the geometry data over the system buses depends directly on the type used to specify the vertex data. Also, especially for pure software-based implementations of OpenGL ES on mobile devices that often lack floating-point units, using floating-point vertex data may force the implementation to fall into a much slower version of the transformation and lighting pipeline. Even with the integer data types, using the more compact data types gives the implementation more freedom to optimize performance. Often GL_SHORT is enough for almost any kind of vertex data in 3D.

The arrays have to be explicitly enabled (or disabled) using

```
void glEnableClientState(GLenum cap)
void glDisableClientState(GLenum cap)
```

where the *cap* parameter is one of

```
GL_COLOR_ARRAY,
GL_NORMAL_ARRAY,
GL_TEXTURE_COORD_ARRAY,
GL_VERTEX_ARRAY, or
GL_POINT_SIZE_ARRAY_OES.
```

OpenGL ES 1.0 supports the multitexturing API but is not required to provide more than one texturing unit, while OpenGL ES 1.1 guarantees the availability of at least two texturing units.

```
void glClientActiveTexture(GLenum texture)
```

is used to select which of texture units is affected by `glTexCoordPointer`, `glEnable ClientState` (`GL_TEXTURE_COORD_ARRAY`), and `glDisableClientState` (`GL_TEXTURE_COORD_ARRAY`) calls. The parameter *texture* defines the new active texture unit (`GL_TEXTURE0`, `GL_TEXTURE1`, etc.).

Default values

OpenGL ES allows a default value to be set for normals, colors, and texture coordinates, and then the corresponding vertex array does not need to be specified. If one of the arrays has not been enabled with `glEnableClientState`, these default values are used instead. The following calls are used to define the default values:

```
void glNormal3{fx}(T nx, T ny, T nz)
void glColor4{fx ub}(T red, T green, T blue, T alpha)
void glMultiTexCoord4{fx}(GLenum target, T s, T t, T r, T q).
```

The *target* is `GL_TEXTURE`i, where $0 \leq i <$ the value of `GL_MAX_TEXTURE_UNITS` which is an implementation-dependent value.

8.1.3 DRAWING THE PRIMITIVES

Once the vertex data has been specified, there are two functions that can be used to draw the resulting shapes. The function

```
void glDrawArrays(GLenum mode, GLint first, GLsizei count)
```

is used to draw consecutive primitives starting from the *first* index in the vertex array. The parameter *mode* defines the type of the primitives to be drawn: GL_POINTS, GL_LINES, GL_LINE_LOOP, GL_LINE_STRIP, GL_TRIANGLES, GL_TRIANGLE_STRIP, or GL_TRIANGLE_FAN. The *count* determines how many vertices are submitted for rendering.

glDrawArrays is typically used in cases where triangles are represented with strips that are organized directly in the correct order. The second drawing function uses a list of indices to the vertex array to define the primitives:

```
void glDrawElements(GLenum mode, GLsize count,
                    GLenum type, const GLvoid * indices)
```

The parameter *mode* is the same as in glDrawArrays. *type* defines the type of the data that is stored in the array *indices* and can be either GL_UNSIGNED_BYTE or GL_UNSIGNED_SHORT. *count* determines the number of indices to process. See Section 6.4 for further discussion about the benefits of indexed rendering, such as better use of vertex caches.

The following example code renders red triangles using both of these methods.

```
static const GLbyte vertices1[8*2] = { 0,0,  0,0,  −20,20,  20,20,
                            −20,40,  20,40,  −20,60,
                             20,60 };
static const GLbyte vertices2[7*2] = { 0,100,  100,0,  0,−100,
                            −100,0,  0,50,  45,20,
                            −45,20 };
static const GLushort indices[9]   = { 0,3,1,  1,3,2,  4,6,5 };
glEnableClientState( GL_VERTEX_ARRAY );
glColor4ub( 255, 0, 0, 255 );
glVertexPointer( 2, GL_BYTE, 0, vertices1 );
/* skip vertex 0, draw five triangles */
glDrawArrays( GL_TRIANGLE_STRIP, 1, 7 );
glVertexPointer( 2, GL_BYTE, 0, vertices2 );
/* draw three triangles, using the first seven vertices */
glDrawElements( GL_TRIANGLES, 9, GL_UNSIGNED_SHORT, indices );
```

8.1.4 VERTEX BUFFER OBJECTS

Since the vertex arrays are stored in user-controlled memory, and the user can change their content between draw calls without the graphics engine being aware of the change, the GL driver cannot cache them. This results in costly data transfers between the system memory and the graphics engine whenever draw calls are issued. *Vertex buffer objects*, introduced in OpenGL ES 1.1, provide a mechanism for storing the vertex arrays into memory controlled by the graphics server and allow buffer data updates only via explicit function calls. A driver may then optimize the vertex buffer usage by storing that data in an optimized memory layout, or by converting the values into a type that executes faster on the hardware.

A buffer object is created with a call to

>   void glBindBuffer(GLenum *target*, GLuint *buffer*)

where *target* is GL_ARRAY_BUFFER and *buffer* is a handle to the buffer. If *buffer* is an unused handle and greater than 0, a new zero-sized memory buffer is created. Otherwise the existing buffer object becomes bound. If 0 is given for *buffer*, the graphics engine will behave as if there were no currently bound vertex buffer object.

A list of existing buffer objects and their resources are deleted with

>   void glDeleteBuffers(GLsizei *n*, const GLuint * *buffers*).

If any of the buffer objects being deleted are bound as active vertex attribute pointers, the bindings are released when the function call returns.

Handles to the buffers can be created by calling

>   void glGenBuffers(GLsizei *n*, GLuint * *buffers*)

which stores *n* buffer object handles to an array specified by *buffers* and marks them as being used. The actual buffers still need to be created with glBindBuffer. A side effect of glDeleteBuffers is to make the deleted handles available again.

The actual data are stored into the currently bound vertex buffer object by calling

>   void glBufferData(GLenum *target*, GLsizeiptr *size*, const GLvoid * *data*,
>   GLenum *usage*).

If the buffer object already contains data, the old data is freed and replaced by the new data. For the vertex data the parameter *target* is set to GL_ARRAY_BUFFER, *size* gives the size of the data to be copied in bytes, *data* is a pointer to the source data, and *usage* gives a hint about the intended usage for this vertex buffer object. GL_STATIC_DRAW advises the driver to optimize for data staying constant across GL draw calls, while GL_DYNAMIC_DRAW indicates that the data for this buffer object are changed dynamically between subsequent frames or even between draw calls.

>   void glBufferSubData(GLenum *target*, GLintptr *offset*, GLsizeiptr *size*, const
>   GLvoid * *data*)

is used to replace some of the data in the server-side store for the currently bound vertex buffer object. *target* is again GL_ARRAY_BUFFER, and *offset* gives an offset in bytes to the location from which the data is to be replaced in the server-side store. *size* gives the length of data to be replaced, and *data* gives the actual data to be copied to the server-side store. Note that this function cannot be used to extend the size of the server side store. If *offset*+*size* extends beyond the data buffer stored originally with a call to glBufferData, a GL error is generated and the data will not be copied.

> **Performance tip:** At first sight, GL_DYNAMIC_DRAW does not seem to improve on the standard vertex arrays, as the driver is assuming that the data is modified often. However, if the data behind the vertex buffer object is shared even for

two draw calls, GL_DYNAMIC_DRAW allows the driver to keep the data in the server-side storage across those invocations, whereas a standard vertex array would have to be sent every time. GL_DYNAMIC_DRAW hints to the implementation that it should not perform particularly costly optimizations for the data representation as it will get replaced many times.

After a vertex buffer object is set up, it can be bound to any vertex attribute array by calling the relevant function such as glColorPointer. The *pointer* argument now does not contain the vertex data, but an offset to the currently bound vertex buffer object. Multiple vertex array pointers can be set up from the same vertex buffer object, e.g., packed vertex data representations can be used the same way as with standard vertex array calls. The vertex buffer objects are disabled with glBindBuffer(GL_ARRAY_BUFFER, 0), after which the vertex pointer calls work as described in Section 8.1.2.

Array indices in buffer objects

It is also possible to store indices that are used with glDrawElements into buffer objects by setting the *target* argument of calls glBindBuffer, glBufferData, and glBufferSubData to GL_ELEMENT_ARRAY_BUFFER. If the currently bound buffer object is a GL_ELEMENT_ARRAY_BUFFER, glDrawElements takes the index data from the buffer, and interprets the *indices* parameter as an offset to the buffer object data.

Example

The following example code renders some colored triangles using vertex buffer objects:

```
static const GLushort indices[9]   = { 0,3,1, 1,3,2, 4,6,5 };
static const GLbyte   vertices[7*2] = { 0,100, 100,0, 0,-100,
  -100,0, 0,50, 45,20, -45,20 };
static const GLubyte  colors[7*4]  = { 0,0,255,255, 0,255,0,255,
  255,0,0,255, 255,255,255,255, 255,0,255,255, 255,255,0,255,
  0,255,255,255 };
/* create handles */
GLuint handle[3];
glGenBuffers( 3, &handle[0] );
/* load the vertex data into the first VBO */
glBindBuffer( GL_ARRAY_BUFFER, handle[0] );
glBufferData( GL_ARRAY_BUFFER, sizeof(vertices),
              &vertices[0], GL_STATIC_DRAW );
/* load the index data into the second VBO */
glBindBuffer( GL_ELEMENT_ARRAY_BUFFER, handle[1] );
glBufferData( GL_ELEMENT_ARRAY_BUFFER, sizeof(indices),
              &indices[0], GL_STATIC_DRAW );
/* load the color data into the third VBO */
glBindBuffer( GL_ARRAY_BUFFER, handle[2] );
glBufferData( GL_ARRAY_BUFFER, sizeof(colors),
              &colors[0], GL_STATIC_DRAW);
```

```
glEnableClientState( GL_VERTEX_ARRAY );
glEnableClientState( GL_COLOR_ARRAY );
glBindBuffer( GL_ARRAY_BUFFER, handle[0] );
glVertexPointer( 2, GL_BYTE, 0, NULL );
glBindBuffer( GL_ARRAY_BUFFER, handle[2] );
glColorPointer( 4, GL_UNSIGNED_BYTE, 0, NULL );
/* skip vertex 0, draw five triangles */
glDrawArrays( GL_TRIANGLE_STRIP, 1, 6 );
glBindBuffer( GL_ELEMENT_ARRAY_BUFFER, handle[1] );
/* draw three triangles, using the first seven vertices */
glDrawElements( GL_TRIANGLES, 9, GL_UNSIGNED_SHORT, NULL );
/* Unbind all VBOs */
glBindBuffer( GL_ARRAY_BUFFER, 0 );
glBindBuffer( GL_ELEMENT_ARRAY_BUFFER, 0 );
```

8.2 VERTEX TRANSFORMATION PIPELINE

This section covers the vertex transformation pipeline, shown in Figure 8.2. First, the vertex coordinates and the vertex normals are transformed from model coordinates to eye coordinates using the *modelview matrix*. Lighting and user clipping are done in the eye coordinate space. Next the *projection matrix* transforms the lit vertices into the clip space, where the primitives formed from the vertices are clipped against the viewing frustum. After clipping, the vertices are transformed into normalized device coordinates by a perspective division, and the primitives are rasterized, i.e., converted into pixels. The *texture matrix* is also applied to texture coordinates during the rasterization to correctly sample the texture maps. Finally the *viewport transformation* determines where and with which depth values the rasterized fragments are stored into the frame buffer. The mathematics behind the transformation pipeline are described in Chapter 2.

8.2.1 MATRICES

The matrix functions operate on the current matrix. The active matrix type is selected using

$$\text{void } \texttt{glMatrixMode}(\texttt{GLenum } \textit{mode}).$$

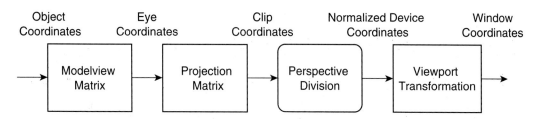

Figure 8.2: The vertex transformation pipeline is parametrized by user-given modelview and projection matrices, and viewport transformation parameters. 4D homogeneous coordinates are mapped from clip coordinates to normalized device coordinates by a division by the fourth, *w*, component.

The *mode* must be one of GL_MODELVIEW, GL_PROJECTION, or GL_TEXTURE. In this section we concentrate on the modelview and projection matrices; texture transformations are discussed in Section 8.2.3. From OpenGL ES 1.1 onward GL_MATRIX_PALETTE_OES is also optionally available (see Section 10.4.3). The color matrix that exists in OpenGL is not supported.

All matrices are 4 × 4 matrices, and are stored in column-first order. The current matrix can be replaced by calling

```
void glLoadMatrix{fx}(const T * m)
```

where *m* is an array of 16 floating-point or fixed-point numbers, ordered as follows:

$$\begin{bmatrix} m[0] & m[4] & m[8] & m[12] \\ m[1] & m[5] & m[9] & m[13] \\ m[2] & m[6] & m[10] & m[14] \\ m[3] & m[7] & m[11] & m[15] \end{bmatrix}. \tag{8.3}$$

It is possible to multiply a new matrix with the current matrix using

```
void glMultMatrix{fx}(const T * m).
```

If C is the current matrix, calling glMultMatrix with M computes $C := C\,M$, that is, the multiplication is from the right side.

As described in Chapter 2, it is often useful to separately transform the vertices from the object coordinates to the world coordinates, and then transform the vertices from the world coordinates to the eye coordinates. The matrices can then be used as follows:

```
GLfloat world_to_eye_matrix[16], object_to_world_matrix[16];
/* calculate matrices */
...
/* set up modelview matrix and draw */
glMatrixMode( GL_MODELVIEW );
glLoadMatrixf( world_to_eye_matrix );
glMultMatrixf( object_to_world_matrix );
glDrawArrays( GL_TRIANGLES, 0, n );
```

The convenience function

```
void glLoadIdentity(void )
```

replaces the current matrix with the identity matrix (see Equation (2.14)), while the following functions

```
void glTranslate{fx}(T x, T y, T z)
void glRotate{fx}(T angle, T x, T y, T z)
void glScale{fx}(T x, T y, T z)
```

multiply the current matrix with one of Equations (2.17), (2.22), and (2.24). The functions

void glFrustum{fx}(T *left*, T *right*, T *bottom*, T *top*, T *near*, T *far*)
void glOrtho{fx}(T *left*, T *right*, T *bottom*, T *top*, T *near*, T *far*)

are used to set up the perspective projection matrix of Equation (2.35) or orthographic projection matrix of Equation (2.39), respectively. The last two arguments set the distance to the near and far frustum clipping planes, while the first four arguments describe where the viewing frustum intersects the near plane. The following example code sets up the projection matrix for a camera with *near* at 10, *far* at 60, with a WINDOW_WIDTH × WINDOW_HEIGHT window, and a 60° horizontal frustum opening angle:

```
GLfloat half_w, half_h, aspect;
/* window size from app or OS */
aspect = GLfloat( WINDOW_WIDTH ) / GLfloat( WINDOW_HEIGHT );
/* near * sin( angle / 2 ) = 10 * sin( 30 ) = 5 */
half_w = 5.0f;
half_h = half_w / aspect;
glMatrixMode( GL_PROJECTION );
glLoadIdentity();
glFrustum( -half_w, half_w, -half_h, half_h, 10, 60 );
/* good practice to leave in modelview mode, used more often */
glMatrixMode( GL_MODELVIEW );
```

8.2.2 TRANSFORMING NORMALS

As described in Section 2.2.4, normal vectors are not transformed using the same transformation as the vertices. OpenGL calculates the inverse transpose for the 3×3 upper left corner of the modelview matrix and applies the result to the normal vector.

The length of the normals may change during this process. However, if the modelview transformation is a rigid transformation, that is, it only consists of a rotation and a translation, and no scale or shear, it does not affect the length of the normal vector. By default OpenGL assumes this and does not normalize the vertex normals before applying the lighting equations.

However, if the modelview matrix includes a scaling component, the lengths do change. For example, if the model is scaled up the normals will shrink as the normals are transformed using the transposed inverse of the modelview matrix. The effect is that the objects appear surprisingly dark. If there is only uniform scaling, i.e., no nonuniform scales or shears, it is possible to calculate a correct rescaling factor from the modelview matrix, and apply that to all normals after the transformation. This is enabled by

```
glEnable( GL_RESCALE_NORMAL );
```

However, in general, if nonuniform scaling or shearing is included, or if the normals were not of unit length to start with, the normal vectors have to be normalized individually, by calculating their lengths and dividing the normal by the length. This is by far the most expensive option, and the geometry pipeline can be instructed to do it by

```
glEnable( GL_NORMALIZE );
```

8.2.3 TEXTURE COORDINATE TRANSFORMATION

The texture matrix mode is turned on with glMatrixMode(GL_TEXTURE), but as every texture unit has its own matrix, the active unit must first be specified with

```
void glActiveTexture(GLenum texture)
```

with *texture* being GL_TEXTUREi, where $0 \leq i <$ the value of GL_MAX_TEXTURE_ UNITS (see the example in Section 9.2.6).

After the texture matrix transformation, the *s* and *t* components of a texture coordinate are divided by the *q* component. The OpenGL ES specification does not require an implementation to do this division on a per-pixel basis—the implementation is allowed to do the division just once per vertex. Taking this shortcut may cause visible differences and artifacts between implementations. The transformed *r* coordinate is discarded, as three-dimensional textures are not supported in OpenGL ES.

While desktop OpenGL supports creation of texture coordinates, for example so that they come from the vertex locations in eye coordinates, or that they are set up for reflections, OpenGL ES does not have this mechanism. Instead, the application must set the appropriate texture coordinates itself. Some of the effects of the texture coordinate generation can be emulated by copying the vertex locations into texture coordinates, and then setting up the texture matrix appropriately.

Below is an example code that draws a simple fake glass object on the screen (see Figure 8.3 for a screenshot). The texture that is used for rendering the glass object is drawn as the background first:

```
static const GLbyte back_coords[] =
{
  1,1,
  1,0,
  0,1,
  0,0
};

static const GLfixed object_coords[] =
{
  ... normalized X,Y,Z coordinates ...
};

void render(void)
{
  glClear( GL_COLOR_BUFFER_BIT | GL_DEPTH_BUFFER_BIT );
```

Figure 8.3: Screen shot of the texture matrix manipulation example code. (Also in the color plate.)

```
/* draw background with two textured triangles */
glMatrixMode( GL_TEXTURE );
glLoadIdentity();
glMatrixMode( GL_PROJECTION );
glLoadIdentity();
glMatrixMode( GL_MODELVIEW );
glLoadIdentity();
glScalef( 2.f, -2.f, 0.f );
glTranslatef( -0.5f, -0.5f, 0.f );
glVertexPointer( 2, GL_BYTE, 0, back_coords );
glTexCoordPointer( 2, GL_BYTE, 0, back_coords );
glDrawArrays( GL_TRIANGLE_STRIP, 0, 4 );
```

Now the object in front is rendered. First the projection matrix is restored and modelview matrix is set so that the object rotates as time passes:

```
/* draw the object in front */
glMatrixMode( GL_PROJECTION );
glLoadIdentity();
glFrustumf( -1.f, 1.f, -1.f, 1.f, 3.f, 1000.f );

glMatrixMode( GL_MODELVIEW );
glLoadIdentity();
glTranslatef( 0, 0, -5.f) ;
glRotatef( time*25, 1.f, 1.f, 0.f );
glRotatef( time*15, 1.f, 0.f, 1.f );
```

The same normalized coordinate set is used as vertex coordinates and texture coordinates. The goal is to rotate the texture coordinates to the same orientation as the vertex coordinates and then use the resulting x and y components as the texture coordinates. This is accomplished by using the same rotation calls as for the modelview matrix and then scaling and translating the coordinates from $[-1,1]$ range to $[0,1]$ range:

```
glMatrixMode( GL_TEXTURE );
glLoadIdentity();
glTranslatef( 0.5f, 0.5f, 0.f );        /* [-0.5,0.5] -> [0,1]     */
glScalef( 0.5f, -0.5f, 0.f );           /* [-1,1]   -> [-0.5,0.5] */
glRotatef( time*25, 1.f, 1.f, 0.f );    /* same rotate calls */
glRotatef( time*15, 1.f, 0.f, 1.f);
glVertexPointer( 3, GL_FIXED, 0, object_coords );
glTexCoordPointer( 3, GL_FIXED, 0, object_coords );
glDrawArrays( GL_TRIANGLES, 0, 16*3 );
```

8.2.4 MATRIX STACKS

Section 2.3.3 introduced the concept of a matrix stack. For every type of matrix there is a corresponding matrix stack, into which a duplicate of the current matrix can be pushed and saved, and from which it can be restored by popping the stack. This is done using the following calls:

```
void glPushMatrix(void )
void glPopMatrix(void )
```

A common pattern is to use `glPushMatrix` to duplicate the top of the stack, then apply one of the matrix manipulation functions, perform rendering, and finally restore the stack to its original state by calling `glPopMatrix`. If the matrix stack becomes full, or you try to pop an empty stack, an error is raised. The modelview stack is guaranteed to be at least 16 elements deep, while the other stacks are guaranteed to be at least 2 elements deep.

8.2.5 VIEWPORT TRANSFORMATION

Two functions control how projected vertex coordinates are mapped into the window coordinates.

```
void glViewport(GLint x, GLint y, GLsizei width, GLsizei height)
```

controls the mapping on the x and y axes and determines the position and the size of the viewport rectangle. The window is initially set to match the size of the render surface. The function

```
void glDepthRange{fx}(T near, T far)
```

determines how the depth coordinates are mapped from the normalized device coordinate range of $[-1, +1]$ into the depth buffer values between 0 and 1. Initially the depth range is set to *near* = 0, *far* = 1, thus covering the range of the entire depth buffer.

Changing these values allows selecting only a subset of the depth buffer range. Here is an example showing how these functions are usually called:

```
glViewport( 0, 0, width, height );
glDepthRangef( 0.f, 1.f );
```

Section 2.6 gives several examples of clever use of `glDepthRange`.

8.2.6 USER CLIP PLANES

The standard transformation pipeline performs clipping of primitives into the canonical view frustum formed by the near, far, left, right, top, and bottom clipping planes. From OpenGL ES 1.1 onward, additional, user-defined clipping planes of arbitrary orientation are also supported. The minimum number of planes an implementation has to support is one, and not many implementations support more than this. The function

```
void glClipPlane{fx}(GLenum plane, const T * equation)
```

is used to define the four-component clipping plane equation. This equation, given in object coordinates, is immediately transformed to the eye coordinate space by multiplying it by the inverse transpose of the current modelview matrix (see Section 3.3.2). The *plane* must be `GL_CLIP_PLANEi` where $0 \leq i <$ `GL_MAX_CLIP_PLANES` are accepted. The clip plane needs to be enabled by `glEnable( GL_CLIP_PLANE0 )`.

8.3 COLORS AND LIGHTING

In this section, we describe the OpenGL ES calls that are required to enable correct lighting. The principles of color and lighting are described in Section 3.2.

8.3.1 SPECIFYING COLORS AND MATERIALS

We have already described the way colors are specified in OpenGL in Section 8.1.2: either all vertices get the same default color set by

```
void glColor4{fx ub}(T red, T green, T blue, T alpha)
```

or each vertex gets an individual color using

```
void glColorPointer(GLint size, GLenum type, GLsizei stride, GLvoid * pointer).
```

If lighting has not been turned on by calling `glEnable( GL_LIGHTING )`, the vertices retain the literal colors they are assigned. However, if lighting is enabled, the surfaces need *material properties*. Section 3.2.3 describes the various material components: *ambient*, *diffuse*, *specular*, and *emissive*. They can be defined by calling

```
void glMaterial{fx}v(GL_FRONT_AND_BACK, GLenum pname, const T * params)
```

where *params* must be a pointer to an array with at least four elements, interpreted as red, green, blue, and alpha values, and *pname* must be one of the following values (the value in parentheses is the corresponding default color):

GL_AMBIENT   (0.2, 0.2, 0.2, 1.0)
GL_DIFFUSE   (0.8, 0.8, 0.8, 1.0)
GL_SPECULAR   (0.0, 0.0, 0.0, 1.0)
GL_EMISSIVE   (0.0, 0.0, 0.0, 1.0)

It is also possible to use GL_AMBIENT_AND_DIFFUSE to set both the ambient and the diffuse component at once to the same value. Note that the material values do not have to lie within [0, 1]. However, the final colors at each vertex, after lighting but prior to rasterization, are clamped to [0, 1]. Whereas in desktop OpenGL one may assign different materials to the front and the back sides of a surface, OpenGL ES only allows the same material on both sides. Therefore, the first argument must always be set to GL_FRONT_AND_BACK.

The shininess of the specular reflectance can be set by calling

    void glMaterial{fx}(GL_FRONT_AND_BACK, GL_SHININESS, T *param*)

where *param* must be in the range [0, 128] and defaults to 0.

It is also possible for individual vertices to have different materials. If you call glEnable (GL_COLOR_MATERIAL) the vertex color array values (set by glColorPointer) are copied into the ambient and the diffuse material components. The specular and the emissive components are not affected by color material.

The handling of colors and materials in OpenGL ES is simplified from that of desktop OpenGL. The second color model, indexed colors, was considered to be a relic not very compatible with modern 3D graphics, and was left out. The desktop version also allows other components than the ambient and the diffuse to be copied from vertex colors, and provides specular shading using a secondary color applied after texture mapping. Such advanced lighting effects are better done using multitexturing effects in OpenGL ES.

8.3.2 LIGHTS

OpenGL ES supports at least eight light sources. The exact number that is supported can be queried by getting the value of GL_MAX_LIGHTS. Each light is disabled by default, and to use a light it must be first enabled by calling, e.g., glEnable(GL_LIGHT0). Additionally, lighting must be enabled by a call to glEnable(GL_LIGHTING).

Lights have various properties described in Section 3.2.4. They have ambient, diffuse, and specular light colors, which have four (red, green, blue, alpha) components. They have a four-component position where the positional and directional lights are defined by the last component (zero for directional, non-zero for positional). A spot light may have a three-component direction as well as single-component exponents for intensity distribution control and for the setting the directional cutoff. Finally, the three attenuation coefficients can be defined.

The single-valued light components (such as GL_LIGHT0) are set by calling

    void glLight{fx}(GLenum *light*, GLenum *pname*, T *param*)

where the *pname*s and their default values are

    GL_SPOT_EXPONENT   0
    GL_SPOT_CUTOFF   180
    GL_CONSTANT_ATTENUATION   1
    GL_LINEAR_ATTENUATION   0
    GL_QUADRATIC_ATTENUATION   0

and multiple components are set by calling

    void glLight{fx}v(GLenum *light*, GLenum *pname*, const T * *params*)

where the *pname*s and their default values are

    GL_AMBIENT   (0, 0, 0, 1)
    GL_DIFFUSE   (1, 1, 1, 1) for GL_LIGHT0, (0,0,0,0) for others
    GL_SPECULAR   (1, 1, 1, 1) for GL_LIGHT0, (0,0,0,0) for others
    GL_POSITION   (0, 0, 1, 0)
    GL_SPOT_DIRECTION   (0, 0, −1)

The ambient, diffuse, and specular colors are quite straightforward to use. They can have arbitrary values, and after Equation (3.3) has been applied, the result for each color channel is clamped to [0, 1] range.

Keeping the attenuation components in their default values (1, 0, 0) in practice disables light attenuation. For more discussion about light attenuation see Section 3.2.4.

The light position is by default at (0, 0, 1, 0), i.e., infinitely far in the positive *z*-direction, making it a directional light source shining toward the negative *z*-direction. The position, when set, is transformed using the current modelview matrix and stored in eye coordinates. If the modelview matrix is identity when the position is set, it means that the light shines from behind the camera, to the viewing direction of the camera. To place the light at the camera, for example, place the light to (0, 0, 0, 1) in the eye coordinates.

Here is a simple example where one light is in the world coordinate system and one is attached to the camera coordinate system:

```
{
  GLfloat lightpos_0[4] = { 0.5f, 0.5f, 0.0f, 1.f };
  GLfloat lightpos_1[4] = { 0.f,  0.f,  0.f,  1.f };

  /* light 1 is fixed to camera (modelview is identity == camera) */
  glLoadIdentity();
  glLightfv( GL_LIGHT1, GL_POSITION, lightpos_1 );
  /* light 0 is in world coordinate system */
  glRotatef( 10, 1.f, 0.f, 0.f );          /* view rotate */
```

```
   glTranslatef( 0, -1.3f, -5.f );         /* view translate */
   glLightfv( GL_LIGHT0, GL_POSITION, lightpos_0 );
   glTranslatef( -1.f, 0.f, 0.f );         /* model translate */
   glScalef( 0.5f, 0.5f, 0.5f );           /* model scale */
   glDrawArrays( GL_TRIANGLES, 0, 512*3 );
}
```

If the spot cutoff angle is 180°, it means there is no cutoff, and the light is a point light shining to every direction, unless it is a directional light infinitely far away shining only to the opposite direction. Otherwise, only values within [0, 90] degrees are allowed. This is the angle around the spot direction where the light is shining. The value 5 would mean that only directions that differ from the spot direction by no more than 5° will receive the light, the total cone opening angle being twice that, i.e., 10°. The spot light exponent is explained in Section 3.2.4. The value 0 means that there is no directional attenuation to the light intensity. The default spot direction of $(0, 0, -1)$, in eye coordinates, means that the light points in the direction in which the camera is looking.

Even though every light may have its own ambient component, there is an implicitly defined global ambient light source. By default its color is $(0.2, 0.2, 0.2, 1)$, and its value can be changed by calling

```
   void glLightModel{fx}v(GL_LIGHT_MODEL_AMBIENT, const T * param),
```

where *param* points to an RGBA color.

8.3.3 TWO-SIDED LIGHTING

By default only the front side of a surface is illuminated by lights. However, it is possible to toggle between two-sided and single-sided lighting by calling

```
   void glLightModel{fx}(GL_LIGHT_MODEL_TWO_SIDE, T param).
```

With a non-zero value in *param* (typically GL_TRUE) you get two-sided lighting, with the value of a zero (or GL_FALSE) you get single-sided lighting. With two-sided lighting, the normals n on the back side are replaced by $-n$.

The vertex ordering determines which side is considered to be the front and which side is the back. By default, counterclockwise order defines the front side of a triangle. That is, if an ant walks around a triangle so that its left side is toward the triangle, and it visits the vertices in order, the ant is on the front side of the triangle. The definition of the front side can be changed by calling

```
   void glFrontFace(GLenum mode)
```

with *mode* either GL_CW or GL_CCW to indicate clockwise and counterclockwise respectively.

8.3.4 SHADING

OpenGL ES supports two shading models: flat and smooth (Gouraud) shading. Flat shading uses a single constant color, whereas smooth shading interpolates the vertex color values (either from the direct color, or the result of illuminating the surface material) within the triangle. The shading model can be changed by calling

```
void glShadeModel(GLenum mode)
```

with *mode* set to GL_SMOOTH (default) or GL_FLAT.

When flat shading is used, it is the last vertex of the primitive that defines the color of the whole primitive. Obviously, for point primitives both shading types produce the same result.

The flat shading model is somewhat awkward to use, and does not usually give the result one might expect as the lighting is calculated using only a single vertex and a single normal per triangle. Even if the faceted look of a polygonal object is desired, you might well use smooth shading and represent the model so that individual triangles have their own vertices and normals. In a typical triangle mesh there are about twice as many vertices than faces, so in order to give each face a unique normal some of the vertices need to be replicated in any case.

8.3.5 LIGHTING EXAMPLE

Here is an extended example on how to set up lighting and materials.

```
static const GLfloat dark_red[4]    = { 0.2f, 0.0f, 0.0f, 1.f };
static const GLfloat dark_gray[4]   = { 0.1f, 0.1f, 0.1f, 1.f };
static const GLfloat white[4]       = { 1.f,  1.f,  1.f,  1.f };
static const GLfloat red_transp[4]  = { 1.f,  0.f,  0.f,  0.f };
static const GLfloat blueish[4]     = { 0.1f, 0.4f, 1.f,  1.f };
static const GLfloat black[4]       = { 0.f,  0.f,  0.f,  1.f };

/* Position at z = +inf creates a directional light toward neg z */
static const GLfloat dir_light[4]  = { 0.f, 0.f, 1.0f, 0.f };
/* Place a spot light close to camera (up and right) */
static const GLfloat spot_light[4] = { 5.f, 5.f, 0.f, 1.f };
/* Direct the spot diagonally down to front of camera */
static const GLfloat spot_dir[3]   = { -1.f, -1.f, -1.f };

/* First disable all lights */
for( i = 0; i < 8; i++ ) glDisable( GL_LIGHT0 + i );

/* Set up the lights in camera coordinates */
glMatrixMode( GL_MODELVIEW );
glLoadIdentity();
```

```
/* Scene ambient light and single-sided lighting */
glLightModelfv( GL_LIGHT_MODEL_AMBIENT,  dark_red );
glLightModelf(  GL_LIGHT_MODEL_TWO_SIDE, GL_FALSE );

/* Set up the directional light */
glLightfv( GL_LIGHT0, GL_POSITION, dir_light );
glLightfv( GL_LIGHT0, GL_AMBIENT,  dark_gray );
glLightfv( GL_LIGHT0, GL_DIFFUSE,  white );
glLightfv( GL_LIGHT0, GL_SPECULAR, red_transp )
glLightf(  GL_LIGHT0, GL_CONSTANT_ATTENUATION,  1.f );
glLightf(  GL_LIGHT0, GL_LINEAR_ATTENUATION,    0.f );
glLightf(  GL_LIGHT0, GL_QUADRATIC_ATTENUATION, 0.f );
glLightf(  GL_LIGHT0, GL_SPOT_CUTOFF,    180.f );

/* Set up the spot light */
glLightfv( GL_LIGHT1, GL_POSITION, spot_light );
glLightfv( GL_LIGHT1, GL_AMBIENT,  white );
glLightfv( GL_LIGHT1, GL_DIFFUSE,  white );
glLightfv( GL_LIGHT1, GL_SPECULAR, white )
glLightf(  GL_LIGHT1, GL_CONSTANT_ATTENUATION,  0.f );
glLightf(  GL_LIGHT1, GL_LINEAR_ATTENUATION,    1.f );
glLightf(  GL_LIGHT1, GL_QUADRATIC_ATTENUATION, 0.f );
glLightf(  GL_LIGHT1, GL_SPOT_CUTOFF,    40.f );
glLightf(  GL_LIGHT1, GL_SPOT_EXPONENT,  10.f );
glLightfv( GL_LIGHT1, GL_SPOT_DIRECTION, spot_dir );

/* Set up materials */
glMaterialfv( GL_FRONT_AND_BACK, GL_AMBIENT, blueish );
glMaterialfv( GL_FRONT_AND_BACK, GL_DIFFUSE, blueish );
glMaterialfv( GL_FRONT_AND_BACK, GL_SPECULAR, red_transp );
glMaterialfv( GL_FRONT_AND_BACK, GL_EMISSION, black );
glMaterialf(  GL_FRONT_AND_BACK, GL_SHININESS, 15.f );

/* Don't forget to normalize normals! Faster if already normalized. */
glDisable( GL_NORMALIZE );

glEnable( GL_LIGHT0 );
glEnable( GL_LIGHT1 );
glEnable( GL_LIGHTING );

/* We use normalized coordinates -> can be used also as normals */
glVertexPointer( 3, GL_FIXED, 0, vertices );
glNormalPointer( GL_FIXED, 0, vertices );
glEnableClientState( GL_VERTEX_ARRAY );
glEnableClientState( GL_NORMAL_ARRAY );

glDrawArrays( GL_TRIANGLES, 0, 512*3 );
```

OPENGL ES RASTERIZATION AND FRAGMENT PROCESSING

This chapter covers everything that happens after the transformation and lighting pipeline. First the primitives are clipped and culled, and the surviving ones are rasterized into fragments. Clipping has already been described in Section 3.3 and will not be repeated here. Texture-mapping, if enabled, is applied to each fragment, and the rest of the fragment pipeline is executed: fog and antialiasing, followed by the alpha, depth, and stencil tests. Finally, the various buffers (color, depth, stencil) are updated. The color buffer updates may use blending or logical operations.

9.1 BACK-FACE CULLING

Back-face culling is used to discard triangles that are facing away from the viewer. This is a useful optimization as roughly half of the triangles of an opaque closed mesh are hidden by the front-facing ones. Culling these early in the pipeline increases the rendering performance. Culling is controlled globally by `glEnable` and `glDisable` using `GL_CULL_FACE` as the argument. Culling affects only triangles; points and lines are never back-face culled.

The user may select which face should be culled by calling

    void glCullFace(GLenum *mode*)

with either GL_FRONT, GL_BACK, or GL_FRONT_AND_BACK as the argument. The last token culls all triangles. Which side of a triangle is considered to be the front is defined using glFrontFace, described in Section 8.3.3.

Culling is conceptually performed during the triangle setup, just prior to rasterization. However, implementations may choose to do this already earlier in the pipeline, and potentially be able to skip, e.g., lighting calculations, for the culled triangles.

By default culling is disabled. The following example enables culling for the clockwise-oriented faces:

```
glFrontFace( GL_CCW );
glEnable( GL_CULL_FACE );
glCullFace( GL_BACK );
```

9.2 TEXTURE MAPPING

Texture mapping plays a fundamental part in the OpenGL ES rendering pipeline. Although the texturing model is slightly simplified from the desktop, it is still a very powerful mechanism that allows many interesting effects. Texturing is conceptually performed during rasterization and prior to the rest of the fragment pipeline. However, some implementations may internally postpone it until after the depth and stencil tests to avoid texturing fragments that would be discarded by these tests. Texturing for the currently active texture unit is enabled or disabled with the GL_TEXTURE_2D flag.

9.2.1 TEXTURE OBJECTS

Texture maps are stored in texture objects. The idea is that you first create a texture object, and then set up the various values that relate to the texture, e.g., the bitmap image to use, or the filtering and blending modes. Finally, just before drawing the primitives, you activate the relevant texture object.

Each texture object is referred by a *texture name* which acts as a handle for texture data and state. The name can be any positive integer (zero is reserved and refers to the default texture). You can ask the driver to provide you a list of unused names with

```
void glGenTextures(GLsizei n, GLuint * textures)
```

which returns *n* new names, stored in the array *textures*. To create a new texture object, or to reactivate a previously created one, call

```
void glBindTexture(GL_TEXTURE_2D, GLuint texture)
```

where *texture* is the name of the texture object. In desktop OpenGL other targets, such as 1D and 3D textures are possible, but OpenGL ES only supports two-dimensional textures.

When a texture map is no longer needed, the resources consumed by it should be freed. This is done by a call to

```
void glDeleteTextures(GLsizei n, const GLuint * textures)
```

which deletes the *n* textures in the array *textures*. If any of these textures is currently bound to one of the texturing units, that unit will have the default texture object (texture 0) assigned to it. Note that in a multi-context environment where different GL contexts share textures, the resources are freed only when a texture is not actively used in any of the contexts.

As a summary, the following code shows a typical pattern of how texture objects are used:

```
GLuint tex_handle[2];
glGenTextures( 2, &tex_handle[0] );
/* set up the textures */
glBindTexture( GL_TEXTURE_2D, tex_handle[0] );
/* specify texture data, filtering, etc. */
glTexImage2D( ... );
...
glBindTexture( GL_TEXTURE_2D, tex_handle[1] );
glTexImage2D( ... );
...
/* now ready to draw, reactivate one of the objects */
glEnable( GL_TEXTURE_2D );
glBindTexture( GL_TEXTURE_2D, tex_handle[1] );
glDrawArrays( ... );
glDisable( GL_TEXTURE_2D );
...
/* release the resources when not needed any longer */
glDeleteTextures( 2, &tex_handle[0] );
```

9.2.2 SPECIFYING TEXTURE DATA

In OpenGL ES the texture image data is managed by the server, which means that the data needs to be copied to it from the client. At this time the image data is usually converted into the internal format best suited for texture mapping. Since both the copy and conversion operations take time, a texture should be created once and used multiple times before being deleted.

```
void glTexImage2D(GL_TEXTURE_2D, GLint level, GLenum internalformat,
                  GLsizei width, GLsizei height, GLint border, GLenum format,
                  GLenum type, const GLvoid * pixels)
```

copies texture image data from client-side memory to the server-side texture object. If mipmapping is not used, or this image is the base mipmap level, *level* should be zero (see Section 9.2.3 for mipmapping and levels). Since OpenGL ES does not support texture borders, the value of *border* must be 0. The dimensions of the texture, in pixels, are given by *width* and *height*, and they have to be powers of two (1, 2, 4, …, 512, 1024, …) but they do not have to be the same (for example 32 × 64 is a valid size). The two format parameters, *internalformat* and *format*, must be the same, and they must be one of the formats in the table below. The table also lists the data *types* that can be matched with the formats. The numbers that are part of a token tell how many bits are allocated to each of the R, G, B, and A channels. *pixels* contains a pointer to the data, the first data row corresponds to the bottom texel row.

Only byte-based data types work the same way on all platforms, as short-based data types are interpreted according to the native platform endianess. Short-based texture data is accessed by the GL implementation as if it were accessed through a native short integer pointer. If the texture data comes from a data file that was stored using the other endianess, texture data must be byte-swapped before any texture upload functions are used. See Table 9.2.

If *pixels* is *NULL*, the server will reserve memory to hold the image data but no image data is copied. The data can be subsequently loaded by using

```
void glTexSubImage2D(GL_TEXTURE_2D, GLint level, GLint xoffset, GLint yoffset,
                     GLsizei width, GLsizei height, GLenum format, GLenum type,
                     const GLvoid * pixels)
```

which updates a subimage within a previously defined texture image. Parameters *level*, *format*, *type*, and *pixels* are the same as for glTexImage2D, and the format needs to

Table 9.1: Texture formats and types.

Texture Format	Data type
GL_LUMINANCE	GL_UNSIGNED_BYTE
GL_ALPHA	GL_UNSIGNED_BYTE
GL_LUMINANCE_ALPHA	GL_UNSIGNED_BYTE
GL_RGB	GL_UNSIGNED_BYTE
	GL_UNSIGNED_SHORT_5_6_5
GL_RGBA	GL_UNSIGNED_BYTE
	GL_UNSIGNED_SHORT_4_4_4_4
	GL_UNSIGNED_SHORT_5_5_5_1

Table 9.2: Endianess in a data file.

Byte Offset	0	1
Texel	0	0
Big Endian	HI: $R_4R_3R_2R_1R_0G_5G_4G_3$	LO: $G_2G_1G_0B_4B_3B_2B_1B_0$
Little Endian	LO: $G_2G_1G_0B_4B_3B_2B_1B_0$	HI: $R_4R_3R_2R_1R_0G_5G_4G_3$

match the original format of the texture map. The lower left corner is at (*xoffset*, *yoffset*) for the *width* × *height* subimage.

The pixel data is copied from the memory block pointed by *pixels*. By default each row of pixels must be aligned to a word boundary, i.e., the alignment must be to an even 4 bytes. The alignment can be changed by

    void glPixelStorei(GL_UNPACK_ALIGNMENT, GLint *param*)

where the allowed values for *param* are 1 (byte-alignment), 2 (rows aligned to even-numbered bytes), 4 (word alignment), and 8 (rows start on double-word boundaries). If your pixel data is continuous, setting the alignment to 1 will always work, but may be slower for unaligned image data.

As OpenGL ES only supports power-of-two texture maps and there is no support for GL_PACK_ROW_LENGTH and GL_PACK_SKIP_PIXELS for glPixelStorei, there is no way to copy a general image that does not have power-of-two dimensions into a texture directly. There are two ways around this problem. The first one is to allocate a memory buffer and to copy power-of-two subpieces of image data into it, then call glTexSubImage2D to construct the texture from these pieces. Another way is to allocate the next larger power-of-two buffer and to copy the original image into a subregion of this buffer, then load the texture data using a single call to glTexImage2D. Which one is faster depends on the texture upload performance and size of the texture, e.g., if the source image size is 260 × 260, the next power of two size is 512 × 512 which would almost quadruple the amount of data to be transferred.

Copying from the frame buffer

If you first render an image that you would like to use as a texture map, you can copy it directly from the frame buffer. Since both the texture maps and the frame buffer reside on the server, i.e., the graphics subsystem, doing the whole operation on the server can be much more efficient than reading the color buffer to the client and then copying the data back to the server using glTexImage2D.

    void glCopyTexImage2D(GL_TEXTURE_2D, GLint *level*, GLenum *internalformat*, GLint *x*,
                          GLint *y*, GLsizei *width*, GLsizei *height*, GLint *border*)

copies a *width* × *height* block of pixels with a lower left corner at (*x*, *y*) in the color buffer into the currently bound texture. The *level*, *internalformat*, and *border* arguments are identical to those of glTexImage. The parameter *internalformat* must be compatible with the color buffer format according to Table 9.3.

Note, however, that glCopyTexImage2D has to flush the graphics pipeline and complete all previous graphics calls, so calling it in the middle of a rendering pass may have a negative performance impact.

Table 9.3: Texture formats compatible with the color buffer formats.

Color Buffer	Texture Format				
	GL_ALPHA	GL_LUMINANCE	GL_LUMINANCE_ALPHA	GL_RGB	GL_RGBA
A	√	—	—	—	—
L	—	√	—	—	—
LA	√	√	√	—	—
RGB	—	√	—	√	—
RGBA	√	√	√	√	√

> void glCopyTexSubImage2D(GL_TEXTURE_2D, GLint *level*, GLint *xoffset*, GLint
> *yoffset*, GLint *x*, GLint *y*, GLsizei *width*,
> GLsizei *height*)

is a variant that takes a screen-aligned *width* × *height* pixel rectangle with lower left corner at (x, y), and replaces a block of the same size in the texture map, with lower left corner at (*xoffset*, *yoffset*).

Compressed texture formats

In order to save texture memory, OpenGL ES supports the concept of *compressed texture formats*. Currently the only supported format uses paletted textures, which contain a palette of colors in the header, followed by a sequence of indices into the palette, one index for each texel. The indices can either use 4-bit indexing for 16 colors, or 8-bit indexing for 256 colors. The palette entries can be either RGB colors stored in 888 or 565 formats, or RGBA colors stored using 8888, 4444, or 5551 formats.

> void glCompressedTexImage2D(GL_TEXTURE_2D, GLint *level*, GLenum *internalformat*,
> GLsizei *width*, GLsizei *height*, GLint *border*,
> GLsizei *imageSize*, const GLvoid * *data*)

is similar to glTexImage2D except that *imageSize* gives the length of *data*, the compressed client-side image data. *internalformat* indicates the format of the compressed data and has to be one of

```
GL_PALETTE4_RGB8_OES,          GL_PALETTE8_RGB8_OES,
GL_PALETTE4_R5_G6_B5_OES,      GL_PALETTE8_R5_G6_B5_OES,
GL_PALETTE4_RGBA8_OES,         GL_PALETTE8_RGBA8_OES,
GL_PALETTE4_RGBA4_OES,         GL_PALETTE8_RGBA4_OES,
GL_PALETTE4_RGB5_A1_OES,       GL_PALETTE8_RGB5_A1_OES.
```

The *level* may be zero if the texture contains only the base level. A negative number indicates the number of mipmap levels in the texture (see the next section about texture filtering).

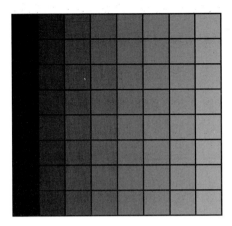

Figure 9.1: Level 0 of the texture in a grid.

An implementation may support other, proprietary compressed texture formats as extensions. Those formats may compress better and provide more colors than paletted textures, but they are less portable as they are not universally supported.

The specification defines an entry point for

```
void glCompressedTexSubImage2D(GL_TEXTURE_2D, GLint level, GLint xoffset,
                               GLint yoffset, GLsizei width, GLsizei height,
                               GLenum format, GLsizei imageSize, const
                               GLvoid * pixels),
```

but currently there are no Khronos-specified formats that support this. The reason is that most implementations expand the paletted texture immediately (and possibly recompress using a proprietary internal format), and being able to update subimages would require also storing the palette and format, creating additional memory overhead.

The following example creates a paletted texture. The colors are 32-bit RGBA, 16 of them are stored in the beginning of the texture map. The base mipmap level is 8 × 8 texels, so the palette is followed by $8 \cdot 8/2 = 32$ bytes of 4-bit indices. The PALTEX macro packs two such indices into a single unsigned byte. The texture contains also 3 mipmap levels (4 × 4, 2 × 2, and 1 × 1). The decompressed texture looks like that in Figure 9.1. For more details about mipmapping, see the next section.

```
#define PALTEX(left,right) ((left << 4) | (right))

static const GLubyte palette_texture[] =
{
    /* 16-entry palette with 32bpp colors */
    0, 0, 0,255,    10,10,10,255,    20,20,20,255,    30,30,30,255,
    40,40,40,255,    50,50,50,255,    60,60,60,255,    70,70,70,255,
```

```
   80,80,80,255,   90,90,90,255,   100,100,100,255, 110,110,110,255,
   120,120,120,255, 130,130,130,255, 140,140,140,255, 150,150,150,255,

   /* mipmap level 0 (base) is (8x8), one palette index is 4 bits */
   PALTEX(0,2), PALTEX(4,6), PALTEX(8,10), PALTEX(12,14),
   PALTEX(0,2), PALTEX(4,6), PALTEX(8,10), PALTEX(12,14),
   PALTEX(0,2), PALTEX(4,6), PALTEX(8,10), PALTEX(12,14),
   PALTEX(0,2), PALTEX(4,6), PALTEX(8,10), PALTEX(12,14),
   PALTEX(0,2), PALTEX(4,6), PALTEX(8,10), PALTEX(12,14),
   PALTEX(0,2), PALTEX(4,6), PALTEX(8,10), PALTEX(12,14),
   PALTEX(0,2), PALTEX(4,6), PALTEX(8,10), PALTEX(12,14),
   PALTEX(0,2), PALTEX(4,6), PALTEX(8,10), PALTEX(12,14),

   /* mipmap level 1 is 4x4 */
   PALTEX(1,5), PALTEX(9,13),
   PALTEX(1,5), PALTEX(9,13),
   PALTEX(1,5), PALTEX(9,13),
   PALTEX(1,5), PALTEX(9,13),

   /* mipmap level 2 is 2x2 */
   PALTEX(3,11),
   PALTEX(3,11),

   /* the last mipmap level (3) is 1x1 */
   PALTEX(7,7)
};
...


/***************************************************
 * Prepare compressed texture.
 * |level|+1 is the number of mipmap levels.
 * Here we have: |-3|+1 = 4 levels.
 ***************************************************/

glGenTextures( 1, &texture_handle );
glBindTexture( GL_TEXTURE_2D, texture_handle );
glCompressedTexImage2D( GL_TEXTURE_2D, -3, GL_PALETTE4_RGBA8_OES,
                        8, 8, 0, sizeof(palette_texture),
                        palette_texture );
```

9.2.3 TEXTURE FILTERING

The basic ideas in texture filtering were introduced in Section 3.4.1 and illustrated in Figure 3.13. The texture coordinates are interpolated for each fragment within a primitive. The coordinates are interpreted so that 0 at the first component (s) maps to the left side of the first texel on a given row of the texture map, and 1.0 maps to the right side of the last texel on that row. The row is determined by the t-coordinate, 0 corresponding to the bottom of the bottom row, and 1.0 to the top of the top row. The texture fetch and filtering machinery then has to come up with a filtered color value from the texture map.

Basic filtering modes

The basic filtering choices are *point sampling* and *linear interpolation*. Point sampling simply returns the value of the texel nearest to the interpolated texture coordinate, while linear interpolation takes a weighted average of the neighboring texel values. These filtering modes can be set separately for *magnification* where one texel maps to several pixels and for *minification* where several texels map to a single pixel. They can be set by calling

```
void glTexParameter{ifx}( GL_TEXTURE_2D, GLenum pname, T param)
void glTexParameter{ifx}v( GL_TEXTURE_2D, GLenum pname, const T * param)
```

where *pname* is either GL_TEXTURE_MAG_FILTER or GL_TEXTURE_MIN_FILTER and *param* is either GL_NEAREST or GL_LINEAR.

Mipmap specification

If a drastic minification is required, that is, a large number of texels would project to a single pixel, neither of those sampling approaches works well. The selection of which texel (or the interpolation of which four texels) is used would essentially be random. This would create both visual artifacts and result in inefficient memory access patterns. *Mipmapping* provides a solution by providing prefiltered texture maps that can be chosen so that the pixel-texel size ratio is sufficiently close to one.

There are three ways of specifying mipmaps: give them one level at a time for regular textures, ask the system to automatically generate them (from OpenGL ES 1.1 onward), or provide them all at once for compressed textures.

If the levels are given one at a time, they are given with glTexImage2D and other related commands using the parameter *level*. The base level is zero, while level 1 needs to be half the size both in width and height, unless one of them is already 1. As an example, for a 64 × 32 texture the level 1 mipmap is 32 × 16, level 2 is 16 × 8, and so on until level 5 is 2 × 1 and the final level 6 is a 1 × 1 texture. The texture will not be *complete* until all mipmaps have been given, they have correct sizes as described above, and the texture formats of the different levels match. Incomplete texture behaves as if texturing was disabled for the texture units where the texture is bound.

OpenGL ES 1.1 supports automatic generation of mipmap levels. The levels are typically obtained by averaging four texels at a finer level to create one texel at a coarser level. Automatic mipmap level generation is not enabled by default, but can be enabled with

```
glTexParameteri( GL_TEXTURE_2D, GL_GENERATE_MIPMAP, GL_TRUE );
```

and disabled with

```
glTexParameteri( GL_TEXTURE_2D, GL_GENERATE_MIPMAP, GL_FALSE );
```

When automatic mipmap generation is activated, the server automatically recomputes the contents of all mipmap levels whenever the base level is updated.

> **Pitfall:** Implementations may free the automatically generated mipmap levels when `GL_GENERATE_MIPMAP` is disabled to save memory. Toggling this parameter on/off may slow down rendering considerably.

The mipmap levels of compressed textures are specified in yet another way. They cannot be generated automatically, and with paletted textures all levels have to be given at once. The *level* argument of `glCompressedTexImage2D` is 0 if only the base level is given, whereas a negative number tells how many mipmap levels are given in the *data* argument. For example, for a texture map where the base is 64 × 32, *levels* must be −6. The example on page 202 illustrates this concept. More generally, the extension specification states for a given texture compression format how the mipmap levels are handled.

Mipmap filtering modes

There are several additional filtering modes available for mipmapping, and they are set with

```
glTexParameteri( GL_TEXTURE_2D, GL_TEXTURE_MIN_FILTER,
                 GL_X_MIPMAP_Y );
```

where you replace `X` and `Y` with either `NEAREST` or `LINEAR`. Specifying `X` to be `NEAREST` means that *within one mipmap level* point sampling will be used, whereas `LINEAR` means that the texel values will be interpolated. Specifying `Y` selects interpolation *across mipmap levels*: `NEAREST` means that only the mipmap level where texels most closely match the pixel size is selected, while `LINEAR` means that two closest-matching mipmap levels are chosen and evaluated separately (using the `X` setting), and the results are finally linearly interpolated. To clarify,

```
glTexParameteri( GL_TEXTURE_2D, GL_TEXTURE_MIN_FILTER,
                 GL_LINEAR_MIPMAP_LINEAR );
```

would perform a full tri-linear filtering whereas

```
glTexParameteri( GL_TEXTURE_2D, GL_TEXTURE_MIN_FILTER,
                 GL_LINEAR_MIPMAP_NEAREST );
```

would just take the closest mipmap level and perform a bilinear filtering on that. Depending on the mode, either 1, 2, 4, or 8 texels will be averaged together.

Recall that mipmapping relates only to minification, as magnification always operates using the highest-resolution mipmap level and you may only choose either `GL_NEAREST` or `GL_LINEAR` to be used as its filter.

Texture filtering can be an expensive operation, especially for a software implementation of OpenGL ES. Typically point sampling is faster than bilinear filtering, and picking the closest mipmap level is less expensive than filtering between two levels. Typically bilinear filtering is as fast as point sampling with hardware rasterizers, at least if only one texture unit is used. The use of mipmaps is *always* a good idea for *both* performance and visual quality, since accessing the coarser mipmap levels reduces the texel fetch bandwidth, improves texture cache coherency, and provides higher-quality filtering.

9.2.4 TEXTURE WRAP MODES

OpenGL ES supports two texture addressing modes: GL_CLAMP_TO_EDGE and GL_REPEAT. GL_CLAMP_TO_EDGE clamps the texture coordinates to $[min, max]$ where $min = 1/(2N)$ and $max = 1 - min$, and N is either the width or height of the texture map. The effect is that texture coordinates that would map to the left of the center of the first texel (in s direction) are clamped to the center of that texel. Similar clamping is applied to coordinates mapping to the right of the center of the last texel. Negative coordinates, or coordinates greater than 1.0, thus fetch a boundary texel. This effect is illustrated in Figure 3.12 (b).

The effect of GL_REPEAT is shown in Figure 3.12 (c). If the texture coordinate at a fragment is outside the [0,1] range, the coordinates are *wrapped* so that the integer part is ignored, and only the fractional part is used to access the texel data. The fractional part of f is defined as $f - \lfloor f \rfloor$ regardless of the sign of f. Let us analyze a 1D situation (not related to Figure 3.12) where one triangle vertex has $s = -0.7$ and the neighboring vertex has $s = 3.0$. The initial -0.7 becomes $-0.7 - (-1) = 0.3$, and as you travel from the first vertex toward the next one, as -0.7 grows toward 0.0, the wrapped coordinate grows from 0.3 toward 1.0. Once the interpolated s reaches 0.0, the wrapped version also repeats from 0.0. This is repeated twice more, at 1.0 and 2.0. The end result is that the texture map repeats 3.7 times between the two vertices.

The wrap modes are set separately for s and t coordinates as follows:

```
glTexParameteri( GL_TEXTURE_2D, GL_TEXTURE_WRAP_S,
                 GL_CLAMP_TO_EDGE );
glTexParameteri( GL_TEXTURE_2D, GL_TEXTURE_WRAP_T, GL_REPEAT );
```

9.2.5 BASIC TEXTURE FUNCTIONS

Each fragment gets a color that is interpolated from the vertex colors. This is combined with the texture source color (obtained through filtering as described above), and a user-given constant color, using one of the functions GL_REPLACE, GL_MODULATE, GL_DECAL, GL_BLEND, or GL_ADD. The details of how these functions work are described in Section 3.4.1. The functions are selected like this:

```
glTexEnvi( GL_TEXTURE_ENV, GL_TEXTURE_ENV_MODE, GL_MODULATE );
```

and the constant color is given like this:

```
glTexEnvfv( GL_TEXTURE_ENV, GL_TEXTURE_ENV_COLOR, color );
```

where color points to a float array storing the RGBA color.

We have now covered enough texture mapping features to show an example that completely sets up a texture object with mipmapping, filtering, and wrapping modes. `texture_data_base` is a pointer to an 8 × 8 texture map data, while `texture_data_mip_1` through `texture_data_mip_3` point to smaller prefiltered versions of the same texture map.

```
glEnable( GL_TEXTURE_2D );
glGenTextures( 1, &tex_handle );
glBindTexture( GL_TEXTURE_2D,  tex_handle );
ver = glGetString( GL_VERSION );

if( ver[strlen(ver)−1] > '0' )
{
  /* the minor version is at least 1, autogenerate mipmaps */
  glHint( GL_GENERATE_MIPMAP_HINT, GL_NICEST );
  glTexParameteri( GL_TEXTURE_2D, GL_GENERATE_MIPMAP, GL_TRUE );
  glTexImage2D( GL_TEXTURE_2D, 0, GL_RGBA, 8, 8, 0, GL_RGBA,
                GL_UNSIGNED_BYTE, texture_data_base );
}
else
{
  /* OpenGL ES 1.0, specify levels one at a time */
  glTexImage2D( GL_TEXTURE_2D, 0, GL_RGBA, 8, 8, 0, GL_RGBA,
                GL_UNSIGNED_BYTE, texture_data_base );
  glTexImage2D( GL_TEXTURE_2D, 1, GL_RGBA, 4, 4, 0, GL_RGBA,
                GL_UNSIGNED_BYTE, texture_data_mip_1 );
  glTexImage2D( GL_TEXTURE_2D, 2, GL_RGBA, 2, 2, 0, GL_RGBA,
                GL_UNSIGNED_BYTE, texture_data_mip_2 );
  glTexImage2D( GL_TEXTURE_2D, 3, GL_RGBA, 1, 1, 0, GL_RGBA,
                GL_UNSIGNED_BYTE, texture_data_mip_3 );
}

glTexEnvi( GL_TEXTURE_ENV, GL_TEXTURE_ENV_MODE, GL_MODULATE );
glTexParameteri( GL_TEXTURE_2D, GL_TEXTURE_MIN_FILTER,
                 GL_NEAREST );
glTexParameteri( GL_TEXTURE_2D, GL_TEXTURE_MAG_FILTER,
                 GL_LINEAR );
glTexParameteri( GL_TEXTURE_2D, GL_TEXTURE_WRAP_S, GL_CLAMP_TO_EDGE );
glTexParameteri( GL_TEXTURE_2D, GL_TEXTURE_WRAP_T, GL_CLAMP_TO_EDGE );
```

9.2.6 MULTI-TEXTURING

OpenGL ES supports multi-texturing, i.e., the results of one texturing unit can be piped to the next one. When using version 1.0 you might get only one texturing unit, whereas 1.1 guarantees at least two units. The actual number of units can be queried with

```
GLint n_units;
glGetIntegerv( GL_MAX_TEXTURE_UNITS, &n_units );
```

Texture mapping calls `glTexImage2D`, `glTexSubImage2D`, and `glTexParameter` affect the state of the current texture object, while `glTexEnv` affects only the active texture unit. Texture object settings affect all texture units where the texture object is bound when a draw call is issued. A unit can be activated with `glActiveTexture`, and then you can both bind a texture object to the unit and modify that unit's texture matrix. The following example sets up a spinning diffuse texture in the first unit, a projective light map in the second unit, and disables the rest of the units.

```
/* the base texture spins around the center of the texture map */
glActiveTexture( GL_TEXTURE0 );
glEnable( GL_TEXTURE_2D );
glBindTexture( GL_TEXTURE_2D, tex_handle );
glMatrixMode( GL_TEXTURE );
glLoadIdentity();
glTranslatef( 0.5, 0.5, 0.0f );
glRotatef( time*20, 0.f, 0.f, 1.f );
glTranslatef( -0.5, -0.5, 0.0f );
/* the second unit has a light map */
glActiveTexture( GL_TEXTURE1 );
glEnable( GL_TEXTURE_2D );
glBindTexture( GL_TEXTURE_2D, lightmap_handle );
glLoadMatrixf( my_projective_light_matrix );
/* make sure the rest of the texture units are disabled */
GLint maxtex, i;
glGetIntegerv( GL_MAX_TEXTURE_UNITS, maxtex )
for( i = 2; i < maxtex; i++ )
{
  glActiveTexture( GL_TEXTURE0 + i );
  glDisable( GL_TEXTURE_2D );
}
```

As described in the previous chapter, for texture coordinates the active texture unit is selected with `glClientActiveTexture`, after which the coordinates are specified with `glTexCoordPointer`.

The output of one texturing unit cascades as input to the next enabled unit. This happens in order, starting from unit 0, and disabled units are simply skipped over as if they did not exist in the first place.

9.2.7 TEXTURE COMBINERS

OpenGL ES 1.1 introduces a set of more powerful texture functions called *texture combiners*. The combiners are activated by calling

```
glTexEnvi( GL_TEXTURE_ENV, GL_TEXTURE_ENV_MODE, GL_COMBINE );
```

With combiners one can specify different texture functions for RGB and alpha, using one of the six functions, which take from one to three arguments *Arg*0, *Arg*1, *Arg*2.

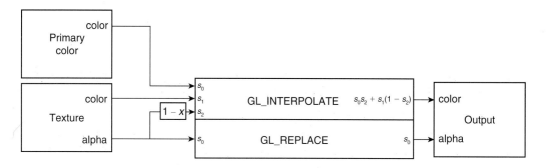

Figure 9.2: Example of combining a texture map into the untextured fragment color in proportion to the texture alpha channel. The resulting color is $C_p * (1 - A_t) + C_t * A_t$, where C_p is the untextured color, and C_t and A_t are the color and alpha of the texture map.

GL_REPLACE simply copies $Arg0$.

GL_MODULATE multiplies two arguments as $Arg0 * Arg1$.

GL_ADD adds them up as $Arg0 + Arg1$, while

GL_ADD_SIGNED treats $Arg1$ as a signed value in $[-0.5, 0.5]$: $Arg0 + Arg1 - 0.5$.

GL_INTERPOLATE linearly interpolates two inputs using the third: $Arg0 * Arg2 + Arg1 * (1 - Arg2)$.

GL_SUBTRACT subtracts the second from the first $Arg0 - Arg1$.

Additionally, GL_DOT3_RGB and GL_DOT3_RGBA can be used only for RGB; they calculate a dot product between the two argument colors as $4 * (s_r + s_g + s_b)$, where s_r is defined as $(Arg0_r - 0.5) * (Arg1_r - 0.5)$ and s_g and s_b are defined in a similar way. The resulting scalar value is copied either to the RGB or RGBA of the output. To illustrate how the texture combiners are used, we give an example that blends a texture map into the triangle color based on the alpha channel of the texture map. Figure 9.2 illustrates the combiner setup for this operation. The combiner functions are set as follows:

```
glTexEnvi( GL_TEXTURE_ENV, GL_COMBINE_RGB, GL_INTERPOLATE );
glTexEnvi( GL_TEXTURE_ENV, GL_COMBINE_ALPHA, GL_REPLACE );
```

The arguments can be taken from the filtered texture color (GL_TEXTURE), untextured fragment color (GL_PRIMARY_COLOR), user-specified constant color (GL_CONSTANT, specified using GL_TEXTURE_ENV_COLOR), or the output color from the previous texture unit (GL_PREVIOUS). In the example above, GL_INTERPOLATE takes three arguments while GL_REPLACE takes only one. They could be specified with

```
glTexEnvi( GL_TEXTURE_ENV, GL_SOURCE0_RGB, GL_PRIMARY_COLOR );
glTexEnvi( GL_TEXTURE_ENV, GL_SOURCE1_RGB, GL_TEXTURE );
glTexEnvi( GL_TEXTURE_ENV, GL_SOURCE2_RGB, GL_TEXTURE );
glTexEnvi( GL_TEXTURE_ENV, GL_SOURCE0_ALPHA, GL_PRIMARY_COLOR );
```

Finally, you need to specify whether you want to use the RGB or alpha as input for the RGB part (for alpha you can only use the alpha component), and these *operands* can be either taken as is (*arg*), or inverted (1 − *arg*), before being passed to the function.

```
glTexEnvi( GL_TEXTURE_ENV, GL_OPERAND0_RGB, GL_SRC_COLOR );
glTexEnvi( GL_TEXTURE_ENV, GL_OPERAND1_RGB, GL_SRC_COLOR );
glTexEnvi( GL_TEXTURE_ENV, GL_OPERAND2_RGB, GL_ONE_MINUS_SRC_ALPHA );
glTexEnvi( GL_TEXTURE_ENV, GL_OPERAND0_ALPHA, GL_SRC_ALPHA );
```

9.2.8 POINT SPRITE TEXTURING

Point sprites are another feature introduced in OpenGL ES 1.1. Many natural phenomena such as fire or smoke can be emulated by overlaying several copies of textures depicting flames or smoke puffs. Using quads (quadrangles made of pairs of triangles) to place the textures is inefficient as four vertices have to be transformed for each quad. It is much more efficient to use a single point for each sprite instead, to specify the point size, and paste the texture image across the point. However, normal points have only a single texture coordinate which is shared by every fragment on the point. With point sprites you can generate texture coordinates so they are interpolated across the point. If you call

```
glEnable( GL_POINT_SPRITE_OES );
glTexEnvi( GL_POINT_SPRITE_OES, COORD_REPLACE_OES, GL_TRUE );
```

the antialiasing mode of the point is ignored, the point is treated as a screen-aligned square, and texture coordinates are interpolated across the point so that the *upper* left corner has coordinates (0,0) while the *lower* right corner has coordinates (1,1). That is, the *t*-coordinate direction is the reverse of the usual OpenGL convention. Note also that you have to enable the texture coordinate interpolation separately for each texturing unit. To disable the interpolation of a unit simply call the function with GL_FALSE. Other features of texture mapping work exactly the same way as triangles.

9.2.9 IMPLEMENTATION DIFFERENCES

Some features of texture mapping are left optional. For example, the OpenGL ES specification does not require an implementation to perform the texture coordinate interpolation in a perspectively correct fashion. Although hardware implementations are likely to handle this correctly, software implementations often use a much cheaper screen-space linear interpolation instead. Some of them support both perspective correct and linear interpolation, and allow choosing between them using glHint (see Section 10.3).

In a similar fashion, some implementations may only choose the closest mipmap level instead of interpolating between them, even if the filtering mode asks for it.

The effects of auto-mipmap generation of OpenGL ES 1.1 may also vary across implementations.

Finally, the OpenGL ES specification does not require that the division of the texture coordinates' *s* and *t* components by the *q* component is performed separately at each pixel. Instead, an implementation may do the division by *q* at vertices, and then interpolate the coordinates.

9.3 FOG

The next step after texture mapping is fog generation. Fog is used to simulate aerial perspective, and to make more distant objects fade into a constant color. A detailed description of fog functions and their parameters can be found in Section 3.4.4. Fragments are blended with a constant fog color; the blending factor is based on the distance to the viewer and the current fog mode. Although the fog distance computation is conceptually performed as a part of the fragment-processing pipeline, implementations often compute the fog values for the vertices of a primitive and then interpolate them. The quality of the fog computation may be controlled with glHint (see Section 10.3).

The fog color is specified with

```
void glFog{fx}v(GL_FOG_COLOR, const T * params)
```

where *params* points to an RGBA color. Other parameters are set by calling

```
void glFog{fx}(GLenum pname, T param)
```

With *pname* GL_FOG_MODE you can select between *params* GL_EXP (default), GL_LINEAR, and GL_EXP2. Further *pname* GL_FOG_DENSITY applies for the exponential modes, and *pname*s GL_FOG_START and GL_FOG_END set the start and end distances for the linear mode.

By default fog is turned off. It can be enabled by calling glEnable(GL_FOG). The following example shows how fog is used. As you can see in Figure 3.20, with these values the GL_LINEAR and GL_EXP2 modes behave in a similar manner, but GL_EXP2 provides a smoother transition.

```
static const GLfloat bluish_fog[4] = { .5f, .5f, .8f, 1.f };
glEnable( GL_FOG )
glHint( GL_FOG_HINT, GL_DONT_CARE );
glFogfv( GL_FOG_COLOR, bluish_fog );
if( linear )
{
  glFogf( GL_FOG_MODE, GL_LINEAR );
  glFogf( GL_FOG_START, 20.0f );
  glFogf( GL_FOG_END, 70.0f );
}
```

```
else
{
  glFogf( GL_FOG_MODE, GL_EXP2 );
  glFogf( GL_FOG_DENSITY, 0.02f );
}
... /* draw the object */
glDisable( GL_FOG );
```

Note that once you enable fog, it is applied to almost every operation, and even if you do not see much effect (depending on the mode and values you set), you pay the penalty of the increased processing load. Do not forget to disable the fog when you do not need it any more.

9.4 ANTIALIASING

There are two basic ways for performing antialiasing in OpenGL ES: edge antialiasing, which is supported for lines and points, and multisampling, which supports all primitives. It is also possible to implement antialiasing by combining other OpenGL ES features.

9.4.1 EDGE ANTIALIASING

OpenGL ES supports edge antialiasing for line and point primitives. This means that a partial pixel coverage percentage is computed for all fragments, and the alpha value of the fragment is then modulated by the coverage percentage. To create the desired antialiasing effect, blending must be enabled.

There are some problems with edge antialiasing, however. First, there are no quality guarantees. There are so many possible ways to implement edge antialiasing that a precise specification would preclude many feasible approaches. Therefore you do not know how the antialiasing is implemented; some implementations may even choose to ignore the request for antialiasing. An even greater problem is that the results depend on the rendering order. Say you first render white lines on a blue background. Some of the edge pixels are going to get a color which is a mix of white and blue. Now if you draw something that is yellow that is farther from the camera than your white line, but closer than the blue background, the result can be pretty ugly. Instead of the white line blending smoothly to the yellow background, many of the boundary pixels have traces of blue.

The advantage is that since an implementation can precalculate analytically how much the line covers each pixel, this method can give much higher quality and more efficient line and point antialiasing than, for example, multisampling. However, for best results the lines and primitives should be sorted by depth, and drawn in a back-to-front order after all other parts of the scene have already been drawn.

Edge antialiasing complicates the triangle rasterization rules, and traditionally edge antialiasing has not been used much for triangles. Therefore OpenGL ES supports it only for points and lines, which makes it relatively straightforward to implement. It is enabled by calling `glEnable` with the arguments `GL_LINE_SMOOTH` or `GL_POINT_ SMOOTH`.

9.4.2 MULTISAMPLING

Some OpenGL ES implementations support *multisampling*, an antialiasing mechanism where each pixel is represented by multiple samples which are combined together at the end of the frame. This is a somewhat expensive feature, and likely to be found only in hardware implementations. Multisampling can be enabled or disabled using the token `GL_MULTISAMPLE`, and by default it is enabled. Basic multisampling is that easy. However, you have to make sure that your EGL configuration supports multisampling (see Chapter 11).

The advantage of multisampling is that it is easy to use: unlike edge antialiasing, it does not require sorting the objects, and blending does not have to be enabled. The disadvantage is the cost of implementation complexity, and higher use of computation resources. Depending on the implementation it may or may not execute at the same speed as single-sampled rendering. The quality of antialiasing depends on the number of samples. Even on mobile hardware engines the number is not likely to be very high: typically two or four samples per pixel are supported.

In order to find out whether multisampling is supported by the currently active EGL surface, query the value of `GL_SAMPLE_ BUFFERS`: here 1 means supported, 0 indicates not supported. `GL_SAMPLES` then tells how many samples per pixel are stored. You cannot usually turn multisampling on or off per primitive; it should be either enabled or disabled for the whole rendering pass.

Blending with multisampling

If multisampling is supported, you can use it for a fast approximation to simple blending. However, beware: on some implementations the overhead of multisampling may be much bigger than that of blending, so this trick may also slow you down.

The idea is that if some of the samples come from one object and others come from another, and the samples are then averaged, we get a reasonable approximation of real blending. For example, if you want to blend two objects 50–50, and your multisampling system takes 4 samples, instead of rendering the 4 samples twice, and reading pixel values from the frame buffer to do the blending, you only need to render 2 samples twice and skip frame buffer reads and blending, resulting in much more than 2 times the performance increase.

The first approach is to use the alpha values to determine the number of samples to be generated: low alpha means fewer samples. This is enabled with `glEnable ( GL_ SAMPLE_ALPHA_TO_MASK )`. In most cases you can now simply ignore the alpha values, as blending is done by the multisampling machinery, but in case you do care (you have an RGBA frame buffer instead of RGB, or blending has been enabled), as you take fewer samples, the alpha of those samples should set to 1.0. For this effect call glEnable (GL_SAMPLE_ALPHA_TO_ONE).

The second possibility is to not use alpha, but to define the sample coverage value directly. For this you enable GL_SAMPLE_MASK and use

```
void glSampleCoverage(GLclampf value, GLboolean invert)
void glSampleCoveragex(GLclampx value, GLboolean invert)
```

where the *value* parameter tells the percentage of the samples that a "fragment mask" selects to pass if *invert* is false. If *invert* is true, the samples that would have passed are killed, and the samples that would have been killed will pass. For example, the following code would take 75% of the samples from the first object, and 25% from the second object, allowing a faster way to blend, for example, two different level-of-detail versions of the same object.

```
glEnable( GL_SAMPLE_MASK );
glSampleCoverage( 0.75f, GL_TRUE );
... /* here draw object 1 */
glSampleCoverage( 0.75f, GL_FALSE );
... /* draw object 2 */
glDisable( GL_SAMPLE_MASK );
```

This guarantees that the objects get different samples. So if every pixel gets 4 samples, 3 of them would sample object 1, and the last one would sample object 2.

9.4.3 OTHER ANTIALIASING APPROACHES

It is possible to do antialiasing by using *feathered* RGBA texture maps. Feathering means that the boundaries are faded, pixels closer to the boundary get progressively smaller alpha value, and beyond the boundaries the alpha values are zero. Like edge antialiasing, blending must be enabled for this approach.

The best alpha mask is obtained by rendering the image at a much higher resolution than the final image, reading it from the server to the client, running a client-side program that filters the image down [GW02], and redrawing using the filtered image. This approach, however, is too slow for real-time interactive applications, but can give high-quality results for still image rendering. A faster but perhaps lower-quality version of this could render the image directly into a texture map in twice the resolution of the desired final image, carefully set the texture coordinates so that pixel centers map between the texels, and use bilinear filtering so that the hardware can do the filtering. This works much faster since the image doesn't have to be fetched from the server (GPU) to the client (CPU), but the whole processing is done at the server.

9.5 PIXEL TESTS

Toward the end of the graphics pipeline the pixels are subjected to a sequence of tests. The first of the tests is the scissor test which allows only pixels within a rectangular box to pass. This is followed by alpha, stencil, and depth tests. All of these tests compare one component of the pixel, i.e., the alpha, stencil, or depth component, to a reference value. The comparison function can be set to always pass the pixel (GL_ALWAYS), never pass it (GL_NEVER), or pass depending on the relative value of the component with respect to the reference value (GL_LESS, GL_LEQUAL, GL_GREATER, GL_GEQUAL, GL_EQUAL, or GL_NOTEQUAL).

9.5.1 SCISSORING

The scissor test, if enabled, allows only pixels within the scissor box to be modified by drawing commands. The scissor box is defined by calling

```
void glScissor(GLint x, GLint y, GLint width, GLint height)
```

By default, the scissor test is not enabled. The scissor box is defined by giving the lower left corner, followed by the width and height in pixels. For example,

```
glEnable( GL_SCISSOR_TEST );
glScissor( 10, 5, 100, 200 );
```

defines a scissor box starting from (10, 5) and extending to (110, 205). If the scissor box is not enabled, the result is the same as if the box covered the entire window. Changing the scissor box may require flushing the graphics pipeline, so it is advisable to set it up only in the beginning of the frame.

9.5.2 ALPHA TEST

The next test after the scissor test is the alpha test. It discards incoming fragments based on a comparison between the fragment's alpha value and a reference value. This can be useful when combined with alpha blending, as it can be used to skip the rest of the pipeline when completely transparent texels are encountered in a texture map. Alpha test is a relatively cheap operation even in software implementations of OpenGL ES, and if a texture contains many discardable texels, using it can even accelerate the rendering.

```
void glAlphaFunc(GLenum func, GLclampf ref)
void glAlphaFuncx(GLenum func, GLclampx ref)
```

is used for selecting the comparison function and the reference alpha value. The parameter *func* should be one of the tests on page 214, while *ref* specifies the reference value. The reference alpha value is clamped to [0, 1] where 0 indicates completely transparent and 1 fully opaque. To allow skipping the fully transparent pixels call

```
glEnable( GL_ALPHA_TEST );
glAlphaFunc( GL_NOTEQUAL, 0.0f );
```

Here is a longer example for the alpha test. If you have a drawing routine that has both opaque and translucent objects, you should first render the opaque ones before blending the translucent ones on top of them. During the first pass depth writing should be enabled, during the second pass it should be disabled, though the depth test itself should be executed. Now transparent objects behind solids will not be drawn, but the ones in front of them will all blend in. To guarantee correct blending the transparent objects should be sorted and drawn in back-to-front order.

```
glEnable(    GL_DEPTH_TEST );     /* enable depth test */
glDepthFunc( GL_LESS );           /* use default depth func */
glDepthMask( GL_TRUE );           /* allow z-buffer update */
glEnable(    GL_ALPHA_TEST );     /* enable alpha test */
glAlphaFunc( GL_GEQUAL, 0.999f ); /* draw only solids */
myDrawFunc();                     /* draw the scene */
glDepthMask( GL_FALSE );          /* disable z-buffer update */
glAlphaFunc( GL_LESS, 0.999f );   /* draw only translucent surfaces */
glEnable(    GL_BLEND );          /* set up blending */
glBlendFunc( GL_SRC_ALPHA,        /* typical blending mode */
             GL_ONE_MINUS_SRC_ALPHA );
myDrawFunc();                     /* draw the scene, again */
glDisable(   GL_ALPHA_TEST );     /* reset to typical state */
glDisable(   GL_BLEND );          /* reset to typical state */
glDepthMask( GL_TRUE );           /* reset to typical state */
```

9.5.3 STENCIL TEST

Stencil testing, in its basic form, is a more general scissoring function. One can first draw an arbitrary 2D shape, or stencil, into the stencil buffer, and then incoming fragments are kept or discarded depending on whether they fall within the stencil shape. However, if your stencil shape is a box, it is much cheaper to use the scissor test instead. Uses for stencil buffer, in addition to the arbitrary-shaped scissor areas, include many advanced algorithms, such as drawing line drawings with hidden lines removed, drawing arbitrary polygons with holes and indentations, and creating volumetric lighting effects and shadows. However, this versatile tool has a high cost: it needs its own buffer, and therefore not all implementations support stenciling. To find out whether the currently active EGL surface has a stencil buffer, and how deep it is, you can query for GL_STENCIL_BITS (8 is a typical number of stencil bits). Of course, at first you should ask for an EGL config that supports stencil buffers as described in Chapter 11.

The stencil test function is set like the alpha test. It needs to be enabled with glEnable (GL_STENCIL_TEST), and you need to select one of the tests on page 214 (the initial mode is GL_ALWAYS) by calling

```
void glStencilFunc(GLenum func, GLint ref, GLuint mask)
```

The reference value *ref* is an integer value $[0, 2^s - 1]$ where s is the number of bits in the stencil buffer. The default reference value is 0. The third argument is *mask*, which is ANDed with both the reference value and the stored stencil value before the comparison test (the default mask has all bits set to one). If there is no stencil buffer, the stencil test always passes.

The values of the stencil buffer are set using

```
void glStencilOp(GLenum sfail, GLenum zfail, GLenum zpass)
```

which instructs how the stencil buffer is updated based on whether the stencil test fails, the depth test fails, or whether the depth test passes. The following update functions are supported

GL_KEEP	leaves the existing stencil buffer contents unmodified
GL_ZERO	sets the stencil buffer value to zero
GL_REPLACE	copies the stencil reference value to the buffer
GL_INCR	increments the stencil buffer value by one (clamps to $2^s - 1$)
GL_DECR	decrements the stencil buffer value by one (clamps to 0)
GL_INVERT	performs a bitwise inversion to the stencil buffer value

The initial state corresponds to `glStencilOp( GL_KEEP, GL_KEEP, GL_KEEP )` which never modifies the stencil buffer.

Here is a simple stencil example, which draws an irregular stencil shape and then uses that to delimit later drawing.

```
glEnable( GL_STENCIL_TEST );
glClearStencil( 0 );                   /* prepare to clear to 0 */
glClear( GL_STENCIL_BUFFER_BIT );      /* actually clear */
glStencilFunc( GL_ALWAYS, 1, 1 );      /* set ref and mask to 1 */
glStencilOp( GL_REPLACE, GL_REPLACE,   /* set to one where you draw */
             GL_REPLACE );
...                                    /* draw the stencil shape */
glStencilOp( GL_KEEP, GL_KEEP,         /* do not modify further */
             GL_KEEP );
glStencilFunc( GL_EQUAL, 1, 1 );       /* draw inside the stencil */
...                                    /* your drawing routine */
glStencilFunc( GL_NOTEQUAL, 1, 1 );    /* draw outside the stencil */
...                                    /* your drawing routine */
glDisable( GL_STENCIL_TEST );
```

The following is a more complex example that uses stencil buffers for volumetric shadows [Hei91]. The idea is to first draw the scene with only ambient lighting. For the parts of the scene that do not get any direct lighting, that is, are in the shadow, that is all there is to do. The shadow volumes are modeled as geometry, and are used to update the stencil buffer. If the front surface of a shadow volume is between the camera and object, that object is potentially in the shadow. Every such shadow will increase the stencil buffer by one. However, if the back surface of the shadow volume is also between camera and the object, then that volume does not reach up to the object, and the stencil buffer is decreased by one. In the end, pixels with stencil values equaling zero are not in shadow, and should be redrawn with full lighting. Note that this example makes several assumptions of light directions and the view frustum setup, and only works for simple cases, as it is meant to illustrate mostly the stencil buffer processing.

```
/* prepare to draw the scene with ambient lights, store depth */
glDisable( GL_STENCIL_TEST );
glEnable( GL_DEPTH_TEST );
glDepthFunc( GL_LESS );
glColorMask( GL_TRUE, GL_TRUE, GL_TRUE, GL_TRUE );
glDepthMask( GL_TRUE );
glCullFace( GL_BACK );

draw_scene_with_ambient_lights();

/* now don't touch color or depth */
glColorMask( GL_FALSE, GL_FALSE, GL_FALSE, GL_FALSE );
glDepthMask( GL_FALSE );
/* Render front triangles only */
glEnable( GL_CULL_FACE );
glCullFace( GL_BACK );
/* INCRement stencil where depth test passes */
glEnable( GL_STENCIL_TEST );
glStencilMask( 0xffffffff );
glStencilFunc( GL_ALWAYS, 0x00000000, 0xffffffff );
glStencilOp( GL_KEEP, GL_KEEP, GL_INCR );

draw_shadow_volumes();

/* render back triangles only */
glCullFace( GL_FRONT );
/* DECRement stencil where depth test passes */
glStencilOp( GL_KEEP, GL_KEEP, GL_DECR );

draw_shadow_volumes();

/* pass stencil test ONLY when stencil is zero (not in shadow) */
glStencilFunc( GL_EQUAL, 0x00000000, 0xffffffff );
/* process only visible surface front pixels */
glCullFace( GL_BACK );
glDepthFunc( GL_EQUAL );
/* redraw color buffer on surviving pixels */
glColorMask( GL_TRUE, GL_TRUE, GL_TRUE, GL_TRUE );

draw_scene_with_normal_light();
```

9.5.4 DEPTH TESTING

Depth testing is the final test in the OpenGL ES fragment pipeline. It is used for sorting the primitives at each pixel based on their distance from the camera. Typically we want the closest object to cover the ones farther away. However, some algorithms exist that need other depth orderings. Depth test is globally turned on or off by calling `glEnable` or `glDisable` with the symbolic constant `GL_DEPTH_TEST`.

> void glDepthFunc(GLenum *func*)

selects between the eight depth comparison functions on page 214. This function is used to compare a fragment's depth value against the one already stored in the depth buffer at the same pixel location. The default function is `GL_LESS`.

The extended shadow volume example in the previous section also illustrates the use of the depth test. When the scene is drawn for the first time, the basic comparison mode `glDepthFunc( GL_LESS )` is used to discard all the fragments but the ones closest to the camera. When it is drawn for the second time, we switch the comparison function to `glDepthFunc( GL_EQUAL )` so that only those fragments that are visible are retained. If the mode would still be `GL_LESS` no fragments would survive the depth test on the second round.

Polygon offsets

Polygon offsets are used for modifying the depth values of triangles. This is a useful feature for, e.g., rendering decals on top of flat surfaces. With polygon offsets you can make sure that the decal is in front of the surface, but not so far that a noticeable gap would show between them. The feature can be turned on or off using `glEnable` or `glDisable` with `GL_POLYGON_OFFSET_FILL`.

> void glPolygonOffset(GLfloat *factor*, GLfloat *units*)
> void glPolygonOffsetx(GLfloat *factor*, GLfixed *units*)

defines the scale *factor* and *units* that are used to modify the fragment's depth value. Both are initially set to 0. See Section 3.5.1 for a more detailed discussion of polygon offsets.

9.6 APPLYING FRAGMENTS TO THE COLOR BUFFER

Once a fragment has been fully processed, it is applied to the color buffer. Three alternative mechanisms exist: the fragment can be copied directly to replace the corresponding pixel in the color buffer, the fragment can be blended with the color buffer, or a logical operation may be applied to combine the fragment with the color buffer. Finally, some frame buffer channels might be masked so that writes are not performed to them.

9.6.1 BLENDING

Blending takes the incoming fragment color (with texturing and fog already applied) and the color that already exists in the frame buffer, and uses them to come up with a new color to be stored in the frame buffer. Blending was described in Section 3.5.2.

Blending can be turned on and off by using glEnable and glDisable with the symbolic constant GL_BLEND. Blending is disabled by default. When enabled, a blend operation multiplies the incoming, or source, fragment color C_s by a source blend factor F_s, and the pixel in the color buffer, or destination color C_d, by a destination blend factor F_d, multiplies and adds component-wise $C_s F_s + C_d F_d$, clamps it to [0,1], and stores the result into the color buffer.

```
void glBlendFunc(GLenum sfactor, GLenum dfactor)
```

sets up the source and destination blend factors. The following table lists the allowed tokens, describes the actual factors, and tells whether they are permissible to be used as a source or a destination factor, or both.

Token	Factor	src	dst
GL_ZERO	$(0, 0, 0, 0)$	√	√
GL_ONE	$(1, 1, 1, 1)$	√	√
GL_SRC_COLOR	(R_s, G_s, B_s, A_s)		√
GL_ONE_MINUS_SRC_COLOR	$(1, 1, 1, 1) - (R_s, G_s, B_s, A_s)$		√
GL_DST_COLOR	(R_d, G_d, B_d, A_d)	√	
GL_ONE_MINUS_DST_COLOR	$(1, 1, 1, 1) - (R_d, G_d, B_d, A_d)$	√	
GL_SRC_ALPHA	(A_s, A_s, A_s, A_s)	√	√
GL_ONE_MINUS_SRC_ALPHA	$(1, 1, 1, 1) - (A_s, A_s, A_s, A_s)$	√	√
GL_DST_ALPHA	(A_d, A_d, A_d, A_d)	√	√
GL_ONE_MINUS_DST_ALPHA	$(1, 1, 1, 1) - (A_d, A_d, A_d, A_d)$	√	√
GL_SRC_ALPHA_SATURATE	$(f, f, f, 1), f = min(A_s, 1 - A_d)$	√	

If the color buffer does not include an alpha channel, the destination alpha A_d is considered to be 1 in the previous equations.

Probably the most common uses for blending are rendering translucent objects and edge antialiasing. You would prepare blending by calling

```
glEnable( GL_BLEND );
glBlendFunc( GL_SRC_ALPHA, GL_ONE_MINUS_SRC_ALPHA );
```

To get the correct blending results, you should first draw the opaque objects, then sort the transparent ones, and render them in a back-to-front order.

9.6.2 DITHERING

Dithering is a mechanism for reducing the visual artifacts generated by quantization of color values to low bit-depth displays (see Figure 3.24). For example, a 5-bit per channel display shows clearly visible banding in smooth color gradients. Dithering masks this banding by applying noise to the image when converting the fragment RGB components from a higher bit depth to a lower one. This usually improves the quality of the resulting image. However, when rendering scenes that contain a lot of overlapping transparent surfaces (e.g., particle systems), the dithering process itself may create visible artifacts as the noise patterns are applied multiple times to each pixel. In such situations it may make sense to manually disable the dithering. This is done by using `glDisable` with the symbolic constant `GL_DITHER` (by default dithering is enabled). Note that dithering is not a required feature for an OpenGL ES implementation.

9.6.3 LOGIC OPS

Logical operations are an alternative to blending. When enabled, the operation between the fragment and the corresponding pixel in the frame buffer is a bit-wise logical one rather than arithmetic, and blending is disabled, regardless of whether `GL_BLEND` is enabled or not. Logic ops are turned on and off using `glEnable` and `glDisable` with the symbolic constant `GL_COLOR_LOGIC_OP`. By default logic ops are disabled.

>   void glLogicOp(GLenum *opcode*)

is used for selecting the logical operation. The following symbols are supported: `GL_CLEAR`, `GL_SET`, `GL_COPY`, `GL_COPY_INVERTED`, `GL_NOOP`, `GL_INVERT`, `GL_AND`, `GL_NAND`, `GL_OR`, `GL_NOR`, `GL_XOR`, `GL_EQUIV`, `GL_AND_REVERSE`, `GL_AND_INVERTED`, `GL_OR _REVERSE`, and `GL_OR_INVERTED`.

> **Pitfall:** Even though the specification requires support of logic ops, there are some hardware implementations that do not support them.

9.6.4 MASKING FRAME BUFFER CHANNELS

The last stage of the graphics pipeline involves optional masking of some channels of the frame buffer to disallow writes to them.

>   void glColorMask(GLboolean *red*, GLboolean *green*, GLboolean *blue*,
>   GLboolean *alpha*)

is used for selecting which of the RGBA channels are active. By default, rendering is performed for all four channels.

> **Pitfall:** Some existing hardware implementations slow down if you mask independent color channels. Disabling and enabling all of the channels is typically fast, however.

```
void glStencilMask(GLuint mask)
```

defines a bitmask that is used to disable writing to individual stencil planes. A stencil plane is enabled if the corresponding bit is set to one. By default all the planes are enabled.

```
void glDepthMask(GLboolean flag)
```

controls whether the depth buffer is updated after a successful depth comparison. By default, depth writes are performed, and this is the wanted behavior for most shaders. However, when transparent surfaces are rendered, it often makes sense not to update the depth buffer. Also in multipass algorithms the latter passes often enable depth test but disable depth writing.

The mask functions are applied to all operations that affect the corresponding buffer, i.e., rendering calls and `glClear`.

MISCELLANEOUS OPENGL ES FEATURES

This chapter covers OpenGL ES functionality that is not part of either the geometry or the rasterization pipelines. Such functionality includes state control, whole-screen operations, state queries, hints, and some extensions.

10.1 FRAME BUFFER OPERATIONS

Several operations affect the entire frame buffer. A number of API calls are provided for clearing the various buffers, and reading back the contents of the color buffer.

10.1.1 CLEARING THE BUFFERS

Typically, the first operation on a new frame is clearing the various buffers to preset values. Often the color buffer is cleared to contain the color of the sky or other background, the depth buffer is initialized to the maximum depth value, and the stencil buffer is set to zero. Although the buffers could also be initialized by rendering a quad that covers the entire screen, using the dedicated `glClear` call is usually much faster.

```
void glClear(GLbitfield mask)
```

is used for clearing the various buffers all at the same time. The input parameter *mask* is a bitwise OR of symbolic constants that indicate which buffers should be cleared. Supported constants are GL_COLOR_BUFFER_BIT, GL_DEPTH_BUFFER_BIT, and GL_STENCIL_BUFFER_BIT. The value that the buffer is filled with during the clearing is set with the following functions:

```
void glClearColor{fx}(T red, T green, T blue, T alpha)
void glClearDepth{fx}(T depth)
void glClearStencil(GLint s)
```

The color or depth argument values are clamped to the range [0, 1], whereas the stencil value is ANDed with $2^s - 1$, where *s* is the number of stencil bits in the stencil buffer. Their initial values, respectively, are (0, 0, 0, 0), 1.0, and 0. Here is an example of how these calls are used:

```
glClearColorf( 1.0f, 0.0f, 0.0f, 0.0f );
glClearDepthf( 1.0f );
glClear( GL_COLOR_BUFFER_BIT | GL_DEPTH_BUFFER_BIT );
```

10.1.2 READING BACK THE COLOR BUFFER

Of the different frame buffer channels only the color buffer can be read back. OpenGL ES 1.x does not provide any mechanism for reading the contents of the depth or stencil buffers. One should note that even reading back the color buffer can be a very time-consuming operation. This is because the call has to flush the rendering pipeline as all buffered rendering commands need to be executed before the function returns. Modern graphics hardware have very deep pipelines, often buffering hundreds or thousands of triangles, in some architectures even from different frames. Also, if the rendering server is implemented on an external accelerator chip, the bus connecting it back to the client can be very slow.

```
void glReadPixels(GLint x, GLint y, GLsizei width, GLsizei height, GLenum
                  format, GLenum type, GLvoid * pixels)
```

is used for reading back the contents of the color buffer. The parameters *x*, *y*, *width*, and *height* are all expressed in pixels, and define a rectangular portion of the screen that is copied. The only supported *format–type* pair copied from desktop OpenGL is GL_RGBA and GL_UNSIGNED_BYTE. OpenGL ES implementations must support one additional *format–type* pair which can be chosen by the implementation. This usually corresponds to the native format of the color buffer, so that no expensive conversion operations need take place while reading pixels, and must be one of the combinations in Table 9.1. The values of *format* and *type* in this case may be obtained by calling glGetIntegerv with the tokens GL_IMPLEMENTATION_COLOR_READ_FORMAT_OES and GL_IMPLEMENTATION_COLOR_READ_TYPE_OES, respectively. The last parameter *pixels* points to a memory block into which the requested portion of the frame buffer is copied.

```
void glPixelStorei(GL_PACK_ALIGNMENT, GLint param)
```

is used to control the packing alignment of pixel transfer operations. As explained in Section 9.2.2, this command specifies the memory alignment at the beginning of each row. The default value is 4, meaning that at the beginning of a new row the storage pointer is advanced between 0 and 3 bytes before writing so that the memory address of the first pixel in the row becomes divisible by 4. If the value is 1 no alignment is done. Other possible values are 2 and 8.

The following code sets word-aligned packing (a word is 4 bytes), and reads in the lower-left 240 × 320 pixel box. Aligned writes are likely to execute faster than unaligned ones.

```
GLubyte buffer[4*240*320 + 3];
/* get aligned pointer */
pixels = ((buffer + 3) >> 2) << 2;
glPixelStorei( GL_PACK_ALIGNMENT, 4 );
glReadPixels( 0, 0, 240, 320, GL_RGBA, GL_UNSIGNED_BYTE, pixels );
```

10.1.3 FLUSHING THE COMMAND STREAM

Some commands, such as glReadPixels, implicitly synchronize the client and the server. You can also perform the synchronization explicitly. Calling

```
void glFlush(void)
```

gives the server an asynchronous signal telling that now would be a good time to start executing all the possibly buffered GL calls—new ones might not be coming for a while. However, you do not know when the rendering has completed, just that it will sometime in the future. A synchronous version that only returns after all the rendering has been completed is

```
void glFinish(void)
```

Even though glFinish guarantees that all calls have been completed, applications using double-buffered window surfaces cannot verify it, as eglSwapBuffers is the actual call that finally triggers the buffer swap. eglSwapBuffers implicitly calls glFinish. With pbuffer surfaces the application really gets the pixels only after eglCopyBuffers or glReadPixels. For more details, see Chapter 11.

10.2 STATE QUERIES

State queries can be divided into two broad categories: static and dynamic. Static queries are the ones that produce the same result throughout the lifetime of a context, such as querying the number of supported texturing mapping units, or the list of supported extensions. Dynamic state queries return information that may vary during the execution of a program, for example the current line width or dimensions of the scissor rectangle.

With the exception of the error state, OpenGL ES 1.0 does not support querying any of the dynamic state. OpenGL ES 1.1, on the other hand, has wide support for dynamic state queries.

10.2.1 STATIC STATE

In OpenGL ES 1.0 only the static state describing the implementation can be queried. With

```
void glGetIntegerv(GLenum pname, GLint * params)
```

you can query for the following values.

GL_ALIASED_POINT_SIZE_RANGE the smallest and largest supported size for aliased points, the range must include 1.

GL_ALIASED_LINE_WIDTH_RANGE the smallest and largest supported width for aliased lines the range must include 1.

GL_ALPHA_BITS the number of alpha bitplanes in the color buffer.

GL_BLUE_BITS the number of blue bitplanes in the color buffer.

GL_COMPRESSED_TEXTURE_FORMATS a list of supported compressed texture formats, `GL_NUM_COMPRESSED_TEXTURE_FORMATS` of them.

GL_DEPTH_BITS the number of bitplanes in the depth buffer.

GL_GREEN_BITS the number of green bitplanes in the color buffer.

GL_IMPLEMENTATION_COLOR_READ_FORMAT_OES the preferred format for pixel read-back.

GL_IMPLEMENTATION_COLOR_READ_TYPE_OES the preferred type for pixel read-back.

GL_MAX_ELEMENTS_INDICES the recommended maximum vertex array index count.

GL_MAX_ELEMENTS_VERTICES the recommended maximum vertex array vertex count.

GL_MAX_LIGHTS the number of supported lights (≥ 8).

GL_MAX_MODELVIEW_STACK_DEPTH the depth of the modelview matrix stack (≥ 16).

GL_MAX_PROJECTION_STACK_DEPTH the depth of the projection matrix stack (≥ 2).

GL_MAX_TEXTURE_SIZE an estimate of the largest texture the engine can handle (≥ 64).

GL_MAX_TEXTURE_STACK_DEPTH the depth of the texture matrix stacks (≥ 2).

GL_MAX_TEXTURE_UNITS the number of supported texture units (≥ 1).

GL_MAX_VIEWPORT_DIMS two numbers: the maximum supported width and height of the viewport. Must be at least as large as the visible dimensions of the display.

GL_NUM_COMPRESSED_TEXTURE_FORMATS the number of supported compressed texture formats.

GL_RED_BITS the number of red bitplanes in the color buffer.

GL_SMOOTH_LINE_WIDTH_RANGE the smallest and largest widths of antialiased lines.

GL_SMOOTH_POINT_SIZE_RANGE the smallest and largest sizes of antialiased points.

GL_STENCIL_BITS the number of bitplanes in the stencil buffer.

GL_SUBPIXEL_BITS an estimate of the number of bits for subpixel resolution for window coordinate positions in rasterization (≥ 4).

```
const GLubyte * glGetString(GLenum name)
```

can be used to query the following null-terminated strings:

GL_EXTENSIONS a space-separated list of supported extensions.

GL_RENDERER the name of the renderer, typically specific to a particular configuration of a hardware platform.

GL_VENDOR the name of the company responsible for this implementation.

GL_VERSION "OpenGL ES-XX Y.Z" where XX = CM for Common Profile, XX = CL for Common Lite Profile, Y is the major version, Z is the minor version. For OpenGL ES Common Profile version 1.0 the string is "OpenGL ES-CM 1.0" (without the quotes).

Here is an example on how to use the query functions.

```
GLint red_bits, max_viewport[2];
GLubyte *str_ptr;
glGetIntegerv( GL_RED_BITS, &red_bits );
glGetIntegerv( GL_MAX_VIEWPORT_DIMS, max_viewport );
str_ptr = glGetString( GL_EXTENSIONS );
```

10.2.2 DYNAMIC STATE QUERIES

OpenGL ES 1.1 introduces many more queries that can be performed with variants of glGet. In addition to glGetIntegerv we have

```
void glGetBooleanv(GLenum pname, GLboolean * params)
void glGetFixedv(GLenum pname, GLfixed * params)
void glGetFloatv(GLenum pname, GLfloat * params)
```

If a `glGet` command is issued that returns value types different from the type of the value being obtained, a type conversion is performed. With `glGetBooleanv`, a zero converts to `GL_FALSE` and other values convert to `GL_TRUE`. With `glGetIntegerv` a boolean converts to 1 or 0, and a float is rounded to the nearest integer, except for colors, depths, or normal coordinates, which are mapped so that 1.0 maps to the most positive representable integer value, and −1.0 to the most negative one. For `glGetFloatv`, a boolean maps to either 1.0 or 0.0, and an integer is coerced to float. If a value is too large to be represented with the requested type, the nearest representable value is returned.

The new *pname*s that are supported in addition to those already in OpenGL ES 1.0 are listed below.

GL_ALPHA_TEST_FUNC the alpha test function.

GL_ALPHA_TEST_REF the reference value for alpha test.

GL_BLEND_DST the destination blend function.

GL_BLEND_SRC the source blend function.

GL_COLOR_ARRAY_BUFFER_BINDING the buffer object name bound to the color array.

GL_COLOR_ARRAY_SIZE the number of components per color in the color array.

GL_COLOR_ARRAY_STRIDE the byte offset between consecutive colors.

GL_COLOR_ARRAY_TYPE the data type of each component in the color array.

GL_COLOR_CLEAR_VALUE four values, the RGBA clear color.

GL_COLOR_WRITEMASK four booleans indicating whether RGBA writes to color buffer are enabled.

GL_CULL_FACE a symbolic constant indicating whether front or back faces are culled.

GL_DEPTH_CLEAR_VALUE the depth buffer clear value.

GL_DEPTH_FUNC the depth comparison function.

GL_DEPTH_RANGE two values, the near and far mapping limits for depth.

GL_DEPTH_WRITEMASK a boolean indicating whether the depth buffer is enabled for writing.

GL_FOG_COLOR four values, the RGBA fog color.

GL_FOG_DENSITY the fog density.

GL_FOG_END the end fog distance for linear fog.

GL_FOG_HINT the current fog hint.

GL_FOG_MODE the current fog equation.

GL_FOG_START the start fog distance for linear fog.

GL_FRONT_FACE whether clockwise or counterclockwise winding is treated as front-facing.

GL_LIGHT_MODEL_AMBIENT the four RGBA components for the global ambient light color.

GL_LIGHT_MODEL_TWO_SIDE a boolean stating whether two-sided lighting is enabled.

GL_LINE_SMOOTH_HINT the current line antialiasing hint.

GL_LINE_WIDTH the current line width.

GL_LOGIC_OP_MODE the current logic operation mode.

GL_MATRIX_MODE which matrix stack is currently the target of matrix operations.

GL_MAX_CLIP_PLANES how many clip planes the implementation supports (≥ 1).

GL_MODELVIEW_MATRIX sixteen values, the matrix on top of the modelview matrix stack.

GL_MODELVIEW_MATRIX_FLOAT_AS_INT_BITS modelview matrix elements as integer array, according to the IEEE 754 floating-point single format bit layout.

GL_MODELVIEW_STACK_DEPTH the number of matrices in the modelview matrix stack.

GL_NORMAL_ARRAY_BUFFER_BINDING the buffer object name bound to the normal array.

GL_NORMAL_ARRAY_STRIDE byte offset between normals.

GL_NORMAL_ARRAY_TYPE type of each normal.

GL_PACK_ALIGNMENT the byte alignment used for writing pixel data to memory.

GL_PERSPECTIVE_CORRECTION_HINT the current perspective correction hint.

GL_POINT_SIZE the current point size.

GL_POINT_SIZE_ARRAY_BUFFER_BINDING_OES the buffer object name bound to the point size array.

GL_POINT_SIZE_ARRAY_STRIDE_OES byte offset between elements.

GL_POINT_SIZE_ARRAY_TYPE_OES type of point sizes.

GL_POINT_SMOOTH_HINT the current point antialiasing hint.

GL_POLYGON_OFFSET_FACTOR the polygon offset scaling factor.

GL_POLYGON_OFFSET_UNITS the units argument for polygon offset.

GL_PROJECTION_MATRIX sixteen values, the matrix on top of the projection matrix stack.

GL_PROJECTION_MATRIX_FLOAT_AS_INT_BITS projection matrix elements as integer array, according to the IEEE 754 floating-point single format bit layout.

GL_PROJECTION_STACK_DEPTH the number of matrices in the projection matrix stack.

GL_SAMPLE_COVERAGE_INVERT a boolean indicating whether the sample coverage set by `glSampleCoverage` is inverted.

GL_SAMPLE_COVERAGE_VALUE the sample coverage value set by `glSample-Coverage`.

GL_SCISSOR_BOX four values describing the current scissor box: *x*, *y*, *width*, *height*.

GL_SHADE_MODEL the current shade model.

GL_STENCIL_CLEAR_VALUE value stencil buffer is cleared to.

GL_STENCIL_FAIL the action that is taken when the stencil test fails.

GL_STENCIL_FUNC the current stencil test function.

GL_STENCIL_PASS_DEPTH_FAIL the action taken when the stencil test passes and the depth test fails.

GL_STENCIL_PASS_DEPTH_PASS the action taken when both the stencil test and the depth test pass.

GL_STENCIL_REF the current reference value used for stencil comparison.

GL_STENCIL_VALUE_MASK the current mask that is applied both to the stencil reference value and the stencil buffer value before comparison.

GL_STENCIL_WRITEMASK the current mask controlling writing to stencil buffer.

GL_TEXTURE_BINDING_2D the name of the texture currently bound to `GL_TEXTURE_2D`.

GL_TEXTURE_ARRAY_BUFFER_BINDING the buffer object name bound to the texture array.

GL_TEXTURE_ARRAY_SIZE the number of coordinates per element.

GL_TEXTURE_ARRAY_STRIDE the byte offset between elements.

GL_TEXTURE_ARRAY_TYPE the coordinate data type.

GL_TEXTURE_MATRIX sixteen values, the matrix on top of the texture matrix stack.

GL_TEXTURE_MATRIX_FLOAT_AS_INT_BITS texture matrix elements as integer array, according to the IEEE 754 floating-point single format bit layout.

GL_TEXTURE_STACK_DEPTH the number of matrices in the texture matrix stack.

GL_UNPACK_ALIGNMENT the byte alignment used for reading pixel data from memory.

GL_VIEWPORT four values describing the current viewport: *x*, *y*, *width*, *height*.

GL_VERTEX_ARRAY_BUFFER_BINDING the buffer object name bound to the vertex array.

GL_VERTEX_ARRAY_SIZE the number of coordinates per element array.

GL_VERTEX_ARRAY_STRIDE the byte offset between elements.

GL_VERTEX_ARRAY_TYPE the coordinate data type.

There are also several additional query functions.

```
void glGetBufferParameteriv( GL_ARRAY_BUFFER, GLenum pname,
                             GLint * params)
```

is used for querying information about buffer objects. Supported *pname*s are:

GL_BUFFER_SIZE size of the data storage.

GL_BUFFER_USAGE expected usage, either GL_STATIC_DRAW or GL_DYNAMIC_ DRAW.

GL_BUFFER_ACCESS access capability, always GL_WRITE_ONLY.

```
void glGetClipPlane{fx}(GLenum pname, T eqn[4])
```

returns the plane equation of the clip plane *pname* (e.g., GL_CLIP_PLANE0) in eye coordinates.

```
void glGetLight{fx}v(GLenum light, GLenum pname, T * params)
```

returns the parameters of the light source *light* such as GL_LIGHT0. The valid *pname*s are

GL_AMBIENT four-component ambient RGBA light intensity.

GL_DIFFUSE four-component diffuse RGBA light intensity.

GL_SPECULAR four-component specular RGBA light intensity.

GL_EMISSION four-component emissive RGBA light intensity.

GL_SPOT_DIRECTION three-component spot light direction.

GL_SPOT_EXPONENT spot exponent [0, 128].

GL_CONSTANT_ATTENUATION attenuation factor.

GL_LINEAR_ATTENUATION attenuation factor.

GL_QUADRATIC_ATTENUATION attenuation factor.

```
void glGetMaterial{fx}v( GL_FRONT_AND_BACK, GLenum pname, T * params)
```

returns material parameter values. Accepted symbols for *pname* are

GL_AMBIENT four-component ambient RGBA reflectance.

GL_DIFFUSE four-component diffuse RGBA reflectance.

GL_SPECULAR four-component specular RGBA reflectance.

GL_EMISSION four-component emissive RGBA reflectance.

GL_SHININESS specular exponent of the material.

```
void glGetPointerv(GLenum pname, void ** params)
```

returns client-side pointer information. Accepted values for *pname* are

GL_COLOR_ARRAY_POINTER

GL_NORMAL_ARRAY_POINTER

GL_TEXTURE_ARRAY_POINTER

GL_VERTEX_ARRAY_POINTER

GL_POINT_SIZE_ARRAY_POINTER_OES

```
void glGetTexEnv{ifx}v( GL_TEXTURE_ENV, GLenum pname, T * params)
```

returns information about the texture environment. Accepted values for *pname* are

> **GL_TEXTURE_ENV_MODE** texture environment mode such as GL_MODULATE.
>
> **GL_TEXTURE_ENV_COLOR** four-component RGBA texture environment color.
>
> **GL_COMBINE_RGB** texture combine function for color.
>
> **GL_COMBINE_ALPHA** texture combine function for alpha.
>
> **GL_SRC012_RGB** texture combine source 012 for color.
>
> **GL_SRC012_ALPHA** texture combine source 012 for alpha.
>
> **GL_OPERAND012_RGB** texture combine operand 012 for color.
>
> **GL_OPERAND012_ALPHA** texture combine operand 012 for alpha.
>
> **GL_RGB_SCALE** texture combine color scale.
>
> **GL_ALPHA_SCALE** texture combine alpha scale.

```
void glGetTexParameter{ifx}v( GL_TEXTURE_2D, GLenum pname, T * params)
```

returns information about the current texture. Accepted values for *pname* are

> **GL_MIN_FILTER** texture minification function.
>
> **GL_MAG_FILTER** texture magnification function.
>
> **GL_TEXTURE_WRAP_S** wrap parameter for texture coordinate *s*.
>
> **GL_TEXTURE_WRAP_T** wrap parameter for texture coordinate *t*.
>
> **GL_GENERATE_MIPMAP** whether mipmap generation is enabled.

```
GLboolean glIsBuffer(GLuint buffer)
```

returns a boolean value indicating whether the specified name corresponds to a buffer object.

```
GLboolean glIsEnabled(GLenum cap)
```

returns a boolean value indicating whether the specified capability is enabled. The valid capabilities are

GL_ALPHA_TEST, GL_ARRAY_BUFFER_BINDING, GL_BLEND, GL_CLIP_PLANEi, GL_COLOR_ARRAY, GL_COLOR_LOGIC_OP, GL_COLOR_MATERIAL, GL_CULL_FACE, GL_DEPTH_TEST, GL_DITHER, GL_FOG, GL_LIGHTi, GL_LIGHTING, GL_LINE_SMOOTH, GL_MULTISAMPLE, GL_NORMAL_ARRAY, GL_NORMALIZE, GL_POINT_SIZE_ARRAY_OES, GL_POINT_SMOOTH, GL_POINT_SPRITE_OES, GL_POLYGON_OFFSET_FILL, GL_RESCALE_NORMAL, GL_SAMPLE_ALPHA_TO_COVERAGE, GL_SAMPLE_ALPHA_TO_ONE, GL_SAMPLE_COVERAGE, GL_SCISSOR_TEST, GL_STENCIL_TEST, GL_TEXTURE_2D, GL_TEXTURE_COORD_ARRAY, GL_VERTEX_ARRAY.

```
GLboolean glIsTexture(GLuint texture)
```

returns a boolean value indicating whether the specified name corresponds to a texture object.

10.3 HINTS

Hints are used to control quality-speed trade-offs for certain features that are regarded as implementation-specific details. They are set by calling

```
void glHint(GLenum target, GLenum mode)
```

The *mode* can be either GL_FASTEST indicating that the highest-performance option should be used, GL_NICEST asking for the highest quality, or GL_DONT_CARE indicating that the user has no preference. The default value for all targets is GL_DONT_CARE.

The valid targets are:

GL_PERSPECTIVE_CORRECTION_HINT gives a hint whether vertex data such as texture coordinates (and maybe even colors) are interpolated using perspective-correct interpolation, as opposed to faster but lower-quality screen-linear interpolation. The effect is usually most visible with large textured polygons (see Figure 3.16 and Section 3.4.2).

GL_POINT_SMOOTH_HINT and GL_LINE_SMOOTH_HINT control the rendering quality of antialiased points and lines.

GL_FOG_HINT relates to the quality of fog calculations. The typical trade-off would be computing fog at each pixel versus only computing it at the vertices and interpolating the resulting gradients across the primitive.

GL_GENERATE_MIPMAP_HINT was introduced in OpenGL ES 1.1. It controls the quality of automatically generated mipmaps.

10.4 EXTENSIONS

OpenGL ES inherits the extension mechanism of the desktop OpenGL. Any vendor can create their own extensions to the basic behavior. Additionally, the OpenGL ES specification defines a few optional extensions that are likely to be implemented by several vendors, as it would not be very useful if the vendors implemented them in slightly different ways.

We first explain the mechanism for querying which extensions are present and obtaining pointers to the extension functions. We continue by describing three extensions: query matrix, matrix palette, and draw texture.

10.4.1 QUERYING EXTENSIONS

The list of supported extensions can be queried by calling `glGetString` with the argument `GL_EXTENSIONS`. This call returns a space-separated string containing the list of all supported extensions. The application can then parse this string and use an OS-specific mechanism for obtaining access to the extension functions. If the platform supports EGL, then the function `eglGetProcAddress` can be used for receiving the address of an extension function:

```
/* define a function pointer of the right type, set to NULL */
void (*_glDrawTexx)(GLfixed, GLfixed, GLfixed, GLfixed, GLfixed) = NULL;

if( strstr( glGetString( GL_EXTENSIONS ), "GL_OES_draw_texture" ) )
{
  _glDrawTexx = (void (*)( GLfixed, GLfixed, GLfixed, GLfixed, GLfixed ))
            eglGetProcAddress( "glDrawTexxOES" );
}
```

In the example the return value from `eglGetProcAddress` is cast to a function pointer that matches the extension function prototype. If your implementation has the `glext.h` header file that contains a ready-made prototype for the extension, you can use it instead.

Note that `eglGetProcAddress` does not work for the core OpenGL ES functions. When extensions are folded into the core in newer versions, the extensions for the same functionality are also left in place so that they can still be queried with `eglGetProcAddress`.

10.4.2 QUERY MATRIX

The `OES_query_matrix` extension introduces the function `glQueryMatrixxOES` that can be used for reading back the top of the current matrix stack. This somewhat surprising function was introduced in OpenGL ES 1.0 as there was no support for any dynamic state queries, yet the working group felt that matrix read-back would be useful at least for debugging purposes. The function returns the matrix components' mantissas and exponents separately, thus providing a representation that is independent of the actual internal implementation of the matrix stack.

```
GLbitfield glQueryMatrixxOES(GLfixed mantissa[16], GLint exponent[16])
```

queries the matrix at the top of the current matrix stack. The *mantissa* array will contain the signed 16.16 mantissas of the 4×4 matrix, and the *exponent* array the exponents. Each entry is then $mantissa * 2^{exponent}$. The function returns *status*, which is a bitfield, which is zero if all the components are valid. If `status & (1<<i) != 0`, then component *i* is invalid (e.g., NaN or $+-$infinity). The following example queries the elements of the current matrix and converts them to floats. The mantissa is first converted to a float, then, depending on the sign of the exponent, it is either multiplied or divided by a suitable power of two.

```
int         i,j;
GLfixed     mantissa[16];
GLint       exponent[16];
GLfloat     matrix[16];
GLbitfield status;

status = glQueryMatrixxOES( mantissa, exponent );

if( 0 == status )
{
  for( i = 0; i < 16; i++ )
  {
    float t = (float)mantissa[i] / 65536.0f;
    matrix[i] = t * pow( 2, exponent[i] );
  }
}
```

Note that this extension has been deprecated in OpenGL ES 1.1. A new extension, `OES_matrix_get` is provided instead. This allows querying the internal floating-point matrices as integer bit patterns.

10.4.3 MATRIX PALETTE

Vertex skinning is brought into OpenGL ES by the optional `OES_matrix_palette` extension. This is a somewhat simplified version of the `ARB_matrix_palette` extension from the desktop world. Matrix palettes were first introduced to OpenGL ES in version 1.1.

Here is a short example code that first checks whether the optional extension is supported, then queries the extension function pointers, sets up the required OpenGL ES state to use the matrix palette, and finally sets up a few matrices in the matrix palette:

```
/* Check if extension is supported, bail out if not */
if( !strstr( glGetString(GL_EXTENSIONS), "GL_OES_matrix_palette" ) )
{
  return NULL;
}
```

```
/* Get the extension function pointers and store to global store */
_glCurrentPaletteMatrix          =
        (void (*)(GLuint))
        eglGetProcAddress( "glCurrentPaletteMatrixOES" );

_glLoadPaletteFromModelViewMatrix =
        (void (*)(void))
        eglGetProcAddress( "glLoadPaletteFromModelViewMatrixOES" );

_glMatrixIndexPointer            =
        (void (*)( GLint, GLenum, GLsizei, const GLvoid * ))
        eglGetProcAddress( "glMatrixIndexPointerOES" );

_glWeightPointer                 =
        (void (*)( GLint, GLenum, GLsizei, const GLvoid * ))
        eglGetProcAddress( "glWeightPointerOES" );

_glWeightPointer( 3, GL_FLOAT, 0, mtxweights );
_glMatrixIndexPointer( 3, GL_UNSIGNED_BYTE, 0, mtxindices );
glEnableClientState( GL_MATRIX_INDEX_ARRAY_OES );
glEnableClientState( GL_WEIGHT_ARRAY_OES );
glEnable( GL_MATRIX_PALETTE_OES );

/* set up basic modelview matrix */
glMatrixMode( GL_MODELVIEW );
glLoadIdentity();
glTranslatef( 0, 0, -4.f );
glScalef( 0.2f, 0.2f, 0.2f);

/* set up matrices in palette indices 0 and 1 */
glMatrixMode( GL_MATRIX_PALETTE_OES );
_glCurrentPaletteMatrix( 0 );
_glLoadPaletteFromModelViewMatrix();
glTranslatef( 0.7f, 0, 0 );
_glCurrentPaletteMatrix( 0 );
_glLoadPaletteFromModelViewMatrix();
glTranslatef( -0.2f, 0, 0 );
```

void glCurrentPaletteMatrixOES(GLuint *matrixpaletteindex*)

defines which matrix is affected by future matrix manipulation calls.

void glLoadPaletteFromModelViewMatrixOES(*void*)

copies the top of the modelview matrix stack to the current matrix palette.

void glMatrixIndexPointerOES(GLint *size*, GLenum *type*, GLsizei *stride*, const
　　　　　　　　　　　　　　GLvoid * *pointer*)

defines an array of matrix indices. The parameter *size* determines the number of indices per vertex, *type* is the data type of the indices (only GL_UNSIGNED_BYTE accepted), *stride* is the stride in bytes between consecutive matrix indices, and *pointer* points to the matrix index of the first vertex in the array. This vertex array is enabled by calling glEnableClientState with the argument GL_MATRIX_INDEX_ARRAY_OES.

```
void glWeightPointerOES(GLint size, GLenum type, GLsizei stride, const
                        GLvoid * pointer)
```

defines an array of matrix weights. The parameter *size* defines the number of weights per vertex, *type* is the data type used for the weights (GL_FIXED and GL_FLOAT are supported), *stride* is the stride in bytes between consecutive weights, and *pointer* points to the first weight of the first vertex. This vertex array is enabled by calling glEnableClientState with the argument GL_WEIGHT_ARRAY_OES.

There are several state queries that become possible if the matrix palette extension is supported. They are

GL_MATRIX_INDEX_ARRAY_BUFFER_BINDING_OES the buffer object name bound to the matrix index array.

GL_MATRIX_INDEX_ARRAY_SIZE_OES the number of matrix indices per vertex.

GL_MATRIX_INDEX_ARRAY_STRIDE_OES the byte offset between elements.

GL_MATRIX_INDEX_ARRAY_TYPE_OES the type of matrix indices.

GL_MAX_PALETTE_MATRICES_OES the number of supported matrix palettes (≥ 9).

GL_MAX_VERTEX_UNITS_OES the number of supported matrices per vertex (≥ 3).

GL_WEIGHT_ARRAY_BUFFER_BINDING_OES the buffer object name bound to weight array.

GL_WEIGHT_ARRAY_SIZE_OES the number of weights per vertex.

GL_WEIGHT_ARRAY_STRIDE_OES byte offset between weights.

GL_WEIGHT_ARRAY_TYPE_OES type of weights.

```
void glGetPointerv(GLenum pname, void ** params)
```

supports two additional tokens:

GL_MATRIX_INDEX_ARRAY_POINTER_OES
GL_WEIGHT_ARRAY_POINTER_OES

```
GLboolean glIsEnabled(GLenum cap)
```

supports these additional capabilities:

GL_MATRIX_PALETTE_OES
GL_MATRIX_INDEX_ARRAY_OES
GL_WEIGHT_ARRAY_OES

> **Pitfall:** Implementations only need to support 9 bones for a single vertex array. However, many models use more bones than 9, for example, a human character typically requires at least 15, even over 40 bones. If the model uses more bones than the OpenGL ES implementation can handle, you have to split the model into smaller partitions and render the mesh with several `glDrawElements` calls.

10.4.4 DRAW TEXTURE

The `OES_draw_texture` extension introduced in OpenGL ES 1.1 provides a mechanism for rendering a two-dimensional texture-mapped pixel rectangle to a rectangular portion of the screen.

```
void glDrawTex{sifx}OES(T x, T y, T z, T width, T height)
```

renders a texture-mapped pixel block to the screen. Here *x* and *y* define the window coordinates of the lower-left corner of the rectangle, and *z* is a value between 0 and 1 where 0 maps to the near plane and 1 maps to the far plane of the current depth range. The parameters *width* and *height* give the size of the screen rectangle in pixels.

```
void glDrawTex{sifx}vOES(const T * coords)
```

provides variants that take the five input coordinates as an array.

10.4.5 USING EXTENSIONS

When using an extension, you should first implement a generic version, and switch to the faster-executing extension only if it is available. The following example shows how this is done. Here point sprites are the preferred method, draw texture comes next, and the ultimate fall-back is to render two texture-mapped triangles. For the complete drawing code, see the full example on the accompanying web site.

```
{
    /* initial values for decision variables */
    int oes11      = 0;
    int drawtexture = 0;
    int pot        = 0;
    int pointsize   = 0;

    /* check GL version */
    ver   = glGetString( GL_VERSION );
    major = ver[strlen(ver)-3];
    minor = ver[strlen(ver)-1];
    if(minor > '0') oes11 = 1;

    /* Check drawtexture extension */
    if( strstr( glGetString(GL_EXTENSIONS), "GL_OES_draw_texture" ) )
```

```
{
  drawtexture = 1;
  _glDrawTexx = (void (*)( GLfixed, GLfixed, GLfixed, GLfixed,
                  GLfixed ))
                  eglGetProcAddress( "glDrawTexxOES" );
}
```

Next, we check whether the dimensions of the source are powers of two and whether the source region size is inside the supported point size range.

```
/* check if dimensions are power-of-two */
if(( getnextpow2( image_width )  == image_width ) &&
   ( getnextpow2( image_height ) == image_height ))
{
  pot = 1;
}

/* is the size supported? Supported point sprite
   range is the same as aliased point size range */
{
  GLfloat pointsizerange[2];
  glGetFloatv( GL_ALIASED_POINT_SIZE_RANGE, pointsizerange );

  if(( image_width >= pointsizerange[0] ) &&
     ( image_height <= pointsizerange[1] ))
  {
    pointsize = 1;
  }
}
```

Now the decision variables are ready for a final decision on which method is going to be used for rendering. The basic fall-back is to draw the region using two triangles.

```
/* if everything else fails, use two triangles */
method = BLIT_DRAW_METHOD_TRIANGLES;

/* if width == height AND power of two AND we have OpenGL ES 1.1 AND
   the point size is inside the supported range we use point sprites */
if( ( BLIT_WIDTH == BLIT_HEIGHT ) && oes11 && pot && pointsize )
{
  method = BLIT_DRAW_METHOD_POINTSPRITE;
}
else if(drawtexture)
{
  /* if draw_texture extension is supported, use it */
  method = BLIT_DRAW_METHOD_DRAWTEXTURE;
}
```

Each of these methods has different setup and drawing codes. Refer to the `blit` example on the companion web site for a fully working example that also does the setup of the methods and actual rendering. The example also shows the correct handling of point clipping for point sprites.

If you end up using a pair of texture-mapped triangles, the easiest approach is to set the modelview matrix, projection matrix, and viewport so that a single step in the x or y direction in vertex data is equal to a step of a single pixel on the display.

EGL

When the desktop OpenGL API was first specified, the windowing system and operating system dependent parts were left out of the core specification. Different windowing systems have their own ways to handle displays, windows, graphics devices, and contexts, and different operating systems developed their own companion APIs for initializing graphics resources. For X11 there is GLX, Mac has AGL, and Windows uses WGL.

Even though all of these APIs differ from each other, it is possible to create a "template API" that mostly abstracts out platform differences, but allows platform-dependent data types to be used where absolutely necessary. EGL unifies the OpenGL ES–related resource management across platforms, and defines standard function names and tokens for the implementations and applications to use. This increases source-level portability for OpenGL ES applications across the many operating systems in the mobile domain, e.g., Symbian, BREW, Linux, and Palm OS.

Some parameter types in EGL are really placeholders for OS-specific types. For example

```
EGLDisplay eglGetDisplay(NativeDisplayType display_id)
```

takes in an OS-dependent display type, initializes EGL to use that display, and returns an OS-independent type EGLDisplay. `NativeDisplayType` is usually typedef'd, as the name implies, to a handle to the native display type.

With this approach application developers ideally need only to change a few lines in their EGL initialization code when porting from one platform to another. Typically, an application developer only needs to take care of initializing the platform-dependent window, and to provide it as a parameter to `eglCreateWindowSurface`. All other EGL calls are portable across the different platforms.

One thing to note is that EGL is an optional API—platforms are free to choose how they bind their windowing with OpenGL ES. Luckily most platforms that have adopted OpenGL ES have also chosen to support EGL. This is good news for application portability.

This chapter begins with an example and an overview of the EGL functionality, then proceeds to describe EGL configuration, the different surface types supported by EGL, and the OpenGL ES/EGL context. We cover EGL extensions and describe how the surfaces can be used to mix OpenGL ES and other graphics library calls. We also cover additions introduced by EGL 1.1: optional support for rendering directly into texture maps, and better support for power events and power optimization.

11.1 API OVERVIEW

Here is a walk-through of a simplified EGL initialization code without error checking.

```
#include <GLES/egl.h>

const EGLint attrib_list[] =
{
    EGL_SURFACE_TYPE,   EGL_WINDOW_BIT,
    EGL_RED_SIZE,       8,
    EGL_GREEN_SIZE,     8,
    EGL_BLUE_SIZE,      8,
    EGL_DEPTH_SIZE,     16,
    EGL_NONE
};

EGLDisplay display;
EGLConfig  config;
EGLContext context;
EGLSurface surface;

void initEgl( void )
{
    int numofconfigs;
    display = eglGetDisplay( EGL_DEFAULT_DISPLAY );
    eglInitialize( display, NULL, NULL );
    eglChooseConfig( display, attrib_list, &config, 1,
                     &numofconfigs );
    context = eglCreateContext( display, config,
                                EGL_NO_CONTEXT, NULL );
    /* replace WINDOW() with the OS dependent window type */
    surface = eglCreateWindowSurface( display, config,
                                      WINDOW(), NULL );
```

```
        eglMakeCurrent( display, surface, surface, context );
    }

    void renderOneFrame( void )
    {
        /* some GL rendering calls ...  */
        eglSwapBuffers( display, surface );
    }

    void terminateEgl( void )
    {
        eglMakeCurrent( display, EGL_NO_SURFACE, EGL_NO_SURFACE,
                        EGL_NO_CONTEXT );
        eglDestroySurface( display, surface );
        eglDestroyContext( display, context );
        eglTerminate( display );
    }
```

First, we need to acquire a display. Some devices may support multiple displays, but in this example we simply use the default display, which we can do in a source-level portable way using the token EGL_DEFAULT_DISPLAY. Other than the default display, the display handling is platform-dependent, and you need to consult platform documentation to find out how displays are controlled. On some systems the display control may partially take place even outside EGL.

EGLDisplay eglGetDisplay void can be used to get the currently active display that is associated with the current context.

After the display handle has been acquired, EGL is initialized with

    EGLBoolean eglInitialize(EGLDisplay *dpy*, EGLint * *major*, EGLint * *minor*)

which returns EGL_TRUE on success, and if *major* and *minor* are not NULL they are filled with the EGL version number. If initialization fails, the function returns EGL_FALSE and sets up an error flag, which can be retrieved with

    EGLint eglGetError(void)

Possible errors returned by eglGetError are listed in Table 11.1.

After EGL has been initialized, you need to select a buffer configuration. Either eglChooseConfig or eglGetConfigs may be used to choose the configuration that best matches the given attributes. In the example code we simply retrieve a configuration that has at least 8 bits for each of the red, green, and blue color channels, at least 16 bits for the depth buffer, and that supports window surfaces (different surface types are covered later).

After a configuration is chosen, a surface and a *context* can be created. Contexts are containers that carry the whole internal state of OpenGL ES. You can use several contexts for each surface or use the same context for different surfaces. Surfaces represent containers where the actual rendered pixels will end up. In this example, we create a window surface, so the pixels will end up inside a window on the device display.

Table 11.1: EGL error codes.

Error	Meaning
EGL_SUCCESS	No errors
EGL_NOT_INITIALIZED	EGL not initialized, or could not be initialized
EGL_BAD_ACCESS	EGL cannot access the requested resource
EGL_BAD_ALLOC	EGL failed to allocate resources
EGL_BAD_ATTRIBUTE	Undefined attribute or attribute value
EGL_BAD_CONFIG	Config is not valid
EGL_BAD_CONTEXT	Context is not valid
EGL_BAD_CURRENT_SURFACE	Current surface is no longer valid
EGL_BAD_DISPLAY	Not a valid display or EGL not initialized on the requested display
EGL_BAD_MATCH	Arguments inconsistent
EGL_BAD_NATIVE_PIXMAP	NativePixmapType is not valid
EGL_BAD_NATIVE_WINDOW	NativeWindowType is not valid
EGL_BAD_PARAMETER	One of the parameters is not valid
EGL_BAD_SURFACE	Surface is not valid
EGL_CONTEXT_LOST	Power management event occurred, context lost

OpenGL ES rendering calls can be made only after a context and surface have been bound to the current thread by calling eglMakeCurrent. After the frame has been rendered, eglSwapBuffers is called to initiate transfer of pixels from the GL color buffer into an EGL surface (in this case the window).

Finally, EGL is terminated by first releasing the active surfaces and contexts with a call to eglMakeCurrent, then destroying them, and finally calling

```
EGLBoolean eglTerminate(EGLDisplay dpy)
```

to free all the resources associated with an EGL display connection.

11.2 CONFIGURATION

Different implementations may support different color depths, depth buffer depths, and so on, and a typical implementation supports 20 to 30 different configurations with different combinations of these attributes. However, the specification does not limit the number of configurations that may be supported. EGLConfig is an opaque handle to a configuration.

Table 11.2 lists all attributes that are specified for a single `EGLConfig`. Out of these attributes, the first thirteen are the ones that typical applications use.

`EGLBoolean eglGetConfigAttrib(EGLDisplay` *dpy*`, EGLConfig` *config*`,`
`EGLint` *attribute*`, EGLint * ` *value*`)`

Table 11.2: EGLConfig attributes, EGL 1.1 attributes marked with asterisk (*).

Attribute	Type	More info
EGL_SURFACE_TYPE	bitmask	surface types configs must supported
EGL_RED_SIZE	integer	red bits in color buffer
EGL_GREEN_SIZE	integer	green bits in color buffer
EGL_BLUE_SIZE	integer	blue bits in color buffer
EGL_ALPHA_SIZE	integer	alpha bits in color buffer
EGL_BUFFER_SIZE	integer	bits in the color buffer
EGL_DEPTH_SIZE	integer	bits in depth buffer
EGL_SAMPLE_BUFFERS	integer	number of multisample buffers
EGL_SAMPLES	integer	number of samples per pixel
EGL_STENCIL_SIZE	integer	bits in stencil buffer
EGL_MAX_PBUFFER_WIDTH	integer	maximum width of pbuffer
EGL_MAX_PBUFFER_HEIGHT	integer	maximum height of pbuffer
EGL_MAX_PBUFFER_PIXELS	integer	maximum size of pbuffer
EGL_BIND_TO_TEXTURE_RGB *	boolean	true if bindable to RGB textures
EGL_BIND_TO_TEXTURE_RGBA *	boolean	true if bindable to RGBA textures
EGL_CONFIG_CAVEAT	enum	caveats for the configuration
EGL_CONFIG_ID	integer	unique EGLConfig identifier
EGL_LEVEL	integer	frame buffer level: 0 = main, > 0 overlays, < 0 underlays
EGL_MAX_SWAP_INTERVAL *	integer	maximum swap interval
EGL_MIN_SWAP_INTERVAL *	integer	minimum swap interval
EGL_NATIVE_RENDERABLE	boolean	true if native APIs can render to surface
EGL_NATIVE_VISUAL_ID	integer	handle of corresponding native visual
EGL_NATIVE_VISUAL_TYPE	integer	native visual type of the associated visual
EGL_TRANSPARENT_TYPE	enum	type of transparency supported
EGL_TRANSPARENT_RED_VALUE	integer	transparent red value
EGL_TRANSPARENT_GREEN_VALUE	integer	transparent green value
EGL_TRANSPARENT_BLUE_VALUE	integer	transparent blue value

can be used to query the value of an *attribute* from a selected *config*.

```
EGLBoolean eglGetConfigs(EGLDisplay dpy, EGLConfig * configs,
                         EGLint config_size, EGLint * num_configs)
```

can be used to find out the `EGLConfig`s supported by the display *dpy*. If *configs* is NULL, the number of configurations the implementation supports is returned in *num_configs*. Otherwise *configs* should have room for *config_size* configurations, and *configs* is filled with at most *config_size* configurations. The actual number of configurations returned is stored in *num_configs*.

```
EGLBoolean eglChooseConfig(EGLDisplay dpy, const EGLint * attrib_list,
                           EGLConfig * configs, EGLint config_size,
                           EGLint * num_config)
```

returns a list of configs that match the specified attributes. Again, if *configs* is NULL, only the number of matching configs is returned. The requirements are stored in *attrib_list*, which contains a token, its value, next token, its value, and so on, until the list is terminated with the token `EGL_NONE`. The list returned in *configs* contains only configurations that fulfill the minimum requirements defined by *attrib_list*. The list returned is sorted using a pre-defined set of rules.

Table 11.3 lists the selection and sorting rules and sort priorities for each attribute. Selection criteria give the function for comparing an application-specified attribute value with the value of the configuration being processed. For example, for `EGL_DEPTH_SIZE` the selection rule is "AtLeast." This means that only configurations whose depth buffer bits equal or exceed the number specified by the application will be matched. In the example code in Section 11.1, only configs with a minimum of 16 bits of depth buffer are matched. "Exact" in the list means that the value must be matched exactly, and "Mask" means that all the bits defined by a bitmask must be set in order to obtain a match.

Sorting criteria for configurations are shown in Table 11.3. First the highest-priority sorting rule is applied to get an initial ordering for the configurations. For configurations that have the same sorting importance the rule with the next-highest priority is applied as a tie-breaker. This process is reiterated until the configurations have a clearly defined order. `EGL_CONFIG_CAVEAT` is sorted first, `EGL_X_SIZE` (where X = RED, GREEN, BLUE, or ALPHA) is sorted next, and so on. `EGL_CONFIG_ID`, which has the lowest priority, guarantees that there always exists a unique sorting order as no two configurations can have the same identifier number.

> **Pitfall:** Specifying `EGL_CONFIG_ID` in the *attrib_list* makes EGL match that ID exactly. The ID enumeration is not standardized, thus code relying on specific ID values is not portable.

The table also lists a sorting order for each attribute. For the depth buffer size the sort order is "Smaller." This means that the smaller depth buffer size values are ranked higher in the returned list. Note however that the sort priority for depth buffer size is

Table 11.3: EGLConfig matching criteria.

Attribute	Default value	Selection rule	Sort order	Sort priority
EGL_CONFIG_CAVEAT	EGL_DONT_CARE	Exact	Special	1
EGL_RED_SIZE	0	AtLeast	Special	2
EGL_GREEN_SIZE	0	AtLeast	Special	2
EGL_BLUE_SIZE	0	AtLeast	Special	2
EGL_ALPHA_SIZE	0	AtLeast	Special	2
EGL_BUFFER_SIZE	0	AtLeast	Smaller	3
EGL_SAMPLE_BUFFERS	0	AtLeast	Smaller	4
EGL_SAMPLES	0	AtLeast	Smaller	5
EGL_DEPTH_SIZE	0	AtLeast	Smaller	6
EGL_STENCIL_SIZE	0	AtLeast	Smaller	7
EGL_NATIVE_VISUAL_TYPE	EGL_DONT_CARE	Exact	Special	8
EGL_CONFIG_ID	EGL_DONT_CARE	Exact	Smaller	9 (last)
EGL_BIND_TO_TEXTURE_RGB	EGL_DONT_CARE	Exact	None	—
EGL_BIND_TO_TEXTURE_RGBA	EGL_DONT_CARE	Exact	None	—
EGL_LEVEL	0	Exact	None	—
EGL_NATIVE_RENDERABLE	EGL_DONT_CARE	Exact	None	—
EGL_MAX_SWAP_INTERVAL	EGL_DONT_CARE	Exact	None	—
EGL_MIN_SWAP_INTERVAL	EGL_DONT_CARE	Exact	None	—
EGL_SURFACE_TYPE	EGL_WINDOW_BIT	Mask	None	—
EGL_TRANSPARENT_TYPE	EGL_NONE	Exact	None	—
EGL_TRANSPARENT_RED_VALUE	EGL_DONT_CARE	Exact	None	—
EGL_TRANSPARENT_GREEN_VALUE	EGL_DONT_CARE	Exact	None	—
EGL_TRANSPARENT_BLUE_VALUE	EGL_DONT_CARE	Exact	None	—

6, so it is processed after many other sorting rules and thus it may not be triggered at all if the previous rules already produce a unique order. Some of the sorting orders are marked "Special" which means that for those attributes a more complex sorting order is specified in the EGL specification. For EGL_X_SIZE (where X can be RED, GREEN, BLUE, or ALPHA) the special rule states that configurations having a larger sum of the bits of the color components get ranked higher. Attributes whose matching values are marked zero (the default) or EGL_DONT_CARE are not considered during the sort. A more in-depth discussion of the other special sorting rules can be found in the EGL specification [Khr03].

> **Pitfall:** Trying to create a surface with a configuration ID that does not support rendering into such a surface type will fail. The best way to avoid this is to always specify `EGL_SURFACE_TYPE` when selecting configurations. Some implementations may support all surface types in every config, others may have configs that only support a particular surface, such as a pbuffer or a window surface.

Do not ask for multisampling in your config selection if it is not strictly needed. See Section 11.10 for an example of how to do proper selection of a multisampling buffer. Also, in some of the antialiasing methods sampling is really a part of the surface and cannot be dynamically enabled or disabled with `GL_MULTISAMPLE`. Although not quite compatible with the OpenGL ES specification, implementations may defer those changes to the next `eglSwapBuffers` call and the change may cause total reinitialization of the surface. Turning multisampling on and off each frame may really slow down the application.

As you may have noticed, the sorting rules and priorities are fixed, which may make it difficult to get exactly what you want. Also, in some cases like multisampling, you need to go through the returned list in the application code to get what you want. An example on how to properly take care of these issues while doing the configuration selection can be found in Section 11.10.

All implementations should provide at least one configuration that supports rendering into a window surface, and has at least 16 bits of color buffer and 15 bits of depth buffer resolution. However, all other bets are off. For example, the implementation may offer you only configurations that have zero bits in alpha or stencil buffers, indicating that destination alpha or stencil buffer operations are not supported. Similarly, if you find a configuration that has 24 bits of color and 8 bits of stencil that can render into pbuffers, there is no guarantee that there is an otherwise similar configuration that can render into window surfaces. Most implementations do support pbuffer surfaces as they usually are easy to implement. However, rendering through a native graphics API may or may not be supported (this can be specified with `EGL_NATIVE_RENDERABLE`).

EGL is becoming a central piece of the various Khronos APIs. It will be used for setting up rendering in other APIs apart from OpenGL ES and OpenVG. Some implementations may also support cross-API rendering. For example, you might be able to render with OpenVG into an OpenGL ES texture, or you could first render a 3D scene with OpenGL ES and then render some 2D overlay information to the same surface with OpenVG. Also, as the OpenGL ES 2.0 API is completely separate from OpenGL ES 1.x, it is addressed in future EGL versions as a different API.

11.3 SURFACES

Surfaces are buffers into which pixels are drawn. With *window surfaces* the color buffer contents will be sent to a window on the display. With *pbuffer surfaces* the contents will be kept in the graphics memory until they are either copied into a native pixmap with a call to `eglCopyBuffers`, or read to the application memory using `glReadPixels`. For *pixmap surfaces* the color buffer is in the same format as the native bitmaps. Out of these surfaces, only the window surfaces are really double-buffered.

> **Pitfall:** The EGL specification does not mandate which surface types must be supported. For maximum portability, applications should be able to cope with any of the three surface types. Typically at least window surfaces are supported.

EGL window surfaces for OpenGL ES are always double-buffered. After completing a swap with `eglSwapBuffers` the contents of the new color buffer are undefined. Certain implementations may have the results of some previous frames in the buffers, but this behavior cannot be guaranteed. For this reason, applications should not make any assumptions on the contents of the new color buffer.

> **Performance tip:** Window surfaces are double-buffered and thus typically provide the best performance of all surface types. Pixmap surfaces have the most constraints from the point of view of the GL engine, and therefore usually have the worst performance. See Section 11.7 for more information.

```
EGLSurface eglCreateWindowSurface(EGLDisplay dpy, EGLConfig config,
                                  NativeWindowType window, const
                                  EGLint * attrib_list)
```

is used to create a window surface. The parameter *config* gives the configuration that the surface is initialized with, and *window* provides the platform-dependent window where the surface should be initialized. For example in Symbian OS the native window type is (`RWindow *`). *attrib_list* is a placeholder for surface attributes to be used in the future. Since EGL 1.1 does not specify any attributes for a window surface, *attrib_list* should either be `NULL`, or it should point to an attribute list that has just `EGL_NONE` as its first element.

On success, this function returns a handle to the window surface. If *window* is not compatible with *config*, or if *config* does not support window surface rendering, the error `EGL_BAD_MATCH` is generated.

> **Pitfall:** As EGL does not specify exactly how the system interacts with the window surface, the behavior may vary, for example, when an OS dialog appears on top of a window surface. Some implementations may simply stop swapping pixels to the window surface but continue to accept GL calls; others may keep updating the part of the OpenGL ES window that remains visible, at a performance cost. The best practice is to pause the application whenever it loses the window focus.

```
EGLSurface eglCreatePbufferSurface(EGLDisplay dpy, EGLConfig config,
                                   const EGLint * attrib_list)
```

is used to create an off-screen surface called a *pbuffer surface*. All the parameters have the same meaning as with `eglCreateWindowSurface`. As pbuffer surfaces do not

have an associated window, the size of the buffer has to be defined using the parameter
attrib_list. Two attributes `EGL_WIDTH` and `EGL_HEIGHT` are supported. An example
of a valid list is { `EGL_WIDTH`, 320, `EGL_HEIGHT`, 240, `EGL_NONE` }. If the values are
not specified, the default value of zero is used instead.

You can use `glReadPixels` to transfer the pixels of a pbuffer into client-side memory,
and then copy them to the display using native graphics APIs. Alternatively you can use

> EGLSurface eglCopyBuffers(EGLDisplay *dpy*, EGLSurface *surface*,
>   NativePixmapType *target*)

which copies the color buffer values from a surface into a native bitmap. In an EGL 1.1
implementation, this function can return `EGL_CONTEXT_LOST` which indicates that a
power management event occurred that caused the GL context to be lost. In this case the
context should be reinitialized. Note also that this function calls internally `glFinish` to
get all of the rendering results into the bitmap. The parameter *surface* is the surface from
which the pixels are copied, and *target* specifies the platform-specific bitmap where the
pixels are stored (in Symbian OS this is defined as `CFbsBitmap`).

The target bitmap should be compatible with the surface. This means that its color depth
should match that of the configuration that was used to initialize the *surface*. However,
implementations may in practice relax this for the alpha value if they do not properly
support bitmaps with an alpha channel. Some platforms, e.g., older Symbian versions,
allow storing alpha channel values only in a separate single-channel bitmap.

Pbuffer surfaces are useful for doing off-screen platform-independent rendering that is
not connected to the native windowing system in any way. Also, pbuffers can be used in
conjunction with the render-to-texture functionality of EGL 1.1. This is covered in more
detail in Section 11.6.

> **Performance tip:** Reading pixels with `glReadPixels` is typically very slow, espe-
> cially if the graphics accelerator is on a separate chip and the read-back channel is slow.
> Typically `eglCopyBuffers` is also many times slower than rendering directly into a
> window surface.

> EGLSurface eglCreatePixmapSurface(EGLDisplay *dpy*, EGLConfig *config*,
>   NativePixmapType *pixmap*, const
>   EGLint * *attrib_list*)

is used to initialize a rendering surface whose render buffer is the underlying buffer
of the bitmap. Parameters are otherwise similar to `eglCreateWindowSurface`
with the exception that the platform-dependent type *pixmap* is here a bitmap. No
attributes are currently supported for pixmap surfaces. If the platform-specific bitmap
is not compatible with the *config*, or *config* does not support pixmap surfaces, the error
`EGL_BAD_MATCH` is returned.

> EGLBoolean eglDestroySurface(EGLDisplay *dpy*, EGLSurface *surface*)

is used to destroy a *surface* that was created using the functions described earlier. Note that if the *surface* is currently bound, the resources may not be freed until the *surface* is unbound.

> EGLBoolean eglQuerySurface(EGLDisplay *dpy*, EGLSurface *surface*,
>   EGLint *attribute*, EGLint * *value*)

is used for querying surface attributes. *surface* indicates the surface we are interested in, *attribute* tells which attribute we want to know, and *value* points to the memory location where the result is stored. For a list of queriable values, see Table 11.4. In the table *create* means that the value can be used when creating the surface, *set* means that it can be set after the surface has been created, and *query* means that it may be queried.

> EGLBoolean eglSurfaceAttrib(EGLDisplay *dpy*, EGLSurface *surface*,
>   EGLint *attribute*, EGLint *value*)

is used for setting surface attributes. Currently only EGL_MIPMAP_LEVEL can be set, and only for pbuffers that are mapped to a texture map.

> EGLSurface eglGetCurrentSurface(EGLint *readdraw*)

returns the current surface. *readdraw* should be either EGL_READ or EGL_DRAW to indicate whether the current read or write surface should be returned.

> EGLBoolean eglSwapBuffers(EGLDisplay *dpy*, EGLSurface *surface*)

is used to copy contents of a *surface* onto the native window on *dpy*. Note that *dpy* should be the same display the surface was initialized to. If an error occurs the function returns EGL_FALSE, and the error code can be fetched with eglGetError. In an

Table 11.4:   Surface attributes. EGL 1.1 attributes marked with asterisk (*).

Attribute	Usage	Meaning
EGL_PBUFFER_WIDTH	create, query	pbuffer width
EGL_PBUFFER_HEIGHT	create, query	pbuffer height
EGL_CONFIG_ID	query	id of EGLConfig that was used to create surface
EGL_LARGEST_PBUFFER	create, query	if true, create largest pbuffer possible
EGL_TEXTURE_FORMAT *	create, query	format of texture: RGB/RGBA/no texture
EGL_TEXTURE_TARGET *	create, query	type of texture: 2D or no texture
EGL_MIPMAP_TEXTURE *	create, query	surface has mipmaps for render-to-texture
EGL_MIPMAP_LEVEL *	set, query	mipmap level to render to

EGL 1.1 implementation, the error can be `EGL_CONTEXT_LOST` which indicates that a power management event occurred that caused the GL context to be lost. In this case the context should be reinitialized.

When rendering into native bitmaps, some synchronization is required between GL and the native rendering system.

```
EGLBoolean eglWaitGL(void)
```

waits until the GL engine has completed rendering to the currently bound surface. All OpenGL ES calls executed previously are guaranteed to have completed after the function returns. Applications using pixmap surfaces should call this function before moving from GL rendering to native 2D operations.

```
EGLBoolean eglWaitNative(EGLint engine)
```

can be used to wait for the native side to finish. All native rendering calls done with the library denoted by *engine* are guaranteed to have executed fully before this function returns. The default engine is selected with token `EGL_CORE_NATIVE_ENGINE`. Applications doing mixed rendering should call this function when moving from native rendering back to GL rendering.

As the native rendering APIs do not typically use depth, stencil, or multisample buffers, all native rendering is always drawn on top of the frame buffer without modifying these buffers. Since native rendering usually draws into the front buffer, mixed rendering into window surfaces should do GL rendering followed by `eglSwapBuffers` followed by native rendering. Note that the results of native rendering calls are only guaranteed to be visible on top of the GL rendering if the selected configuration supports `EGL_NATIVE_RENDERABLE`.

Pitfall: Not every EGL implementation is guaranteed to support multithreaded use. With Symbian OS, for example, the `RWindow` handle that is given as a parameter to `eglCreateWindowSurface` is thread-specific. Calling EGL commands that require access to the native window (such as `eglSwapBuffers`) from a different thread than the one that created it may panic and exit the application. For ultimate portability, limit EGL and GL usage to the main application thread.

11.4 CONTEXTS

A context is a container for the internal state of OpenGL ES. Entities such as texture objects, vertex buffer objects, matrix stacks, and lighting and material values are stored in a context. The application must create at least one context and make it active in order to perform any OpenGL ES rendering.

```
EGLContext eglCreateContext(EGLDisplay dpy, EGLConfig config,
                            EGLContext share_context, const
                            EGLint * attrib_list)
```

creates a rendering context that is compatible with *config* and *dpy*. This context can then be made current with a compatible rendering surface. The context shares all the shareable data with *share_context* and with the contexts that *share_context* shares data with, unless *share_context* is set to EGL_NO_CONTEXT. With OpenGL ES 1.0 and EGL 1.0 only texture objects could be shared across contexts. With OpenGL ES 1.1 and EGL 1.1 it is also possible to share vertex buffer objects. There are no supported attributes for *attrib_list*, but extensions may define some if needed.

    EGLBoolean eglDestroyContext(EGLDisplay *dpy*, EGLContext *ctx*)

destroys the context *ctx*. Note that if the context is currently bound, the resources may not be freed until *ctx* is unbound.

    EGLBoolean eglQueryContext(EGLDisplay *dpy*, EGLContext *ctx*,
                              EGLint *attribute*, EGLint * *value*)

is used to query value of *attribute* from the context *ctx*. The result is stored to the memory location pointed by *value*. Currently the only supported attribute is EGL_CONFIG_ID.

    EGLBoolean eglMakeCurrent(EGLDisplay *dpy*, EGLSurface *draw*,
                             EGLSurface *read*, EGLContext *ctx*)

binds the *draw* and *read* surfaces and the context *ctx* to the current rendering thread. *draw* specifies the surface where rendering results will appear, whereas *read* specifies the surface from which operations such as glReadPixels and glCopyTexImage2D will read data. In most cases *read* and *write* point to the same surface.

Applications may create multiple contexts and surfaces and make them current at any time by calling eglMakeCurrent. However, some context changes may be expensive. For example, binding rendering to a recently created context and surface can cause full hardware reconfiguration.

    EGLContext eglGetCurrentContext(void)

returns the currently bound context, or EGL_NO_CONTEXT if none exists.

    EGLDisplay eglGetCurrentDisplay(void)

returns the currently active display, or EGL_NO_DISPLAY if there is none.

11.5 EXTENSIONS

The EGL API provides a mechanism for adding extensions to both EGL itself and to the core rendering APIs, such as OpenGL ES and OpenVG. Extensions may add new tokens for existing functions, e.g., by adding a new texture format GL_RGBA_9675_XXX, or they can add new functions such as glPrintfXXX, where XXX is replaced with the vendor ID such as ATI, NV, or SGI. The extension EXT is used for multi-vendor extensions and OES for extensions specified by the OpenGL ES working group.

You can find out the extensions supported by OpenGL ES by calling `glGetString` (`GL_EXTENSIONS`) which returns a space-separated list of extension names. An equivalent function call in EGL is

```
const char * eglQueryString(EGLDisplay dpy, EGLint name)
```

which returns information about EGL running on display *dpy*. The queried *name* can be `EGL_VENDOR` for obtaining the name of the EGL vendor, `EGL_VERSION` for getting the EGL version string, or `EGL_EXTENSIONS` for receiving a space-separated list of supported extensions. The format of the `EGL_VERSION` string is

```
<major_version>.<minor_version><space><vendor specific info>
```

The extension list only itemizes the supported extensions; it does not describe how they are used. All the details of the added tokens and new functions are presented in an extension specification. There is a public extension registry at `www.khronos.org/registry/` where companies can submit their extension specifications. The Khronos site also hosts the extension header file `glext.h` which contains function prototypes and tokens for the extensions listed in the registry.

If the extension merely adds tokens to otherwise existing functions, the extension can be used directly by including the header `glext.h`. However, if the extension introduces new functions, their entry points need to be retrieved by calling

```
void (* eglGetProcAddress(const char * procname))()
```

which returns a pointer to an extension function for both GL and EGL extensions. One can then cast this pointer into a function pointer with the correct function signature.

11.6 RENDERING INTO TEXTURES

Pbuffers with configurations supporting either `EGL_BIND_TO_TEXTURE_RGB` or `EGL_BIND_TO_TEXTURE_RGBA` can be used for rendering directly into texture maps. The pbuffer must be created with special attributes as illustrated below.

```
EGLint pbuf_attribs[] =
{
  EGL_WIDTH,            width,
  EGL_HEIGHT,           height,
  EGL_TEXTURE_FORMAT,   EGL_TEXTURE_RGBA,
  EGL_TEXTURE_TARGET,   EGL_TEXTURE_2D,
  EGL_MIPMAP_TEXTURE,   EGL_TRUE,
  EGL_NONE
};
```

```
surface = eglCreatePbufferSurface( eglGetCurrentDisplay(),
                                   config, pbuf_attribs );

eglSurfaceAttrib( eglGetCurrentDisplay(), surface,
                  EGL_TEXTURE_LEVEL, 0 );
```

Texture dimensions are specified with EGL_WIDTH and EGL_HEIGHT, and they must be powers of two. EGL_TEXTURE_FORMAT specifies the base internal format for the texture, and must be either EGL_TEXTURE_RGB or EGL_TEXTURE_RGBA. EGL_TEXTURE_TARGET must be EGL_TEXTURE_2D. EGL_MIPMAP_TEXTURE tells EGL to allocate mipmap levels for the pbuffer.

EGL_TEXTURE_LEVEL can be set with eglSurfaceAttrib to set the current target texture mipmap level.

After rendering into a pbuffer is completed, the pbuffer can be bound as a texture with

EGLBoolean eglBindTexImage(EGLDisplay *dpy*, EGLSurface *surface*,
                           EGLint *buffer*)

where *buffer* must be EGL_BACK_BUFFER. This is roughly equivalent to freeing all mipmap levels of the currently bound texture, and then calling glTexImage2D to define new texture contents using the data in *surface* with texture properties such as texture target, format, and size being defined by the pbuffer attributes.

Mipmap levels are automatically generated by the GL implementation if the following hold at the time eglBindTexImage is called:

• EGL_MIPMAP_TEXTURE is set to EGL_TRUE for the pbuffer
• GL_GENERATE_MIPMAP is set for the currently bound texture
• value of EGL_MIPMAP_LEVEL is equal to the value of GL_TEXTURE_BASE_LEVEL

No calls to swap or to finish rendering are required. After *surface* is bound as a texture it is no longer available for reading or writing. Any read operations such as glReadPixels or eglCopyBuffers will produce undefined results.

After the texture is not needed anymore, it can be released with

EGLBoolean eglReleaseTexImage(EGLDisplay *dpy*, EGLSurface *surface*,
                              EGLint *buffer*)

11.7 WRITING HIGH-PERFORMANCE EGL CODE

As the window surface is multi-buffered, all graphics system pipeline units (CPU, vertex unit, fragment unit, display) are able to work in parallel. Single-buffered surfaces typically require that the rendering be working on a frame N while the vertex unit is working on frame $N+1$ completed when some synchronous API call to read pixels is performed. Only after the completion can new hardware calls be submitted for the same frame or the next one. When multi-buffered surfaces are used, the hardware has the choice of parallelizing between the frames, e.g., the fragment unit can be working on frame N while the vertex unit is working on frame $N+1$.

EGL buffer swaps may be implemented in various ways. Typically they are done either as a copy to the system frame buffer or using a flip chain. The copy is simple: the back buffer is copied as a block to the display frame buffer. A flip chain avoids this copy by using a list of display-size buffers. While one of the buffers is used to refresh the display, another buffer is used as an OpenGL ES back buffer. At the swap, instead of copying the whole frame to another buffer, one hardware pointer register is changed to activate the earlier OpenGL ES back buffer as the display refresh buffer, from which the display is directly refreshed.

A call to `eglSwapBuffers` can return immediately after the swap command, either a flip or a frame copy, is inserted into the command FIFO of the graphics hardware. See also Section 3.6.

> **Performance tip:** To get the best performance out of window surfaces, you should match the configuration color format to that of the system frame buffer. You should also use full-screen window surfaces if possible, as that may enable the system to use direct flips instead of copies.

Window surfaces can be expected to be the best-performing surfaces of most OpenGL ES implementations since they provide more opportunities for parallelism. However, the application can force even double-buffered window surfaces into a nonparallel mode by calling `glReadPixels`. Now the hardware is forced to flush the rendering pipeline and transfer the results to the client-side memory before the function can return. If the implementation was running the vertex and fragment units in parallel, e.g., vertex unit is on a DSP chip and the fragment unit runs on dedicated rasterization hardware, the engine needs to complete the previous frame on the rasterizer first and submit that to flip. After that, the implementation must force a flush to the vertex unit to get the results for the current frame and then force the fragment unit to render the pixels, while the vertex unit remains idle. Finally all the pixels are copied into client-side memory. During all this time, the CPU is waiting for the call to finish and cannot do any work in the same thread. As you can see, forcing a pipeline flush slows the system down considerably even if the application parallelizes well among the CPU, vertex unit, and rasterizer within a single frame. To summarize: calling `glReadPixels` every frame effectively kills all parallelism and can slow the application down by a factor of two or more.

Pbuffer surfaces have the same performance penalty as `glReadPixels` has for window surfaces. Using pbuffers forces the hardware to work in single-buffered mode as the pixels are extracted either via `glReadPixels` or`eglCopyBuffers`. Out of these two,`eglCopyBuffers` is often better as it may allow the buffer to be copied into a hardware-accelerated operating system bitmap instead of having to transmit the pixel data back to the host memory. If pbuffers are used to render into texture, the results remain on the server. However, using the results during the same frame may still create a synchronization point as all previous operations need to complete before the texture map can be used. If at all possible, you should access that texture at the earliest during the next frame.

You should also avoid calling EGL surface and context binding commands during rendering. Making a new surface current may force a flush of the previous frame before the new surface can be bound. Also, whenever the context is changed, the hardware state may need to be fully reloaded from the host memory if the context is not fully contained in a server-side object.

11.8 MIXING OPENGL ES AND 2D RENDERING

There are several ways to tie in the 3D frame buffer with the 2D native windowing system. The actual implementation should not be visible to the programmer, except when you try to combine 3D and 2D native rendering into the same frame. One reason to do so is if you want to add native user-interface components into your application or draw text using a font engine provided by the operating system. This is when the different properties of the various EGL surfaces become important.

As a general rule, double-buffered window surfaces are fastest for pure 3D rendering. However, they may be implemented so that the system's 2D imaging framework has no awareness of the content of the surface, e.g., the 3D frame buffer can be drawn into a separate overlay buffer, and the 2D and 3D surfaces are mixed only when the system refreshes the physical display. Pbuffers allow you to render into a buffer in server-side memory, from which you can copy the contents to a bitmap which can be used under the control of the native window system. Finally, pixmap surfaces are the most flexible choice, as they allow both the 3D API and the native 2D API to directly render into the same surface. However, not all systems support pixmap surfaces, or window surfaces that are also EGL_NATIVE_RENDERABLE.

In the following we describe three ways to mix OpenGL ES and native 2D rendering. No matter which approach you choose, the best performance is obtained if the number of switches from 3D to 2D or vice versa is minimized. For best results you should implement them all, measure their performance when the application is initialized, and dynamically choose the one that performs best.

11.8.1 METHOD 1: WINDOW SURFACE IS IN CONTROL

The most portable approach is to let OpenGL ES and EGL control the final compositing inside the mixing window. You should first draw the bitmaps using a 2D library, either the one that is native to the operating system, or for ultimate portability your own 2D library. You should then create an OpenGL ES texture map from that bitmap, and finally render the texture into the OpenGL ES back buffer using a pair of triangles. A call to `eglSwapBuffers` transfers all the graphics to the display. This approach works best if the 2D bitmap does not need to change at every frame.

11.8.2 METHOD 2: PBUFFER SURFACES AND BITMAPS

The second approach is to render with OpenGL ES into a hardware-accelerated pbuffer surface. Whenever there is a switch from 2D to 3D rendering, texture uploading is used as in the previous method. Whenever there is a switch from 3D rendering into 2D, `eglCopyBuffers` copies the contents of the pbuffer into a native pixmap. From there the native 2D API can be used to transfer the graphics to the display, or further 2D-to-3D and 3D-to-2D rendering mode switches can be made. `glReadPixels` can also be used to obtain the color buffer from OpenGL ES, but `eglCopyBuffers` is faster if the implementation supports optimized server-side transfers of data from pbuffers into OS bitmaps. With `glReadPixels` the back buffer of OpenGL ES has to be copied into CPU-accessible memory.

Note that the texture upload may be very costly. If there are many 2D-to-3D-to-2D switches during a single frame, the texture transfers and the cost of `eglCopyBuffers` begin to dominate the rendering performance as the graphics hardware remains idle most of the time.

> **Performance tip:** Modifying an existing texture that has already been transferred to the server memory may be more costly than you think. In fact, in some implementations it may be cheaper to just create a new texture object and specify its data from scratch.

11.8.3 METHOD 3: PIXMAP SURFACES

EGL pixmap surfaces, if the system supports them, can be used for both native 2D and OpenGL ES 3D rendering. When switching from one API to another, EGL synchronization functions `eglWaitNative` and `eglWaitGL` are used. When all rendering passes have been performed, pixels from the bitmap may be transferred to the display using an OS-specific bit blit operation.

On some systems the pixel data may be stored on the graphics server at all times, and the only data transfers are between the 3D subsystem and the 2D subsystem. Nevertheless, switching from one API to another typically involves at least a full 3D pipeline flush at each switch, which may prevent the hardware from operating in a fully parallel fashion.

11.9 OPTIMIZING POWER USAGE

As mobile devices are battery-powered, minimizing power usage is crucial to avoid draining the battery too quickly. In this section we cover the power management support of EGL. We first discuss what the driver may do automatically to manage power consumption. We then tell what the programmer may do to minimize power consumption in the *active mode* where the application runs in the foreground, and then consider the *idle mode* where the application is sent to the background. Finally we find out how power consumption can be measured, and conclude with actual power measurements using some of the presented strategies.

11.9.1 POWER MANAGEMENT IMPLEMENTATIONS

Mobile operating systems differ on how they handle power management. Some operating systems try to make application programming easier and hide the complexity of power management altogether. For example, on a typical S60 device, the application developer can always assume that the context is not lost between power events. Then again, others fully expose the power management handling and events to the applications. For example, the application may be responsible for restoring the state of some of the resources, e.g., the graphics context, when returning from power saving mode.

For the operating systems where applications have more responsibility for power management, EGL 1.1 provides limited support for recognizing power management events. The functions `eglSwapBuffers` and `eglCopyBuffers` indicate a failure by returning `EGL_FALSE` and setting the EGL error code to `EGL_CONTEXT_LOST`. In these cases the application is responsible for restoring the OpenGL ES state from scratch, including textures, matrices, and other states.

In addition to the EGL power management support, driver implementations may have other ways to save power. Some drivers may do the power management so that whenever the application is between `eglInitialize` and `eglTerminate`, no power saving is performed. When EGL is not active, the driver may allow the system to enter a deeper sleep mode to save power. For such implementations, 3D applications that have lost their focus should terminate EGL to free up power and memory resources.

Some drivers may be more intelligent about power saving and try to do it by analyzing the activity of the software or hardware and determining from that whether some automatic power state change events should be made. For example, if there have been no OpenGL ES calls in the previous 30 seconds, the driver may automatically allow the system to enter deeper sleep modes. In these cases, EGL may either set an `EGL_CONTEXT_LOST` error on `eglSwapBuffers`, or it may handle everything automatically so that when new GL calls are made, the context is restored automatically. In some cases the inactivity analysis may be done at various granularity levels, also within a single frame of rendering.

In certain cases the clock frequency and voltage of the graphics chip can be controlled based on the activity of the graphics hardware. Here the driver may attempt to detect how much of the hardware is actually being used for graphics processing. For example, if the graphics hardware is only used at 30% capacity for a duration of 10 seconds, the hardware may be reset to a lower clock frequency and voltage until the graphics usage is increased again.

A power-usage aware application on, for example, the S60 platform could look like the one below. The application should listen to the foreground/background event that the application framework provides. In this example, if the application goes to background, it starts a 30-second timer. If the timer triggers before the application comes to the foreground again, a callback to free up resources is triggered. The timer is used to minimize EGL reinitialization latency if the application is sent to background only for a brief period. For a complete example, see the example programs provided in the accompanying web site.

```
void CMyAppUI::HandleForegroundEventL( TBool aForeground )
{
  if( !aForeground )
  {
    /* we were switched to background */
    ... disable frame loop timer ...
    ... start a timer for 30 seconds to call to a callback ...
    iMyState->iWaitingForIdleTimer = ETrue;
  }
  else
  {
   /* we were switched to foreground */
   if( !iMyState->iInitialized )
   {
     /* we are not initialized */
     initEGL();
     iMyState->iWaitingForTimer = EFalse;
   }
  }
}


void CMyAppUI::initEGL()
{
  ... calls to initialize EGL from scratch ...
  ... calls to reload textures & setup render state ...
  ... restart frame loop timer ...
  iMyState->iInitialized = ETrue;
}

void myTimerCallBack( TAny *aPtr )
{
  ... cast aPtr to appui class ...
  appUI->iWaitingForTimer  = EFalse;
  appUI->iInitialized      = EFalse;
```

```
    ... calls to terminate EGL ...
  }

  void myRenderCallBack( TAny *aPtr )
  {
    ... cast aPtr to appui class ...
    ... GL rendering calls ...

    if( !eglSwapBuffers( iDisplay, iSurface ) )
    {
      EGLint err = eglGetError();
      if(err == EGL_CONTEXT_LOST)
      {
        /* suspend or some other power event occurred, context lost */
        appUI->initEGL();    /* reinitialize EGL */
      }
    }
  }
```

11.9.2 OPTIMIZING THE ACTIVE MODE

Several tricks can be employed to conserve the battery for a continuously running application. First, the frame rate of the application should be kept to a minimum. Depending on the EGL implementation, the buffer swap rate is either capped to the display refresh rate or it may be completely unrestricted. If the maximum display refresh is 60Hz and your application only requires an update rate of 15 frames per second, you can cut the workload roughly to one-quarter by manually limiting the frame rate.

A simple control is to limit the rate of `eglSwapBuffers` calls from the application. In an implementation that is not capped to display refresh this will limit the frame rate roughly to your call rate of `eglSwapBuffers`, provided that it is low enough. In implementations synchronized to the display refresh this will cause EGL to miss some of the display refresh periods, and get the swap to be synchronized to the next active display refresh period.

There is one problematic issue with this approach. As the display refresh is typically handled completely by the graphics driver and the screen driver, an application has no way of limiting the frame rate to, e.g., half of the maximum display refresh rate. This issue is remedied in EGL 1.1 which provides an API call for setting the swap intervals. You can call

```
EGLBoolean eglSwapInterval(EGLDisplay dpy, EGLint interval)
```

to set the minimum number of vertical refresh periods (*interval*) that should occur for each `eglSwapBuffers` call. The *interval* is silently clamped to the range defined by the values of the `EGL_MIN_SWAP_INTERVAL` and `EGL_MAX_SWAP_INTERVAL` attributes of the `EGLConfig` used to create the current context. If *interval* is set to zero, buffer swaps are not synchronized in any way to the display refresh. Note that EGL implementations may set the minimum and maximum to be zero to flag that only unsynchronized swaps are supported, or they may set the minimum and maximum to one to flag that only normal synchronized refreshes (without frame skipping) are supported. The swap interval may in some implementations be only properly supported for full-screen windows.

Another way to save power is to simplify the rendered content. Using fewer triangles and limiting texture mapping reduces both the memory bandwidth and the processing required to generate the fragments. Both of these factors contribute to the system power usage. Combining content optimizations with reduced refresh rates can yield significant power savings. Power optimization strategies can vary significantly from one system to another. Using the above tricks will generally optimize power efficiency for all platforms, but optimizing the last drop of energy from the battery requires device-specific measurements and optimizations.

11.9.3 OPTIMIZING THE IDLE MODE

If an application knows in advance that graphics processing is not needed for a while, it should attempt to temporarily release its graphics resources. A typical case is where the application loses focus and is switched to the background. In this case it may be that the user has switched a game to background because a more important activity such as a phone call requires her attention.

Under some power management schemes, even if the 3D engine does not produce any new frames, some reserved resources may prevent deeper sleep modes of the hardware. In such a case the battery of the device may be drained much faster than in other idle situations. The application could then save power by releasing all EGL resources and calling `eglTerminate` to free all the remaining resources held by EGL.

Note, however, that if`eglTerminate` is called, the application needs to restore its context and surfaces from scratch. This may fail due to out-of-memory conditions, and even if it succeeds, it may take some time as all active textures and vertex buffer objects need to be reloaded from permanent memory. For this reason applications should wait a bit before freeing all EGL resources. Tying the freeing of EGL resources to the activation of the screen saver makes sense assuming the operating system signals this to the applications.

11.9.4 MEASURING POWER USAGE

You have a couple of choices for verifying how much the power optimizations in your application code improve the power usage of the device. If you know the pinout of the battery of your mobile device, you can try to measure the current and voltage from the battery interface and calculate the power usage directly from that. Otherwise, you can use a simple software-based method to get a rough estimate.

The basic idea is to fully charge the battery, then start your application, and let it execute until the battery runs out. The time it takes for a fully charged battery to become empty is the measured value. One way to time this is to use a regular stopwatch, but as the batteries may last for several hours, a more useful way is to instrument the application to make timed entries into a log file. After the battery is emptied, the log file reveals the last time stamp when the program was still executing.

Here are some measurements from a simple application that submits about 3000 small triangles for rendering each frame. Triangles are drawn as separate triangles, so about 9000 vertices have to be processed each frame. This test was run on a Nokia N93 mobile phone. The largest mipmap level is defined to be 256 × 256 pixels. In the example code there are five different test runs:

1. Render textured (not mipmapped), lit triangles, at an unbounded frame rate (about 30–35 FPS on this device);

2. Render textured (not mipmapped), lit triangles, at 15 FPS;

3. Render textured, mipmapped, lit triangles, at 15 FPS;

4. Render nontextured, lit triangles, at 15 FPS;

5. Render nontextured, nonlit triangles (fetching colors from the vertex color array), at 15 FPS.

From these measurements two figures were produced. Figure 11.1 shows the difference in the lengths of the power measurement runs. In the first run the frame rate was unlimited, while in the second run the frame rate was limited to 15 frames per second. Figure 11.2 shows the difference between different state settings when the frame rate is kept at 15 FPS.

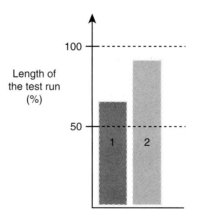

Figure 11.1: Duration of the test with unbounded frame rate (test 1) and with frame rate capped to 15 FPS (test 2).

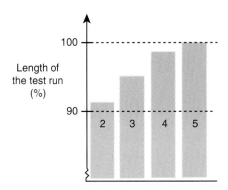

Figure 11.2: Duration with frame rate capped to 15 FPS but with different features enabled. 2 = textured and lit, 3 = textured with mipmaps and lit, 4 = nontextured and lit, 5 = nontextured, no lighting.

Studying Figure 11.1 one can see that dropping the frame rate has the biggest effect on how long the batteries last (about 30%). Enabling mipmapping also saves some energy by allowing more coherent memory access patterns, as can be seen in Figure 11.2. Disabling texture mapping has some effect, as well as dropping lighting altogether. Although on this particular hardware the optimizations in examples 2–5 did not provide significant wins, on some other hardware the effect may be more noticeable, especially if the vertex pipeline is not hardware accelerated.

11.10 EXAMPLE ON EGL CONFIGURATION SELECTION

The criteria for optimal EGL configuration selection logic depend on the application, so no generic optimal solution can be implemented. If it were possible, it would already be implemented in EGL! In this example, the primary goal is to find a configuration that matches at least the minimum color buffer and depth buffer bit depths requested by the application. A secondary goal is to find a configuration that has at least as many stencil bits as requested by the application. If such a configuration does not exist, stencil selection will be completely ignored by the rest of the code. Finally, a configuration with the best antialiasing quality is selected among the configurations that otherwise match the requirements. The example function does not return any information about the configuration that was selected, as these can be queried using the various `glGet` functions.

An alternate way for compactly specifying the requirements in the application would be to let the application specify both the minimum and optimal requirements for the attributes, and then sort the requirements in the order of importance. In this case the configuration that matches the optimal requirements would be searched for, and if multiple candidates are found, the one with the best antialiasing support would be picked. If no configurations fulfill the optimal requirements, a configuration that matches at least the minimum requirements would be selected. If no configuration is found that supports even the minimum requirements, none would be returned, and the application would have to exit.

In the first code snippet, we construct a list of configuration attributes and filter out with `eglChooseConfig` the configurations that clearly do not match our surface type requirements (set by the caller), color depth, and depth buffer bits. If stencil bits are requested, they are also set as a requirement to the attribute list.

```
EGLConfig select_config( int surfacetype, int framebuf_bits,
                         int depthbuf_bits, int stencil_bits )
{
  EGLBoolean  err;
  EGLint      amount;
  EGLint      attrib_list[5*2];
  EGLConfig   configs[64], best_config;
  EGLint *ptr = &attrib_list[0];

  *ptr++ = EGL_SURFACE_TYPE;
  *ptr++ = surfacetype;
  *ptr++ = EGL_BUFFER_SIZE;
  *ptr++ = framebuf_bits;
  *ptr++ = EGL_DEPTH_SIZE;
  *ptr++ = depthbuf_bits;

  if( stencil_bits )
  {
    *ptr++ = EGL_STENCIL_SIZE;
    *ptr++ = stencil_bits;
  }
  *ptr++ = EGL_NONE;

  err = eglChooseConfig( eglGetDisplay( EGL_DEFAULT_DISPLAY ),
                         &attrib_list[0], &configs[0],
                         64, &amount);
```

Now, `amount` contains the number of configurations that fulfill our requirements. If no configurations were returned, a new call to `eglChooseConfig` is made with an attribute list where the stencil requirement is dropped.

```
  if( amount == 0 )
  {
    attrib_list[6] = EGL_NONE;
    err = eglChooseConfig( eglGetDisplay( EGL_DEFAULT_DISPLAY ),
                           &attrib_list[0], &configs[0],
                           64, &amount );
  }
```

At this stage, we either have a list of configurations supporting stencil, or we have configurations that do not support stencil, or we have zero configurations if the basic requirements are not met. If no configurations exist, we just exit the code. Otherwise, we continue by finding the one with the best antialiasing, i.e., most samples per pixel.

```
if( amount > 0 )
{
  int i, best_samples;

  best_samples    = 0;
  best_config     = configs[0];

  for( i = 0; i < amount; i++ )
  {
    int samp;

    eglGetConfigAttrib( eglGetDisplay( EGL_DEFAULT_DISPLAY ),
                        configs[i], EGL_SAMPLES, &samp );

    if( samp > best_samples )
    {
      best_config  = configs[i];
      best_samples = samp;
    }
  }
  return best_config;
}
else
{
  return (EGLConfig) 0;
}
}
```

PART III
M3G

INTRODUCING M3G

Practically all mobile phones sold in developed countries are equipped with Java Micro Edition (Java ME), making it the most widely deployed application platform in the history of computing. A rapidly growing subset of those devices come pre-installed with M3G (Mobile 3D Graphics API for Java ME; also known as JSR 184) [JCP05]. As of 2007, there are more than a dozen device vendors shipping M3G-enabled devices, with yearly shipments in the order of hundreds of millions. To get hold of such a device, just pick up—for example—any Nokia or Sony Ericsson phone with a quarter-VGA display (240 × 320 pixels).

This chapter introduces M3G, putting it in the context of the mobile Java environment, OpenGL ES, and other scene graph engines. The later chapters will get you started with programming on M3G. Our presentation is aligned with Part I of this book, and builds on concepts introduced there. In other words, we assume that you are familiar with the OpenGL (ES) rendering model, scene graphs, keyframe animation, mesh deformation, and so on. Reading Part II will give you further insight to the inner workings of M3G, but it is not a prerequisite for understanding the following chapters or for utilizing M3G in practice.

This book is not about teaching Java programming; you should already have working knowledge of objects, classes, inheritance, exceptions, garbage collection, Java virtual machines, and other basic concepts of object-oriented programming. Neither is this book about mobile Java per se; we do not explain how to use its 2D graphics libraries, or how to write well-behaving applications. Familiarity with these topics may help, but is not strictly necessary, as our example framework (available on the companion web site) takes care of all the non–3D-related code.

12.1 OVERVIEW

The Mobile 3D Graphics API provides Java programmers with an efficient and compact interface for managing and rendering 3D scenes. It is based on the established OpenGL rendering pipeline, yet designed for Java with an object-oriented mindset, providing for a shallow learning curve for beginners, and high productivity for seasoned 3D programmers. Due to its retained-mode design, it minimizes the performance overhead of the Java virtual machine. The strict specifications and rigorous conformance tests of M3G ensure application portability from one device to another, allowing developers to reach hundreds of millions of devices from different vendors with a reasonable effort.

12.1.1 MOBILE JAVA

Figure 12.1 shows an overview of the mobile Java software architecture and the positioning of M3G in it. At the top of the diagram, we have the applications, called *midlets* in this environment. The term originates from MIDP, the Mobile Information Device Profile, which is shown in the diagram just beneath the application layer. MIDP defines the structuring and packaging of mobile Java applications, as well as the basic features that are available to them in the runtime execution environment.

All midlets must adhere to an event-driven framework that is intended to make them better behaved with respect to shared resources and system events, such as incoming phone calls. To this end, midlets cannot have a `main` method, but must instead implement

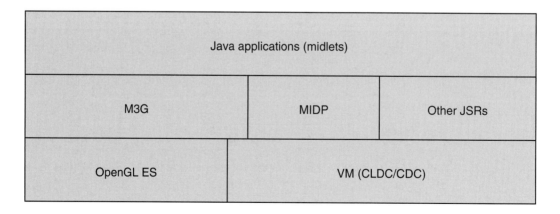

Figure 12.1: The mobile Java software stack.

a set of event handlers like `startApp` and `pauseApp`, as shown in Figure 12.2. Along with the application framework, MIDP also provides basic facilities for controlling the display, polling the keypad, rendering 2D graphics and text, accessing the network, playing back audio, and so on.

A contemporary mobile handset has a dozen or so built-in APIs that are standardized under various Java Specification Requests. The most widely available ones include the Mobile Media API (JSR 135), the Wireless Messaging API (JSR 120), and of course M3G. Some devices also include vendor-specific packages, residing in namespaces other than the standard `javax.microedition`. For example, the fairly widespread Nokia UI API resides in the `com.nokia.mid.ui` package.

Going back to Figure 12.1 and proceeding to the bottom layer there, we first encounter OpenGL ES. As discussed in Section 5.2.4, M3G is conceptually based on OpenGL ES,

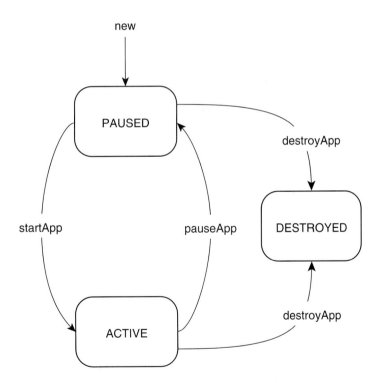

Figure 12.2: The life cycle of an application in Java MIDP. The application may be in one of three states: paused, active, or destroyed. State transitions are controlled by the application framework, and signaled to the midlet via the three event handlers shown in the diagram. All midlets must implement these event handlers, as well as a constructor; some of the methods may be empty, though. The midlet is responsible for acquiring and releasing its resources as appropriate upon each event.

but some implementations use tailor-made software rasterizers instead. All hardware-accelerated devices are probably using OpenGL ES, though.

Finally, at the bottom right of Figure 12.1, we have the Java Virtual Machine (VM) with its core libraries. The core libraries are defined in CLDC (Connected Limited Device Configuration) for typical devices, or the less limited CDC on some high-end devices. There are other flavors of mobile Java than the one presented here, mainly in Japan, but the CLDC/MIDP combination is so dominant that we will use it as a synonym to Java Micro Edition in this book. Besides, M3G has been deployed on all variants of mobile Java, as well as on desktop Java, and it works the same way on all of them.

Compared to desktop Java, some of the most important differences in mobile Java (CLDC/MIDP) are the lack of the Java Native Interface (JNI), lack of dynamic class loading, and limited built-in libraries. These restrictions are in place to help guarantee security and to reduce hardware requirements. As a result, you cannot include native code with your midlet, load and unload classes to optimize memory use, or load classes over the network to dynamically extend your application. You must also implement some basic things like inverse trigonometric functions in your own code. Appendix B provides further information on the inner workings of Java virtual machines.

12.1.2 FEATURES AND STRUCTURE

M3G can be thought of as an object-oriented interface to OpenGL ES at the low level, and as a link to digital content creation tools—such as 3ds Max or Maya from Autodesk,[1] Softimage,[2] or the freely available Blender[3]—at the high level.

Figure 12.3 shows the class diagram of M3G. All the classes are defined in the `javax.microedition.m3g` package. We will refer to this figure in the later chapters as we discuss each class in detail. The base class of the hierarchy is `Object3D`; all objects that can be rendered or be part of a scene graph are derived from it. These objects are collectively known as *scene graph objects*, and they form the bulk of the API. There are only four classes that are not derived from `Object3D`: `Graphics3D` takes care of all rendering; `Loader` is for importing art assets and scenes from files or over the network; `Transform` represents a generic 4 × 4 matrix; and `RayIntersection` is used for picking objects in the scene.

At its foundation, M3G wraps coherent blocks of OpenGL ES state into *retained-mode* objects that are controlled by the M3G engine, and can thus be stored and processed completely in native code (see Section 5.3). Classes that can be considered simple wrappers for OpenGL concepts are indicated by the dashed outline in Figure 12.3. Nearly all

---

1   www.autodesk.com

2   www.softimage.com

3   www.blender.org

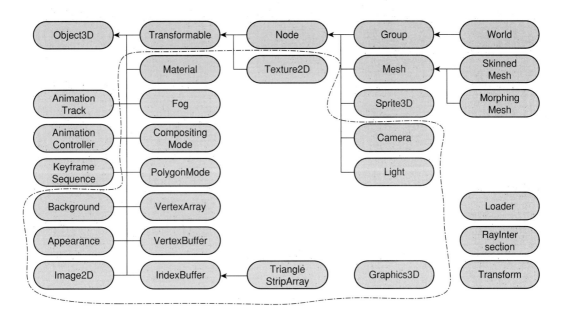

Figure 12.3: The M3G class hierarchy consists of 30 classes, all but four of them derived from `Object3D`. Classes that are simple wrappers for OpenGL ES and EGL functionality are demarcated by the dashed line. The other classes provide capabilities that are beyond the scope of OpenGL, such as object and scene representation, keyframe animation, and content loading.

features of OpenGL ES 1.0 are available through M3G, although a few were abstracted into a simplified form, e.g., blending and depth testing, and certain rarely used features were dropped altogether, e.g., logic ops, points, and lines. Also, to provide developers with a less fragmented platform, anything that is optional in OpenGL ES or poorly supported in hardware was left out, e.g., stencil buffering. Refer back to Figure 3.1 to see how the rendering pipeline differs from that of OpenGL ES 1.1.

Building on the core rendering features, M3G defines a scene graph where the retained-mode components can be linked with each other to form complete objects, groups of objects, and ultimately an entire scene. M3G supports the types of scene graph *nodes* that one would expect to find in a scene graph API, including `Camera`, `Light`, `Group`, and a basic rigid-body `Mesh`. In addition, there are two deformable variants of `Mesh`: the `SkinnedMesh` that is animated by a bone hierarchy, and the `MorphingMesh` that is deformed by linear blending of morph targets. Figure 12.4 illustrates how these and other high-level features relate to the OpenGL ES vertex pipeline. The scene graph nodes also include `Sprite3D`, which is useful for 2D billboards and overlays, and `World`, which is the scene graph root. A simple example of a scene graph is shown in Figure 12.5.

To keep the scene graph lightweight and uncomplicated, M3G does not include explicit support for terrains, shadows, portals, particles, and other advanced high-level features.

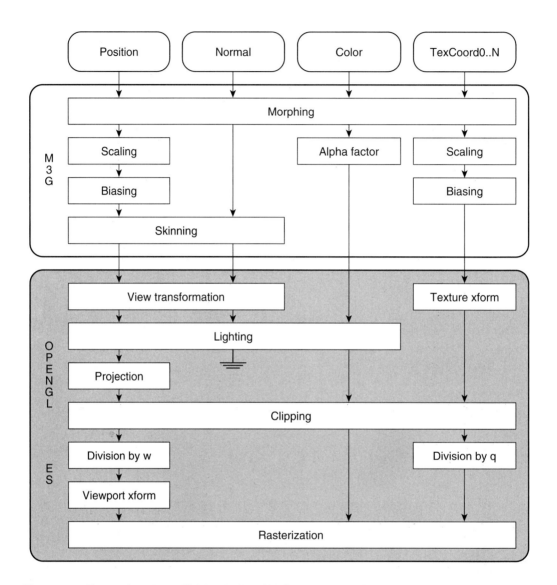

Figure 12.4: The transformation and lighting pipeline of M3G. The back end of the pipeline is the same as in OpenGL ES. The front end provides morphing, skinning, scaling, biasing, and the alpha factor. These are described in Chapters 14 through 16. Although not indicated by this diagram, morphing and skinning are mutually exclusive.

Also, the scene graph nodes can have at most one parent, i.e., there is no support for instancing at the node level. However, all substantial data, e.g., textures, vertices, indices, and animations, are in the node components, and can be shared by arbitrarily many nodes. Node instancing was dropped to keep things simple; many scene graph operations are easier to define and implement on a tree, as compared to a directed acyclic graph.

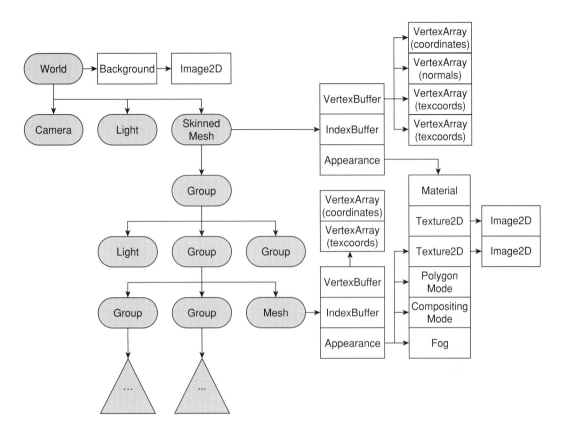

Figure 12.5: An example scene graph. The gray, rounded boxes are scene graph nodes, while the square boxes are node components. Note how some of the Appearance components are shared by the `SkinnedMesh` and the regular `Mesh`.

The recommended way of using M3G is to set up a complete scene graph in the beginning, and only make relatively minor modifications to it on a per-frame basis. It is possible to render individual objects in the *immediate mode*, but rendering an entire scene graph in one go, using the *retained mode*, is far more efficient. Using the retained mode reduces the amount of Java code executed and the number of methods called, allows the engine to draw the objects in an optimal order, enables the use of hierarchical view frustum culling, and so on. In some cases, the best approach is to render most of the scene in retained mode, adding perhaps a player character and some special effects into the scene using the immediate mode.

One of the key features of M3G is its keyframe animation engine. It can animate any property of any object by sampling a user-specified animation curve. It is conceptually simple, yet allows almost any arbitrary animation curve to be exported from DCC tools using only a modest number of keyframes. The animation engine is decoupled from rendering, allowing you to first apply some predefined animations, add in some programmatic animation on top, and only then render the scene. Any properties targeted by the animation engine can be equally well modified by calling individual methods in the API. The animation engine merely adds a conceptual model on top, allows complex animations to be predefined in authoring tools, and provides better performance by running in native code. You can use it for simple playback of predefined animations, or as the back-end of a more comprehensive system driven by physics or AI, for instance.

The keyframe animation system is composed of three classes. `KeyframeSequence` stores the actual keyframes and specifies the interpolation mode and whether the sequence is looping or not. `AnimationController` defines the speed of the animation as a function of *world time*, which is provided by the application at each call to `animate`. This is demonstrated in the "Hello, World" example below. `AnimationTrack` links together the keyframe sequence, the animation controller, and the target object.

Finally, M3G offers a binary file format that has a one-to-one mapping with the API. The file format and the related utility functions facilitate separation of artistic content from programmable application logic.

12.1.3 HELLO, WORLD

To give you a quick glimpse of how the API is used, without yet explaining things in detail, let us introduce the "Hello, World" of M3G. This piece of code, shown below, is possibly the shortest fully functional M3G animation player you can write. The midlet first loads a complete scene from a `.m3g` file, and then proceeds to animate and render it at the maximum frame rate until the user presses a key.

```
import javax.microedition.m3g.*;
import javax.microedition.lcdui.*;
import javax.microedition.lcdui.game.GameCanvas;
import javax.microedition.midlet.MIDlet;

// The ``main'' class of a midlet is always derived from MIDlet,
// and must implement the three event handlers discussed earlier.
// Here we are leaving pauseApp and destroyApp empty, and using
// an implicit constructor, which is also empty.
//
public class HelloWorld extends MIDlet
{
    public void startApp() {
        MyCanvas myCanvas = new MyCanvas();
        Display.getDisplay(this).setCurrent(myCanvas);
        myCanvas.animateAndRender();
        notifyDestroyed();
    }
    public void pauseApp() {}
    public void destroyApp(boolean unconditional) {}
}
```

```
class MyCanvas extends GameCanvas
{
   MyCanvas() { super(true); }

   public void animateAndRender() {
      try {
         World world = (World)Loader.load("/res/world.m3g")[0];
         Graphics graphics = getGraphics();
         Graphics3D g3d = Graphics3D.getInstance();
         long start = System.currentTimeMillis();
         for (long time=0; getKeyStates()==0; ) {
            time = System.currentTimeMillis() - start;
            world.animate((int)time);
            g3d.bindTarget(graphics);
            g3d.render(world);
            g3d.releaseTarget();
            flushGraphics();
            Thread.yield();
         }
      } catch (Exception e) {}
   }
}
```

The public class `HelloWorld` implements the three event handlers that are mandatory for all midlets. In `startApp`, we first create a `GameCanvas` and make it appear on the screen, then invoke our rendering loop, and finally terminate. The other two event handlers do nothing in this bare-bones example. Note that this midlet is not very well-behaved: it uses almost all the available processing time, does not handle pauses or exceptions properly, and so on.

In our `GameCanvas`, we first use the M3G `Loader` to import a complete `World` from the midlet's JAR package. Next, we obtain a `Graphics` object, which you can think of as a handle to the frame buffer, and the singleton `Graphics3D`, which takes care of 3D rendering.

All the interesting stuff happens in the `for` loop: updating animations in the scene to the current `time`, binding the frame buffer to the `Graphics3D`, rendering the scene, releasing the frame buffer, and finally flushing it to the screen. After rendering each frame, we give any other threads in the system a chance to do their job by calling `Thread.yield`. Note that we animate the scene to wall-clock time; this way, the animation will not go into fast-forward mode if the device is very fast, but will only play back more smoothly.

12.2 DESIGN PRINCIPLES AND CONVENTIONS

The design goals of M3G were described in Section 1.3: the standardization group wanted a system that is small, fast, and easy to use for both novices and experts. The API should also work the same way on all devices, save for the unavoidable performance differences. In this section, we discuss some of the key decisions that were made in an effort to meet these goals. We also introduce some general programming conventions of M3G that will help you navigate the API and the rest of this book.

12.2.1 HIGH ABSTRACTION LEVEL

Choosing the right level of abstraction for the M3G API was difficult because of conflicting requirements. On one hand, desktop and console developers are often demanding uninhibited access to the GPU, and of course the CPU. High-level game engines and middleware are gaining popularity, but a lot of major titles are still built from the ground up. Some developers regard any single abstraction layer between their code and the hardware as one too many, despite the fact that popular engines like Gamebryo,[4] Unreal Engine,[5] Torque,[6] or Vicious Engine[7] ship with full source code to enable deep customization for each title. Mobile developers often share that point of view, and many consider even software implementations of OpenGL ES too abstract and too slow when compared to a renderer that is tailored to a particular game.

On the other hand, the rules of desktop and console development do not apply to mobile Java. First of all, mobile devices are so many and so heterogeneous that tuning your code and content to perfectly match the capabilities of any single device only makes sense as a hobby, whereas in console development it is almost a prerequisite. Such tuning would be hard anyway, because device vendors are notoriously secretive about their hardware and software configurations, and Java isolates you even further from the details. Furthermore, the performance differential between native code and Java (see Appendix B) suggests that as much processing and data as possible should be shifted to the native side—but that is something only the device vendor can do.

The M3G standardization group first considered doing direct bindings to OpenGL ES, but settled on a higher-level design for three main reasons: First, to compensate for the Java performance overhead by building in more functionality; second, to provide a closer match with modeling tools; and third, to make for a less fragmented platform by abstracting the underlying renderer. The renderer need not be any particular version of OpenGL ES, or in fact *any* version of OpenGL ES at all—it may as well be a proprietary software rasterizer, which is indeed very common, or even Direct3D Mobile.

Having decided on a retained-mode API, the group first tried taking a subset of Java 3D (version 1.3) as the basis of M3G, augmenting it with new functionality where necessary. We went pretty far along that route, but it turned out to be a dead end. The number

---

4   www.gamebryo.com

5   www.unrealtechnology.com

6   www.garagegames.com/products/torque/tge

7   www.viciousengine.com

one problem was the sheer size of Java 3D: by any measure, it is an order of magnitude more complex than M3G eventually came to be. Despite its size, it still lacks many of the features that we considered essential, such as keyframe animation, skinning, or importing of complete scene graphs. We ended up pruning, collapsing, merging, and augmenting the class hierarchy in such a radical way that the result bore very little resemblance to Java 3D. Yet another problem was that the Java 3D specification was not detailed enough to let us really figure out what each method should be doing—the "standard" was in fact defined by the sole existing implementation.

The exercise of trimming down Java 3D was hugely beneficial, though. Compared to starting from scratch, we had a much better idea of what we did and did not want. There were a lot of good things in Java 3D that we readily copied, and a lot of things that everyone in the group was happy to design in a completely different way. Starting from a clean table, we could also better match the feature set of OpenGL ES 1.0, which was being defined concurrently with M3G.

Some critics considered the retained-mode approach to be short-lived as Java would surely catch up with native performance very soon, making an immediate-mode API like OpenGL ES more attractive. Java virtual machines have indeed improved by leaps and bounds, but recently the law of diminishing returns appears to have taken over, while native code still remains in the lead by a comfortable margin. As of this writing, the jury is still out on whether the current level of Java acceleration is adequate for a low-level API like OpenGL ES; it will be interesting to observe the performance of JSR 239 (which implements a direct binding to OpenGL ES) when it becomes available on real devices in the market.

Note that the immediate mode in M3G is not as immediate as in OpenGL ES, which allows all attributes and data, except for textures, to be held in application memory (or the *client side* in OpenGL parlance). M3G, on the other hand, keeps everything wrapped up into Java objects whose contents can only be accessed through the API. This design allows a rendering call to run completely in native code, without having to access any information from the garbage-collected Java heap. The inevitable downside is that dynamic updates to mesh data, such as vertex arrays, are slower than in native OpenGL ES.

12.2.2 NO EVENTS OR CALLBACKS

Strictly speaking, M3G is not really an object-oriented scene graph. Sure, there is a hierarchy of classes, even some dynamic binding here and there, but there are no interfaces, event handlers, or abstract classes that the application could implement, no methods that it could override to change the behavior of the built-in methods. The ability to extend API classes is a cornerstone of object-oriented programming, and that is missing from M3G.

The way that you use M3G is almost as if you were programming in C. You set up some structures, and then pass them as parameters to a function like `animate` or `render`. The main difference to a C API is that those data structures are hidden. Thus, rather than reading and writing some public variables directly, you need to use *setter* and *getter* methods. Having a lot of setters and getters is, again, not very good object-oriented design, but is necessary so that the data can be retained on the native side for good performance.

All methods in M3G are fully *synchronous*. This means that when you call a method, you will not regain control until the method either completes its operation or throws an exception. In particular, there is nothing that would interrupt the animation and rendering methods. For example, there is no user-defined method that would be called after queuing objects up for rendering but before dispatching them to OpenGL ES. Also, no M3G methods will block waiting for system resources (such as a rendering surface) to become available, but will instead throw an error or exception. This is to ensure that the system will never go into a deadlock.

Callbacks are eliminated from the API for a number of reasons. First, allowing the scene graph to be modified while the implementation is processing it is a risk to system stability and security. Second, any visibility-culling or state-sorting optimizations would be thwarted if the position, shape, or rendering attributes of scene graph objects could change after the system has queued them up for rendering (or while it is doing that). Third, interrupting the relatively tight rendering traversal code to jump into an arbitrary Java method is bound to slow down the rendering. Finally, the procedure of calling Java code from native code tends to be slow and not portable from one Java virtual machine to another.

Callbacks could be restricted to work around these issues—as is done in Java 3D, for instance—by limiting the number of callbacks per frame or by disallowing modifications to scene graph objects. However, that would more or less defeat the purpose of having callbacks in the first place, as there would no longer be much in the way of added flexibility or developer control over the rendering process. In the end, the M3G expert group considered it more important to keep scene graph traversal and rendering as simple and robust as possible.

12.2.3 ROBUST ARITHMETIC

Unlike in OpenGL ES, there is no Common Lite profile or any other provisions for limited-dynamic-range arithmetic in M3G. All scene graph operations and vertex transformations, including skinning, have to be done at the full dynamic range. This guarantees that overflows do not occur in practical use, which is crucially important when porting content across different devices and implementations.

The full dynamic range in M3G is equivalent to a 24-bit floating-point format having seven bits of exponent, sixteen bits of mantissa, and one sign bit. This yields 16-bit precision across a dynamic range of about 38 orders of magnitude, compared to just four orders of magnitude at the same precision for signed 16.16 fixed point.

There are many ways to fulfill these requirements even if no FPU is available. For example, custom floating-point routines that dispense with denormals and other special cases can easily achieve double the performance of standard library routines. Switching to a custom floating-point representation, with perhaps mantissas and exponents stored separately, can yield even greater speed-up. Also, it often pays off to use specialized routines for different tasks, e.g., skinning. Finally, it may be possible to switch to fixed-point routines altogether if the inputs have narrow enough dynamic range. See Appendix A for further details.

Of course, operations that are not susceptible to disastrous overflows are allowed to use a much reduced precision and range. In particular, color operations in the pixel pipeline are clamped to [0, 1] in any case, so they only need to match the precision of the frame buffer. Similarly, rasterization can be done entirely in fixed point, because the maximum viewport dimensions set predefined limits to the accuracy and range.

12.2.4 CONSISTENT METHODS

There are thirty classes and some four hundred methods and enumerations in the M3G API, so it is important that their names be consistent, and the syntax and behavior of each method predictable. Although the specification is in Javadoc format, and therefore easy to browse, it would quickly become a burden for the developer if he or she were forced to constantly look things up from the documentation.

There are very few methods in the API whose names consist of a single verb, but these methods are doing almost all the work, i.e., `animate`, `align`, `render`, `clear`, `pick`, `load`, `find`, `duplicate`, and maybe a dozen others that are related to matrix arithmetic. The methods have descriptive enough names that you should be able to make an educated guess about what each of them is for.

The vast majority of methods in the API are simple getters and setters, also known as *accessors*, that just read or write an attribute of the Java object that they are invoked on. As a naming convention, setters are prefixed by `set` and getters by `get`, followed by one or more nouns designating the attribute that they set or get (e.g., `setTexture`). To make for more readable code, getters that retrieve boolean flags are prefixed by `is`, as in `isDepthTestEnabled`. In addition to getters and setters, there are also a few "adders" and "removers" in the API (e.g., `addChild` and `removeChild`); they operate on data structures that can grow and shrink depending on the number of elements.

M3G includes getters corresponding to almost everything that the application can set or change, as well as a special *static* getter for properties that are constant for each device. Static properties include information such as whether the device supports antialiasing; we will discuss the static properties in detail in Section 13.1.4.

There is generally one getter for each parameter that can be set. For example, the `setWrapping(int *wrapS*, int *wrapT*)` method in `Texture2D` is accompanied by `getWrappingS` and `getWrappingT`. If the parameter is a vector or matrix, it is returned in an array instead of having separate getters for each component. For example, getScale(float[] *scale*) fills in the **X**, **Y**, and **Z** scaling factors into the given array. Note that the method does not return a new array, as that would create garbage, but fills in an array provided by the user. This is again a general principle that is followed by all getters in the API.

Note that the value returned by a getter may not be the same value that was set; instead, it may be any value that produces an equivalent result. This typically happens with floating-point values, as they may be converted into lower-precision formats to speed up internal computations. Having to store both the value that was set and the value that is used internally would place an unnecessary burden on the implementations with no obvious benefit.

We mentioned above that there are getters for *almost* everything in the API. Indeed, there is only one thing in M3G 1.1 that you cannot read back—the pixels in an Image2D— and that limitation is imposed by OpenGL ES. However, some three dozen getters were omitted from M3G 1.0 to minimize the footprint of the API, and then reinstated in version 1.1. As it turned out, spending some ten or twenty kilobytes of extra memory was not an issue for anybody, after all. The getters that are only available in M3G 1.1 are listed in Section 12.3.

12.2.5 PARAMETER PASSING

The parameter-passing semantics of Java are very easy to remember: int, float, and other primitive types are passed by value, everything else by reference. However, what happens to a referenced object is up to each method. It may be written to, its contents may be copied in, or the reference itself may be copied in. The only way to find out for sure is to read the documentation of each method, or by trial and error. To alleviate that burden, the following two rules for parameter handling were adopted throughout the API.

The first rule is that scene graph objects—that is, all objects derived from Object3D— are copied in by reference. This means that your application and M3G will share each instance of Object3D that you pass in. As you construct a Mesh, for example, you give the constructor a VertexBuffer that you created earlier. The constructor copies in the *reference* to your VertexBuffer, but does not copy any of the vertex data. If you later modify some vertices in the buffer, the mesh will change accordingly. You are also free to lose your copy of the reference, since you can get it back from the Mesh at any time, using getVertexBuffer.

The second rule is that all *non*-scene graph objects are copied in by value. This means that M3G creates its own private copy of the object that you pass in, effectively taking a snapshot of its contents. For example, you can set up the projection matrix in Camera by passing in a Transform object:

```
myCamera.setProjection(myTransform); // matrix is copied in by
                                     // value
myTransform.setIdentity();           // this does not affect
                                     // myCamera
```

Since `Transform` is not derived from `Object3D`, it is copied in by value, that value being a 4 × 4 matrix. There is no reference from `myCamera` to `myTransform`, so you may freely reset the `Transform` to identity and start using it for something else without affecting the `Camera`.

There are two exceptions to the second rule, but they are obvious given their context. The first exception is the arbitrary *user object* that can be attached to any scene graph object. The user object is quite obviously stored by reference, because otherwise we would not be storing the same object as the user. The other special case is when a rendering target is bound to M3G. The target is held by reference, but you are not supposed to access it while it is bound. If you do that, the rendered image may become corrupt.

The way that arrays of `Object3D`s are treated is a logical consequence of the two rules. Using the `Mesh` again as an example, you also provide its constructor an array of `IndexBuffer`s. The array itself is copied in by value, but the values happen to be `IndexBuffer` references, which are copied in by reference. If you thereafter let the array and its contents go out of scope, the garbage collector will reclaim the array, but not the `IndexBuffer`s, because they are also held by the `Mesh`.

12.2.6 NUMERIC VALUES

The default numeric formats in M3G are `float` and `int`. Almost everything is read and written in these formats. In fact, only images and vertices are handled differently.

Pixels are fed into `Image2D` in byte arrays, one byte per color component in RGBA order. This is the format that raw images are usually stored in, and it is accepted as such by OpenGL ES. On the other hand, colors that are passed in to setters individually, such as material colors, are packed into integers in the `0xAARRGGBB` order. For example, fully opaque dark red would be `0xFF800000`. This cuts the number of parameters from four to one, reducing method call overhead significantly. The same format is also used in MIDP.

Vertex attributes in `VertexArray` are read and written in either `byte` or `short` arrays. Supporting `float` and `int` vertex arrays was also considered, but ultimately rejected due to their high memory requirements, the performance penalty of floating-point transformation and lighting in absence of dedicated hardware, and finally the lack of compelling use cases. We adopted a cheaper alternative instead, whereby the transformation matrices are in floating point, allowing accurate placement and smooth animation of objects in the 3D world without fear of overflowing.

Note also that there is no fixed-point data type in M3G, and no methods that would take 16.16 fixed-point parameters. This is mainly because there would not be much performance benefit to it, because the time-consuming internal operations are subject to the floating-point precision and range criteria regardless of the input format. Another reason is the lack of `typedef` in Java: there is no efficient way to define a `fixed` data type to distinguish 16.16 fixed-point values from ordinary `int` variables. Without this capability, fixed-point code becomes even more unreadable and error-prone than otherwise. Finally, the benefit of doing fixed-point arithmetic may not be as great in Java as in native code, because you cannot use assembly language, and because the extra bit-shifting requires more bytecodes than the corresponding `float` operations. See the Java section in Appendix A for more information.

12.2.7 ENUMERATIONS

As the Java programming language has no support for enumerations, they are represented as constant integer values (i.e., `static final int`). Enumerations are defined in the class where they are needed, and do not apply anywhere else. For example, the `RGB` pixel format token in `Image2D` has the decimal value 99, and is the only token in the API having that particular value.

Having to prefix all enumerations by their class name is cumbersome, but if you need a particular enumeration very often, you can copy it into a local variable or instance variable like this:

```
int REPEAT = Texture2D.WRAP_REPEAT;
myTexture1.setWrapping(REPEAT, REPEAT);
myTexture2.setWrapping(REPEAT, REPEAT);
```

12.2.8 ERROR HANDLING

As in any proper Java API, error handling in M3G is based on the built-in exception mechanism. Thanks to exceptions, no methods in the API need to return error codes or set internal error flags that the application would have to check separately. There are seven different types of exceptions the API may throw, roughly indicating the type of error. The exceptions are listed in Table 12.1.

M3G is generally more stringent about error checking than OpenGL ES. For example, indexing a vertex array out-of-bounds has "undefined" effects in OpenGL ES, but causes a well-defined exception in M3G. The extra error checking may have a minor impact on performance, but it also makes debugging easier and the implementations more robust against buggy or malicious code. Debugging facilities on mobile devices tend to be poor or nonexistent, so any help in that area is particularly welcome. To minimize the performance overhead, errors are checked at the earliest possible occasion, typically at constructors and setters. Final validation of the scene graph must be deferred until rendering time, however. This is because the validity of an object often depends on other objects that the application may change at any time.

Table 12.1: The exceptions that may be thrown by M3G, and their typical causes. Note that the list of causes is not exhaustive.

Type	Typical Causes
`ArithmeticException`	Supplying an uninvertible transformation as a parameter
`IllegalArgumentException`	Supplying a wrong enumeration as a parameter
`IllegalStateException`	Attempting to render an incomplete or invalid object, such as a `Mesh` with no `VertexBuffer` attached
`IndexOutOfBoundsException`	Attempting to read or write beyond the boundaries of some internal data structure, such as the list of child nodes in `Group`, or the list of textures in `Appearance`
`NullPointerException`	Supplying a `null` reference as a parameter
`SecurityException`	Attempting to load a remote file without having sufficient network access permissions
`IOException`	Attempting to load an invalid file, or attempting to load a remote file when the device is out of network coverage

12.3 M3G 1.1

To combat market fragmentation, the upgrade cycle of M3G has been kept relatively slow. M3G 1.1 was released in June 2005, a year and a half after the original, but unlike OpenGL ES 1.1, it does not add any new rendering features. It is focused on merely improving the performance and interoperability of the existing functionality—in other words, fixing errors and omissions in the original spec. Importantly, the file format was not changed at all. A complete change log is available on the Overview page of the specification [JCP05]; here we review only the changes that have practical significance.

12.3.1 PURE 3D RENDERING

The most important addition to M3G 1.1 is the `OVERWRITE` hint. It lets you tell the implementation that you intend to do full-screen 3D rendering, so any pre-existing contents of the designated render target may be discarded. Having to preserve the old frame buffer contents is generally very expensive on hardware-accelerated devices (see the next chapter for details), so we advise you to use this hint whenever possible.

12.3.2 ROTATION INTERPOLATION

A persistent interoperability issue that was resolved in M3G 1.1 was due to keyframe-animated rotations, or more precisely, interpolation of quaternions (see Section 4.1.2). Some devices and content exporters had taken the liberty to interpolate along the shortest path in 3D space, which is not always the same as the shortest path in 4D quaternion space.

If the content producer (i.e., the exporter) assumes that the shortest 3D path is taken, and the runtime engine takes the shortest 4D path, or vice versa, the resulting animation will look fascinating, to say the least. The typical symptom is some occasional flickering in the animation sequence; when examined more closely and in slow motion, it turns out that the object does a full 360° spin around multiple axes when it should only rotate a degree or two. This happens between two successive keyframes, which is often just a blink of an eye, and is thus perceived as flickering.

This issue has been fixed in all the publicly available exporters, as far as we know, but you may well run into it if you pull some generic quaternion interpolation routine from the web, and use that in your application or proprietary content processing tools. See page 372 in Section 16.2 for more information.

12.3.3 PNG AND JPEG LOADING

Another frequent source of problems prior to M3G 1.1 was loading of PNG images that contain transparency information. The PNG file format supports various forms of transparency, including color-keying, palette entries with alpha information, and complete alpha channels. M3G 1.1 makes it explicit that all these formats must be supported, regardless of whether the base image is grayscale, indexed color (paletized), or true color. The mapping of these formats to the `Image2D` internal formats is now well-specified, too.

Support for JPEG images was left optional in both M3G 1.0 and 1.1, for fear of risking the royalty-free status of M3G and thereby hindering its adoption. Thus, depending on the device, you may or may not be able to load JPEG files using the built-in `Loader`. On the other hand, including them into `.m3g` files was ruled out completely, as that would have compromised the portability of art assets.

However, these decisions have been later reversed by the new Mobile Service Architecture (MSA, JSR 248) standard [JCP06]: it requires full JPEG support across the board, including in `.m3g` files.[8] JPEG is clearly superior to PNG for photographic images, and everyone in the industry has a license for it these days, so it makes sense to use it as widely as possible. The downside is that we now have three kinds of devices in the market with respect to the availability of JPEG: those with full support, those with no support, and those with partial support. As a further complication, some pre-MSA devices may expand grayscale JPEGs into RGB, increasing their size by a factor of two to four.

If you wish to target your application for all M3G-enabled devices that have ever shipped, with a minimum effort, we advise you to use `.png` for images that have no transparency, and `.m3g` for those that include alpha.

---

8   Luckily, this is the only material change that MSA imposes on M3G.

12.3.4 NEW GETTERS

As we mentioned in the previous section, M3G 1.1 also adds more than thirty getters that were missing from the original release. With the complete set of getters available, applications need no longer keep duplicate copies of M3G state attributes on the Java side. The getters are also useful for debugging, diagnostics, and content processing purposes. The complete list of new getters in each class is shown below.

```
AnimationController:
  int getRefWorldTime()

Graphics3D:
  Object getTarget()
  boolean isDepthBufferEnabled()
  int getHints()
  int getViewportX()
  int getViewportY()
  int getViewportWidth()
  int getViewportHeight()
  float getDepthRangeNear()
  float getDepthRangeFar()
  Camera getCamera()
  int getLightCount()
  Light getLight(int index, Transform transform)

IndexBuffer:
  int getIndexCount()
  void getIndices(int[] indices)

KeyframeSequence:
  int getComponentCount()
  int getKeyframeCount()
  int getInterpolationType()
  int getKeyframe(int index, float[] value)
  int getValidRangeFirst()
  int getValidRangeLast()

Node:
  int getAlignmentTarget(int axis)
  Node getAlignmentReference(int axis)

PolygonMode:
  boolean isLocalCameraLightingEnabled()
  boolean isPerspectiveCorrectionEnabled()

SkinnedMesh:
  void getBoneTransform(Node bone, Transform transform)
  int getBoneVertices(Node bone, int[] indices, float[] weights)

Texture2D:
  int getLevelFilter()
  int getImageFilter()
```

```
VertexArray:
  int getVertexCount()
  int getComponentCount()
  int getComponentType()
  void get(int firstVertex, int numVertices, byte[] values)
  void get(int firstVertex, int numVertices, short[] values)
```

12.3.5 OTHER CHANGES

The other incompatibilities addressed in M3G 1.1 were very minor, and many of them had been discovered by proofreading the specification, not because they would have posed problems for developers. One thing perhaps worth mentioning is that the Loader now treats file names as case sensitive; previously this was left ambiguous.

Finally, the new version relaxes error checking on situations where the added security or diagnostic value of throwing an exception was questionable. For example, M3G 1.0 used to throw an exception if a polygon mesh had lighting enabled but was lacking normal vectors. Now, M3G 1.1 just leaves the normals undefined. Viewing the erroneously shaded mesh on the screen probably makes it easier for the developer to figure out what is wrong than getting an exception that may be caused by half a dozen other reasons.

BASIC M3G CONCEPTS

Now is the time to get your hands dirty and begin programming with M3G. To get started, you will need a device that supports M3G; almost any mid-category or high-end phone will do. For your development PC, you will need a software development kit (SDK) such as the Java Wireless Toolkit by Sun Microsystems[1] or Carbide.j by Nokia.[2] We also recommend that you download the official M3G 1.1 specification [JCP05], available as either zipped HTML or PDF. Forum Nokia are also hosting an online, browser-friendly copy in their Java ME Developers Library.[3] More detailed instructions for setting up your development environment are provided on the companion web site of this book.

The first thing that a well-behaved M3G application needs to do is to check the availability of M3G, as it may not be present on some older devices. If M3G is available, its version number should be verified, as many devices only support the 1.0 version. The examples in this book are based on M3G 1.1; subtle changes may be needed in some cases to make the code work robustly on a 1.0 implementation. The version number can be queried from the system property microedition.m3g.version, as shown below:

```
String version = System.getProperty("microedition.m3g.version");
if (version == null) { ... }                // M3G not supported
else if (version.equals("1.0")) { ... }     // M3G 1.0
```

---

1 java.sun.com/products/sjwtoolkit/
2 www.forum.nokia.com/carbide
3 www.forum.nokia.com/ME_Developers_Library/

```
else if (version.equals("1.1")) { ... }    // M3G 1.1
else { ... }                                // M3G 2.0+
```

Once you have confirmed that M3G is indeed supported on your target device, you can go ahead and start using the `javax.microedition.m3g` package. The first class that you are going to need from that package is most probably `Graphics3D`, and that is also the logical starting point for learning the API.

13.1 `Graphics3D`

The only class in M3G that you cannot avoid if you want to draw anything at all is the 3D rendering context, `Graphics3D`. This is where all rendering and render target management takes place, so you can think of it as a combination of OpenGL ES and EGL. It is a lot simpler, though, because most of the OpenGL ES state information is stored elsewhere, leaving only the viewport, camera, lights, and a few hints to be managed by `Graphics3D`. Most of EGL is not exposed at all. Instead, you just provide a render target, and all the complexities of managing surfaces and configurations are taken care of under the hood.

13.1.1 RENDER TARGETS

There is only one instance of `Graphics3D` in the system, and that has been graciously created for you in advance. All you need to do is to get a handle on that single object, bind a rendering target to it, render your scene, and release the target. This is shown in the example below. Since we have not yet discussed rendering, let us just clear the screen:

```
void paint(Graphics graphics) {
  Graphics3D g3d = Graphics3D.getInstance();
  try {
    g3d.bindTarget(graphics);
    g3d.clear(null);
  }
  finally {
    g3d.releaseTarget();
  }
}
```

This example shows a typical scenario, in which you implement the `paint` callback for your `Canvas`. A `Canvas` represents a displayable surface in MIDP that may or may not be visible, and may or may not cover the entire display, but for all practical purposes you can think of it as the screen. The rendering target that you bind is not the `Canvas` itself, however, but its 2D rendering context, a `Graphics` object. This is because a `Canvas` is guaranteed to have access to the frame buffer (or back buffer) only when its `Graphics` is available to the application. Binding to a `Graphics` also simplifies things for the developer: you can get a `Graphics` for off-screen images as well, which means that your code will work unmodified for both on-screen and off-screen targets. Rendering to a texture works the same way, except that you bind an `Image2D` object (see Section 13.2) instead of a `Graphics`.

So what exactly happens when you bind and then later release a target? From the developer's point of view, nothing much: `bindTarget` simply flushes all 2D drawing commands so that 3D rendering can proceed, and `releaseTarget` does the opposite. As a result, the pre-existing contents of the target are nicely overlaid or overwritten by the 3D scene. There are only three ground rules: First, do not touch the target while it is bound, as that may yield unpredictable results. In particular, do not try to render any 2D graphics with MIDP. Second, do not assume anything about the contents of the depth buffer after `bindTarget`, because the contents are undefined. Third, make sure that your render target gets released no matter what exceptions occur, so that your application has a chance to recover, or at least make a clean exit. The easiest way to do that is a `try—finally` construct as shown in the example above.

If you care about performance, there are two more things to keep in mind. First, minimize the number of render targets that you use. Binding to a new target may require setting up a new OpenGL ES rendering context and/or a new back buffer. Second, minimize the number of binds and releases that you do per frame. Every bind and release bears some amount of overhead, and on hardware-accelerated devices that overhead can be dramatic. The reasons boil down to the notoriously poor interworking of 2D and 3D rendering on most Java ME implementations.

Synchronizing 2D and 3D

In a typical MIDP implementation, the font engine and all other 2D routines are running on the CPU, and can only use a back buffer that resides in main memory, while the 3D hardware can only use a back buffer that resides in its local memory. The 2D back buffer is copied from the main memory to the graphics memory at each `bindTarget`, and a reverse copy takes place at each `releaseTarget`. The extra copying is bad in itself, but the hidden penalties are even worse. First of all, reading the 3D frame buffer defeats all parallelism among the CPU and the different stages of the GPU. As explained in Section 3.6, this can cut two-thirds of the potential performance. Second, the only way to copy the 2D back buffer into the 3D back buffer may be to upload it into an OpenGL ES texture and then render a full-screen quad mapped with that texture. Texture uploading is a very costly operation on some architectures.

There is no sure-fire way to completely avoid the expensive 2D/3D synchronization points on all devices; sometimes all you can do is to give some hints to MIDP and M3G and then cross your fingers, hoping for the best. A reasonably good advice is to make your application pure, full-screen 3D: keep your `Canvas` in full-screen mode, and do not allow anything other than M3G to access it. The best and most explicit hint you can provide, however, is the OVERWRITE flag at bindTarget:

```
g3d.bindTarget(graphics, ..., Graphics3D.OVERWRITE);
```

This tells the implementation not to burn cycles on preserving the pre-existing contents of the 2D back buffer. We have observed frame rates increasing two-, three-, even five-fold on some devices just because of this. The OVERWRITE hint is only available since M3G 1.1, but some 1.0 devices provide an indirect means to achieve the same effect: just clear the entire screen before drawing anything. The implementation may then conclude that the 2D back buffer does not have to be copied in, as it will be completely cleared anyway.

Antialiasing and dithering

There are three other hint bits available in Graphics3D besides OVERWRITE. If you want to use more than one of them at a time, you need to bitwise-OR them together:

```
int hints = Graphics3D.OVERWRITE | Graphics3D.ANTIALIAS;
g3d.bindTarget(graphics, ..., hints);
```

This example shows the overwrite hint combined with ANTIALIAS, requesting the implementation to turn on antialiasing if possible, even at the expense of reduced performance. No specific method of antialiasing is mandated, but some form of full-scene antialiasing (FSAA) is recommended, and in practice the industry has converged on multisampling (see Section 3.4.5). There are very few devices on the market that support any kind of antialiasing, as not even all the hardware-accelerated models can do it, but those few devices do a pretty good job at it. They achieve good quality without much performance overhead, so we recommend that you at least try the ANTIALIAS hint. To find out if antialiasing is supported on your target platform, use the static Graphics3D.getProperties method (see Section 13.1.4).

The remaining two hint bits in Graphics3D are DITHER and TRUE_COLOR. The former turns on dithering to increase the apparent color depth of the display (see Section 3.5.3). The latter instructs the renderer to use its maximum internal color precision, even if the display can only reproduce, say, 256 or 4096 colors. These hints seemed useful back in 2002, but the incredibly fast development of color displays soon made them obsolete—no M3G-enabled device ever shipped with less than 65K colors! Today, most implementations render in true color regardless of the display color depth or the TRUE_COLOR hint, and any dithering takes place automatically at the display controller, also regardless of the DITHER hint.

Disabling the depth buffer

One final thing to mention about bindTarget is the depth buffer enable flag:

```
boolean enableDepthBuffer = false;
g3d.bindTarget(graphics, enableDepthBuffer, hints);
```

This lets you disable depth buffering at the outset if you are drawing some very simple content that is independent of rendering order, or if you are resolving the visibility by yourself, such as when using a height map for simple terrain rendering. The implementation can then decide not to allocate a depth buffer at all, saving some 150K bytes of memory on the typical quarter-VGA device. Those savings may not be realized in practice, though. Situations where depth buffering is not needed are so few and far between that M3G implementations generally allocate the buffer just in case. Besides, depth buffering is typically very efficient, particularly on hardware implementations, and things may only slow down if you come up with clever tricks to avoid it.

13.1.2 VIEWPORT

M3G rendering does not necessarily affect the entire rendering target. The area that will be rendered to is determined by the intersection of the *viewport* defined in `Graphics3D` and the *clipping rectangle* defined in `Graphics`. `Image2D` targets do not have a clipping rectangle, so the renderable area is defined by the viewport alone. If you go with the default settings in `Graphics3D`, the viewport will cover the entire `Canvas`, which is usually a good thing. If you nonetheless want to restrict your rendering to some rectangular sub-area of the screen, you need to call the `setViewport` method after `bindTarget`. Note that you will have to do that every frame, as `bindTarget` resets the viewport back to its default, full-screen state.

As described in Section 2.6, the viewport transformation maps vertices from normalized device coordinates (NDC) to screen or window coordinates. The mapping is parameterized by the width, height, and top-left corner of the viewport, all specified in screen pixels. To illustrate, let us expand our earlier screen clearing example so that the top half is cleared with the red color and the bottom half with blue. This is done by setting up a `Background` object and supplying it as a parameter to `clear`:

```
int width = graphics.getClipWidth();
int height = graphics.getClipHeight();
try {
  g3d.bindTarget(graphics, true, hints);
  g3d.setViewport(0, 0, width, height/2);   // top half
  myBackground.setColor(0x00FF0000);        // red in 0xARGB format
  g3d.clear(myBackground);
  g3d.setViewport(0, height/2, width, height); // bottom half
  myBackground.setColor(0x000000FF);        // blue
  g3d.clear(myBackground);
} ...
```

The `Background` class is pretty self-explanatory. It defines whether and how the viewport and the corresponding area in the depth buffer are cleared. In this example we used a constant clear color, but with a few more lines of code we could have used a tiled or scaled background image; see Section 14.4.1 for details.

> **Performance tip:** On hardware-accelerated devices, it is a good idea to clear the color buffer and depth buffer completely and in one go, even if the whole screen will be redrawn. Various hardware optimizations can only be enabled when starting from a clean table, and some devices can clear the screen by just flipping a bit. Even with software implementations, clearing everything is typically faster than clearing a slightly smaller viewport.

Note that the viewport need not lie inside the render target; it can even be larger than the render target. The view that you render is automatically scaled to fit the viewport. For example, if you have a viewport of 1024 by 1024 pixels on a QVGA screen, you will only see about 7% of the rendered image (the nonvisible parts are not really rendered, of course, so there is no performance penalty); see the code example in Section 13.1.4. The maximum size allowed for the viewport does not depend on the type of rendering target, but only on the implementation. All implementations are required to support viewports up to 256 by 256 pixels, but in practice the upper bound is 1024 by 1024 or higher. The exact limit can be queried from `Graphics3D.getProperties`.

> **Pitfall:** Contrary to OpenGL ES, there is no separate function for setting the scissor rectangle (see Section 3.5). Instead, the scissor rectangle is implicitly defined as the intersection of the viewport and the `Graphics` clipping rectangle.

A concept closely related to the viewport is the *depth range*, set by `setDepthRange(float` *near,* `float` *far)*, where *near* and *far* are in the range [0, 1]. Similar to the viewport, the depth range also defines a mapping from normalized device coordinates to screen coordinates, only this time the screen coordinates are depth values that lie in the [0, 1] range. Section 2.6 gives insight on the depth range and how it can be used to make better use of the depth buffer resolution or to speed up your application.

13.1.3 RENDERING

As we move toward more ambitious goals than merely clearing the screen, the next step is to render some 3D content. For simplicity, let us just assume that we have magically come into possession of a complete 3D scene that is all set up for rendering. In case of M3G, this means that we have a `World` object, which is the root node of the scene graph and includes by reference all the cameras, lights, and polygon meshes that we need. To render a full-screen view of the world, all we need to do within the `bindTarget-releaseTarget` block is this:

```
g3d.render(myWorld);
```

This takes care of clearing the depth buffer and color buffer, setting up the camera and lights, and finally rendering everything that there is to render. This is called *retained-mode* rendering, because all the information necessary for rendering is retained by the `World` and its descendants in the scene graph. In the *immediate mode*, you would first clear the screen, then set up the camera and lights, and finally draw your meshes one by one in a loop.

The retained mode and immediate mode are designed so that you can easily mix and match them in the same application. Although the retained mode has less overhead on the Java side, and is generally recommended, it may sometimes be more convenient to handle overlays, particle effects, or the player character, for instance, separately from the rest of the scene. To ease the transition from retained mode to immediate mode at the end of the frame, the camera and lights of the `World` are automatically set up as the current camera and lights in `Graphics3D`, overwriting the previous settings.

The projection matrix (see Chapter 2) is defined in a `Camera` object, which in turn is attached to `Graphics3D` using `setCamera(Camera` *camera*, `Transform` *transform*). The latter parameter specifies the transformation from camera space, also known as eye space or view space, into world space. The `Camera` class is described in detail in Section 14.3.1. For now, it suffices to say that it allows you to set an arbitrary 4×4 matrix, but also provides convenient methods for defining the typical perspective and parallel projections. The following example defines a perspective projection with a 60° vertical field of view and the same aspect ratio as the `Canvas` that we are rendering to:

```
Camera camera = new Camera();
float width = myCanvas.getWidth();
float height = myCanvas.getHeight();
camera.setPerspective(60.0f, width/height, 10.0f, 500.0f);
g3d.setCamera(camera, null);
```

Note that we call `setCamera` with the `transform` parameter set to `null`. As a general principle in M3G, a `null` transformation is treated as identity, which in this case implies that the camera is sitting at the world-space origin, looking toward the negative *Z* axis with *Y* pointing up.

Light sources are set up similarly to the camera, using `addLight(Light` *light*, `Transform` *transform*). The *transform* parameter again specifies the transformation from local coordinates to world space. Lighting is discussed in Section 14.3.2, but for the sake of illustration, let us set up a single directional white light that shines in the direction at which our camera is pointing:

```
Light light = new Light();
g3d.addLight(light, null);
```

Now that the camera and lights are all set up, we can proceed with rendering. There are three different `render` methods in immediate mode, one having a higher level of abstraction than the other two. The high-level method `render(Node` *node*, `Transform` *transform*) draws an individual object or scene graph branch. You can go as far as rendering an entire `World` with it, as long as the camera and lights are properly set up in

Graphics3D. For instance, viewing myWorld with the camera that we just placed at the world space origin is as simple as this:

```
g3d.render(myWorld, null);
```

Of course, the typical way of using this method is to draw individual meshes rather than entire scenes, but that decision is up to you. The low-level render methods, on the other hand, are restricted to drawing a single triangle mesh. The mesh is defined by a vertex buffer, an index buffer, and an appearance. As with the camera and lights, a transformation from model space to world space must be given as the final parameter:

```
g3d.render(myVertices, myIndices, myAppearance, myTransform);
```

The other render variant is similar, but takes in an integer *scope mask* as an additional parameter. The scope mask is bitwise-ANDed with the corresponding mask of the current camera, and the mesh is rendered *if and only if* the result is non-zero. The same applies for lights. The scope mask is discussed further in Chapter 15, as it is more useful in retained mode than in immediate mode.

13.1.4 STATIC PROPERTIES

We mentioned in Section 12.2 that there is a static getter for retrieving implementation-specific information, such as whether antialiasing is supported. This special getter is defined in Graphics3D, and is called getProperties. It returns a java.util. Hashtable that contains Integer and Boolean values keyed by Strings. The static properties, along with some helpful notes, are listed in Table 13.1. To illustrate the use of static properties, let us create a viewport that is as large as the implementation can support, and use it to zoom in on a high-resolution rendering of myWorld:

```
Hashtable properties = Graphics3D.getProperties();
maxViewport = ((Integer)properties.get("maxViewportDimension")).
              intValue();
...
g3d.bindTarget(graphics, true, hints);
int topLeftX = -(maxViewport - graphics.getClipWidth())/2;
int topLeftY = -(maxViewport - graphics.getClipHeight())/2;
g3d.setViewport(topLeftX, topLeftY, maxViewport, maxViewport);
g3d.render(myWorld);
g3d.releaseTarget();
```

We first query for maxViewportDimension from the Hashtable. The value is returned as a java.lang.Object, which we need to cast into an Integer and then convert into a primitive int before we can use it in computations. Later on, at the paint method, we set the viewport to its maximum size, so that our Canvas lies at its center. Assuming a QVGA screen and a 1024-pixel-square viewport, we would have a zoom factor of about 14. The zoomed-in view can be easily panned by adjusting the top-left *X* and *Y*.

Table 13.1: The system properties contained in the `Hashtable` returned by `Graphics3D.getProperties`. There may be other properties, as well, but they are not standardized.

Key (String)	Value	Notes
supportAntialiasing	Boolean	`true` on some hardware-accelerated devices
supportTrueColor	Boolean	`false` on all devices that we know of
supportDithering	Boolean	`false` on all devices that we know of
supportMipmapping	Boolean	`false` on surprisingly many devices
supportPerspectiveCorrection	Boolean	`true` on all devices, but quality varies
supportLocalCameraLighting	Boolean	`false` on almost all devices
maxLights	$\mathtt{Integer} \geq 8$	typically 8
maxViewportWidth	$\mathtt{Integer} \geq 256$	typically 256 or 1024; M3G 1.1 only
maxViewportHeight	$\mathtt{Integer} \geq 256$	typically 256 or 1024; M3G 1.1 only
maxViewportDimension	$\mathtt{Integer} \geq 256$	typically 256 or 1024
maxTextureDimension	$\mathtt{Integer} \geq 256$	typically 256 or 1024
maxSpriteCropDimension	$\mathtt{Integer} \geq 256$	typically 256 or 1024
maxTransformsPerVertex	$\mathtt{Integer} \geq 2$	typically 2, 3, or 4
numTextureUnits	$\mathtt{Integer} \geq 1$	typically 2

13.2 `Image2D`

There are a few cases where M3G deals with 2D image data. Texturing, sprites, and background images need images as sources, and rendering to any of them is also supported.

`Image2D`, as the name suggests, stores a 2D array of image data. It is similar in many respects to the `javax.microedition.lcdui.Image` class, but the important difference is that `Image2D` objects are fully managed by M3G. This lets M3G implementations achieve better performance, as there is no need to synchronize with the 2D drawing functions in MIDP.

Similarly to the MIDP `Image`, an `Image2D` object can be either mutable or immutable. To create an immutable image, you must supply the image data in the constructor:

```
Image2D(int format, int width, int height, byte[] image)
```

The *format* parameter specifies the type of the image data: it can be one of `ALPHA`, `LUMINANCE`, `LUMINANCE_ALPHA`, `RGB`, and `RGBA`. The *width* and *height* parameters determine the size of the image, and the *image* array contains data for a total of *width* × *height* pixels. The layout of each pixel is determined by *format*: each image component takes one byte and the components are interleaved. For example, the data for a LUMINANCE_ALPHA image would consist of two bytes giving the luminance and alpha of the first pixel, followed by two bytes giving the luminance and alpha of the second pixel, and so on. The pixels are ordered top-down and left to right, i.e., the first *width* pixels provide the topmost row of the image starting from the left. Upon calling the constructor, the data is copied into internal memory allocated by M3G, allowing you to discard or reuse the source array. Note that while the image is input upside-down compared to OpenGL ES (Section 9.2.2), the *t* texture coordinate is similarly reversed, so the net effect is that you can use the same texture images and coordinates on both OpenGL ES and M3G.

Unfortunately, there is no support in M3G for packed image formats, such as RGB565. This is partially because OpenGL ES does not give any guarantees regarding the internal color depth of a texture image, but also because the image formats were intentionally kept few and simple. In retrospect, being able to input the image data in a packed format would have been useful in its own right, regardless of what happens when the image is sent to OpenGL ES.

As a form of image compression, you can also create a paletted image:

    Image2D(int *format*, int *width*, int *height*, byte[] *image*, byte[] *palette*)

Here, the only difference is that the *image* array contains one-byte indices into the *palette* array, which stores up to 256 color values. The layout of the color values is again as indicated by *format*. There is no guarantee that the implementation will internally maintain the image in the paletted format, though.

Pitfall: The amount of memory that an Image2D consumes is hard to predict. Depending on the device, non-palletized RGB and RGBA images may be stored at 16 or 32 bits per pixel, while palletized images are sometimes expanded from 8 bpp to 16 or 32 bpp. Some implementations always generate the mipmap pyramid, consuming 33% extra memory. Some devices need to store two copies of each image: one in the GL driver, the other on the M3G side. Finally, all or part of this memory may be allocated from somewhere other than the Java heap. This means that you can run out of memory even if the Java heap has plenty of free space! You can try to detect this case by using smaller images. As for remedies, specific texture formats may be more space-efficient than others, but you should refer to the developer pages of the device manufacturers for details.

A third constructor lets you copy the data from a MIDP Image:

    Image2D(int *format*, java.lang.Object *image*)

Note that the destination *format* is explicitly specified. The source format is either RGB or RGBA, for mutable and immutable MIDP images, respectively. Upon copying the data, M3G automatically converts it from the source format into the destination format.

As a general rule, the conversion happens by copying the respective components of the source image and setting any missing components to 1.0 (or 0xFF for 8-bit colors). A couple of special cases deserve to be mentioned. When converting an RGB or RGBA source image into LUMINANCE or LUMINANCE_ALPHA, the luminance channel is obtained by converting the RGB values into grayscale. A similar conversion is done when converting an RGB image into ALPHA. This lets you read an alpha mask from a regular PNG or JPEG image through Image.createImage, or create one with the 2D drawing functions of MIDP, for example.

Often the most convenient way to create an Image2D is to load it from a file. You can do that with the Loader, as discussed in Section 13.5. All implementations are required to support the M3G and PNG formats, but JPEG is often supported as well.[4] Loading an image file yields a new Image2D whose format matches that of the image stored in the file. JPEG can do both color and grayscale, yielding the internal formats RGB and LUMINANCE, respectively, but has no concept of transparency or alpha. PNG supports all of the Image2D formats except for ALPHA. It has a palletized format, too, but unfortunately the on-device PNG loaders tend to expand such data into raw RGB or RGBA before it ever reaches the Image2D. M3G files obviously support all the available formats, including those with a palette.

Pitfall: The various forms of transparency supported by PNG are hard to get right. For example, the M3G loader in some early Nokia models (e.g., the 6630), does not support any form of PNG transparency, whereas some later models (e.g., the 6680) support the alpha channel but not color-keying. Possible workarounds include using Image.createImage or switching from PNG files to M3G files. These issues have been resolved in M3G 1.1; see Section 12.3.

Finally, you can create a mutable Image2D:

```
Image2D(int format, int width, int height)
```

The image is initialized to opaque white by default. It can be subsequently modified by using set(int x, int y, int width, int height, byte[] pixels). This method copies a rectangle of *width* by *height* pixels into the image, starting at the pixel at (*x*, *y*) and proceeding to the right and down. The origin for the Image2D is in its top left corner.

A mutable Image2D can also be bound to Graphics3D as a rendering target. The image can still be used like an immutable Image2D. This lets you, for example, render dynamic reflections or create feedback effects.

---

4   JPEG support is in fact required by the Mobile Service Architecture (MSA) specification, also known as JSR 248. MSA is an umbrella JSR that aims to unify the Java ME platform.

Table 13.2: The available `Image2D` formats and their capabilities. The shaded cells show the capabilities of *most* devices, as these cases are not dictated by the specification. Mipmapping is entirely optional, and palletized images may be silently expanded into the corresponding raw formats, typically RGB. Most devices support mipmapping and palletized images otherwise, but will not generate mipmaps for palletized textures, nor load a palletized PNG without expanding it. There are some devices that can do better, though. Finally, note that JPEG does not support the alpha channel, and that PNG does not support images with *only* an alpha channel.

	Mutable	Render Target	Texture	Mipmap	Background	Sprite	Load from M3G	Load from PNG	Load from JPEG	Copy from Image
ALPHA	✓	✗	✓	✓	✗	✓	✓	✗	✗	✓
LUMINANCE	✓	✗	✓	✓	✗	✓	✓	✓	✓	✓
LUM_ALPHA	✓	✗	✓	✓	✗	✓	✓	✓	✗	✓
RGB	✓	✓	✓	✓	✓	✓	✓	✓	✓	✓
RGBA	✓	✓	✓	✓	✓	✓	✓	✓	✗	✓
Palette	✗	✗	✓	✗	✗	✓	✓	✗	✗	✗

> **Performance tip:** Beware that updating an `Image2D`, whether done by rendering or through the setter, can be a very costly operation. For example, the internal format and layout of the image may not be the same as in the `set` method, requiring heavy conversion and pixel reordering. If your frame rate or memory usage on a particular device is not what you would expect, try using immutable images only.

While `Image2D` is a general-purpose class as such, there are various restrictions on what kind of images can be used for a specific purpose. For example, textures must have power-of-two dimensions, and render targets can only be in RGB or RGBA formats. Table 13.2 summarizes the capabilities and restrictions of the different `Image2D` formats.

13.3 MATRICES AND TRANSFORMATIONS

One of the most frequently asked questions about M3G is the difference between `Transform` and `Transformable`. The short answer is that `Transform` is a simple container for a 4 × 4 matrix with no inherent meaning, essentially a `float` array wrapped into an object, whereas `Transformable` stores such a matrix in a componentized, animatable form, and for a particular purpose: constructing the modelview matrix or the texture matrix. The rest of this section provides the long answer.

13.3.1 `Transform`

`Transform` stores an arbitrary 4 × 4 matrix and defines a set of basic utility functions for operating on such matrices. You can initialize a `Transform` to identity, copy it in from another `Transform`, or copy it from a `float[]` in row-major order (note that this is different from OpenGL ES, which uses the unintuitive column-major ordering). `setIdentity` resets a `Transform` back to its default state, facilitating object reuse.

Creating a matrix

To give an example, the following code fragment creates a matrix with a uniform scaling component [2 2 2] and a translation component [3 4 5]. In other words, a vector multiplied by `this` matrix is first scaled by a factor of two, then moved by three units along the *x* axis, four units along *y*, and five units along *z*:

```
Transform myTransform = new Transform();
myTransform.set(new float[] { 2f, 0f, 0f, 3f,
                              0f, 2f, 0f, 4f,
                              0f, 0f, 2f, 5f,
                              0f, 0f, 0f, 1f });
```

Matrix operations

Once you have created a `Transform`, you can start applying some basic arithmetic functions to it: You can `transpose` the matrix ($M' = M^T$), `invert` it ($M' = M^{-1}$), or multiply it with another matrix ($M' = MA$). Note that each of these operations overwrites the pre-existing value of the `Transform` with the result (M'). The matrix multiplication functions come in several flavors:

void postMultiply(Transform *transform*)

void postScale(float *sx*, float *sy*, float *sz*)

void postTranslate(float *tx*, float *ty*, float *tz*)

void postRotate(float *angle*, float *ax*, float *ay*, float *az*)

void postRotateQuat(float *qx*, float *qy*, float *qz*, float *qw*)

The `post` prefix indicates that the matrix is multiplied *from the right* by the given matrix (e.g., $M' = MA$); `pre` would mean multiplying from the left (e.g., $M' = AM$), but there are no such methods in `Transform`. Going through the list of methods above, the first three probably need no deeper explanation. The rotation method comes in two varieties: `postRotateQuat` uses a quaternion to represent the rotation (see Section 2.3.1), whereas `postRotate` uses the *axis-angle* format: looking along the positive rotation axis $\begin{bmatrix} ax & ay & az \end{bmatrix}$, the rotation is *angle* degrees clockwise.

To make things more concrete, let us use `postScale` and `postTranslate` to construct the same matrix that we typed in manually in the previous example:

```
Transform myTransform = new Transform();
myTransform.postTranslate(3f, 4f, 5f);
myTransform.postScale(2f, 2f, 2f);
```

Transforming vertices

As in OpenGL, you should think that the matrix operations apply to vertices in the reverse order that they are written. If you apply the transformation TS to a vertex v, the vertex is first scaled and then translated: $T(Sv)$. Let us write out the matrices and confirm that the above code fragment does indeed yield the correct result:

$$\mathbf{M}' = \mathbf{ITS} = \begin{bmatrix} 1 & 0 & 0 & 0 \\ 0 & 1 & 0 & 0 \\ 0 & 0 & 1 & 0 \\ 0 & 0 & 0 & 1 \end{bmatrix} \begin{bmatrix} 1 & 0 & 0 & 3 \\ 0 & 1 & 0 & 4 \\ 0 & 0 & 1 & 5 \\ 0 & 0 & 0 & 1 \end{bmatrix} \begin{bmatrix} 2 & 0 & 0 & 0 \\ 0 & 2 & 0 & 0 \\ 0 & 0 & 2 & 0 \\ 0 & 0 & 0 & 1 \end{bmatrix} = \begin{bmatrix} 2 & 0 & 0 & 3 \\ 0 & 2 & 0 & 4 \\ 0 & 0 & 2 & 5 \\ 0 & 0 & 0 & 1 \end{bmatrix}$$

One of the most obvious things to do with a transformation matrix is to transform an array of vectors with it. The `Transform` class defines two convenience methods for this purpose. The first, `transform(float[]` *vectors*) multiplies each 4-element vector in the *vectors* array by `this` matrix and overwrites the original vectors with the results ($v' = Mv$, where v is a column vector). The other `transform` variant is a bit more complicated:

```
void transform(VertexArray in, float[] out, boolean w)
```

Here, we take in 2D or 3D vectors in a `VertexArray`, set the fourth component to zero or one depending on the *w* parameter, and write the transformed 4-element vectors to the *out* array. The input array remains unmodified.

The `transform` methods are provided mostly for convenience, as they play no role in rendering or any other function of the API. Nonetheless, if you have a large number of vectors that you need to multiply with a matrix for whatever purpose, these built-in methods are likely to perform better than doing the same thing in Java code. The `VertexArray` variant also serves a more peculiar purpose: it is the only way to read back vertices from a `VertexArray` on many devices, as the necessary `VertexArray.get` methods were only added in M3G 1.1.

Other use cases

Now that you know how to set up `Transform` objects and use them to transform vertices, let us look at what else you can use them for. First of all, in `Graphics3D` you need them to specify the local-to-world transformations of the immediate-mode camera, lights, and meshes. In both immediate mode and retained mode, you need a `Transform` to set up an oblique or otherwise special projection in `Camera`, or any kind of projection for texture coordinates in `Texture2D`. Finally, you can (but do not have to) use a `Transform` in the local-to-parent transformation of a `Node`. Each of these cases will come up later on in this book.

13.3.2 `Transformable`

`Transformable` is an abstract base class for the scene graph objects `Node` and `Texture2D`. Conceptually, it is a 4 × 4 matrix representing a node transformation or a texture coordinate transformation. The matrix is made up of four components that can be manipulated separately: translation *T*, orientation *R*, scale *S*, and a generic 4 × 4 matrix *M*. During rendering, and otherwise when necessary, M3G multiplies the components together to yield the *composite transformation*:

$$C = T\,R\,S\,M \qquad (13.1)$$

A homogeneous vector $\boldsymbol{p} = \begin{bmatrix} x & y & z & w \end{bmatrix}^T$, representing a vertex coordinate or texture coordinate, is then transformed into $\boldsymbol{p}' = \begin{bmatrix} x' & y' & z' & w' \end{bmatrix}^T$ by:

$$\boldsymbol{p}' = C\,\boldsymbol{p} \qquad (13.2)$$

The components are kept separate so that they can be controlled and animated independent of each other and independent of their previous values. For example, it makes no difference whether you first adjust *S* and then *T*, or vice versa; the only thing that matters is what values the components have when *C* needs to be recomputed. Contrast this with the corresponding operations in `Transform`, which are in fact matrix multiplications and thus very much order-dependent.

Note that for node transformations, the bottom row of the *M* component is restricted to [0 0 0 1]—in other words, projections are not allowed in the scene graph. Texture matrices do not have this limitation, so projective texture mapping is fully supported (see Section 3.4.3).

Methods

The following four methods in `Transformable` allow you to set the transformation components:

    void setTranslation(float *tx*, float *ty*, float *tz*)

    void setOrientation(float *angle*, float *ax*, float *ay*, float *az*)

    void setScale(float *sx*, float *sy*, float *sz*)

    void setTransform(Transform *transform*)

The complementary methods, `translate`, `preRotate`, `postRotate`, and `scale`, each modify the current value of the respective component by applying an additional translation, rotation, or scaling. The user-provided rotation can be applied to the left (pre) or to the right (post) of the current R; scaling and translation are order-independent. These methods take the same parameters as their setter counterparts.

Transformable also defines a getter for each of the four components, as well as for the composite transformation C:

```
void getTranslation(float[] translation)

void getOrientation(float[] angleAxis)

void getScale(float[] scale)

void getTransform(Transform transform)

void getCompositeTransform(Transform transform)
```

Note that there is indeed only one getter for each component, not separate ones for tx, ty, tz, $angle$, and so on. Consistent with the API conventions, the values are filled in to a float array or Transform object designated by the user, thus facilitating object reuse.

Rotations

Rotations in Transformable are specified in the axis-angle format, which is very intuitive, but unfortunately less robust and sometimes less convenient than quaternions. There are no utility methods in the API to convert between the two representations, but luckily this is quite simple to do in your own code. Denoting a normalized axis-angle pair by $[\hat{a}\,\theta] = [a_x\,a_y\,a_z\,\theta]$, and a unit quaternion by $\hat{q} = [q_v\,q_w] = [q_x\,q_y\,q_z\,q_w]$, the conversions are as follows:

$$[q_v\,q_w] = [\hat{a}\sin(\theta/2) \quad \cos(\theta/2)] \tag{13.3}$$

$$[\hat{a} \quad \theta] = \left[q_v/\sqrt{1 - q_w^2}\ \ 2\arccos(q_w)\right]. \tag{13.4}$$

Both formulas assume the input axis or quaternion to be normalized, and will produce normalized output. If the axis-angle output is intended for M3G, however, you do not need to normalize the axis because M3G will do that in any case. You may therefore skip the square root term, yielding a significantly faster conversion from quaternion to axis-angle:

$$[a \quad \theta] = [q_v\ 2\arccos(q_w)]. \tag{13.5}$$

In other words, only the rotation angle needs to be computed, because q_v can be used as the rotation axis as such. Remember that the angle needs to be degrees, and if your acos() returns the angle in radians, the resulting θ must be multiplied with $180/\pi$. Note that the input quaternion must still be normalized, or else $\arccos(q_w)$ will yield an incorrect value for θ. A quaternion can be normalized just like any other vector:

$$\hat{q} = q/\sqrt{q_x^2 + q_y^2 + q_z^2 + q_w^2}. \tag{13.6}$$

> **Pitfall:** Due to the unfortunate lack of inverse trigonometric functions in mobile Java, you will have to write an `acos` routine yourself, or download one from the web. In any case, ensure that the routine has sufficient precision, or otherwise you will not get smooth animation.

Pivot transformations

The scale, orientation, and translation components are not sufficient to fully represent affine transformations (that is, all 3×4 matrices). For that, we would also need *scale orientation* O and *pivot translation* P. Scale orientation provides for scaling along arbitrary orthonormal axes, rather than just the primary axes. Pivot translation allows any 3D point to be set as the center of rotation, instead of just the origin. The composite transformation would then become

$$C = T P R P^{-1} O S O^{-1} M \tag{13.7}$$

Scale orientation and pivot translation were omitted from M3G, because they are rarely needed in practice. They would also add substantial storage and processing overhead to scene graph nodes, even when not used. If you do need a full affine transformation, however, you can composite one in your own code, and feed it in as the generic M component. This works for both texture transformations and node transformations. For node transformations, you have an easier alternative: use some extra `Group` nodes and split the transformation into multiple parts, depending on which components you need to control separately. Typically, P and O remain constant, while the translation, rotation, and scale are animated. In this case, you could assign the components into one extra `Group` and the original leaf node as shown in Figure 13.1. Note that T and P are combined into T_A.

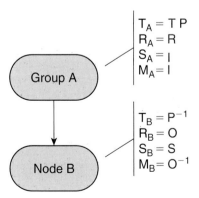

Figure 13.1: Using an extra `Group` node to implement rotation around a pivot point ($P\,R\,P^{-1}$) and oriented scaling ($O\,S\,O^{-1}$).

This works fine with `translate`, but if you use `setTranslation`, you must remember to factor in the pivot translation.

13.4 `Object3D`

`Object3D` is an abstract base class for all objects that can be part of a 3D scene. As shown in Figure 12.3, all but four classes in the whole API are derived from `Object3D`. It defines properties and capabilities that are common to all scene graph objects, including the ability to be keyframe-animated, duplicated, or imported from a file.

13.4.1 ANIMATING

Arguably the single most powerful method in `Object3D` is `animate(int *time*)`, which invokes the built-in keyframe animation system. The `animate` method first updates all animated properties in the `Object3D` that it is called on, then in all `Object3D`s that are referenced from it, and so on in a recursive manner. In other words, `animate` updates all objects that are *reachable* from the initial object by following a chain of references. There are two kinds of references that are not followed, though: those that go upward in the scene graph, and those that go sideways, jumping from one branch to another. This is all very intuitive—if you animate a particular branch of the scene graph, you expect all objects in that branch to be updated, not just the root node. On the other hand, you do not expect the rest of the scene to be animated with it.

Recalling that `World` is derived from `Object3D`, and correctly deducing that there must be a chain of references from a `World` object to everything in the scene graph, it follows that we can animate an entire scene with this single line of code:

```
myWorld.animate(myWorldTime);
```

This updates all animated properties in `myWorld` to the given time. You can then render the updated scene as such, or further animate it using ordinary Java code. `animate` is typically called once per frame, and the world time increased by the number of milliseconds elapsed since the previous frame. The keyframe animation system is described in detail in Chapter 16.

13.4.2 ITERATING AND CLONING

There are three other methods in `Object3D` that follow the same principles of traversing the scene graph as `animate`. Let us start with `getReferences`, which helps you iterate through the scene graph in your own code:

```
int getReferences(Object3D[] references)
```

This method retrieves all objects that are directly referenced by an Object3D, again not including references to parent nodes or other branches. The integer return value tells you how many such direct references there are. Typically you would first invoke getReferences(null) to get the number of references, then allocate an array of sufficient size and call the method again to get the list of objects. Note that there may be duplicate objects in the list, as each reference is treated separately.

To illustrate a case when getReferences is highly useful, consider the following utility method that retrieves all objects of the given class type that are reachable from the given root object, eliminating duplicates along the way. For example, to retrieve all cameras in the scene, you would call getUniqueObjects(cameras, myWorld, Class.forName("javax.microedition.m3g.Camera")), just making sure that the cameras array is large enough.

```
// A recursive method to find all Object3Ds of given 'type' that
// are reachable from 'root'.  Returns the number of unique,
// matching objects and inserts them into the 'found' array.
// This method is not very efficient: it takes O(N^2) time and
// O(N) memory, where N is the number of objects traversed.
// On the other hand, finding objects in the scene graph is
// typically a one-off process.
//
int getUniqueObjects(Object3D[] found, Object3D root, Class type)
{
  int i, numUnique = 0;

  // Retrieve the scene graph objects that are directly referenced
  // by 'root' and process them recursively.  Note that we create
  // a new 'references' array at each step of the recursion; this
  // is not recommended as a general practice, but in this case we
  // are favoring brevity and clarity over efficiency.
  //
  Object3D[] references = new Object3D[root.getReferences(null)];
  root.getReferences(references);
  for (i=0; i < references.length; i++) {
    numUnique += getUniqueObjects(found, references[i], type);
  }

  // Check whether 'root' is an instance of 'type', and if so,
  // insert it at the end of the 'found' array, provided that
  // there is at least one empty slot left.  Then loop through
  // the array, checking if 'root' has been inserted before.
  // If not, we let it remain in the array and increase the
  // count of unique objects by one.
  //
  if (type.isAssignableFrom(root.getClass()) &&
      numUnique < found.length) {
    found[numUnique] = root;
    for (i=0; found[i] != root; i++);
```

```
        if (i == numUnique) numUnique++;
    }
    return numUnique;
}
```

That is just fifteen lines of code, excluding comments, of which only five are spent actually traversing the scene graph. If it were not for `getReferences`, those five lines would be replaced with a horrendous `switch-case` construct, probably using up several hundred lines of code.

The second utility method in `Object3D` that deals with chains of references is `duplicate`. This method creates a copy of the object that it is called on. For most objects that amounts to a *shallow copy*, in which the instance variables and references are copied, but the referenced objects themselves are not. However, for non-leaf scene graph nodes, a *deep copy* is necessary to maintain the integrity of the duplicated scene graph branch. Given the rule that scene graph nodes can have at most one parent in M3G, how should we go about cloning a `Group` node, for instance? The children of that group cannot be in both the new and the old group at the same time, so there are two choices: leave the new group empty, or clone the entire subtree. M3G does the latter, because creating a "duplicate" that has none of the original contents would be rather misleading and pointless.

Now that you know how `duplicate` works, you may wonder why it has to exist in the first place. We already have `clone` in `java.lang.Object`, right? Wrong: there is no `clone` in CLDC/MIDP. It does exist on the higher-end CDC platform, though, and may some day exist on CLDC. On such platforms, `Object3D` will include both `duplicate` and `clone`. However, the behavior of `clone` on `Object3D` and its derived classes is left undefined in the M3G specification, so we recommend using `duplicate` instead.

13.4.3 TAGS AND ANNOTATIONS

The one remaining scene graph traversal method, `find(int *userID*)`, is best utilized together with the M3G file format. Importing content from `.m3g` files is discussed in the next section, but what is important for understanding the benefits of `find` is that since you can load an arbitrarily large number of objects in one go, locating the objects that you need may be difficult. If there are a thousand meshes in the scene, how do you identify the flashlight object that your player character should be able to pick up? That is when `find` and `userID` come in handy.

Finding objects by ID

Despite being just a simple integer, the `userID` is a very powerful tool that allows the graphics designer and application programmer to synchronize their work. First, the designer assigns a unique `userID` for each object that needs individual treatment at runtime. For instance, the player character might be tagged with the ID 1000, her right hand with 1010, and different items that she can hold with IDs 2000-2010. The designer then exports the 3D scene into a .m3g file. Finally, at runtime, the scene is loaded in and the relevant objects retrieved using find:

```
Node player = (Node)myWorld.find(1000);
Node playerRightHand = (Node)player.find(1010);
Mesh flashlight = (Mesh)myWorld.find(2000);
...
Mesh knife = (Mesh)myWorld.find(2010);
```

Formally, Object3D.find retrieves the first Object3D that has the given userID and is reachable from the object where the search is started. The definition of being reachable is the same as with animate.

Adding metadata

The UserObject is another mechanism that allows the designer to communicate with the runtime engine. The user object is simply an arbitrary block of metadata that can be associated with any scene graph object. The interpretation of that metadata is up to you; M3G itself never touches the user object. You can associate a user object with an Object3D either at runtime, in which case it can be anything derived from java.lang. Object, or through the M3G file format, in which case it will be a java.util.Hashtable filled with byte[] elements that are keyed by Integers. It is then up to the application to parse the byte arrays to extract their meaning.

Advanced annotations

As an advanced example that leverages both the UserID and the UserObject, let us associate symbolic names with those bones of a SkinnedMesh that we need to manipulate at runtime. The names of the bones have been agreed on by the designer and the programmer, and they are of the form "left_arm." The designer identifies the relevant bones in the authoring tool, assigns the agreed-upon names and any arbitrary userIDs to them, and finally, with a little support from the exporter, stores the (userID, name) pairs into the UserObject field of the SkinnedMesh.

At runtime, having loaded the M3G file, we first retrieve the UserObject that has by now taken the form of a Hashtable with (Integer, byte[]) pairs. In this case, the integers are actually our user IDs, while the byte arrays are the names. We then iterate through the hash table: take the user ID, find the bone that corresponds to it, and finally build a new hash table (called bones) that associates each bone with its name:

```
// Load the SkinnedMesh and get the table of (userID, name) pairs,
// then set up a new hash table that will associate bones with
```

```
// their symbolic names.
//
SkinnedMesh creature = (SkinnedMesh)Loader.
                          load("/creature.m3g")[0];
Hashtable names = (Hashtable)creature.getUserObject();
Hashtable bones = new Hashtable(names.size());

// For each UserID in the (userID, name) table:
//  1. Get the name corresponding to that UserID.
//  2. Convert the name from a byte array into a Java String.
//  3. Find the bone Node corresponding to the UserID.
//  4. Insert the String and the Node into the new hash table.
//
Enumeration userIDs = names.keys();
while (userIDs.hasMoreElements()) {
  Integer userID = (Integer)userIDs.nextElement();
  String name = new String( (byte[])names.get(userID) );
  Node bone = (Node)creature.find(userID.intValue());
  bones.put(name, bone);
}

// Finally, bind the (name, bone) table as the UserObject
// of our SkinnedMesh, replacing the (userID, name) table
// (assuming that it will not be needed anymore).
//
mySkinnedMesh.setUserObject(bones);
```

Now that we have some semantics associated with our bones, it becomes a breeze to animate any specific part of the character in our main loop. For example, to move the left arm into a certain position relative to the left shoulder, you just do this:

```
Node leftArm = (Node)bones.get("left_arm");
leftArm.translate(...);
```

Note that if you are going to update leftArm very often, it may be smart to cache it in an instance variable rather than looking it up from the hash table every time.

Annotating bones—or any scene graph objects, for that matter—with symbolic names is a good idea, because it allows the designer to change the scene representation without the programmer having to change the application code. If the application relies on the left arm being a certain number of steps from the skinned mesh root, for example, things will break down immediately if the artist decides to add a few fix-up bones to the shoulder region. Furthermore, using plain-text names rather than just integers leaves less room for typing errors for both the artist and the programmer, and is of great help in debugging.

13.5 IMPORTING CONTENT

The easiest way to construct a scene graph in M3G is to import it from the JAR package or a network URL using the built-in `Loader`. The loader can import individual images from PNG and JPEG files, and complete or partial scene graphs from M3G files. There are numerous M3G exporters available for 3ds Max, Maya, Softimage, Lightwave, and Blender; see the companion web site for an up-to-date list. For a step-by-step tutorial on creating some M3G content in Blender, see Chapter 10 of *Mobile 3D Graphics: Learning 3D Graphics with the Java Micro Edition* by Claus Höfele [Hö07].

We begin this section by explaining how to use the `Loader`, then proceed to discuss the M3G file format in enough detail to get you started with your own content processing tools.

13.5.1 `Loader`

The `Loader` will accept at least PNG and M3G files on any device, but JPEG is also supported on many devices.[5] Loading a PNG or JPEG yields a single `Image2D` object (see also Section 13.2). M3G files, on the other hand, can store anything up to and including an array of complete scene graphs. They may even include an arbitrary number of other files by reference. The number of objects per file and the total size of those objects are bounded only by the available memory in each device.

Methods

`Loader` is one of the four special classes in M3G that are not derived from `Object3D` (see the class diagram in Figure 12.3). Moreover, it cannot be instantiated, and its only members are these two static `load` methods:

    Object3D[] load(String *name*)

    Object3D[] load(byte[] *data*, int *offset*)

The first variant loads the content from a *named resource*, which can be a file in the JAR package or a URL (typically of the form `http://...`). Named resources are treated as case-sensitive, and must specify an absolute path (e.g., `/bg.png` rather than just `bg.png`). This method is what you will probably use in most cases.

The other form of `load` reads the data from a byte array. This method may be useful in special cases: if you need to embed some art assets into your Java class files for whatever reason, this method allows you to do that. It also lets you manually load and preprocess your content before forwarding it to the loader. For example, you could make it harder to

---

5   At least on those that conform to the MSA (JSR 248) specification.

rip off or reverse-engineer your assets by keeping them in encrypted form, only decrypting them at runtime.

Both `load` methods are synchronous, i.e., they only return when the entire contents of the given input have been successfully loaded, along with any files that are included by reference. It is therefore not possible to render or otherwise process a partially loaded file. There is also no way to get any progress information from the loader. If loading takes a lot of time in your application and you need a good progress bar, our advice is to split your assets into multiple files that are loaded separately.

Output

Both `load` methods return an `Object3D` array. This array contains the *root objects* of the file. A root object is one that is not referenced by any other object in the file. There may be an arbitrary number of root objects in a file, and the root objects may, in turn, reference an arbitrary number of non-root objects. Finding the objects that you need from within that mass of objects is made easier by the `Object3D` methods `find(int` *userID*`)` and `getReferences`, as discussed in the previous section.

All the returned objects, whether root or non-root, are guaranteed to be consistent, meaning that you might as well have constructed them with the API without getting any exceptions thrown. However, they are not guaranteed to be in a renderable condition. For example, there may be textures or other components missing, causing an exception if you try to render the scene. This is fully intentional, as it allows you to store a partial scene graph in a file and patch in the missing pieces at runtime.

Pitfall: The peak memory consumption of many applications occurs at the setup stage, and asset loading plays a big role in that. Let us hypothesize what may be happening behind the scenes when you load a PNG image into a MIDP `Image` and then convert it into an `Image2D`. The PNG file is first decompressed from the JAR; then the PNG itself is decompressed into the `Image`; finally, the `Image` is copied into `Image2D`. In the worst case, you may have one compressed copy and *two* uncompressed copies of the image in memory at the same time! The temporary copies are of course released in the end, but that does not help with your peak memory consumption. If you keep running out of memory while loading, we would suggest you to split your content into parts that are loaded separately.

Example

The following code fragment gives a concrete example of using the `Loader`. The code first loads the file `myscene.m3g` from the `/res` subdirectory of the JAR package, and then uses the runtime type information provided by Java to find the first `World` object among the potentially many root objects. Note that if there are any `Worlds` in the file, they are guaranteed to be among the root objects.

```
try {
  Object3D[] objects = Loader.load("/res/myscene.m3g");
  for (int i=0; i < objects.length; i++) {
    if (objects[i] instanceof World) {
      myWorld = (World)objects[i];
      break;
    }
  }
} catch (Exception e) { ... }
```

Catching any exceptions that might occur during the loading is not only good programming practice, but actually required: the `Loader` may throw an `IOException`, which is a special kind of exception in that it must be either explicitly caught or declared to be thrown to the calling method. You cannot just not mention it and let the caller take care of it.

Note that the above example will not work reliably if there are several `World` objects in the file, because the `Loader` does not guarantee that they are returned in any particular order. On the other hand, if we are certain that there is never going to be more than one root object in the file, that being our desired `World`, we can omit the `for` loop altogether and just do this:

```
myWorld = (World)Loader.load("/res/myscene.m3g")[0];
```

Using `Loader.load` is so straightforward that there is not much else to say about it, so let us continue with the M3G file format instead. You may now want to fast-forward to the next chapter if you do not intend to debug any `.m3g` files or develop any M3G content processing tools in the foreseeable future.

13.5.2 THE FILE FORMAT

The graphics industry is certainly not suffering from a shortage of file formats. There must be a thousand 3D file formats in existence, so why did the M3G standardization group have to invent yet another one? Well, probably for the same reasons as most of the file format designers before us: we needed a format that matches the runtime API perfectly, not just so-and-so. We wanted to leave as little room for interpretation as possible, and that is best achieved if every object and field in the file format has a one-to-one mapping with the API.

One of the key features of the file format is its simplicity. We opted for quick and easy reading and writing, rather than extensibility, maximum compression, random access, streaming, error concealment, or a number of other things that are best handled elsewhere or not required at all. You will no doubt value that decision if you ever need to write your own exporters, viewers, or optimization tools for M3G content, or simply need to debug an existing file.

The simplicity is achieved by four primary means: First, there is a one-to-one mapping between object types in the file format and Java classes in the run-time API. Second, there are no forward references, so objects can only refer to objects that reside earlier in the file. Third, compression is based on the widely available zlib, rather than specialized encodings for different data types, or complex algorithms such as arithmetic coding. Finally, the Loader has an all-or-nothing policy: a file is either loaded completely or not at all. No attempt is made to recover from errors.

We will now go through the structure of the file format, shown at a high level in Figure 13.2. To shed light on individual details, we will refer to the example file in Figure 13.3. Note that what follows is not intended to be an exhaustive description or a replacement for the specification, but only to give you an idea of how things are laid out. Having read this, you should be able to more quickly dig up whatever details you need in the spec.

File structure

M3G files are easy to recognize in a text editor by their *file identifier*, <<JSR184>>, located at the very beginning. To be exact, the identifier consists of that string and a few special characters to quickly catch file transmission errors, for a total of twelve bytes (in hexadecimal): AB 4A 53 52 31 38 34 BB 0D 0A 1A 0A.

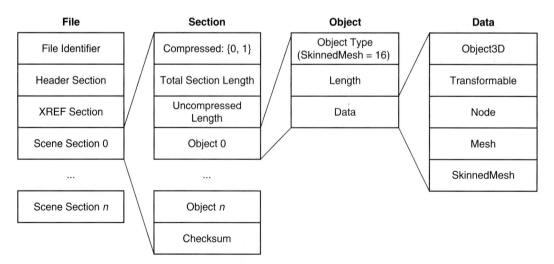

Figure 13.2: M3G files are divided into sections, each containing one or more objects, which are further divided into fields. The fields are laid out in the order of class inheritance; for example, a SkinnedMesh object is derived from Object3D, Transformable, Node, and Mesh, as shown in Figure 12.3.

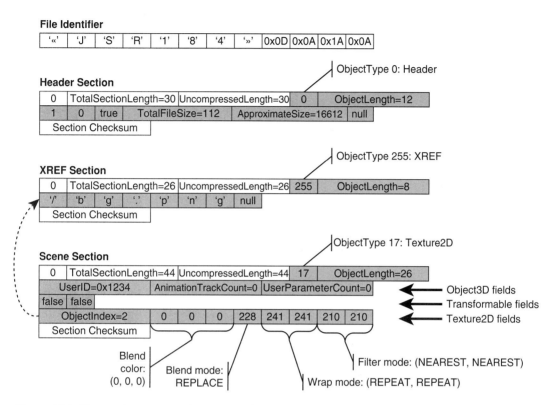

Figure 13.3: The complete contents of our example file, byte by byte. There is one root object in the file, a `Texture2D`, and one non-root object, an `Image2D` that is loaded from the external file `/bg.png`. All sections are uncompressed. Object data are shown in gray boxes, section data in white.

Beyond the file identifier, M3G files are divided into *sections* that contain one or more *objects* each. Sections may be individually compressed with `zlib`; this allows you to selectively compress the sections for which it makes most sense. Each section also has an Adler32 checksum (provided by `zlib`) to allow the `Loader` to quickly reject a corrupt file without parsing it further. Note that the loader will make no attempt to recover the contents of a damaged file, but will simply throw an `IOException`.

There are three kinds of sections. The *header section* must be present in every file, must be uncompressed, and must be located right after the file identifier. The *external reference section* is optional, but must immediately follow the header section if present. The rest of the file is composed of an arbitrary number of *scene sections*. Any legal M3G file must have at least one section besides the header, and must not have any empty sections.

Data types

The file format has data types corresponding to the built-in `boolean`, `byte`, `short`, `int`, and `float` types in Java. Booleans are encoded as a single byte, such that 1 indicates `true`, 0 indicates `false`, and other values are disallowed. The integer and float types are stored so that the least significant byte comes first.

Besides the basic types, M3G files may also contain null-terminated strings, 3-element floating-point vectors, 4 × 4 matrices, RGB and RGBA colors encoded at 8 bits per color component, references to other objects, and arbitrary-length arrays of any basic or compound type.

Object references

Upon loading, objects are read sequentially from the beginning of the file and assigned a running number as their *index*. The first object in the file, which is a special header object, gets the index one, the first actual scene object gets the index two, and so on. The index zero is reserved for `null` references.

Objects can only reference other objects that reside at *lower* indices, i.e., those that have already been imported. This is to guarantee that the `Loader` can parse any M3G file from start to finish in one pass, and also to allow it to type-check the references immediately. Note that the lack of forward references means that a scene graph loaded from a file can never have cycles, although they are permitted in the runtime scene graph for node alignment; see Section 15.3.2.

Header section

The header section contains exactly one object, the header object, which cannot be present anywhere else in the file. As shown in Figure 13.3, the header object begins with a two-byte version number, identifying variants of the file format. The only legal version number at this time is 1.0. Note that the file format does not necessarily have the same version number as the M3G API.

Following the version number is a boolean flag telling whether the external reference section is present (in our example, it is). The header object also stores the total size of the file, both with and without the external references. The size that includes the external references is regarded to be a hint and need not be accurate, so as to allow the referenced files to be modified independently of the root file. In our example, the root file is 112 bytes (exactly), and the externally referenced PNG is (estimated to be) 16500 bytes.

The final item in the header object is the `AuthoringField` where the authoring tool or the author herself may store an arbitrary null-terminated string of text, such as a copyright notice. In our example the field is left empty, containing just the terminating `null`.

External reference section

The external reference section stores one or more external references, or XREFs for short. External references allow you to build up your scene from a collection of separate M3G and image files. Images are typically included by reference rather than embedded into the host file, because dedicated image formats provide better compression than plain `zlib`. A minor disadvantage with external image files is that they have no user ID or user parameters.

External references are simply null-terminated strings pointing at named resources, such as network URLs or files in the JAR package. Each external reference yields exactly one root-level `Object3D`. Our example file in Figure 13.3 has just one XREF, pointing at `/bg.png` in the JAR package. It will be imported as a single `Image2D`.

M3G files may reference an arbitrary number of other M3G files, which in turn may freely reference another set of M3G files, and so on, but the references are not allowed to form a cycle. Also, if you intend an M3G file to be referenced from another, make sure that it only has one root object. If there are many root objects, the `Loader` will pick only the first one and discard the rest.

Scene sections

Scene sections store the actual scene graph—or several scene graphs. Each scene section can contain one or more objects, and again each object corresponds to exactly one `Object3D` in the runtime API. The contents of each object are generally the same as that of the corresponding class in the API.

In our example file, there is one scene section, containing a single `Texture2D`. The base class data for `Object3D` comes first, followed by the other base class `Transformable`. The data for the concrete class is stored last. This is the case with all types of objects in the file format.

For simplicity, we have no animation tracks or user parameters in our example, and no texture matrix in `Transformable`. The two `false` entries in `Transformable` indicate that the *T R S* components as well as the *M* component will assume their default values, i.e., the identity matrix. The fields of the `Texture2D` object itself are pretty obvious. The main thing to note is that the image in `/bg.png` must have power-of-two dimensions. Also note that the `Image2D` is assigned the object index 2, because the header object always gets the index one, and zero is reserved for `null`.

Special compression

We said in the beginning of this section that there are no special compression formats for different data types in the M3G file format, just `zlib` for everything, but that is not strictly true. The `VertexArray` and `KeyframeSequence` classes do in fact have special encodings as an option. However, the encodings are almost trivial.

Vertex arrays—including colors, normals, texture coordinates and vertex positions—can be compressed with *delta encoding*. This means that each vertex attribute is stored as a difference vector relative to the previous value. The differences are unsigned, so for example a difference of −2 is encoded as 254 (in case of a `byte` array) or 65534 (in case of a `short` array). Thus, the deltas take up the same number of bits as the raw integers (8 or 16 bits per component), making the whole encoding seem rather pointless. However, the deltas tend to have fewer significant bits, causing the same bit patterns to repeat more often across the array. This, in turn, allows `zlib` to compress the array more efficiently. Note that delta encoding and `zlib` are both lossless.

Keyframes, which are 32-bit `float` values in raw format, can be encoded by quantizing them to 16-bit or 8-bit integers which are then scaled and offset using a bias value. The quantized keyframes consume only a half or a quarter of the file size compared to the raw format, and that is further reduced by `zlib`. Floating-point bit patterns, on the other hand, are poorly compressed by `zlib`.

LOW-LEVEL MODELING IN M3G

M3G builds upon the common low-level concepts set forth in Chapter 3. It offers most of the same functionality that OpenGL ES provides for native applications, but with an object-oriented Java interface. Some features are slightly more abstracted in order to reduce API complexity, but the underlying rendering pipeline, be that implemented in software or hardware, can be shared with OpenGL ES. Also, while familiarity with OpenGL ES is not a prerequisite for understanding M3G, existing knowledge on OpenGL ES will not be wasted on M3G.

In this chapter, we walk through the lowest-level parts of M3G. By the end of the chapter, you will know how to use M3G to draw polygon meshes in immediate mode, similarly to OpenGL ES. The components discussed here will also serve as building blocks for the higher-level functions which are covered in the following chapters.

14.1 BUILDING MESHES

Meshes in M3G are built out of vertex array and buffer objects, triangle buffer objects, and shading parameters specified in various rendering state objects.

14.1.1 `VertexArray`

Low-level modeling begins by defining your vertex data. The `VertexArray` class stores an array of vectors that can then be used for any per-vertex data: positions, normals, colors, or texture coordinates. The class constructor is `VertexArray(int` *numVertices*, `int` *numComponents*, `int` *componentSize*), where the parameters are the number of vertices, number of components per vertex, and size of the data type used, respectively. *componentSize* is 1 for `byte`, and 2 for `short` data. For a mesh with 100 vertices having vertex positions and colors only, for example, you could create two arrays:

```
myPositions = new VertexArray(100, 3, 2);   // 16-bit positions
myColors    = new VertexArray(100, 4, 1);   // 8-bit RGBA colors
```

Vertex data is loaded into the arrays using the `set` function, which copies a range of vertex values from a `byte` or `short` array:

```
void  set(int firstVertex, int numVertices, byte[] values)
void  set(int firstVertex, int numVertices, short[] values)
```

Pitfall: If you plan on reading data back from `VertexArray`, you may soon find that the `get` method for that is not included in M3G 1.0—it was one of the many getters dropped to minimize the API footprint.

The `get` methods were added to `VertexArray` in M3G 1.1, but if you absolutely need equivalent functionality with M3G 1.0, it can be done using the `Transform.transform` method as described in Section 13.3. Even then, you will only get the vertex data in floating-point format, not the original 8-bit or 16-bit integers.

Now, assume that you have your positions in a `short` array `myPositionData` and your colors in a `byte` array `myColorData`. The arrays should have at least 300 and 400 elements, respectively. We can then load the data values for all 100 vertices into the previously created vertex arrays:

```
myPositions.set(0, 100, myPositionData);
             myColors.set(0, 100, myColorData);
```

M3G makes a copy of the data you load into a `VertexArray`, so `myPositionData` and `myColorData` can be discarded at this point. In fact, all data in M3G is stored internally—client-side arrays are only referenced when copying data from them. This allows M3G to internally organize the data in the most efficient way.

14.1.2 VertexBuffer

Once you have the vertex arrays you need, they must be combined into a `VertexBuffer` to form the actual vertices. The constructor for `VertexBuffer` simply creates an empty set of vertices. The necessary component arrays are added using the `setPositions`, `setNormals`, `setColors`, and `setTexCoords` functions. Note that there are certain restrictions on what kind of vertex data you can use for

Table 14.1: Supported vertex array types in M3G (ticks), relative to OpenGL ES 1.1 (ticks and crosses). The grayed-out boxes indicate combinations that are supported in neither API.

	Byte	**Short**	**Fixed**	**Float**	**2D**	**3D**	**4D**
Vertices	✓	✓	✗	✗	✗	✓	✗
Texcoords	✓	✓	✗	✗	✓	✓	✗
Normals	✓	✓	✗	✗		✓	
Colors	✓		✗	✗		✓	✓

each vertex component—those are summarized in Table 14.1. The setters for colors and normals are trivial, only taking in the array you wish to use for that vertex component. Normals are automatically normalized. For positions, however, additional *scale* and *bias* values must be supplied:

```
void setPositions(VertexArray positions, float scale, float[] bias)
```

Since M3G only supports 8- and 16-bit vertices, *scale* and *bias* let you map the quantized vertices into a wider floating-point domain. Before M3G uses any of your vertex data, each quantized vertex v_i is converted into an equivalent floating-point vertex v_i':

$$v_i' = sv_i + b \qquad (14.1)$$

where s and b are the values of *scale* and *bias*, respectively. This way, you can author your model in floating point, quantize the vertices to 16 or 8 bits, and still use the resulting VertexArray in M3G as you would the original data. The precision is sufficient for just about any model, while the memory usage is only a half or one-quarter of full floating-point vertices. M3G implementations are also made more efficient, as there is no need to implement a full floating-point vertex pipeline.

Again, using our example arrays, let us set up a VertexBuffer:

```
myVertices = new VertexBuffer();
myVertices.setColors(myColors);
myVertices.setPositions(myPositions, 100.f / (1<<16), null);
```

In this case, we set *bias* to null, signaling a default bias of $(0, 0, 0)$. The *scale* parameter scales our 16-bit position data so that the coordinates span 100 units in floating point domain. If the full 16-bit range is utilized in myPositions, our model therefore extends from −50 to +50 on each coordinate axis.

> **Performance tip:** Always make use of the full range available for your vertex positions and texture coordinates. Quantize your floating-point coordinates so that they fill the 8- or 16-bit numeric range optimally, then map the data back to floating point by using the scale and bias values. There is no additional runtime cost from doing this, but it will let you achieve the maximum precision possible.

Texture coordinates take one more additional parameter, the index of the texturing unit:

```
void setTexCoords(int index, VertexArray texcoords, float scale, float[] bias)
```

When using multi-texturing, `VertexBuffer` must contain a set of texture coordinates for each texture unit. Of course, you can—and often will—also set the same `VertexArray` for each texture unit; no data replication is required. Arrays can also be shared between any number of vertex buffers, and nothing prevents you from, for example, using the same array for both vertex normals and texture coordinates.

> **Performance tip:** Always prefer multi-texturing over multi-pass rendering. With multi-texturing, you get multiple layers of texture by only rendering the geometry once, whereas multi-pass rendering incurs the transformation and lighting overhead for each pass. Blending and other frame buffer processing will also add to this overhead.

Vertex positions are the only piece of data that is required for all rendering. If you want to use lighting, your `VertexBuffer` will also need normal vectors, and we already mentioned that texture coordinates are required to apply a texture. For vertex colors, you have a choice of using either a per-vertex color array or a single color for the entire buffer, set using `setDefaultColor`. To construct a buffer where all the vertices are red, you can do:

```
myVertices = new VertexBuffer();
myVertices.setPositions(myPositions, 100.f / (1<<16), null);
myVertices.setDefaultColor(0xFF0000);
```

> **Pitfall:** M3G versions 1.0 and 1.1 specify slightly different error handling for vertex components, with M3G 1.0 being more strict. It throws exceptions for many cases of missing data, such as texturing without valid texture coordinates. This was viewed as an extra burden on implementations, and in M3G 1.1 error checking was relaxed so that vertex normals and texture coordinates default to some undefined value if the respective arrays do not exist during rendering.
>
> As an application developer, you should be aware of the fact that you may *not* get an exception if you are missing a required piece of vertex data. Instead, your rendering results will simply be incorrect. The reason may be tricky to identify even if you know what to look for, so if you want to use lighting or texturing, remember to supply those normals or texture coordinates!

> **Performance tip:** Note that you can use `set` at any time to modify the contents of a `VertexArray`, and you can also use the setters on `VertexBuffer` to change the arrays being used. Be aware, however, that this may not be cheap, as the implementation may have to recompute bounding volumes or other cached data that is dependent on

the vertex values. As a rule, create your vertex arrays and buffers during the initialization phase of your application and only modify their contents after that if you really need to.

14.1.3 `IndexBuffer` AND RENDERING PRIMITIVES

Vertices alone do not let you render anything. You also need to specify the kind of primitives you want to draw. For this purpose, M3G has the abstract `IndexBuffer` class that is specialized for each type of primitive. With the primitive types, M3G takes rather an ascetic approach, as the only kind of primitive currently supported is a triangle strip (see Section 3.1.1). Comparing to OpenGL ES in Table 14.2, we see that this is quite a cut in features. Lines and points were dropped because they would have added a lot of complexity to support quite a few use cases; if necessary, they can be emulated with triangles, which is how most renderers implement them in any case.

The reasoning behind supporting triangles as strips only was that they are an efficient primitive both for storing a shape and for rendering it, and most M3G content will come from authoring tools that can easily generate the strips. It was perceived that quite a bit of implementation complexity could be dropped this way. Looking back now, this was one of the decisions where features were a little too aggressively cut down in the effort to minimize complexity—having to use triangle strips instead of triangle lists is quite an annoyance when generating meshes in code, for example.

The `TriangleStripArray` class lets you construct an array of several triangle strips. You have a choice of two flavors of strips: *implicit* and *explicit*. The former assumes that the source vertices are ordered sequentially in the ascending order of indices, and you only have to specify the starting vertex and the length of each subsequent strip:

```
TriangleStripArray(int firstVertex, int[] stripLengths)
```

The number of entries in the *stripLengths* array gives the number of strips. For example, if *stripLengths* is {3, 4, 3}, the call `TriangleStripArray(2, stripLengths)` will create three strips with the indices {2, 3, 4}, {5, 6, 7, 8}, and {9, 10, 11}. This

Table 14.2: Supported rendering primitives in M3G, relative to OpenGL ES 1.1. The grayed-out boxes indicate combinations that are supported in neither API.

	Byte	Short	Implicit	Strip	Fan	List
Triangles	✗	✓	✓	✓	✗	✗
Lines	✗	✗	✗	✗	✗	✗
Points	✗	✗	✗			✗
Points sprites	✗	✗	✗			✗

is not very useful for most real-world meshes, but can save some space in certain special cases and procedurally generated meshes.

The other alternative, explicit strips, is what you normally want to use. Here, the difference is that instead of a starting vertex, you give a list of indices:

```
TriangleStripArray(int[] indices, int[] stripLengths)
```

The *indices* array is then split into as many separate triangle strips as specified in the *stripLengths* array. For a simple example, let us construct an `IndexBuffer` containing two strips, one with five and the other with three vertices; this translates into three and one triangles, respectively.

```
static final int myStripIndices[] = { 0, 3, 1, 4, 5, 7, 6, 8 };
static final int myStripLengths[] = { 5, 3 };
myTriangles = new TriangleStripArray(myStripIndices, myStripLengths);
```

> **Performance tip:** While triangle strips in general are very efficient, there is a considerable setup cost associated with rendering each strip. Very small strips are therefore not efficient to render at all, and it is important to try to keep your strips as long as possible. It may even be beneficial to join several strips together using degenerate triangles, duplicating the end index of the first and the beginning index of the second strip so that zero-area triangles are created to join the two strips. Such degenerate triangles are detected and quickly discarded by most M3G implementations.
>
> As usual, your mileage may vary. With the large spectrum of M3G-enabled devices out there, some software-only implementations may in fact be able to render short strips fairly efficiently, whereas some other implementations may optimize the strips themselves regardless of how you specify them. Submitting already optimized strips may therefore yield little or no benefit on some devices.

Note that unlike vertex arrays and buffers, the index buffers cannot be modified once created—this was seen as an unnecessary feature and left out in the name of implementation complexity, but perhaps overlooked the fact that someone might still want to recycle an `IndexBuffer` rather than create a new one. Nevertheless, index buffers need not have a one-to-one correspondence to vertices, and you can use as many index buffers per vertex buffer as you want to. The index buffer size does not have to match the size of the vertex buffer, and you can reference any vertex from multiple index buffers, or multiple times from the same index buffer. The only restriction is that you may not index outside of the vertex buffer. As a concrete use case, you could implement a level-of-detail scheme by generating multiple index buffers for your vertex buffer, with fewer vertices used for each lower detail level, and quickly select one of them each time you render based on the distance to the camera or some other metric.

14.1.4 EXAMPLE

Now we know how to build some geometry in M3G and draw it. Let us illustrate this with a more comprehensive example where we create some colored triangles and render them. We assume that you have set up your `Graphics3D` and `Camera` as described in Chapter 13; make sure your `Camera` sits at its default position and orientation at the origin. You will also see that we construct an `Appearance` object, which we have not described yet. In this example, it merely tells M3G to use the default shading parameters— we will cover `Appearance` in detail in the next section.

First, let us define our vertex and triangle data. You could put these as static members in one of your Java classes.

```
static final byte positions[] = { 0,100,0, 100,0,0, 0,-100,0, -100,0,0,
                                   0,50,0, 45,20,0, -45,20,0 };
static final byte colors[] = { 0,0,255,255, 0,255,0,255, 255,0,0,255,
                               255,255,255,255, 255,0,255,255,
                               255,255,0,255, 0,255,255,255 };

static final int indices[] = { 0,3,1, 1,3,2, 4,6,5 };
static final int strips[]  = { 3, 3, 3 };
```

Note that since M3G only supports triangle strips, individual triangles must be declared as strips of three vertices each. This is not a problem when exporting from a content creation tool that creates the strips automatically, but is a small nuisance when constructing small test applications by hand. In this case, we could also easily combine the first two triangles into a single strip like this:

```
static final int indices[] = { 0,3,1,2, 4,6,5 };
static final int strips[]  = { 4, 3 };
```

Once we have the vertex and index data in place, we can create the objects representing our polygon mesh. You would typically place this code in the initialization phase of your application.

```
// Create the vertex arrays
VertexArray myPositionArray = new VertexArray(7, 3, 1);
VertexArray myColorArray = new VertexArray(7, 4, 1);

// Set values for 7 vertices starting at vertex 0
myPositionArray.set(0, 7, positions);
myColorArray.set(0, 7, colors);

// Create the vertex buffer; for the vertex positions,
// we set the scale to 1.0 and the bias to zero
VertexBuffer myVertices = new VertexBuffer();
myVertices.setPositions(myPositionArray, 1.0f, null);
myVertices.setColors(myColorArray);

// Create the indices for five triangles as explicit triangle strips
IndexBuffer myTriangles = new TriangleStripArray(indices, strips);
```

```
// Use the default shading parameters
Appearance myAppearance = new Appearance();

// Set up a modeling transformation
Transform myModelTransform = new Transform();
myModelTransform.postTranslate(0.0f, 0.0f, -150.0f);
```

With all of that done, we can proceed to rendering the mesh. You will normally do this in the `paint` method for your MIDP `Canvas`.

```
void paint(Graphics g) {
  Graphics3D g3d = Graphics3D.getInstance();
  try {
    g3d.bindTarget(g);
    g3d.clear(null);
    g3d.render(myVertices, myTriangles, myAppearance, myModelTransform);
  }
  finally {
    g3d.releaseTarget();
  }
}
```

Assuming everything went well, you should now see your geometry in the middle of the screen. You can play around with your vertex and index setup, modeling transformation, and camera settings to see what happens.

14.2 ADDING COLOR AND LIGHT: Appearance

You can now create a plain polygon mesh and draw it. To make your meshes look more interesting, we will next take a closer look at the `Appearance` class we met in the previous section. This is one of the most powerful classes in M3G, providing a wide range of control over the rendering and compositing process of each mesh. An `Appearance` object is needed for everything you render in M3G, so let us begin with the simplest possible example—use the default rendering parameters as we already did above.

```
Appearance myAppearance = new Appearance();
```

In fact, the `Appearance` class in itself does very little. There is only one piece of data native to an `Appearance` object—the rendering layer—and we will not need that until we start using the M3G scene graph. Instead, the functionality of `Appearance` is split into five component classes. Each of the component classes wraps a logical section of the low-level rendering pipeline, so that together they cover most of the rendering state of OpenGL ES. You can then collect into an `Appearance` object only the state you want to control explicitly and leave the rest to `null`, saving you from the hassle of doing a lot of settings, and letting you share state data between different meshes. We will see how this works in practice, as we follow the rendering pipeline through the individual component classes.

14.2.1 `PolygonMode`

The `PolygonMode` class affects how your input geometry is interpreted and treated at a triangle level. It allows you to set your winding, culling, and shading modes, as well as control some lighting parameters and perspective correction.

By default, M3G assumes that your input triangles wind counterclockwise and that only the front side of each triangle should be drawn and lit. Triangles are shaded using Gouraud shading, and local camera lighting and perspective correction are not explicitly required. You can override any of these settings by creating a `PolygonMode` object, specifying the settings you want to change, and including the object into your `Appearance` object. For example, to render both sides of your mesh with full lighting and perspective correction, use `PolygonMode` as follows:

```
PolygonMode myPolygonMode = new PolygonMode();
myAppearance.setPolygonMode(myPolygonMode);

myPolygonMode.setCulling(PolygonMode.CULL_NONE);
myPolygonMode.setTwoSidedLightingEnable(true);
myPolygonMode.setPerspectiveCorrectionEnable(true);
myPolygonMode.setLocalCameraLightingEnable(true);
```

For the `setCulling` function, you can set any of `CULL_BACK`, `CULL_FRONT`, and `CULL_NONE`. The `setTwoSidedLightingEnable` function controls whether the vertex normals are flipped when computing lighting for the back side of triangles (should they not be culled), and `setWinding` controls which side of your triangles *is* the front side. For `setWinding`, you have the options `WINDING_CCW` and `WINDING_CW`. Additionally, there is `setShading`, where the default of `SHADE_SMOOTH` produces Gouraud-shaded and `SHADE_FLAT` flat-shaded triangles. You may wish to refer to Section 9.1 for the equivalent OpenGL ES functions.

Finally, it is worth pointing out that the perspective correction and local camera lighting flags are only hints to the implementation. The very low-end implementations may not support perspective correction at all, and local camera lighting is unsupported in most implementations that we know of. If supported, both come at a cost, especially on software renderers, so you should pay attention to only using them where necessary. *Do* use them where necessary, though: when rendering slanted, textured surfaces made of large triangles, the possible performance gain of disabling perspective correction is not usually worth the resulting visual artifacts.

> **Pitfall:** There is quite a lot of variety in the speed and quality of perspective correction among different M3G implementations. What works for one implementation, may not work for others. For quality metrics you can refer to benchmark applications such as JBenchmark.

14.2.2 Material

The `Material` class is where you specify the lighting parameters for a mesh in M3G. Putting a non-`null` `Material` into your `Appearance` implicitly enables lighting for all meshes rendered using that `Appearance`.

M3G uses the traditional OpenGL lighting model as explained in Section 3.2. If you are familiar with OpenGL lighting (see Section 8.3.1), you will find the same parameters in M3G.

The `setColor(int` *target*`, int` *argb*`)` function lets you set each of the material parameters with *target* set to `AMBIENT`, `DIFFUSE`, `SPECULAR`, and `EMISSIVE`, respectively. The alpha component of the color is only used for `DIFFUSE`. You can also make the ambient and diffuse components track the vertex color with `setVertexColorTrackingEnable(true)`. Additionally, you can specify the specular exponent with `setShininess`. If you want something resembling red plastic, you could set it up like this:

```
redPlastic = new Material();
redPlastic.setColor(Material.AMBIENT, 0xFF0000);   // red
redPlastic.setColor(Material.DIFFUSE, 0xFFFF0000); // opaque red
redPlastic.setColor(Material.SPECULAR, 0xFFFFFF);  // white
redPlastic.setColor(Material.EMISSIVE, 0x000000);  // black
redPlastic.setShininess(2.0f);
```

A shinier material, something like gold, could look like this:

```
golden = new Material();
golden.setColor(Material.AMBIENT, 0xFFDD44);   // yellowish orange
golden.setColor(Material.DIFFUSE, 0xFFFFDD44); // opaque yellowish orange
golden.setColor(Material.SPECULAR, 0xFFDD44);  // yellowish orange
golden.setColor(Material.EMISSIVE, 0x000000);  // black
golden.setShininess(100.0f);
```

You can also bitwise-OR the color specifiers for `setColor`, for example `setColor (Material.AMBIENT | Material.DIFFUSE, 0xFFFFFFFF)`, to set multiple components to the same value.

Materials need light to interact with. If you try to use `Material` alone, only the emissive component will produce other than black results. Light is provided through light sources, which we will discuss later in Section 14.3.2, but for a quick start, you can just create a default light source and put it into your `Graphics3D` like this:

```
Light myLight = new Light();
g3d.addLight(myLight, null);
```

Since both the light and the camera have the same transformation (now `null`), that light will be shining from the origin in the same direction as your camera is looking, and you should get some light on the materials.

14.2.3 `Texture2D`

Texturing lets you add detail beyond vertex positions, colors, and normals to your surfaces—look at the low-polygon bikers in Figure 14.1 for an example. After lighting, your triangles are rasterized and converted into *fragments* or, roughly, individual pixels. Texturing then takes an `Image2D` and combines that with the interpolated post-lighting color of each fragment using one of a few predefined functions.

To enable texturing, add a `Texture2D` object into your `Appearance`. A valid texture image must be specified at all times, so the constructor takes a reference to an `Image2D` object. You can, however, change the image later with a call to `setImage`. Texture images must have power-of-two dimensions, and neither dimension may exceed the maximum texture dimension queriable with `Graphics3D.getProperties`. Assuming that we have such an image, called `myTextureImage`, we can proceed:

```
Texture2D myTexture = new Texture2D(myTextureImage);
myAppearance.setTexture(0, myTexture);
```

Note the 0 in the `setTexture` call: that is the index of the texturing unit. At least one unit is guaranteed to exist, but multi-texturing support is optional for M3G implementations. You can query the number of texturing units available in a particular implementation, again via `Graphics3D.getProperties`. If the implementation supports two texturing units, you will also have unit 1 at your disposal, and so forth. In this case each additional texturing unit further modifies the output of the previous unit.

Wrapping and filtering modes

When sampling from the texture image, M3G takes your input texture coordinates, interpolated for each fragment, and maps them to the image. The top left-hand corner of the image is the origin, $(0, 0)$. The bottom right corner is $(1, 1)$. By default, the texture coordinates wrap around so that if your coordinates go from -1.0 to $+3.0$, for example,

Figure 14.1: Texturing can add a lot of detail to low-polygon models, allowing large numbers of them on-screen without excessive geometry loads. (Images copyright © Digital Chocolate.)

the texture image will repeat four times. You can control this behavior with setWrapping(int *wrapS*, int *wrapT*), where *wrapS* and *wrapT* can be either WRAP_REPEAT or WRAP_CLAMP. The latter will, instead of repeating, clamp that coordinate to the center of the edge pixel of the image. These are equivalent to the texture wrapping modes in OpenGL ES (Section 9.2.4). If your texture has a pattern that is only designed to tile smoothly in the horizontal direction, for example, you may want to disable wrapping in the vertical direction with

```
myTexture.setWrapping(Texture2D.WRAP_REPEAT, Texture2D.WRAP_CLAMP);
```

Once the sampling point inside the texture is determined, M3G can either pick the closest texel or perform some combination of mipmapping and bilinear filtering, similarly to OpenGL ES (Section 9.2.3). This is controlled with setFiltering(int *levelFilter*, int *imageFilter*). You can choose between FILTER_NEAREST and FILTER_LINEAR for *imageFilter*, to use either point sampling or bilinear filtering within each mipmap image. For *levelFilter*, you can choose the same for nearest or linear filtering between mipmap levels, or FILTER_BASE_LEVEL to use just the base-level image. If you enable mipmapping, the other mipmap levels will be automatically generated from the base-level image. However, all filtering beyond point-sampling the base level is optional; you will encounter a lot of devices that do not even support mipmapping.

Performance tip: Always enable mipmapping. Not only does it make your graphics look better, it also allows the underlying renderer to save valuable memory bandwidth and spend less time drawing your better-looking graphics. In rare cases, you may want to opt for the small memory saving of not using mipmapping, but depending on the M3G implementation, this saving may not even be realized in practice.

Unlike mipmapping, choosing between FILTER_NEAREST and FILTER_ LINEAR *is* a valid trade-off between quality and performance, especially when using a software renderer.

Texture application

Once the texture samples are fetched, they are combined with the input fragments according to the texture blending function you choose—blending was a somewhat unfortunate choice of name here, as it is easy to confuse with frame-buffer blending, but we shall have to live with that. The setBlending function lets you select one of FUNC_ADD, FUNC_BLEND, FUNC_DECAL, FUNC_MODULATE, and FUNC_REPLACE. These directly correspond to the texture functions described in Section 3.4.1—refer there for details on how each function works. The texture blend color used by FUNC_DECAL can be set via setBlendColor.

As an example, a common case in texturing is combining a texture with per-vertex lighting; it makes no difference whether you have M3G compute the lighting dynamically or use an off-line algorithm to bake the lighting into per-vertex colors—the texture is applied the same way. To do this, we only need to *modulate* (multiply) the interpolated fragment colors with a texture. Assuming we have, say, a repeating brick pattern in an `Image2D` called `brickImage`:

```
// Create a repeating texture image to multiply with the incoming color
Texture2D myTexture = new Texture2D(brickImage);
myTexture.setWrapping(Texture2D.WRAP_REPEAT, Texture2D.WRAP_REPEAT);
myTexture.setBlending(Texture2D.FUNC_MODULATE);
myTexture.setFiltering(Texture2D.FILTER_NEAREST,
                       Texture2D.FILTER_NEAREST);

// Set as the first texture to an Appearance object created earlier;
// the other texture slots are assumed to be null
myAppearance.setTexture(0, myTexture);
```

In fact, `WRAP_REPEAT` and `FUNC_MODULATE` are the default settings for a `Texture2D`, so the related two lines in the example above could be skipped. Depending on your target hardware, you may also want to experiment with different filtering modes to see which one is the best compromise between performance and image quality.

Multi-texturing

If you are targeting an M3G implementation capable of multi-texturing, you may want to bake your static lighting into a *light map* texture instead—this lets you get detailed lighting without excess vertices, which can be useful if the vertex transformations would otherwise become the performance bottleneck; for example, if rasterization is hardware-accelerated but transformations are done in software. If you have your light map in an `Image2D` called `lightmapImage`, you could then implement the above example using two textures only, without any per-vertex colors or lighting:

```
// Create the textures for the brick pattern and our light map.
// We omit the default wrapping settings for the brick image;
// light maps do not normally repeat, so we clamp that
Texture2D myTexture = new Texture2D(brickImage);
myTexture.setFiltering(Texture2D.FILTER_NEAREST,
                       Texture2D.FILTER_NEAREST);
Texture2D myLightmap = new Texture2D(lightmapImage);
myLightmap.setFiltering(Texture2D.FILTER_NEAREST,
                        Texture2D.FILTER_LINEAR);
myLightmap.setWrapping(Texture2D.WRAP_CLAMP, Texture2D.WRAP_CLAMP);

// Create the final fragment color by just multiplying the two textures
myAppearance.setTexture(0, myLightmap);
myLightmap.setBlending(Texture2D.FUNC_REPLACE);
myAppearance.setTexture(1, myTexture);
myTexture.setBlending(Texture2D.FUNC_MODULATE);
```

Note that you will also need to include texture coordinates in your `VertexBuffer` for each texturing unit you are using. With multi-texturing, however, you may be able to share the same coordinates among many of your textures.

> **Pitfall:** As in OpenGL, textures in M3G are applied *after* lighting. If you want your lighting to modulate the texture, which is the common case when representing surface detail with textures, this only works well with diffuse reflection. You should then render a second, specular-only pass to get any kind of specular highlights on top of your texture, or use multi-texturing and add a specular map. Either of these will give you the effect you can see in the specular highlight in Figure 3.2—compare the images with and without a separate specular pass.

Texture transformations

Now that we have covered the basics, note that the `Texture2D` class is derived from `Transformable`. This means that you can apply the full transformation functionality to your texture coordinates prior to sampling the texture. The transformation constructed via the `Transformable` functions is applied to the texture coordinates in exactly the same way as the modelview matrix is to vertex coordinates.

> **Performance tip:** The scale and bias parameters of `VertexBuffer` are all you should need for normal texturing. To avoid an unnecessary performance penalty, especially on software-only implementations, limit the use of the texture transformation to special effects that really need it.

Finally, note that you can share the `Image2D` object used as the texture image with as many `Texture2D` objects as you want. This lets you use different texture transformations, or even different wrapping and filtering modes on the same image in different use cases. If the texture image is mutable, you can also render into it for dynamic effects.

14.2.4 Fog

The next component of `Appearance` to affect your rendering results is `Fog`. It is a fairly simple simulation of atmospheric effects that gets applied to your fragments after they have been textured. Let us add some `Fog` into our `Appearance`:

```
myFog = new Fog();
myAppearance.setFog(myfog);
```

This creates a default black fog that obscures everything more than one unit away from the camera, so it may not be very useful as such. To get something more like atmospheric perspective, let us set some parameters:

```
myFog.setMode(Fog.EXPONENTIAL};
myFog.setDensity(0.01f);
myFog.setColor(0x6688FF); // pale blue tint
```

We have a choice between two flavors in the `setMode` function: EXPONENTIAL and LINEAR fog. For the former, we just set the density of the fog using `setDensity`. The latter has a linear ramp from no fog to fully fogged, specified with `setLinear(float` *near*, `float` *far*). Finally, there is the fog color, set via `setColor`. Refer to Section 3.4.4 for the details of fog arithmetic.

Pitfall: Despite the name, `setLinear` does not make the fog LINEAR—you must set the fog mode and parameters separately:

```
myFog.setMode(Fog.LINEAR);
myFog.setLinear(0.0, 10.0);
```

Note that there is no `EXP2` fog mode in M3G, although it is frequently used in OpenGL (see Section 3.4.4). This was, again, done to drop one code path from proprietary software implementations; today, it may seem like rather an arbitrary choice.

14.2.5 `CompositingMode`

After fog has been applied to your fragments, they are ready to hit the frame buffer. By default, anything you render is depth-tested and, should the depth test pass, replaces the previously existing frame buffer values. The `CompositingMode` class lets you control what is written to the frame buffer and how it blends with the existing pixels for compositing and multi-pass rendering effects.

```
myCompositingMode = new CompositingMode();
myAppearance.setCompositingMode(myCompositingMode);
```

Fragment tests

The first operation done on any fragment at the compositing stage is the alpha test. M3G simplifies this down to a single threshold alpha value that your fragment must have in order to pass. The threshold is set via `setAlphaThreshold`, and must have a value between zero and one. Any fragment with an alpha value less than the threshold gets rejected right away. The default value of 0.0 lets all pixels pass. A common use for the alpha channel is transparency, and you usually want to reject fragments with small alpha values so that the transparent regions do not mess up the depth buffer:

```
myCompositingMode.setAlphaThreshold(0.5f);
```

Note that this is equivalent to enabling the alpha test in OpenGL ES and calling `glAlphaFunc(GL_GEQUAL, 0.5f)`. See Section 9.5.2 for more details on the OpenGL ES functionality.

Performance tip: The alpha test is the fastest way to discard individual fragments, as it does not require a comparison with the depth buffer. For example, your rendering speed may improve by using alpha testing to discard transparent areas already before the blending stage. In practice, many implementations detect these discarded fragments much earlier in the rendering pipeline, providing savings from other stages as well.

If the alpha test passes, the depth test then compares the depth value of the fragment with the depth buffer at the screen location of the fragment. If the depth test passes, the fragment will be written into the color and depth buffers. Depth testing in M3G is also simplified from OpenGL ES so that the test is hard coded to "less than or equal" (GL_LEQUAL). That is, fragments farther away than the existing depth buffer value are discarded. It is, however, possible to disable the depth test entirely with setDepthTestEnable(false). Pixels in the frame buffer can then be overwritten even if they were closer to the camera than the fragments being drawn.

Prior to depth testing, you can optionally add an offset value to all fragment depth values, similarly to glPolygonOffset shown in Section 9.5.4. This helps solve *z*-fighting problems that you may encounter with multi-pass rendering algorithms. The offset can be set with setDepthOffset(float *factor*, float *units*). Here, *factor* is a multiplier for the maximum depth gradient and *units* the number of smallest resolvable depth buffer units to add. For example:

```
myCompositingMode.setDepthOffset(−1.0f, −1.0f);
```

brings your geometry closer to the camera by an amount equal to one depth buffer unit plus the largest depth difference between two adjacent pixels in a triangle. The depth offset is constant for each individual polygon. For more details, see Section 3.5.1.

All fragments that pass the depth test are written to both the color buffer and the depth buffer by default, but you can disable writing to either if you need to. Depth buffer writes are controlled with setDepthWriteEnable. Note that disabling depth writes does *not* disable the depth test, and vice versa. Controlling color buffer writes is split between setColorWriteEnable and setAlphaWriteEnable. The RGB channels are lumped together and cannot be individually disabled—the equivalent OpenGL ES call would be glColorMask(colorWrite, colorWrite, colorWrite, alphaWrite).

> **Performance tip:** Disabling color writes or alpha writes can force certain hardware implementations into hugely expensive workarounds. If your frame rate is much less than you would expect, first make sure that all objects in the scene have alpha writes enabled. Note that this does *not* concern depth writes.

Blending

Color and alpha channels can be blended with the existing color buffer pixels in a number of ways. To reduce implementation complexity, M3G simplifies the blending arithmetic somewhat from OpenGL ES, exposing a predefined set of blending modes rather than independent source and destination operands—this is another restriction that nowadays exists mostly for historical reasons. The blending mode is set with setBlending, and the available modes are summarized in Table 14.3. The default value, REPLACE, does not perform blending but overwrites the existing pixels. ALPHA is traditional alpha blending, where the fragment alpha value controls the amount of fragment color blended with the color buffer—1.0 results in pure fragment color, 0.5 in a 50:50 mix, and so on. It is most often used for per-pixel transparency and translucency. `ALPHA_ADD` adds the alpha-weighted fragment color to the color buffer instead of blending. This is good for additive light effects such as lens flares. `MODULATE` and `MODULATE_X2` multiply the fragment and color buffer colors to produce the final color, with the latter multiplying the end result by two (the result is still clamped before writing to the depth buffer, though). A common use case for these is light mapping, where the light map is rendered first and modulated with a detail texture in a second pass.

Example: separate specular pass

Let us illustrate multi-pass rendering with an example that renders a *separate specular pass* on top of textured geometry, with the level of specularity additionally controlled by the alpha channel of the texture. Figure 14.2 demonstrates this technique. Assuming that

Table 14.3: The blending modes supported in M3G. C_s is the incoming fragment color, A_s is the fragment alpha, and C_d is the color in the color buffer.

Mode	Function
ALPHA	$C_d = C_s A_s + C_d(1 - A_s)$
ALPHA_ADD	$C_d = C_d + C_s A_s$
MODULATE	$C_d = C_s C_d$
MODULATE_X2	$C_d = 2C_s C_d$
REPLACE	$C_d = C_s$

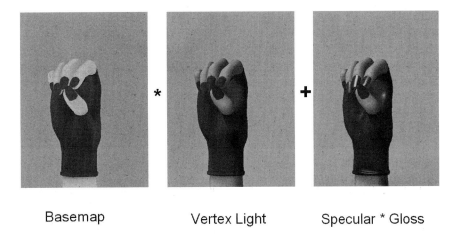

Basemap   *   Vertex Light   +   Specular * Gloss

Figure 14.2: Demonstrating a separate specular pass with controllable degree of glossiness. The per-pixel gloss factors can be stored in the alpha channel of the base texture map. (Image copyright © AMD.) (See the color plate.)

you have your texture in an RGBA `javax.microedition.lcdui.Image` object
`myTextureImage`, you need to construct two `Appearance` objects:

```
// First pass applies diffuse lighting modulated by the texture

Appearance diffusePass = new Appearance();

Image2D   myTextureColor = new Image2D(Image2D.RGB, myTextureImage);
Texture2D diffuseTexture = new Texture2D(myTextureColor);
diffuseTexture.setFiltering(Texture2D.FILTER_NEAREST,
                            Texture2D.FILTER_NEAREST);
diffusePass.setTexture(0, diffuseTexture);

Material diffuseMaterial = new Material();
diffuseMaterial.setColor(Material.AMBIENT|Material.DIFFUSE,
                         0xFFFFFFFF);
diffusePass.setMaterial(diffuseMaterial);

// Second pass adds specular lighting on top of the previous pass

Appearance specularPass = new Appearance();

Image2D   myTextureGloss  = new Image2D(Image2D.ALPHA, myTextureImage);
Texture2D specularTexture = new Texture2D(myTextureGloss);
specularTexture.setFiltering(Texture2D.FILTER_NEAREST,
                             Texture2D.FILTER_NEAREST);
specularTexture.setBlending(Texture2D.FUNC_REPLACE);
specularPass.setTexture(0, specularTexture);

Material specularMaterial = new Material();
specularMaterial.setColor(Material.AMBIENT|Material.DIFFUSE, 0);
specularMaterial.setColor(Material.SPECULAR, 0xFFFFFF);
specularMaterial.setShininess(50.f);
specularPass.setMaterial(specularMaterial);

CompositingMode additiveAlphaBlend = new CompositingMode();
additiveAlphaBlend.setBlending(CompositingMode.ALPHA_ADD);
```

Now, when you render your geometry first with `diffusePass` and then
`specularPass`, you get specular highlights over your diffuse texturing based on the
per-pixel alpha value. You may also want to disable the depth writes on the second pass,
as the same depth values are already written in the first pass.

> **Pitfall:** Blending has no effect on depth writes. If you have an alpha-blended surface
> and you want anything from behind it to show through, you must order your rendering
> carefully so that the blended geometry is rendered last. You may also be able to just use
> the alpha test if your transparency boundaries are sharp enough. Note that transparent
> parts may also overlap within the same object.

We have now reached the end of the fragment pipeline and our fragments have been
written to the frame buffer. With its combination of blending modes and write masks,

`CompositingMode` can be used to build more complex multi-pass rendering effects than shown here. With the layer mechanism in `Appearance`, all of those can also be incorporated into M3G scene graphs, as we shall discuss in Chapter 15.

Now, you can play around with the various `Appearance` settings we have constructed so far in the example. Make note of how they affect the rendering results, but also be aware of the fact that, for example, the `CompositingMode` settings are greatly dependent on what you are compositing with and in which order, and `Material` really needs some light to work properly.

14.3 LIGHTS AND CAMERA

So far, we have hinted at lighting and cameras, and the `Light` and `Camera` classes, without going into much detail. Let us now take a closer look at how to manipulate the camera from our examples, and how to use the built-in lighting functionality.

14.3.1 `Camera`

Similarly to a real-life camera, through `Camera` you can control your projection and viewpoint. `Camera` can be used in both scene graphs and immediate mode.

Using the `Camera` class is actually rather simple. First, create your camera:

```
myCamera = new Camera();
```

This gives you a camera with a default projection—an identity projection matrix, to be more precise—as we have seen in the examples so far. The default projection maps your 3D coordinates onto the screen so that X at -1 maps to the left and $+1$ to the right edge of the screen; Y at -1 to the bottom and $+1$ to the top; and only objects within Z range from -1 at the *near* and $+1$ at the *far* clipping plane are visible. There is no perspective in this projection; in other words, it is a parallel projection.

Projections

To keep the parallel projection, but change the parameters, call:

```
setParallel(float fovy, float aspectRatio, float near, float far)
```

Here, *fovy* is the height of the view volume in camera coordinates, *aspectRatio* is the ratio of width to height, and *near* and *far* give the distances to the near and far clipping planes. By using a negative distance, you can place one or both of the planes behind the camera location. Note that you can also specify the clipping planes in arbitrary order—if *far* is less than *near*, then objects farther down the Z axis will appear to be closer.

For a perspective projection, call:

```
setPerspective(float fovy, float aspectRatio, float near, float far)
```

Again, *fovy* gives the vertical size of the viewing volume, but as an angle of anything between]0, 180[degrees. *aspectRatio* is the ratio of viewport width to viewport height, and *near* and *far* give the clipping distances. With perspective projection, the distances must be positive, and *near* must be less than *far*.

Finally, if you need a more customized projection, you can call:

```
setGeneric(Transform transform)
```

This lets you handle special cases such as off-center projections and infinitely far clipping planes, should you need them.

Camera transformations

The camera, by default, looks from the origin in the direction of the negative *Z* axis. This is boring, so you can supply a camera transformation when setting the camera to your `Graphics3D` for immediate mode rendering:

```
Graphics3D g3d = Graphics3D.getInstance();
g3d.setCamera(myCamera, myCameraTransform);
```

This makes `myCamera` the camera to use for subsequent immediate mode rendering, after transforming it with the `Transform` object `myCameraTransform`. You can also keep calling this to just update the camera transformation as necessary. Your `Camera` is transformed exactly like light sources and polygon meshes. You can also use a `null Transform` to indicate identity.

Let us illustrate how you could position and aim your camera based on your own position, yaw, and pitch variables, as well as set a desired maximum field of view from another variable. We assume that `myCanvas` points to your MIDP `Canvas` object:

```
Camera myCamera = new Camera();

Transform cameraTransform = new Transform();
cameraTransform.postTranslate(cameraX, cameraY, cameraZ);
cameraTransform.postRotate(cameraYaw, 0, -1.f, 0);
cameraTransform.postRotate(cameraPitch, 1.f, 0, 0);
g3d.setCamera(myCamera, cameraTransform);

float width = myCanvas.getWidth();
float height = myCanvas.getHeight();
if (height >= width) {
  myCamera.setPerspective(cameraFOV, width/height, 1.0f, 100.0f);
}
```

```
else {
  myCamera.setPerspective(cameraFOV*height/width, width/height,
                          1.0f, 100.0f);
}
```

Note that this will not give you an exactly fixed field of view on a wide display—that would require using the `atan` function, which is not available in the Java ME math package. Barring extreme cases, though, the accuracy of the example above should suffice for normal use.

Pitfall: Make sure that your scene is in front of your camera. It is easy to get confused with the various coordinate systems and to lose track of where everything needs to be in relation to the camera. In particular, do remember that the positive Z axis points out of the screen, i.e., *behind* the camera. To make sure that your camera is working, you can always revert back to an identity camera transformation and try placing your objects at a suitable distance away on the negative Z axis. If this makes them visible, you probably have moved something or rotated the camera in the wrong direction.

Note that as the camera is conceptually the eye that everything is rendered through, the renderer actually needs to transform *everything else* relative to the camera as discussed in Section 2.4. For that purpose, the camera transformation is not applied to the camera, instead the inverse of that transformation is applied to everything else to move the world into the camera's coordinate system, the eye coordinates. If the camera transformation is not invertible, your whole world vanishes into a singularity before the camera has a chance to see it. But if you simply place your camera in the 3D world like any other object, everything works just fine.

In summary, the modelview transformation in M3G is really composed of two parts: model, which you supply with each rendered mesh, and view, which comes from the camera transformation. This is then combined with the projection matrix to give the full vertex transformation to normalized device coordinates

$$T_{NDC} = PC^{-1}M \tag{14.2}$$

where P is the projection matrix, C the camera transformation, and M the modeling transformation.

14.3.2 `Light`

Lights in M3G are represented by the `Light` class. It is also a scene graph node, but serves a second function as an immediate mode light source. We will concentrate on the general functionality here, and revisit the scene graph related aspects of lighting in the next chapter.

Similarly to `Material`, `Light` is a very straightforward wrapper for equivalent parts of the OpenGL lighting model. Some of the details are arranged differently in the interest of user-friendliness and to make it more obvious how things work, and some simplifications have been made to the capabilities of individual light sources. However, using multiple light sources, you can get the same functionality with both APIs, with one exception: M3G only lets you control the specular and diffuse lighting contributions separately at material level, not in light sources.

Let us begin by creating a light source:

```
myLight = new Light();
```

This creates a directional light that is white. Directional and spot lights in M3G always shine in the direction of the negative Z axis in their local coordinate system. The light direction is changed with transformations applied to the light. Similarly, the default position of the light source at the origin can only be modified through transformations.

Managing lights

To use the light for immediate mode rendering, we have to add it to the `Graphics3D` object:

```
Transform myLightTransform = new Transform();
myLightTransform.postRotate(90.0f, -1.0f, 0, 0);
g3d.addLight(myLight, myLightTransform);
```

The `Graphics3D.addLight` function inserts a new light source into the `Graphics3D` object. You can insert as many lights as you want, and these lights will be used for lighting in subsequent immediate mode rendering. However, only a fixed maximum number of lights will be used to light any single mesh—this value can be queried using `Graphics3D.getProperties`. If you exceed this limit, M3G will automatically select a subset of the light sources currently set to `Graphics3D`.

Pitfall: Basically, there is no guarantee that a particular M3G implementation will select a *good* subset of lights if you have set a large number of them. For best results, select the most important light sources yourself, and only add those to `Graphics3D`, or use the scoping functionality (Section 15.6.2) to control light selection.

The `Transform` object, `myLightTransform`, gives the transformation from the local coordinate system of the light source to world coordinates—in other words, lights are transformed exactly like polygon meshes. You can also specify `null` to indicate an identity transformation. In our example, the light will be shining down the negative Y axis after the transformation. The transformation is copied in, so any changes made to it after calling `Graphics3D.addLight` have no effect on the light. The transformation of the

`Light` node itself is also ignored when used for immediate mode lighting, but changes to other light source parameters do, however, affect subsequent rendering.

In addition to `addLight`, `Graphics3D` also offers `setLight`, which you can use to modify the lights added with `addLight`. `addLight` returns an integer index for each light you add, and you can pass this index to `setLight` to set a new light source or new light transformation for that slot. You can also remove a light by setting its slot to `null`. You can remove all lights by calling `Graphics3D.resetLights`.

Types of light sources

The type of light source is selected via `setMode(int mode)`. The default, as we have seen, is `DIRECTIONAL` for a directional light. `AMBIENT` makes the light shine equally from all directions, whereas `OMNI` makes the light shine from its position *toward* all directions. `SPOT` adds directionality and the spot cone parameters. These are set using `setSpotAngle(float angle)` and `setSpotExponent(float exponent)`.

> **Performance tip:** The different light types have different runtime performance costs. `AMBIENT` is virtually free, and `DIRECTIONAL` is cheap enough that it can often be used with software-only M3G implementations. `OMNI` and especially `SPOT` are considerably more expensive, so their use should be limited to where absolutely necessary.

Regardless of the light type, you can set the light color through `setColor` using the familiar hexadecimal `0xAARRGGBB` color notation. For example, `myLight.setColor(0x00FF3311)` gives `myLight` a strong red tint. The intensity of the light is set separately in floating point using the `setIntensity` function— this lets you animate either one independently of the other. Multiplying the color and intensity gives the light value used in the lighting computations. Note that "overbright" and even negative intensities are quite acceptable. As a simplification from the OpenGL model, the same color and intensity are used for both specular and diffuse lighting.

Finally, you can specify attenuation parameters for `OMNI` and `SPOT` lights through `setAttenuation(float constant, float linear, float quadratic)`. For `AMBIENT` and `DIRECTIONAL` lights, attenuation has no effect. For a detailed explanation of the attenuation parameters, as well as other lighting parameters, refer to Section 3.2.

> **Performance tip:** In general, lighting is rather complex and should only be used when you really need it. Features like spot lights and attenuation are particularly expensive performance-wise.
>
> For static scenes, you will always get better results by baking the lighting information into your vertex colors or texture maps. For dynamic scenes, you can use texture maps

and texture transformations to very cheaply simulate diffuse lighting and even add some reflections.

Be especially warned that some of the early mobile graphics hardware may have hardware-accelerated transformations, but run the lighting pipeline in software. This means that using the traditional lighting can completely kill your otherwise good rendering performance—the Sony Ericsson W900i is one example you might encounter in the real world.

Example

Let us conclude with an example on setting up lights and materials.

```java
static final int red        = 0xFFFF0000;
static final int white      = 0xFFFFFFFF;
static final int red_transp = 0x00FF0000;
static final int blueish    = 0xFF2066FF;
static final int black      = 0;

Graphics3D g3d = Graphics3D.getInstance();

// Create a scene global ambient light

Light ambient = new Light();
ambient.setMode(Light.AMBIENT);
ambient.setColor(red);
ambient.setIntensity(0.2f);
g3d.addLight(ambient, null);

// Create a directional light at the origin, shining in the direction
// of the negative Z axis

Light dirLight = new Light();
dirLight.setMode(Light.DIRECTIONAL);
dirLight.setColor(white);
dirLight.setIntensity(1.0f);
g3d.addLight(dirLight, null);

// Create a spot light close to the origin, aimed diagonally down
// and to the left -- note that in immediate mode, the transformation
// in the Light object is ignored, so we pass it as a separate object

Light spotLight = new Light();
spotLight.setTranslation(5.f, 5.f, 0.f);
spotLight.setOrientation(60.f, -1.f, 1.f, 0.f);
spotLight.setMode(Light.SPOT);
spotLight.setColor(white);
spotLight.setIntensity(5.0f);
spotLight.setSpotAngle(40.f);
spotLight.setSpotExponent(10.f);
spotLight.setAttenuation(0.f, 1.f, 0.f);

Transform t = new Transform();
spotLight.getCompositeTransform(t);
g3d.addLight(spotLight, t);
```

```
// Create a material to receive the lights

Material material = new Material();
material.setColor(Material.AMBIENT|Material.DIFFUSE, blueish);
material.setColor(Material.SPECULAR, red_transp);
material.setColor(Material.EMISSIVE, black);
material.setShininess(15.f);
```

14.4 2D PRIMITIVES

In addition to polygon meshes, M3G can also render 2D graphics to some extent. The `Background` class allows you to clear the viewport with a solid color or an image. `Sprite3D` represents a slightly more versatile object, letting you draw a 2D image that has a 3D position and interacts with the 3D graphics. Both of these can be used in both immediate and retained mode rendering.

The 2D features were some of the more controversial topics discussed by the M3G standardization group, with opinions strung between compatibility with the coming OpenGL ES standard, and enabling proprietary optimizations on software engines that would not be using hardware acceleration. In the end, the group tried to compromise between the two camps, which unfortunately meant including some nasty limitations and special cases in the 2D feature set. It soon turned out, however, that this lean toward proprietary software engines was largely in vain, as all the major implementations were moving toward full OpenGL ES compatibility more quickly than anticipated. This left the possibility for software 2D graphics optimizations mostly unused. Nevertheless, the 2D feature set exists in the API and can be used for the intended purposes, barring a few loopholes which we will highlight below.

14.4.1 Background

By default, the color buffer is cleared with transparent black and the depth buffer with the maximum depth value. The color buffer can also be cleared with a given color and alpha, or with a background image that can be independently scaled, tiled and centered in the horizontal and vertical directions. The depth buffer can only be cleared with the maximum depth value of 1.0, or not cleared at all.

Recall that in immediate mode, you need to clear the screen manually. In retained mode, we will see how the `Background` object can be associated with your `World`.

To enable and disable clearing the color and frame buffers and to set the clear color, use the following methods:

```
void setColor(int ARGB)
void setColorClearEnable(boolean enable)
void setDepthClearEnable(boolean enable)
```

If you want to use a background image, you will need the following methods in `Background`:

```
void setImage(Image2D image)
void setImageMode(int modeX, int modeY)
void setCrop(int cropX, int cropY, int width, int height)
```

Only `RGB` and `RGBA` formats are allowed for a background image, and the format must match that of the rendering target. In other words, you can use an RGBA format background image only when rendering into an M3G `Image2D` that has an alpha channel; RGB is the only allowed format for MIDP rendering targets, as `Canvas` and mutable `Image` objects never have an alpha channel. This restriction was incorporated to save software M3G implementations from having to implement dedicated blitting functions for each combination of formats. However, implementations today typically rely on OpenGL ES texturing for drawing background images, making the restriction completely unnecessary—if you wish, you can also easily implement your background as a textured quad, a skybox, or any other suitable geometry, and side-step the whole issue.

The size and position of the background image is controlled with `setCrop(int cropX, int cropY, int width, int height)`. The point (*cropX*, *cropY*) in the image is placed in the top left corner of the viewport, with the *width* by *height* pixels to the right and down from there scaled to fill the viewport.

The `setImageMode` function controls whether the background image should be tiled or not, separately in either direction. Specifying BORDER fills areas outside of the image with the specified background color, whereas REPEAT tiles the image *ad infinitum*. The tiling modes can be different for *X* and *Y* directions.

Example: scrolling background

Pulling all this together, let us clear our QVGA screen so that the background image resides at the top of the screen and is scrolled in the horizontal direction, while the area below the image is cleared with a light green color and later filled by rendering some 3D content. The code to do that is shown below, and the end result is shown in Figure 14.3.

```
// initialization

myBg = new Background();
myBg.setColor(0x00CCFFCC);
myBg.setImage(new Image2D(Image2D.RGB, 256, 128, myBgImage));
myBg.setImageMode(Background.REPEAT, Background.BORDER);

// per frame stuff: scroll the background horizontally.
// the screen is 240 pixels wide

cropX = (cropX+1) % 240;
myBg.setCrop(cropX, 18, 240, 320);
g3d.clear(myBg);
```

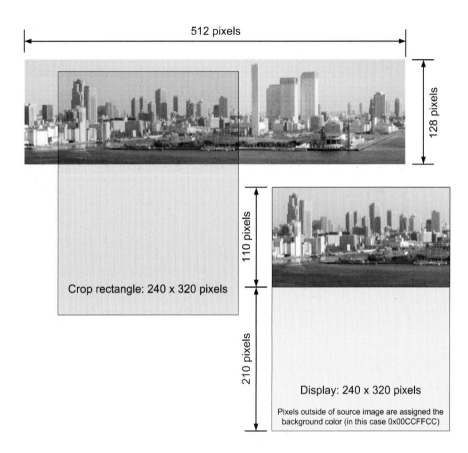

Figure 14.3: An illustration of what our example code for `Background` does.

It should be noted, however, that since the crop rectangle is specified in integers, it is not possible to achieve entirely smooth scrolling or zooming at arbitrary speeds, since there is no way to address the image at sub-pixel precision. This is another limitation you can easily overcome with textured quads.

> **Pitfall:** Background images are allowed to have any size, but in practice, M3G implementations usually render them using OpenGL ES textures. This means that internally, background images are still subject to the same limitations as images used for texturing. This may adversely affect the quality or performance of your backgrounds if you use images that map poorly to the restrictions of the underlying renderer. We strongly advise you to only use background images that could as well be used as texture images on your target implementation; in other words, use power-of-two dimensions and keep the size within the limits allowed for textures. The limit can be queried with `Graphics3D.getProperties`.

14.4.2 `Sprite3D`

The name "sprite" originates from Commodore 64-era home computers that had specialized circuitry for drawing a movable block of pixels on the screen. That is almost exactly what `Sprite3D` does, only with slightly more features and, in all cases we know of, without the specialized circuits. `Sprite3D` takes an `Image2D` and draws it on the screen at the projected position of its 3D location. The image can additionally be scaled with distance, and different regions of the image can be selected to be displayed.

The `Sprite3D` class was originally introduced into M3G in order to allow fast 2D primitives on software engines, and considerable effort was put into specifying how sprites should function. In retrospect, this was largely a wasted effort, as it soon became evident that all major implementations would have to be compatible with OpenGL ES, making proprietary optimizations impractical. `Sprite3D` also turned out to be a nuisance to implement using OpenGL ES textures, as its specification is not quite aligned with the limitations on texture size in OpenGL ES. As a result, sprites remain something of a niche feature in the API. They are little more than wrappers for textured quads, but they are still available and do make common 2D effects somewhat easier to implement.

There are two main use cases for `Sprite3D`: you can use it as an *impostor* for 3D objects, or for 2D overlays such as lighting effects or text labels on top of your 3D graphics. For impostors, you can use a static image of a complex object and draw multiple instances quickly. Alternatively, you can take advantage of the support for using a mutable `Image2D` for a sprite, and re-render your 3D object into the impostor when the projection has changed by a significant amount. A simple lighting effect could be to draw a light bloom around a light source: use a suitable bloom image, place your sprite at the location of the light source, and enable additive blending for the sprite.

Performance tip: Do not confuse `Sprite3D` with point sprites in OpenGL ES. Because each instance of `Sprite3D` incorporates its own transformation, it is too slow for most use cases of point sprites. The scaling computations are also more complex than for point sprites. Particle systems, for example, are far more efficiently created in M3G by explicitly constructing quads to represent the particles. The essential bit here is that you can then draw all the particles at once from a single `VertexBuffer`, even though you have to animate them manually.

Sprite functions

Let us create a scaled sprite for starters:

```
Sprite3D mySprite = new Sprite3D(true, mySpriteImage, myAppearance);
```

The first parameter tells whether our sprite is scaled or not—in our example, we specified `true` for a scaled sprite. A scaled sprite is drawn like a unit quad filled with the sprite image, centered about the 3D location of the sprite, and facing the camera. An unscaled sprite is otherwise similar, but drawn with a 1:1 match between the sprite image and the screen pixels, regardless of the distance between the camera and the sprite. The depth of the sprite is, however, equal to the depth of its 3D position for both scaled and unscaled sprites.

As in the `Texture2D` class, you have to specify the sprite image in the constructor but can change it with the `setImage` function later on if you need to. Unlike texture images, however, `Sprite3D` imposes no restrictions on the image dimensions—any image will do.

> **Performance tip:** Like background images, most implementations simply implement `Sprite3D` using textured quads, and in practice the limits of texture images apply. To maximize performance and quality, stick to the texture image restrictions with sprites as well.

You can specify only a subset of the image to be shown with the function `setCrop(int x, int y, int width, int height)`. The image rectangle of *width* by *height* pixels starting at (x, y), relative to the upper left corner of the image, is used to draw the sprite. Note that for scaled sprites, this only changes the contents of the projected rectangle, whereas for unscaled sprites, the on-screen size is changed to match the crop rectangle size. Additionally, you can mirror the image about either or both of the **X** and **Y** axes by specifying a negative *width* or *height*.

One thing you can do using `setCrop` is an animated sprite. For example, assume that we have a set of eight animation frames, 32 × 32 pixels each. If we put those into a 256 × 32 `Image2D`, called `myAnimationFrames` in this example, we can easily flip between the frames to animate the sprite:

```
// Create the sprite
Sprite3D mySprite = new Sprite3D(true, myAnimationFrames, myAppearance);
int frame = 0;

// Animation (per frame)
mySprite.setCrop(frame * 32, 0, 32, 32);
frame = ++frame % 8;
```

Compositing sprites

Sprite rendering is also controlled by an `Appearance` object. The only `Appearance` attributes that concern sprites are `CompositingMode`, `Fog`, and the layer index. All of them function exactly as with mesh rendering, whereas all other `Appearance` components are simply ignored. You must give the `Appearance` object to the constructor, too, but unlike the image, you can specify a `null` `Appearance` initially and set it later with the `setAppearance` function. The one thing you will often want to include into your sprite appearance is a `CompositingMode` with `setAlphaThreshold(0.5f)`. This lets you set the shape of the sprite with the alpha channel, as pixels below the alpha threshold are discarded when rendering. In our example above, we should add

```
myAppearance.setCompositingMode(new CompositingMode());
myAppearance.getCompositingMode().setAlphaThreshold(0.5f);
```

into the initialization code.

To draw your sprite, call `Graphics3D.rendermySprite, myTransform`, where `myTransform` is the world-space transformation for your sprite. The attached `Appearance` object is used for the shading.

Pitfall: Remember that sprites reside at their true depth in the 3D scene. If you want your sprite as a 2D overlay on top of the 3D graphics, make sure you draw it last with depth testing disabled.

THE M3G SCENE GRAPH

M3G has been designed from the ground up to be a retained-mode scene graph API. While low-level rendering is all fine and dandy, to really make the most of M3G you will want to take advantage of the scene graph functionality. In this chapter we will take what we learned about low-level rendering so far, and see how that fits into the concept of scene graphs.

While the scene graph is an elementary component of M3G that you really should understand, you have the freedom to use as much or as little of it as you want. Immediate and retained mode rendering in M3G are not mutually exclusive—on the contrary, M3G has been intentionally designed to let you mix the two as you like.

For background information on scene graphs, as well as some insight into the actual design process of the M3G scene graph model, please refer to Chapter 5.

15.1 SCENE GRAPH BASICS: `Node`, `Group`, AND `World`

Scene graphs are built from `Node` objects. `Node` is an abstract base class with certain common functions and properties. Each node has a transformation relative to its parent, and rendering can be enabled and disabled individually for each node. There is also an *alpha factor* that you can use to control the transparency of each node or group of nodes. The basic `Node` class is specialized into different scene graph objects, of which `Camera`,

Light, and Sprite3D are already familiar. In this chapter, we will introduce Group, Mesh, and World. With these classes you can create a simple scene graph:

```
Mesh myCarBody, myCarWheel[];
float wheelX[], wheelY[], wheelZ[];
Light mySpotLight;
Background myBackground;

// Some initialization code would go here -- omitted for brevity

World myCarScene = new World();
myCarScene.setBackground(myBackground);

Group myCar = new Group();
myCar.addChild(myCarBody);
for (int i = 0; i < 4; ++i) {
  myCar.addChild(myCarWheel[i]);
  myCarWheel[i].setTranslation(wheelX[i], wheelY[i], wheelZ[i]);
}

myCarScene.addChild(myCar);
myCar.setScale(0.1f, 0.1f, 0.1f);
myCar.setOrientation(-30.f, 0.f, 1.f, 0.f);

myCarScene.addChild(spotLight);
spotLight.setTranslation(10.f, 20.f, 30.f);
spotLight.setOrientation(40.f, -1.f, 1.f, 0.f);

Camera camera = new Camera();
myCarScene.addChild(camera);
camera.setTranslation(0.f, 3.f, 20.f);

myCarScene.setActiveCamera(camera);
```

Note how, unlike in immediate mode, the node transformations are directly used in the scene graph—there is usually no need to use separate Transform objects to move nodes around.

Groups and inherited properties

One special kind of Node is Group. This lets you group several Node objects together and treat them as one—for example, it lets you transform or animate the entire group instead of having to do that for each object separately. In other words, grouping allows partitioning the scene into logical entities. An obvious example is creating composite objects, such as a car with individual wheels; another could be putting all objects of a particular type into a group so that you can apply some operation to all of them at once.

We already mentioned that node transformations are relative to the parent node. Similarly, flags enabling rendering and alpha factor values from groups are cumulatively inherited by their children: disabling rendering of a group will also disable rendering of its children, and putting a half-opaque node inside a half-opaque group will result in a one-quarter-opaque node. Rendering is enabled or disabled via `setRenderingEnable`, and alpha factors can be set with `setAlphaFactor`. The alpha factor is effectively multiplied into the post-lighting vertex alpha value of `Mesh` objects, and the per-pixel alpha value of `Sprite3D` objects.

> **Pitfall:** Alpha factor is a poor fit with per-vertex colors, as it has to be premultiplied into them in certain cases. Especially avoid using alpha factors, at least other than 0 and 1, in combination with per-vertex alpha and texturing. Depending on the implementation, there may be other performance bottlenecks triggered by alpha factors as well.

We will show some more use cases for groups later, but for now, it suffices to say that to add a child `Node` into a `Group`, you call the function

```
void addChild(Node child).
```

The group into which you add *child* is then said to be the *parent* of the *child*. You can query the parent of any `Node` with the `getParent` function. Since M3G does not allow loops in the scene graph, each node can only have a single parent, and consequently *child* must have a `null` parent when calling `addChild`. You are still free to reassign nodes into groups as you please—just call `removeChild(Node child)` to remove a node from its current group prior to adding it into a different one.

World

There is also a special kind of `Group` called `World`. It is special in one particular way: it cannot be a child of any other `Node`. `World` serves as the root of your scene graph, a container for all other scene graph objects, and it defines `Camera` and `Background` objects used by your entire scene graph. It is possible to use scene graphs without using `World`, but `World` is what ultimately allows you to draw all of it with what is perhaps the single most powerful command in M3G: `render(myWorld)`. This call clears the screen with the selected background, sets up the currently active camera and lights, and renders the entire scene, all in a single operation.

You should now have a fairly good idea about the basics of using scene graphs in M3G. In the rest of this chapter, we will look at the new classes in detail, as well as introduce some advanced scene graph concepts.

15.2 Mesh OBJECTS

In immediate mode, we used `VertexArray`, `VertexBuffer`, `IndexBuffer`, and `Appearance` to build our polygon meshes. The scene graph equivalent is the `Mesh` class. It takes exactly the same data as one would use in immediate mode rendering:

```
myMesh = new Mesh(myVertices, myTriangles, myAppearance);
```

The parameters above are, respectively, a `VertexBuffer`, an `IndexBuffer`, and an `Appearance`. In essence, the `Mesh` object serves as a container for your immediate mode render call. You can place it in the scene graph, move, rotate, and animate it, and have it drawn with the rest of the scene.

You can also group multiple batches of triangles, or *submeshes* in M3G parlance, into a single `Mesh` object:

```
IndexBuffer[] mySubMeshes;
Appearance[] myAppearances;

// Set up the above arrays here...

myMesh2 = new Mesh(myVertices, mySubMeshes, myAppearances);
```

This lets you create composite objects with patches having different rendering properties. It also allows multi-pass rendering for simulating more complex material properties, especially when combined with the layer index mechanism of `Appearance`. We will discuss that later in Section 15.4.

> **Performance tip:** The number of submeshes is best kept to a minimum, as rendering each submesh typically has some fixed amount of overhead. When rendering lots of triangles in small batches, the individual low-level drawing calls that M3G will have to perform internally may become the main bottleneck of the whole system.

The submeshes themselves cannot be changed once the mesh is created, but you can use `setAppearance` to change the `Appearance` of each submesh. This lets you change the material properties on the fly, or to exclude the submesh from rendering altogether by setting its appearance to `null`. The submeshes can share vertices across the entire mesh, so you can also, for example, represent different levels of detail with dedicated index buffers and use `setAppearance` to control which LOD level gets rendered:

```
// Initialization -- create an LOD Mesh.

VertexBuffer vertices;
IndexBuffer highDetail, mediumDetail, lowDetail;

// (initialization of buffers omitted -- each index buffer should
// contain successively fewer polygons)

IndexBuffer triangleLODs[3] = { highDetail, mediumDetail, lowDetail };
static final float maxLODDistance[3] = { 10.f, 20.f, 40.f };

Mesh myLODMesh = new Mesh(vertices, triangleLODs, null);
Appearance myMeshAppearance = new Appearance();

// Rendering time -- select the LOD to draw based on some distance
```

```
// metric, called ``distanceToMesh'' here.  Note that the mesh will
// not be drawn at all when exceeding the threshold distance for the
// lowest level of detail.

int lod = 0;
for (int i = 0; i < 3; ++i) {
  myLODMesh.setAppearance(i, null);
  if (distanceToMesh > maxLODDistance[lod]) {
    ++lod;
  }
}
if (lod < 3) {
  myLODMesh.setAppearance(lod, myMeshAppearance);
}
```

Data instancing

All the data you put into a Mesh can be shared by several Mesh instances. While you cannot directly create several instances of the same Mesh, you can duplicate it as you please without worrying about excessive memory usage. As an example, assume that you want to create a new instance of myMesh, but with a different material color. A shallow copy is made by default, so you can change just the properties you want to:

```
Mesh copyMesh = myMesh.duplicate();
copyMesh.setAppearance(copyMesh.getAppearance().duplicate());
Material copyMaterial = copyMesh.getAppearance().getMaterial().
                        duplicate();
copyMesh.getAppearance().setMaterial(copyMaterial);
copyMaterial.setColor(Material.AMBIENT|Material.DIFFUSE,
                      0xFF88FF44);
```

In this example, the Appearance object and its Material are duplicated so that they can be changed without affecting the original, but any other Appearance components are shared between the two meshes.

There are also two subclasses of the basic Mesh: MorphingMesh and SkinnedMesh, used for animating your meshes. We will return to them in Chapter 16.

Performance tip: Make sure that you only include the data you really need in your Mesh objects. In particular, some content authoring tools may include vertex normals by default, even if you do not intend to use lighting. This can get expensive when skinning is used, as M3G may end up doing unnecessary work transforming the normal vectors that never get used. It is possible for the implementation to detect the case and skip processing the normals when lighting is not enabled, but it is equally likely that the implementation simply assumes that any data you have supplied is needed. In any case, excess data will always use up memory for no good reason. This applies to data such as texture coordinates and vertex colors as well—if you have no use for some piece of data, drop it *before* putting it into the M3G format.

Next, let us figure out how to move the objects around in the `World`.

15.3 TRANSFORMING OBJECTS

Remember how in immediate mode rendering you had to pass in a modeling transformation for each rendering call? In the scene graph, all you have to do is to move the objects themselves. Let us move the meshes we created in the previous section:

```
myMesh.setTranslation(0.0f, 0.0f, -20.0f);
myMesh2.setTranslation(10.0f, 0.0f, -20.f);
myMesh2.setOrientation(30.0f, 1.0f, 1.0f, 0.0f);
```

`Node` is derived from `Transformable`, which provides you with the functions for setting various transformation components as discussed in Section 13.3: translation T, rotation R, scale S, and an arbitrary 4 × 4 matrix M. These are combined into a single composite transformation in each node:

$$C = TRSM \qquad (15.1)$$

For scene graph `Node` objects, there is an additional restriction that the bottom row of the matrix component must be $(0\ 0\ 0\ 1)$—in other words, the W component will retain its value of 1 in all scene graph node transformations. There is normally no need for projective transformations in this context, so supporting them would unnecessarily complicate M3G implementations.

Querying transformations

In addition to the getters for each of the transformation components, you can also query the composite transformation C directly. To do this, call `Transformable.getCompositeTransform(Transform transform)`. Upon return, *transform* will contain the composite transformation matrix. This is usually faster than combining the individual components in Java code.

The node transformations are concatenated hierarchically within the scene graph. If you have a `Group` with a `Mesh` inside it, the composite world-space transformation of the `Mesh` object is

$$C_{mesh\text{-}to\text{-}world} = C_{group} C_{mesh} \qquad (15.2)$$

where C_{group} and C_{mesh} are the composite transformations of the group and mesh, respectively. Note that the transformation of `World` nodes is always ignored, as only observers outside a world would notice when the whole world moves.

Often, you will want to do some computation between two objects in the scene graph. For that, you need to know the transformation from one object to the other so that you can do your computations in a single coordinate system. To get the composite transformation from one `Node` to another, call the `Node` member function:

```
boolean getTransformTo(Node target, Transform transform)
```

where *target* is the node you want to transform *to*, and *transform* is the resulting composite transformation. M3G will automatically find the shortest path between the two nodes or return `false` if no path exists, i.e., the two nodes are not in the same scene graph. The only restriction is that all transformations along the path must be nonsingular, as inverse node transformations may be needed in order to compute the composite transformation. As an example, this will return the world space transformation of `myMesh`:

```
boolean pathFound = myMesh.getTransformTo(myWorld,
                                    myMeshToWorldTransform);
```

Reversing the nodes will give you the transformation *from* world space *to* your node:

```
boolean pathFound = myWorld.getTransformTo(myMesh,
                                    myWorldToMeshTransform);
```

Note that this is mathematically equivalent to calling `invert` on `myMeshToWorld-Transform`. Numeric precision issues may, however, cause the results to differ, and M3G may be able to compute the inverse faster if it knows to look for it in the first place.

15.3.1 `Camera`, `Light`, AND VIEWING TRANSFORMATIONS

Concatenating the node transformations up to world space gives us the modeling transformation for each object. As discussed in Section 14.3.1, the viewing part of the model-view transformation is obtained from the `Camera` class.

Moving to the scene graph world, the only difference from our treatise of the subject in Section 14.3.1 is that you no longer have to give the viewing transformation explicitly. Instead, you can place your camera—or as many cameras as you like—in the scene graph like any other nodes. They can be placed directly into the `World`, or inside `Group` objects. The inverse of the camera-to-world transformation is then automatically computed and concatenated with each modeling transformation when rendering the scene.

Let us add some light and cameras to our world:

```
Light sunLight = new Light();
sunLight.setMode(Light.DIRECTIONAL);
sunLight.setColor(0xFFEE88);
sunLight.setIntensity(1.5f);
sunLight.setOrientation(20.f, -1.f, 0.f, 1.f);
myWorld.addChild(sunLight);
```

```
// Note that these getters are only available in M3G 1.1
float aspectRatio = g3d.getViewportWidth() /
                    g3d.getViewportHeight();
float fovXToY = 1.f / aspectRatio;

Camera myWideCamera = new Camera();
myWorld.addChild(myWideCamera);
myWideCamera.setPerspective(60.f*fovXToY, aspectRatio, 1.f, 100.f);

Camera myTeleCamera = new Camera();
myWorld.addChild(myTeleCamera);
myTeleCamera.setTranslation(-50.f, 20.f, -30.f);
myTeleCamera.setOrientation(30.f, 0.f, -1.f, 0.f);
myTeleCamera.postRotate(10.f, -1.f, 0.f, 0.f);
myTeleCamera.setPerspective(20.f*fovXToY, aspectRatio, 1.f, 100.f);

myWorld.setActiveCamera(myWideCamera);
```

Now, you can use `setActiveCamera` to switch between the two cameras. This saves you the trouble of having to move a single camera around the scene graph to switch between different predefined viewpoints.

> **Pitfall:** Your camera must be a part of your `World`! Otherwise, M3G will be unable to compute the camera-to-world transformation, and will raise an exception.

> **Pitfall:** If you want an entire `World` garbage-collected, it will not happen as long as its camera and lights are referenced from `Graphics3D` (see Section 13.1.3). It is therefore not enough to do `myWorld = null` in your cleanup code; you also need to do `g3d.setCamera(null, null)` and `g3d.resetLights()`.

15.3.2 NODE ALIGNMENT

In addition to setting the transformations explicitly, there is a semi-automatic mechanism for orienting nodes of which you can take advantage in some cases. *Node alignment* lets you, for example, force an object to always face some other object or maintain an upright position in the world. Alignment can be forced for any `Node` and the entire subtree of its descendants with a single function call. Typically, you would place alignment after all animations, just before rendering:

```
myWorld.align(myWorld.getActiveCamera());  // apply node alignments
g3d.render(myWorld);                        // draw the world
```

Let us leave the details of that `align` call for later, though. First, we will discuss how alignment works and what you can do with it.

The specification for node alignment is rather involved because it attempts to ensure that all implementations work in the same way. The actual operation is much simpler. For both the *Z* and the *Y* axis of a node, you can specify that the axis should always point toward a specific point or direction in the scene. If you specify alignment for both of the axes, it is the Z axis that rules: it will always be exactly aligned, while the Y axis will only make its best effort thereafter. We will clarify this with a couple of examples in a moment.

> **Pitfall:** Some early M3G implementations lack sufficient numeric range and precision to compute alignments accurately. You may not be able to rely on alignment working reliably across the entire range of M3G-enabled devices.

Setting up node alignment

To set up alignment for a `Node`, call:

```
void setAlignment(Node zRef, int zTarget, Node yRef, int yTarget)
```

This looks complicated, but note that there are two identical sets of parameters comprising a reference node and an alignment target for each axis. Looking at the Z parameters, the reference node *zRef* is what you want your node to use as a guide when aligning itself; *zTarget* is what *in zRef* you want your node to align to. The same goes for the equivalent Y parameters.

Valid values for *zTarget* and *yTarget* are `NONE`, `ORIGIN`, `X_AXIS`, `Y_AXIS`, and `Z_AXIS`. `NONE`, fairly obviously, disables alignment for that axis. `ORIGIN` makes the axis point toward the origin of the reference node. The three axis targets make the aligned axis point in the same direction as the specified axis of the reference node. Here are two examples:

```
myMesh.setAlignment(null, Node.NONE, myWorld, Node.Y_AXIS);
myMesh2.setAlignment(myWorld, Node.ORIGIN, null, Node.NONE);
```

Now, the Y axis of `myMesh` will always point *in the same direction as* the Y axis of `myWorld`; and the Z axis of `myMesh2` will always point *toward* the origin of `myWorld`.

Note that we are specifying no alignment for the Y axis of `myMesh2`—this means that the Y axis will point in whatever direction it happens to point after `myMesh2` is rotated to align its Z axis. The M3G specification states that the alignment rotation will always start from a fixed reference orientation, without any rotation applied. Therefore, even though you may not know the exact orientation of your object after the alignment, you can still rely on the Y axis behaving nicely: given a target Z axis direction, you will always get a deterministic Y axis direction, and it will change smoothly rather than jump around randomly each frame.

> **Pitfall:** Make sure that your alignment reference nodes are in the same scene graph as the nodes being aligned! Otherwise, M3G will be unable to compute the alignment and will throw an exception that may be hard to track down.

In addition to fixed nodes, you can also easily align objects based on the current camera, without giving an explicit node reference to it. To make a *billboard* that always faces the camera, you could apply this setting on a piece of flat geometry:

```
myNode.setAlignment(null, Node.ORIGIN, null, Node.NONE);
```

Note that we left *zRef* and *yRef* `null` in this example. Then, return to our first code example on alignment and notice how we passed in the active camera of the world. The only argument to `align` is a `Node` to be used as the alignment reference in all cases where you have specified a `null` *zRef* or *yRef*. The most common use for this is passing in the currently active camera as in our example. You could of course specify any `Camera` node as a reference to `setAlignment`—however, if you have multiple cameras in your scene graph, using `null` instead lets you switch between them, or even create new cameras, without having to reset the alignment for any camera-aligned nodes. It is therefore good practice to use `null` to mean "align to my current camera."

Alignment examples

Now, let us try a couple of more examples to illustrate what you can do with alignment. These examples, again, assume that you are passing the active camera of your world to each `align` call.

As an alternative to our billboard example above, you may want to align the billboard with the *Z* axis of the camera rather than aiming it at the camera origin:

```
myNode.setAlignment(null, Node.Z_AXIS, null, Node.NONE);
```

This may be faster on some M3G implementations, but the result will also look slightly different—especially with a wide field of view—because the billboard will align to the *orientation* of the camera rather than its position. You can see this difference in Figure 15.1. Which alternative looks better depends on the desired effect of the billboard.

Of course, we can also make a billboard and align its *Y* axis. If you want to emulate `Sprite3D`, you can align the billboard with both the *Z* and *Y* axes of the camera:

```
myNode.setAlignment(null, Node.Z_AXIS, null, Node.Y_AXIS);
```

Note that unlike `Sprite3D`, this still lets you use any geometry you want, as well as apply multi-texturing and multi-pass rendering. Of course, if you just want to draw a sprite, the dedicated sprite class is optimized for that and may give you better performance, but on many practical implementations you are unlikely to notice a difference.

To simulate complex objects such as trees, as in Figure 15.1, you may want to have the impostor geometry and textures oriented vertically with respect to the world, while turning about the vertical axis to face the camera—in other words, have the orientation of your billboard *constrained* by a fixed axis. Since *Y*-axis alignment is subordinate to *Z*-axis alignment in M3G, we must use the *Z* axis as the constraint. Assuming that the *Y* axis represents the vertical direction, or height, in your world, you would align your impostor trees like this:

```
myNode.setAlignment(myWorld, Node.Y_AXIS, null, Node.ORIGIN);
```

Of course, you must also model your geometry so that the *Z* axis is the vertical axis of your impostor geometry.

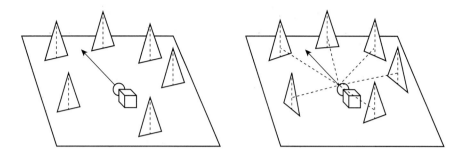

Figure 15.1: Two variants of billboard trees. On the left, the trees are aligned with the Z axis of the camera; on the right, they are aligned to face the camera origin. In both cases, the vertical axis of each tree is constrained to be perpendicular to the ground plane.

> **Performance tip:** Alignment comes at a price, as it involves quite a bit of computation. It may therefore not be the best idea to use our example above to make *lots* of trees using aligning billboards—note that you cannot just group them and align the group as one object, because you want each tree to stay at a fixed location, so you would have to align them individually. You will likely get better performance if you limit that technique to a few close-by or medium distance trees, and implement the faraway ones using static impostor objects representing larger portions of the forest.

Targeting the camera and lights

Our final example is also a common one: a target camera. Often, you will want your camera or lights to track an object. To do this, let us aim the Z axis at the object `myTarget`, and align the Y axis with the world Y axis so that the camera stays upright while tracking:

```
myCamera.setAlignment(myTarget, Node.ORIGIN, myWorld, Node.Y_AXIS);
myCamera.setScale(-1, 1, -1);
```

What is it with that `setScale` line? Remember that the camera in M3G looks in the direction of the *negative* Z axis. Alignment aims the *positive* Z axis at `myTarget`, so the camera will by default look *away* from the target. We need to rotate the camera by 180° after the alignment to aim it in the right direction. We could wrap the camera in an extra `Group` node and align that instead, but reversing the X and Z axes of the camera itself achieves the same result for free. The scale component of the node transformation does not affect alignment computations; if you refer to Equation 15.1, you will see that the rotation component, which is replaced by the alignment rotation, resides on the left side of the scale and matrix components. In practice, this means that the scale and matrix components of the node itself are ignored when computing the alignment rotation.

What we said about cameras above applies equally to lights, except that the *Y* axis does not matter for them: all M3G lights are symmetric about the *Z* axis, so you only need to align that. You can therefore save some processing time by specifying `null` and `Node.NONE` for *yRef* and *yTarget*, respectively.

15.4 LAYERING AND MULTI-PASS EFFECTS

There is a default sorting rule in the M3G scene graph that all blended primitives, i.e., primitives using a blending mode of anything other than `REPLACE` in `CompositingMode`, are drawn after all nonblended primitives. This is sufficient to cover many cases where semitransparent geometry and opaque geometry are used—such as our example on rendering a separate specular lighting pass in Section 14.2.5, which is easily enough wrapped into a `Mesh` object:

```
IndexBuffer primitives[2] = { myTriangles, myTriangles };
Appearance passes[2] = { diffusePass, specularPass };
Mesh mesh = new Mesh(myVertexBuffer, primitives, passes);
```

This works, regardless of the order in which you specify your rendering passes, because `diffusePass` used the default `REPLACE` blending mode, whereas `specularPass` used `ALPHA_ADD` (refer back to page 336 for the details). However, sometimes you will want to override this default sorting, or force sorting based on some other criteria. This is where rendering layers come into the picture.

Pitfall: Other than the default sorting rule, the M3G specification does not require implementations to sort semitransparent primitives in any particular way—such as back-to-front. This was intentionally left out, as sorting can be an expensive operation and it still does not quite solve all of the problems associated with rendering semitransparent geometry. In the end, it is *your* responsibility to make sure that your blended triangles get drawn in the correct order. However, if transparency is rare enough that you do not routinely expect to view transparent objects through other transparent objects, the default rule will be quite sufficient.

Rendering layers

When discussing `Appearance` in Section 14.2, we already mentioned the subject of rendering layers, but dismissed it as something that is only useful in scene graphs. Each `Appearance` object has a rendering layer index that you can set with `setLayer(int layer)`. Valid values for *layer* range from −63 to 63, with the default being 0.

The layer index overrides the default sorting rule when determining the rendering order for submeshes and sprites. The default rule is still obeyed within each layer, but the layers are sorted in ascending order. The layer with the smallest index gets drawn first. For example, we could use a sprite as a waypoint or some other marker overlaid on top of the 3D scene:

```
Image2D markerImage = ...

CompositingMode alphaOverlay = new CompositingMode();
alphaOverlay.setBlending(CompositingMode.ALPHA);
alphaOverlay.setDepthTestEnable(false);
alphaOverlay.setDepthWriteEnable(false);

Appearance overlay = new Appearance();
overlay.setCompositingMode(alphaOverlay);
overlay.setLayer(63);

Sprite3D myMarker = new Sprite3D(false, markerImage, overlay);
```

Setting the rendering layer to 63, the maximum value, ensures that our marker is drawn last, and not overwritten by anything in the scene.

You can use the layer index to separate things into discrete passes or to do a coarse sorting. For example, if you know that some semitransparent geometry will always be close to the viewer, put it in one of the higher layers (that is, larger-numbered) to have it drawn on top of anything behind it. If you have two-sided transparent geometry, use an `Appearance` with a lower index on the "inside" polygons to make them correctly visible through the "outside" polygons drawn in front. Any lens flares and other light blooming effects should be in the highest layers so that they are drawn on top of the entire scene.

> **Performance tip:** If you have a sky cube, draw it last to save fill rate. If you have geometry that you know will always be close to the viewer, draw that first to occlude larger parts of the scene early on. This way, depth buffering can drop the hidden pixels before they are drawn at all, saving the work of shading and texturing them. Translucent objects will naturally need different sorting for blending to work.

Multi-pass `Meshes`

In multi-pass rendering, you can just put the same `IndexBuffer` into your `Mesh` multiple times, with a different `Appearance` object for each rendering pass, and use the layer index to indicate the order in which to render the passes. This way, you can easily do shading beyond simple light mapping without having to explicitly draw your objects multiple times.

> **Performance tip:** When rendering multiple passes of the same geometry, make the first pass opaque and disable depth writes for all subsequent passes. Depth testing is still needed, but you save the cost of rewriting the existing values into the depth buffer. Also note that the layer sorting works across all objects in the scene, so the first opaque pass will save on fill rate for all subsequent passes of any occluded geometry.

Once the layer indices are set, M3G handles the sorting of multiple rendering passes automatically. The specified depth test function also guarantees that multiple passes of the same geometry get drawn at the same depth, allowing you to blend arbitrarily many layers on top of a single opaque layer.

15.5 PICKING

Picking is one more thing you can only do with the scene graph. Put briefly, picking lets you fire a ray into a `Group` in the scene graph and see what you hit.

> **Pitfall:** The performance of picking varies widely from one implementation to another. As a rule of thumb, consider picking a once-in-a-while utility function rather than a tool that your physics engine can make extensive use of.

Picking through the camera

You can use picking in either of two ways: picking through a camera plane, or picking from a 3D point. To use the first alternative, call the `Group` member function:

```
boolean pick(int scope, float x, float y, Camera camera,
             RayIntersection ri).
```

The first parameter, *scope*, is tested for a match with the scope mask of each node (Section 15.6.2) prior to performing the actual picking test. The *x* and *y* parameters specify a point on the image plane of *camera* that the ray is fired from. The origin is in the upper left corner of the viewport, with (1, 1) being in the lower right corner, so you can fire a ray through the center of the camera image by specifying (0.5, 0.5). The direction of the ray is always away from the eye, i.e., the origin of the `Camera` node. Note that you can pick from any camera in the scene, not just the current active camera. By using the active camera, though, it is easy to pick the object in the center of your current view:

```
    RayIntersection hitInfo;
    if (myWorld.pick(-1, 0.5f, 0.5f, myWorld.getActiveCamera(),
        hitInfo)) {
      Node objectHit = hitInfo.getIntersected();
      float distance = hitInfo.getDistance();
      ...
    }
```

Note that the ray is fired *from the near clipping plane*—you cannot hit objects closer to the camera than that. The unit of distance is equal to the distance between the near and far clipping planes, as measured along the picking ray, so that distance 0 is at the near clipping plane and 1 at the far clipping plane. This lets you easily determine whether the hit object is actually visible when rendered. The actual origin and direction of the ray, in the coordinates of the world or group node being picked, can also be queried from the `RayIntersection` object.

> **Performance tip:** If you really want to fire the ray from the origin of your camera, you can use `getTransformTo` to get the transformation from your camera to world space: `myCamera.getTransformTo(myWorld, myMatrix)`. Now, the last column of `myMatrix` gives you the origin of the ray, and the third one is the (positive) Z axis of the camera, which you can use as the ray direction. You can then pass these to the other picking variant which we introduce below.

Picking with an explicit ray

The other `pick` variant lets you specify the picking ray explicitly:

```
boolean pick(int scope, float ox, float oy, float oz, float dx, float dy,
             float dz, RayIntersection ri).
```

The point (*ox*, *oy*, *oz*) is the origin of the picking ray and (*dx*, *dy*, *dz*) is its direction. Both are expressed in the local coordinate system of the node that `pick` is invoked from. Obviously, you do not need a camera to use this variant:

```
RayIntersection hitInfo;
if (myWorld.pick(-1, 0.f, 0.f, 0.f, 0.f, 0.f, 1000.f, hitInfo)) {
  Node objectHit = hitInfo.getIntersected();
  ...
}
```

The example fires a picking ray from the origin of `myWorld` along the positive Z axis. Here, the unit of distance is the length of the given direction vector. In this case, we gave a non-unit direction vector, so our distance would be scaled accordingly; if the world coordinates are in meters, for example, the picking distance returned would be in kilometers.

Picking traversal

In either case, the picking ray will only be tested against objects inside the scene subtree spanned by the group you invoked `pick` for. The return value tells you if anything was hit in the first place. If it is `true`, details about the closest object intersected are returned in the `RayIntersection` object. Table 15.1 lists the functions you can use for retrieving data about the intersection.

Like rendering, picking is controlled hierarchically via the `setPickingEnable` function. If you disable picking on a group node, picking from higher up in the scene graph, such as from your root `World` object, will ignore everything inside that group. However, if you fire your picking ray from a child of a disabled group, picking traversal will proceed normally to all enabled nodes inside that child group.

> **Performance tip:** Always choose the smallest possible group of objects for picking. For example, if you only want to test against the terrain, create a separate group to hold just your terrain, and fire your picking ray into that. This saves the picking traversal from visiting all the non-terrain objects in your scene.

Table 15.1: `RayIntersection` member functions for querying data about the closest intersection when picking. The surface normal at the intersection point is interpolated if vertex normals are present, otherwise its value is undefined.

Function	Data returned
`float getDistance()`	The distance from the origin of the ray to the intersection point. The unit corresponds to the length of the direction vector of the ray—see `getRay` below.
`Node getIntersected()`	The `Mesh` or `Sprite3D` object intersected.

`float getNormalX()`
`float getNormalY()`
`float getNormalZ()`
	The *X*, *Y*, or *Z* component of the surface normal at the intersection point.

`void getRay(float[]` *ray*`)`	The origin, in elements 0 to 2, and direction, in elements 3 to 5 of *ray*, of the pick ray.
`int getSubmeshIndex()`	The index of the submesh intersected. Always zero for sprites.
`float getTextureT(int` index`)` `float getTextureS(int` index`)`	The *S* or *T* texture coordinate, for texture unit *index*, at the intersection point. For sprites, this is the point within the sprite crop rectangle, with (0, 0) being at the top left corner of the displayed area and (1, 1) at the bottom right.

> **Performance tip:** Picking complex models can be very slow. To speed it up, use separate picking geometry. Make two `Mesh` objects for your model: one for rendering, and another, simplified one, for picking. Disable picking on the rendering model, and disable rendering on the picking model. Group them together and use the transformation of the `Group` node to transform them.

15.6 OPTIMIZING PERFORMANCE

It is easy to fill your scene graph with more objects than M3G can handle with reasonable performance. When building real-life applications, you will almost certainly run into problems where M3G is not drawing your world quite as quickly as you would like. While M3G seems to offer very few tools explicitly geared for helping you with performance problems, there are a few relatively easy things you can do with the scene graph that may help you along the way.

15.6.1 VISIBILITY OPTIMIZATION

M3G as a specification takes no position on visibility optimization; it neither mandates nor recommends any specific method. However, most if not all commercially deployed implementations are doing view frustum culling, either on a per-mesh basis, or also hierarchically at the group node level.

> **Pitfall:** Early M3G-enabled devices from many vendors were plagued with bugs related to view frustum culling, causing meshes and/or sprites to disappear when they were definitely not supposed to. Some devices are known to exhibit problems when a `VertexBuffer` is shared by multiple `Mesh` objects, others fail to update the bounding box for animated meshes, and so forth. If you are developing for older devices and are experiencing weird visibility problems, we suggest that you pay a visit to the handset vendor's developer forums.

As a rule, any visibility optimization that a generic scene graph API does, a carefully crafted game specific engine can do better, and do it without burning cycles on optimizations that are not helpful with the particular game genre that the engine is designed for. This is one of the reasons that generic scene graphs have not met with great success on PCs, game consoles, and other native platforms. But again, the mobile Java platform is different. A complex culling scheme written in Java is not likely to compare well with a scheme that is running in native code, even if the complex system would be able to cull a larger percentage of objects.

Fortunately, the developer has the option to combine the best of both worlds: to employ a spatial data structure that is optimized for the specific application, but also leverage retained-mode rendering. The scene can be organized into an appropriate spatial hierarchy, for example an octree, by using `Group` nodes. The application must do a pre-render traversal of the scene graph, marking the *potentially visible* and *definitely hidden* groups of objects by setting or clearing the rendering enable flags of the corresponding `Group` nodes with `Node.setRenderingEnable`. M3G can then render the potentially visible set efficiently in one `render(World)` call. This approach is likely to perform much better than rendering the leaf nodes one by one in immediate mode.

15.6.2 SCOPE MASKS

Every `Node` object in M3G has a 32-bit integer scope mask that you can freely set with `setScope`. Scope masks are another way to reduce the workload of M3G in complex scenes. You can use scope masks to exclude objects from rendering or picking, as well as reduce the number of lights affecting an object.

When rendering via any of the `render` variants, the scope mask of each rendered mesh or sprite is compared with the scope mask of the current camera, and the object is rendered only if the masks share at least one bit that is set to 1. The same is done for each light source prior to computing lighting, in immediate as well as retained mode. Also, the *scope* parameter of `pick` is similarly compared with the scope mask of each object, and the object is only tested if the masks share at least one bit. Note, however, that scope masks are *not* inherited—the scope masks for `Group` nodes are therefore effectively ignored.

To give a concrete example, imagine a scene with lots of objects and light sources scattered among multiple rooms. Each light can only interact with a small subset of the objects, so it is advantageous for you to inform M3G about that in advance. If you can determine which rooms each light can illuminate, you can encode that information into the scope masks:

```
static final int LIVING_ROOM = 1<<0;
static final int KITCHEN = 1<<1;
static final int BEDROOM = 1<<2;
static final int STAIRCASE = 1<<3;
static final int HALL = 1<<4;
...
Light kitchenLight, bedroomLight, livingRoomLight, hallLight;
...
kitchenLight.setScope(KITCHEN|LIVING_ROOM|HALL);
bedroomLight.setScope(BEDROOM|STAIRCASE);
livingRoomLight.setScope(LIVING_ROOM|KITCHEN);
hallLight.setScope(HALL|STAIRCASE|KITCHEN);
```

Then, for each object you can just mark the room it is in:

```
sofa.setScope(LIVING_ROOM);
armchair.setScope(LIVING_ROOM);
kitchenSink.setScope(KITCHEN);
bed.setScope(BEDROOM);
```

Finally, you can dynamically set the scope of the camera based on which rooms it can see from its current position:

```
camera.setScope(LIVING_ROOM|HALL);
```

Now, when you render, you will already have significantly reduced your set of visible objects and light interactions, saving a lot of work for the M3G implementation. You will still have to determine the potentially visible rooms each time the camera moves, though.

Essentially, scope masks let you segment your scene into 32 groups or regions that are independent of the scene graph topology. For each camera and light, you can then decide which of those 32 groups it can see or affect. Similarly, for picking you can choose to detect different kinds of objects at different times. 32 groups may not sound like much, but since the scoping mechanism is completely orthogonal to the scene topology, you can use both scoping and `Group` nodes together when segmenting the scene.

CHAPTER

ANIMATION IN M3G

The final part of our tour of the M3G API is animation. M3G boasts a simple, yet flexible, animation engine with advanced features geared for the needs of modern games. The thinking behind the engine is to provide you with the basic building blocks you need, while leaving you in charge of using them in the way that best suits your application. You can use the animation engine as such or build a more comprehensive animation system on top of it, whichever best suits your particular needs.

Fundamentally, animation in M3G is nothing more than a way to quickly set a number of object properties to pre-programmed, time-dependent values upon command. All of the properties modified by animation can be equally modified by calling setters and getters. The animation engine merely adds a conceptual model on top, enables pre-authoring of complex animations through the binary file format, and provides better performance via its native math engine.

For background information on the animation concepts we will be dealing with in this chapter, please refer to Chapter 4.

16.1 KEYFRAME ANIMATION: `KeyframeSequence`

The principal component of the M3G animation engine is keyframe animation (see Section 4.1). You can create keyframe sequences for most settable properties and

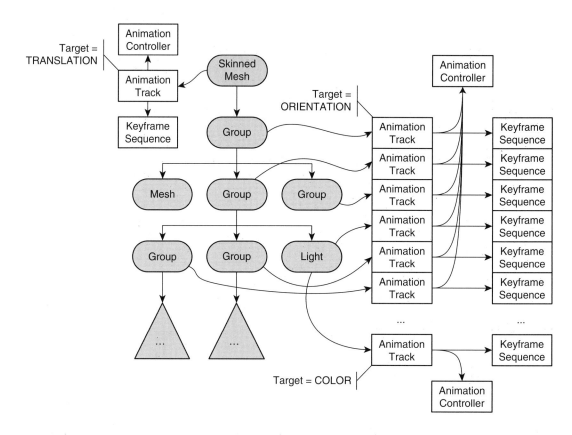

Figure 16.1: A `SkinnedMesh` object with animations applied to the translation of the root node and the orientations of the bone nodes. The `AnimationTrack` class links a keyframe sequence into its target property, while `AnimationController` supplies timing and control data.

attach them to different objects for animation. Figure 16.1 shows an example of how the different animation classes link together; we will describe the classes in detail in the rest of this chapter.

The `KeyframeSequence` class lets you create sequences of parameter values placed on a timeline and choose how to interpolate between them. For example, `KeyframeSequence(10, 3, KeyframeSequence.LINEAR)` creates a sequence of ten 3-vector keyframes for linear interpolation. Table 16.1 lists the available interpolation types, which are explained in more detail in Sections 4.1.1 and 4.1.2. The keyframe values for `STEP`, `LINEAR`, and `SPLINE` can be vectors with arbitrarily many components—including scalars as 1-vectors—whereas `SLERP` and `SQUAD` require quaternion keyframes represented as 4-vectors. In all cases, all keyframes must have the same dimensionality within any single sequence.

Table 16.1: Types of keyframe interpolation available in M3G.

Name	Description
STEP	Step function, no interpolation.
LINEAR	Linear interpolation.
SPLINE	Spline interpolation.
SLERP	Linear interpolation of quaternions.
SQUAD	Spline interpolation of quaternions.

Note that when creating a keyframe sequence, you must decide both the number of keyframes and the interpolation type beforehand. This allows M3G to select all the required resources at construction time, avoiding potentially costly data reorganization later on. While fixing the number of keyframes may seem restrictive, you can still modify them dynamically and use only a subset of the sequence at any given time. More on that later.

Setting up the keyframes

After creating your new `KeyframeSequence`, you will want to put some data into it. Often, you will be loading pre-authored animations from resource files using the `Loader` class, but you could as well want to create your sequences at runtime for a number of reasons—for example, if you are streaming the animation data over a network connection or generating it procedurally at runtime. You can set your desired values to the keyframes by calling `int` *time*, *float[]*value, where *index* is the index of the keyframe in the sequence, *time* is the time position of the keyframe, and *value* is a floating-point vector that gives the actual data value to be assigned to the keyframe. The keyframe times are given relative to the beginning of the sequence, and must be monotonically increasing so that no keyframe has a time preceding any of the previous keyframes. In other words, the keyframes must be on the timeline in the same order as their indices. It is acceptable to have multiple keyframes at the *same* point in time, though.

pitfall: The M3G file format offers a choice between 16-bit integer and 32-bit floating-point keyframes to enable potential space savings in the JAR file. However, some early M3G implementations (including the Sun Wireless Toolkit) exhibit problems when loading 16-bit keyframes, so you may find that your target platform can only use the floating-point variant.

pitfall: There are no getters for keyframe times or values in M3G 1.0; they were only added in 1.1. The same goes for the number of keyframes and components, the interpolation mode, and the valid range. However, you can extract that data by abusing the exceptions defined in `setValidRange`, `setKeyframe` and `Object3D.animate`.

The interpolation mode can be inferred by interpolating between known keyframes. Extracting all the hidden data takes some 200 lines of code and is dog-slow, but you can do it if you must for some pressing reason, such as for debugging purposes. Our companion web site includes example code implementing a class that you can readily use for this purpose.

Note that we are talking about time without specifying any time unit. This is intentional, since M3G leaves the choice of time units to you. Feel free to use milliseconds, seconds, or microseconds for your keyframes, and M3G will happily produce the results you want as long as you are consistent. In fact, you can even use different time units for different sequences if you happen to need that sort of thing. Refer to Section 16.3 for information on doing that.

Duration and looping

After setting all your keyframes, you must also set the duration of your keyframe sequence by calling setDuration. This information is used by M3G when you want your keyframe sequences to loop, but it also serves as a sanity check for your keyframe times.

pitfall: Your keyframe sequences are not valid until a valid duration is set. This concerns all sequences, regardless of whether they loop or not.

We mentioned looping sequences, and often you will use exactly those. For example, the motion of a helicopter rotor is easily defined using just two quaternion keyframes that repeat over and over. To enable looping, call setRepeatMode(Keyframe-Sequence.LOOP)—the default value of KeyframeSequence.CONSTANT means that the sequence maintains the value of the first or last keyframe when sampled outside of the beginning or end of the sequence, respectively. With looping enabled, the keyframes are conceptually repeated in time at intervals of the sequence duration d, to infinity and beyond in both directions. An example is shown in Figure 16.2. The effect is exactly the same as replicating each keyframe at every time instant $(\ldots, t-2d, t-d, t, t+d, t+2d, \ldots)$, where t is the original time of the keyframe, but without any additional memory use.

To wrap up the basic steps of keyframe sequence creation, let us create a looping sequence that you can use to perpetually rotate an object about the Z axis at a steady pace. This sequence will interpolate quaternion keyframes, using spherical linear interpolation, so that the target object completes one revolution every one thousand time units:

```
static float kf0[4] = { 0.f, 0.f,  0.000f,  1.0f };
static float kf1[4] = { 0.f, 0.f,  0.866f, −0.5f };
static float kf2[4] = { 0.f, 0.f, −0.866f, −0.5f };

KeyframeSequence rotationSeq = new KeyframeSequence(3, 4,
                                  KeyframeSequence.SLERP);
```

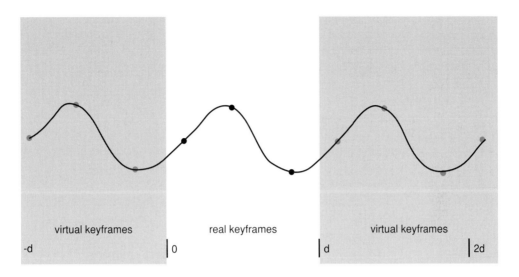

Figure 16.2: A looping KeyframeSequence: virtual keyframes are created around the original sequence at intervals of duration d.

```
rotationSeq.setDuration(2000);
rotationSeq.setRepeatMode(KeyframeSequence.LOOP);
rotationSeq.setKeyframe(0, 0, kf0);
rotationSeq.setKeyframe(1, 667, kf1);
rotationSeq.setKeyframe(2, 1333, kf2);
```

The keyframe values are unit quaternions corresponding to rotations of 0, 240, and 480 degrees, respectively—since we are using quaternions, we will complete *two* revolutions in 3D when rotating one full circle in the quaternion space (refer to Sections 2.3.1 and 4.1.2). Hence, we set the duration to 2000 time units to match our desired time for one revolution. Alternatively, we could set keyframes at 0, 180, and 360 degrees at 0, 500, and 1000 milliseconds, respectively, and set the sequence duration at 1000 milliseconds. However, that would introduce a discontinuity into our interpolated quaternion data, which would cause awkward jumps in the animation if we later tried to blend (Section 16.5.2) our rotation with another orientation sequence.

Valid keyframe range

One more feature of KeyframeSequence is the *valid range*. As we already hinted, this lets you choose a subset of the entire sequence. That subset is then used exactly like a sequence comprising just those keyframes. For example, calling setValidRange (3, 7) would only take the keyframes with indices 3 to 7 into account when you use the sequence. You can also specify a valid range that wraps around: setValidRange (8, 2) would treat your 10-keyframe sequence as if it comprised keyframes 8, 9, 0, 1, and 2, in that order—keyframe 8 would then have to have the lowest time value for the sequence to be valid. The valid range is useful if, for any reason, you want to dynamically modify the contents or length of your animation sequence, as it saves you from creating new sequences and inducing garbage collection. We will show some example use cases later on.

16.2 ANIMATION TARGETS: `AnimationTrack`

A `KeyframeSequence` on its own does very little—you need something to connect the animation to. In M3G parlance, each animatable property on each object is called an *animation target*. To connect a keyframe sequence with an animation target, you create an `AnimationTrack` object and add it to your target object via `Object3D.addAnimationTrack`.

Animatable properties are enumerated in the `AnimationTrack` class as listed in Table 16.2. `AnimationTrack` associates a keyframe sequence with one of these properties. To create a track for animating the position of the scene graph node `myNode` using the `KeyframeSequence` object `mySequence`, for example, you could use this piece of code:

```
AnimationTrack myPositionTrack;
myPositionTrack = AnimationTrack(mySequence,
                                 AnimationTrack.POSITION);
myNode.addAnimationTrack(myPositionTrack);
```

We can also animate `myNode` with the rotation sequence we created in the earlier example:

```
AnimationTrack rotationTrack;
rotationTrack = new AnimationTrack(rotationSeq,
                                   AnimationTrack.ORIENTATION);
myNode.addAnimationTrack(rotationTrack);
```

Every object can be animated with multiple tracks at the same time, so doing both of the above would make `myNode` both move and rotate.

All properties are animated as floating-point values interpolated from the keyframes. For boolean properties, values of 0.5 or higher are interpreted as "true," and values under 0.5 as "false." Values for certain properties, such as colors, are clamped between 0 and 1 after interpolation. For the `ORIENTATION` property, the quaternion values are automatically normalized after interpolation.

Performance tip: Quaternions do not require `SLERP` or `SQUAD` interpolation. Due to the automatic normalization, using plain `LINEAR` or `SPLINE` interpolation will make you only lose the constant velocity property. For many animations this is good

Table 16.2: List of animatable properties in M3G 1.1.

Name	Applicable properties
ALPHA	Alpha component of `Background`, `Material`, and `VertexBuffer` color; `Node` alpha factor.
AMBIENT_COLOR	Ambient color in `Material`.
COLOR	Color of `Light`, `Background`, `Fog`, and `VertexBuffer`; `Texture2D` blend color.
CROP	Cropping rectangle in `Background` and `Sprite3D`.
DENSITY	`Fog` density.
DIFFUSE_COLOR	Diffuse `Material` color.
EMISSIVE_COLOR	Emissive `Material` color.
FAR_DISTANCE	Far distance in `Camera` and `Fog`.
FIELD_OF_VIEW	`Camera` field of view.
INTENSITY	`Light` intensity.
MORPH_WEIGHTS	`MorphingMesh` weights.
NEAR_DISTANCE	Near distance in `Camera` and `Fog`.
ORIENTATION	`Transformable` orientation.
PICKABILITY	Picking enable flag of `Node`.
SCALE	`Transformable` scale.
SHININESS	`Material` shininess.
SPECULAR_COLOR	Specular `Material` color.
SPOT_ANGLE	Spotlight angle of `Light`.
SPOT_EXPONENT	Spotlight exponent of `Light`.
TRANSLATION	`Transformable` translation.
VISIBILITY	Rendering enable flag in `Node`.

enough, and if you can use simpler interpolation on most of the animations, you will save valuable processing time for other things. For example, try the simple LINEAR or SPLINE modes on your bone orientations.

pitfall: There is something of an infamous problem regarding SLERP interpolation in several M3G 1.0 implementations as well as early content authoring tools, as discussed in Section 12.3.2

This issue was resolved in M3G 1.1, but if you want your content to be compatible with the faulty M3G 1.0 implementations as well as with the correctly implemented ones, you must take extra precautions in constructing your SLERP keyframe sequences: make sure that the angle between the orientations described by adjacent keyframes is less than 180° in 3D space. In practice, this means that the dot product of any two adjacent quaternion keyframes must be positive. If this is not the case with your source data, you can enforce it by adding extra keyframes for segments that rotate 180° or more in 3D space.

Note that each `AnimationTrack` object only defines the type of property to be animated, without specifying an object. An `AnimationTrack` can therefore be associated with multiple objects to animate the same property, in the same way, for each one. Similarly, a `KeyframeSequence` can be associated with multiple `AnimationTrack` objects, and hence multiple animation targets of possibly different types. The only restriction is that the keyframe types and animated properties must be compatible. This makes it possible to share the keyframe data between multiple objects, while being able to control the animation of each one individually.

16.3 TIMING AND SPEED: `AnimationController`

In addition to a `KeyframeSequence` and an `AnimationTrack`, each individual animation needs an `AnimationController` to "drive" the animation. The controller is attached to each `AnimationTrack` object to define the speed and timing of that particular animation. Again, a single controller can be attached to multiple animation tracks, and in noninteractive animation, a single controller will often handle the entire scene. However, using multiple controllers will give you the degree of flexibility you want for playing back multiple animations simultaneously.

For example, assuming one object with two animation tracks, `motionTrack` and `rotationTrack`, it makes sense to control both using a single controller:

```
myObject.addAnimationTrack(motionTrack);
myObject.addAnimationTrack(rotationTrack);

AnimationController control = new AnimationController();
control.setActiveInterval(10000, 25000);
control.setPosition(0.f, 10000);
control.setSpeed(0.5f);

motionTrack.setController(control);
rotationTrack.setController(control);
```

Assuming milliseconds for the time unit, this would begin the animation of your object at ten seconds into the animation, animate it at half speed for fifteen seconds, and then stop. The animation would start playing from the beginning of your keyframe sequences.

World time and sequence time

Before we look at `AnimationController` in more detail, we must be more specific about time as it applies to M3G animation. With `KeyframeSequence`, we are talking in terms of *sequence time*: time 0 (zero) is the start of our keyframe sequence, and all keyframes in the sequence are defined relative to that. What you want to feed to the animation system from the application, however, is usually *world time*: that can be time passed since the start of your application, game session, or composite animation, or it may be the time of day if you so desire. Individual animation tracks may start and stop at arbitrary points in world time. It would often be impractical to build your keyframe sequences using world time, so `AnimationController` lets you easily map world time to the time of each keyframe sequence.

`AnimationController` uses two pieces of data to convert between world time and sequence time: a *reference point* and relative speed. You set the reference point by calling `setPosition(float `*sequenceTime*`, int `*worldTime*`)`. This is exactly equivalent to saying "I want my sequence time to be *sequenceTime* when the world clock reaches *worldTime*." Often, your desired *sequenceTime* will be zero and you are just saying "I want my sequence to start at *worldTime*," but M3G gives you a bit more flexibility in mapping the times.

In addition to setting the position of your animation sequence, you may want to set the speed at which the sequence time passes relative to the world clock. Figure 16.3

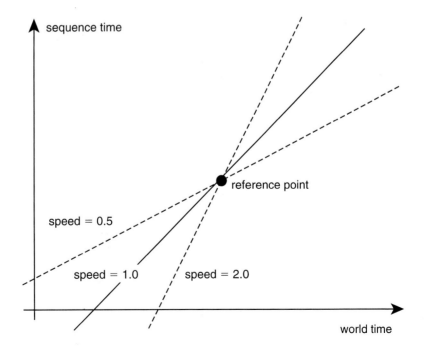

Figure 16.3: Relationship of world time and sequence time with different speed settings.

illustrates the relationship of the reference times and speed. By default, sequence time and world time are synchronized, but you can speed up or slow down a particular animation, or specify different units of time for your keyframes. You do this by calling `setSpeed(float` *speed*, `int` *worldTime*). A *speed* of 0.5, for example, will make your sequence run at half the normal speed, whereas 2.0 makes it twice as fast. A *speed* of 0.001 would let you specify your keyframes as whole seconds if your world time is in milliseconds.

Note the other parameter, *worldTime*. Why do you need to specify that? That is the point in world time at which your sequence speed change occurs. Imagine you have been running a long animation sequence for a while, and suddenly want to speed it up for one reason or another. You will still want to continue the animation from the current position, so if you were to just change the speed factor, you would have to adjust the reference time point to avoid a sudden jump. Instead, `setSpeed` takes the current world time as input and automatically makes that the new reference point. The sequence time at the new reference point is changed to match whatever it was for your animation before you decided to change the speed. As a result, you will only notice that your animation continues to run smoothly at the new speed.

Weight and active interval

In addition to the speed of a controller, you can also set its weight via `setWeight` (`float` *weight*). The interpolated animation data is then multiplied by *weight* prior to applying it to its animation target. This is useful for animation blending, which we will describe in more detail in Section 16.5.2.

> **Performance tip:** You can speed up the animation process by telling M3G to ignore any animations you do not need at any given moment. You can do that by either setting the weight of the respective controller to zero, or setting the controller of an animation track to NULL.

Finally, each `AnimationController` has an *active interval*, set via `setActiveInterval(int` *start*, `int` *end*). *start* and *end* are the world times at which the activity of this animation controller begins and ends, respectively. Each controller is only considered in animation calculations if the current world time falls within its active interval; otherwise, it is as if the animations controlled by that controller did not exist at all.

> **pitfall:** The animations controlled by an inactive controller (either zero weight or outside of the active interval) are not updated *at all*. In other words, the animation targets are not reset to any default values when a controller becomes inactive. In particular, if you make a jump in your animation that lands the world time outside of the active interval of any controller, the values animated through that controller will retain the values they had before the jump.

On a related note, an animated M3G scene will contain initial values for everything when loaded from an M3G file, but there is no direct way to reset those initial values. You must either reload the file, or have your animations active at time zero to set the correct values.

16.4 ANIMATION EXECUTION

So, you have set up your `KeyframeSequence`, `AnimationTrack`, and `AnimationController`. You have added the track to an object—say, `myMesh`. How do you effect your animation to the mesh? You call `animate(int` *worldTime*`)`, passing in the time currently displayed by the world clock you maintain in your application:

```
static long startTime = System.currentTimeMillis();
...
myMesh.animate(System.currentTimeMillis() - startTime);
```

You can call `animate` on `myMesh`, or if `myMesh` happens to be a part of `myWorld`, you can animate all of `myWorld` with a single `animate` call.

```
myWorld.addChild(myMesh);
...
myWorld.animate(System.currentTimeMillis() - startTime);
```

Animation in M3G is always requested by the application. There are no timers or events involved unless you want to involve them. Neither does the animation engine have any state that you need to change to play, stop, or rewind your animations. All you do is pass in your desired world time to `animate`, and everything is updated to reflect that point in time.

Let us look at an example on event-based animation. Assume an animation controller, `actionController`, controls a composite animation representing an action that a game entity would perform in response to some event. To trigger the animation upon receiving that event, we only need one line of code in addition to the previous example:

```
actionController.setPosition(0.0f, eventTime);
```

Here, `eventTime` is the world time of the event. When `myWorld.animate()` is next called, the animation controlled by `actionController` is automatically effected on the target objects. To re-trigger the animation in the future, another call to `setPosition` is sufficient.

Performance tip: There is no way to read back the current state of a particular animation in M3G, but you may want to know the phase of an animation in order to execute some corresponding action in the game logic. The duration of each animation could be encoded in the user data field of the animation controller, but you can also link that information directly to your animation: create an empty `Group` node and attach an animation track to its alpha factor. You can then set the keyframe values so that the alpha factor will contain any desired data values, synchronized to the actual animation, which you can query directly. If you only need a binary state, you can use the node enable flags instead.

Animation proceeds recursively: all objects reachable from the object being animated, according to the rules set forth in Section 13.4.1, are automatically animated as well. If you call `animate` on a `World` object, for example, everything in your `World` is animated; if you animate a `Group`, only objects within that group are touched. Note, however, that all referenced objects are animated—if your `Group` has a `Mesh` using a `Texture2D` via an `Appearance`, the transformation of the `Texture2D` will also update if it has an animation attached. Normally, you need not worry about this—M3G just handles it automatically for you, and the result is what you would expect in most cases.

We mentioned at the beginning of this chapter that animation in M3G is essentially just a way of quickly setting a number of parameters, and that is exactly what happens. When your `animate` function call returns, all the animated parameters will have their new values and the animation engine leaves the rest up to you. Normally, you will just proceed to `Graphics3D.render` and draw your scene, but you are free to modify anything between animation and rendering if you want to. One common step is to call `align` on your entire world or some specific nodes to compute any node alignments you have defined. However, you can do any other processing before rendering. You do not even have to render; you can just keep on animating if you have a special use case for that—for example, you could use the spline interpolation to generate vertex data by reading back the animated values after each animation call, then assigning the data to a vertex array.

16.5 ADVANCED ANIMATION

We have now covered the basic setup and execution of keyframe animation in M3G. By now, you can get simple animations up and running to modify your object parameters. We can now look at how to make more complex animations involving animated meshes, blending between multiple animation sequences, and some useful animation features not explicitly described in the M3G specification.

16.5.1 DEFORMABLE MESHES

In Section 4.2 we discussed how morphing and skinning can be used to bring polygon meshes to life. M3G has support for both of these techniques via the `MorphingMesh` and `SkinnedMesh` classes. The former allows morphing between sets of vertex attributes, and the latter implements skinning.

MorphingMesh

Creating a `MorphingMesh` is very similar to creating a regular `Mesh`. In fact, the only difference is that you need to pass in an additional *targets* parameter:

```
MorphingMesh(VertexBuffer base, VertexBuffer[] targets, IndexBuffer[]
             submeshes, Appearance[] appearances)
```

The *targets* array is your set of morph targets. The *base* vertex buffer gives the vertices for your undeformed mesh, and each buffer in the *targets* array is one morphed version of the original mesh. The morph targets only need to contain the vertex properties that change. For example, if all of the morph targets share the same texture coordinates, those may be specified only in the base mesh. Morph targets *cannot* contain vertex attributes that are not present in the base mesh, and the set of attributes in each morph target must be the same. Refer to the M3G specification for more details.

In the common case, you want to blend vertex positions and normals between multiple shapes, while retaining per-vertex colors or texture coordinates. This is illustrated in Figure 16.4, and easily achieved in code:

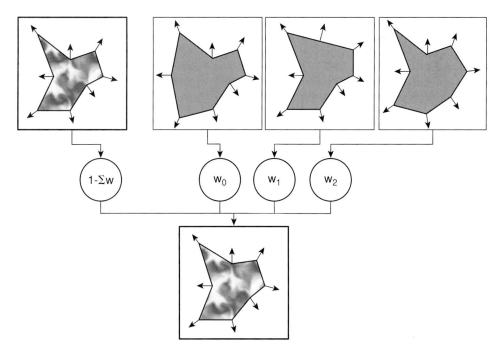

Figure 16.4: An example of morphing in M3G. The base mesh, top left, is modified by blending in positions and normals from three morph targets. See the code example in text.

```
VertexArray basePositions, baseNormals, colors, texCoords;
VertexArray morphedPositions[3], morphedNormals[3];
IndexBuffer primitives;
Appearance appearance;

// Array initialization omitted...

// Initialize the base vertex buffer

VertexBuffer baseVertices = new VertexBuffer();
baseMesh.setPositions(basePositions, 1.f, null);
baseMesh.setNormals(baseNormals);
baseMesh.setTexCoords(0, texCoords, 1/128.f, null);
baseMesh.setColors(colors);

// Initialize the morph target vertex buffers -- note that
// only the morphed attributes, i.e., positions and normals,
// are needed for these

VertexBuffer morphedVertices[] = new VertexBuffer[3];
for (int i = 0; i < 3; ++i) {
  morphedVertices[i] = new VertexBuffer();
  morphedVertices[i].setPositions(morphedPositions[i], 1.f, null);
  morphedVertices[i].setNormals(morphedNormals[i]);
}

// Create the final mesh object

MorphingMesh mesh = new MorphingMesh(baseVertices,
                                     morphedVertices,
                                     primitives,
                                     appearance);

// Set to an even blend between the base mesh and each morph target

float weights[3] = { 0.25f, 0.25f, 0.25f };
mesh.setWeights(weights);
```

Once you have the `MorphingMesh` constructed, you can animate it via the morph target weights. You can either call `setWeights(float[]` *weights*) to set them directly, or animate the `MORPH_WEIGHTS` property of the mesh. The keyframes in that case will be vectors that have one floating-point weight corresponding to each morph target. However you apply the weights, each morph target will contribute to the final mesh shape according to its weight. The actual equation is

$$M = B + \sum w_i(T_i - B) = (1 - \sum w_i)B + \sum w_i T_i, \qquad (16.1)$$

that is, the *difference* between the base mesh B and each morph target T is weighted and added to the base mesh to produce the final shape M. Note that if the weights sum to one, the effect of the base mesh is canceled out and you are only blending between your morphed shapes. You are free to use any weights, though, including negative ones. An alternative way of thinking about this is that each morph target represents a single feature, and you can blend these features to alter your base mesh. This approach is often used to produce facial animation, with different expressions being blended in.

> **pitfall:** In morphing, it is *your* responsibility to make sure that the morphed vertex coordinates do not overflow the numeric range of your vertex buffer. M3G can handle very large intermediate results (from weighting each morph target), but the end result must still fit within the original range of either 8 or 16 bits.

SkinnedMesh

Now, let us build a complete animated character using skinning. Most of this will already be familiar, so we will begin with a practical example before introducing the new functions in detail. While the code is fairly straightforward, there is quite a bit of it, so we have split it into a couple of sections. The entire example is also available from the companion web site.

Example: Building a Skinned Character

Our skinned character is shown in Figure 16.5. First, we will construct the skinned mesh object with the various bones that we can control separately:

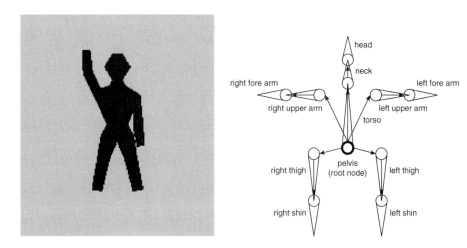

Figure 16.5: Our example of a skinned character. The rendered figure is shown on the left, and the skeleton group on the right. The illustration shows the origin (sphere) and primary axis (triangle) of each bone, while the arrows indicate parent-child relationships in the scene graph. The torso node is co-located with the root node, pelvis, emphasized.

```
private SkinnedMesh stickMan;
private Group torso, neck, head;
private Group leftThigh, rightThigh, leftShin, rightShin;
private Group leftUpperArm, rightUpperArm, leftForeArm,
              rightForeArm;
```

We have defined simple 2D vertex data along the outlines of our character. From this, we construct the vertex and index buffers as well as the actual mesh object in a way that is similar to past examples:

```
static private byte vertices[] = {
  // Head and neck
  -10, 127, 0,   10, 127, 0,   -25, 103, 0,   25, 103, 0,
  -10,  80, 0,   10,  80, 0,   -15,  70, 0,   15,  70, 0,
  // Arms and torso
  -120, 55, 0, -120, 40, 0,  -80,  60, 0,  -80, 40, 0,  -40, 65, 0,
  -40,  40, 0,  120, 55, 0,   120, 40, 0,   80, 60, 0,   80, 40, 0,
   40,  65, 0,   40, 40, 0,  -20,   0, 0,   20,  0, 0,
  // Lower body and legs
  -30, -20, 0,    0, -30,  0,   30, -20,  0,  -30, -60, 0,
  -5,  -60, 0,  -30, -120, 0,  -10, -120, 0,    5, -60, 0,
   30, -60, 0,   10, -120, 0,   30, -120, 0
};

static private int tristrips[] = {
  1, 0, 3, 2, 5, 4, 7, 6,
  8, 9, 10, 11, 12, 13, 6, 20, 7, 21, 18, 19, 16, 17, 14, 15,
  20, 22, 21, 23, 24,
  23, 22, 26, 25, 28, 27,
  24, 23, 30, 29, 32, 31
};

  static private int striplens[] = { 8, 16, 5, 6, 6 };

  // Create the vertices and triangle strips for the mesh

  VertexArray pos = new VertexArray(vertices.length / 3, 3, 1);
  pos.set(0, vertices.length / 3, vertices);

  VertexBuffer vb = new VertexBuffer();
  vb.setPositions(pos, 1.f, null);
  vb.setDefaultColor(0x000000);

  IndexBuffer ib = new TriangleStripArray(tristrips, striplens);

  stickMan = new SkinnedMesh(vb, ib, new Appearance(),
                             new Group());
```

Connecting the Bones

So far, our mesh is no different from regular `Mesh` class objects, except that there is an empty group to serve as a skeleton. Next, we will create the bones and connect them into a skeleton as shown in Figure 16.5, starting with the group we already inserted above:

```
Group pelvis = stickMan.getSkeleton();

// Connect the torso, neck, and head

torso = new Group();
pelvis.addChild(torso);

neck = new Group();
torso.addChild(neck);
neck.setTranslation(0.f, 60.f, 0.f);

head = new Group();
neck.addChild(head);
head.setTranslation(0.f, 20.f, 0.f);

// Connect the arms to the torso

leftUpperArm = new Group();
torso.addChild(leftUpperArm);
leftUpperArm.setTranslation(30.f, 50.f, 0.f);
leftUpperArm.setOrientation(-90.f, 0.f, 0.f, 1.f);

leftForeArm = new Group();
leftUpperArm.addChild(leftForeArm);
leftForeArm.setTranslation(0.f, 50.f, 0.f);

...
```

Note how the arms, for example, are offset inside the torso group. The translation of each bone determines the location of its hinge point (origin) relative to the hinge point of its parent bone. We have also used a convention where the Y axis of each bone runs along the length of the bone, so we are rotating some of the bones. The character defined by the untransformed vertices is standing with arms stretched out to the sides, and our bones now match that rest pose.

Attaching the Skin

The final step in creating a skinned character is attaching flesh to the bones. We must tell M3G which vertices each bone should affect, and if multiple bones affect any single vertex, M3G will average their influences based on the weights assigned to each bone. You can use any integer values for the weights—in this example, we use a nominal scale of 0 to 100. We have also laid out the vertex data so that we can attach each bone to a group of vertices at once:

```
stickMan.addTransform(torso, 100, 6, 2);    // Vertices 6, 7,
stickMan.addTransform(torso, 100, 12, 2);   // 12, 13,
stickMan.addTransform(torso, 100, 18, 2);   // 18, 19,
stickMan.addTransform(torso, 100, 20, 2);   // 20, and 21

stickMan.addTransform(neck, 30, 4, 4);      // Vertices 4, 5, 6, and 7
stickMan.addTransform(head, 100, 0, 6);     // etc.

stickMan.addTransform(rightForeArm, 100, 8, 4);
stickMan.addTransform(rightUpperArm, 100, 10, 4);

...
```

Our mesh is now ready for animation. Any further transformations to the bones will deform the mesh accordingly, so let us make our character raise his right hand to say hello:

```
leftUpperArm.postRotate(-80.f, 0.f, 0.f, 1.f);
rightUpperArm.postRotate(-60.f, 0.f, 0.f, 1.f);
rightForeArm.postRotate(-30.f, 0.f, 0.f, 1.f);
```

API review

Constructing a `SkinnedMesh` is, again, similar to creating a regular `Mesh` except for the extra *skeleton* parameter:

```
SkinnedMesh(VertexBuffer vertices, IndexBuffer[] submeshes, Appearance[]
            appearances, Group skeleton)
```

The set of bones for your skinning animation are contained by the *skeleton* group. It is actually a completely generic scene graph branch that can contain any objects—even other `SkinnedMesh` nodes are permitted. Each node to be used as a bone is defined by calling addTransform(Node *bone*, int *weight*, int *firstVertex*, int *numVertices*). This specifies that transformations of the skeleton node *bone* will influence the *numVertices* vertices starting at *firstVertex* with a given *weight*. The weights for skinning are normalized during vertex transformation by dividing the bone weights with the sum of all weights contributing to each vertex. After adding all bone influences, animating the transformations of the bone nodes will automatically deform the `SkinnedMesh`.

Note that the transformations B_i for the rest pose (Section 4.2.2) are not explicitly given to the API. These are inferred from the bone node transformations *at the time of the* addTransform *function call*. So, before using addTransform, be sure to set your bones to their initial positions.

Skinning in OpenGL and graphics hardware usually uses a fixed maximum number of per-vertex transformations—that is, you can specify a maximum of, for example, only four matrices to be used for each particular vertex. Whereas M3G conceptually allows you to specify an unlimited number of bone influences per vertex, the lowest-weighted transformations will be ignored if the capacity of the underlying renderer is exceeded.

You can check how many transformations per vertex it makes sense to use, though. If you call `Graphics3D.getProperties`, the *maxTransformsPerVertex* property returned gives the number of transformations per vertex that M3G will actually use. No more than *maxTransformsPerVertex* bones will ever influence a single vertex.

Altogether, the setup for skinning is quite involved. Even though the operations are simple, you need to do a lot of them. However, you will rarely have to explicitly set up a `SkinnedMesh`. Because a good-looking skinned character will require tweaking the vertex weights and bone positions by hand, they are practically always exported directly from a modeling tool such as 3ds Max, Maya, or Blender. What is left for you to do in code, then, is to identify the parts of the skeleton that you need to animate, or the predefined animation controllers that you use for the different animations built into the ready-made model. The M3G user ID mechanism can be a big help here, as discussed in Section 13.4.3.

Combined Morphing and Skinning

We mentioned that morphing is often used for facial animation, whereas skinning handles characters. Now, if you want to combine skinning and morphing—if, for example, your skinned character has a face that you wish to morph—you will find that you can only choose one or the other per mesh. In practice, you can use a `MorphingMesh` for the head or face of your character and `SkinnedMesh` for all other parts, then hide the seams as best as you can. For example, the texture below the chin and on the neck is often smooth enough that you can split your mesh there without anyone noticing. Note that you can still use your "head" mesh as a part of the skeleton, attaching it directly to your "neck" bone or equivalent. You can even use it for skinning, like any other bone node.

16.5.2 ANIMATION BLENDING

In interactive applications, you often have cases where you have multiple predefined animation sequences between which you want to switch. For example, your game character could have a walking sequence, a running sequence, a jumping sequence, and a swinging-a-sword sequence. When the player wants to go from walking to running, you need to switch between animation sequences, but you still want to keep the motion fluid and avoid a discontinuity. Animation blending can help you there.

As we already mentioned, `AnimationController` has a weight that you can set and use for blending. In the example of transitioning between walking and running, you can use one controller for each of the sequences—for example `myWalkController` and `myRunController`. When the player is walking, you have the weight for `myWalkController` set to one, and the weight for `myRunController` set to zero; for running, the opposite is true. Now, when the player hits the "run" button, you do not instantly switch to the running sequence. Instead, you gradually, over several frames or a fixed time delay, ramp the weight of myRunController up while simultaneously reducing the weight of myWalkController to zero:

```
static int transitionTime = 400;
walkController.setWeight(1.f);
runController.setWeight(0.f);

// Log the starting time when you begin the transition
static long transitionStart = System.currentTimeMillis();
...

// At rendering time, adjust the blend for each frame
protected void paint(Graphics g) {
  ...
  long time = System.currentTimeMillis();
  int delta = time - transitionStart;
  if (delta < transitionTime) {
    runController.setWeight(delta / (float) transitionTime);
    walkController.setWeight((transitionTime - delta) /
                             (float) transitionTime);
  }
  else {
    runController.setWeight(1.f);
    walkController.setWeight(0.f);
  }
  ...
}
```

As a result, there is no sudden jump, and the motion will smoothly change from walking to running.

There are a few points to observe in blending animations, though. You need to synchronize your sequences so that, for example in our walk-to-run example above, each foot is moving in the same direction in both sequences—that is, the *phase* of the animation is maintained during blending. If your running sequence has the left foot touching the ground and the walking sequence the right foot touching the ground when you blend between them, the result will no doubt look odd. Synchronization is easily achieved if both of the animations being blended take the same time to complete one cycle, as they will then always stay in sync. Otherwise, you will have to tweak the position and/or speed of one or both animations when you begin (and possibly during) the transition from one sequence to another. The details of such blending are beyond the scope of this book; instead, look into papers on the topic of motion blending [BW95, KG03] or motion graphs [KGP02]. However, the M3G animation engine gives you the basic tools you need to get it done.

Another point worth noting is that the blended animations need not target all the same features. You can have one AnimationController controlling only the feet of your character, while another controls both the feet and the upper body. Mixing those two animations is, again, not readily solved for you by M3G. Rather, it is something you can take advantage of in special cases.

16.5.3 CREATING DISCONTINUITIES

Sometimes you want to make sudden jumps in the middle of an animated sequence, or wish to control the tangents more precisely. A common case is camera animation. You may want your camera to pan, track, or dolly for one shot, then cut into a completely different viewpoint for the next shot. For other shots, you may want the camera to remain absolutely stationary. Splitting your animation into multiple keyframe sequences is cumbersome, so it is easier to introduce discontinuities into the animation track.

Adding discontinuities is actually quite easy once you know how. Just introduce a segment that has a duration of zero, and M3G will jump over it when animating. In other words, place two keyframes at the same point in time, but with different data values, as illustrated in Figure 16.6. The intermediate values will never be produced by the animation engine. This is all you need for linear interpolation.

For spline interpolation, recall from Chapter 4 that M3G looks at four keyframes in total to determine the tangent vectors for each segment. To control the tangents around the discontinuity, you need four coincident keyframes in total—two on each side of the jump. As a matter of fact, this allows you explicit control over tangents *anywhere* you may need it, not just around discontinuities.

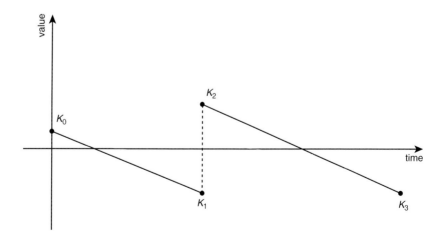

Figure 16.6: Creating a discontinuity in a LINEAR keyframe sequence by duplicating a keyframe. Keyframes 1 and 2 are at the same position in time, but have different data values.

Referring to Section 4.1.1 and Equations 4.6, 4.4, and 4.5, we can generate any tangent value anywhere in an M3G animation sequence. Given our three keyframes, a, b, and c, and placing a and b at the same point in time, we see that Equation 4.5 becomes

$$b'_+ = \frac{\Delta t_{bc}}{\Delta t_{bc}} b'$$
$$= \frac{c - a}{2} \tag{16.2}$$

after substituting for b' from Equation 4.6. In other words, the value of the tangent coming out of the discontinuity can be controlled simply by changing the value of keyframe a. The zero-length segment between a and b is never used by the M3G spline interpolator, so a only affects the tangent. If we place b and c at the same point in time instead, the tangent b'_- can be similarly controlled with the value of c.

16.5.4 DYNAMIC ANIMATION

Sometimes static animation sequences may not be suitable for your needs. For example, you could use splines to create motion paths for nonplayer entities in a game in order to avoid explicitly moving them around, yet you want them to react dynamically to game events. Alternatively, you might want to stream a long piece of animation over a network connection. In either case, you have an unbounded number of keyframes coming from some source, and you cannot create a single, long `KeyframeSequence` to contain all of them.

We have already hinted at how the valid range in `KeyframeSequence` can be useful if you want to change the contents of your sequences. In particular, it allows you to use a single `KeyframeSequence` object as a *circular buffer* in which you can cache the currently required part of any dynamic or streaming animation.

Let us assume that you get a stream of spline keyframes from some source—be it your game's AI subsystem, a network connection, or something else—and you want to use them to drive the motion of some game entity. You will create your `AnimationTrack` and `AnimationController` as usual. For the `KeyframeSequence`, you only need to allocate a minimum of four keyframes, as needed for a single spline segment:

```
myBuffer = new KeyframeSequence(4, 3, KeyframeSequence.SPLINE);
```

Initially, you will retrieve the first four keyframes of your sequence and set them to `myBuffer`. Then set the duration of `myBuffer` to the time of the *last* keyframe inserted into the buffer; the duration will be used to keep track of the length of animation you have "downloaded" into the buffer so far.

Now you will run your animation exactly as before, except for one additional check before each `animate` call. Each time you run out of data, you need to retrieve a new keyframe and insert that into the buffer. You can easily check for this by comparing the sequence time with the duration of your buffer:

```
if (myController.getPosition(worldTime) >= myBuffer.getDuration()) {
    float[] nextKeyframe = new float[3];
    int nextKeyframeTime = myGetNextKeyframeFunction(nextKeyframe);
```

Then, insert your new keyframe into the buffer, replacing the oldest keyframe and cycling the valid range forward by one keyframe:

```
    int firstValid = myBuffer.getValidRangeFirst();
    int lastValid = firstValid;
    firstValid = (firstValid + 1) % myBuffer.getKeyframeCount();
    myBuffer.setValidRange(firstValid, lastValid);

    myBuffer.setKeyframe(lastValid, nextKeyframeTime, nextKeyframe);
    myBuffer.setDuration(nextKeyframeTime);
}
```

That is all there is to it! The sequence `myBuffer` now has the latest segment of your dynamically created spline, and you can proceed to animating as usual. With this simple added step, you can create or stream arbitrarily long animations. In a real-life application, especially if streaming over an uncertain and laggy network connection, you will want to use a longer buffer, but the basic mechanism remains the same.

PART IV
APPENDIX

FIXED-POINT MATHEMATICS

OpenGL is a floating-point API, but practically no mobile phones at the time when OpenGL ES 1.0 was defined had any hardware support for floating-point arithmetic. Most C compilers support floating-point operations, but emulating IEEE floats using integer hardware can be painfully slow.

However, integers can be used to represent decimal numbers. For example, to store a number such as 87.65432 with the accuracy of four decimal points, you could store it as 876543, and either instruct a decimal point to be moved four steps left, or, equivalently, say that the number we really mean is the number we store, only divided by 10000. Now you can do your arithmetic using integer operations which can run much faster than emulating floats.

We can do the same with 32-bit two's complement (signed) binary integers. In the example before, we used powers of ten, but since computers naturally use powers of two, we also switch to that base. Since we want to allocate as many bits for numbers smaller than one as for numbers greater than one, it makes sense to divide by $2^{16} = 65536$. That is, to convert a floating-point value to fixed point, you should multiply it by 65536 and round, and to convert a fixed-point value into a float you should divide it by 65536.0. We call these numbers 16.16 fixed-point numbers. Here the first number denotes the integer bits and the second the decimal bits.

When using 16.16 fixed-point values we get the a from −32768 to almost 32768, whereas single precision IEEE floating-point values may have magnitudes up to 10^{38}. OpenGL does not require this large a range, as only magnitudes up to 2^{32} need to be representable, and for colors even 2^{10} is enough. The precision of these fixed-point numbers is fixed: (1/65536), whereas the precision of floats depends on the magnitude of the values. Values close to zero have a very high accuracy: two consecutive floats at around 1.0 have a precision of 1/16777216, floats at around 250.0 have roughly the same precision as fixed-point numbers, while larger numbers become more inaccurate (two consecutive floats around 17 million are further than 1.0 units apart). OpenGL requires only accuracy of one part in 10^5, which is a little under 17 bits; single-precision floats have 24 bits of accuracy.

Below are C macros for converting from float to fixed and vice versa:

```
#define float_to_fixed( a )    (int)  ((a) * (1<<16))
#define fixed_to_float( a )    (((float)a) / (1<<16))
```

These are "quick-and-dirty" versions of conversion. `float_to_fixed` can overflow if the magnitude of the float value is too great, or underflow if it is too small. `fixed_to_float` can be made slightly more accurate by rounding. For example, asymmetric arithmetic rounding works by adding 0.5 to the number before truncating it to an integer, e.g., `(int)floor((a) / 65536.0f + 0.5f)`.

Finally, note that some of these conversions are expensive on some processors and thus should not be used in performance-critical code such as inner loops.

Here are some 16.16 fixed-point numbers, expressed in hexadecimal, and the corresponding decimal numbers:

0x 0001 0000	1.0
0x 0002 0000	2.0
0x 0010 0000	16.0
0x 0000 8000	0.5
0x 0000 4000	0.25
0x 0000 2000	0.125
0x 0000 0001	1.0/65536
0x ffff ffff	−1.0/65536
0x fffe 0000	−2.0

Depending on the situation it may make sense to move the decimal point to some other location, although 16.16 is a good general choice. For example, if you are only interested in numbers between zero and one (but excluding one), you should move the decimal point all the way to the left; if you use 32 bits denote that with u0.32 (here *u* stands for unsigned). In rasterization, the number of sub-pixel bits and the size of the screen in pixels determine the number of bits you should have on the right side of the decimal point. Signed 16.16 is a compromise that is relatively easy to use, and gives the same relative importance to numbers between zero and one as to values above one.

In the upcoming examples we also use other fixed-point formats. For example, a 32.32 fixed-point value would be stored using 64 bits and it could be converted to a float by dividing it by 2^{32}, whereas 32.16 would take 48 bits and have 32 integer and 16 decimal bits, and 32.0 would denote a regular 32-bit signed integer. To distinguish between unsigned (such as u0.32) and signed two's complement fixed-point formats we prepend unsigned formats with *u*.

In this appendix, we first go through fixed-point processing in C. We then follow by showing what you can do by using assembly language, and conclude with a section on fixed-point programming in Java.

A.1 FIXED-POINT METHODS IN C

In this section we first discuss the basic fixed-point operations, followed by the shared exponent approach for vector operations, and conclude with an example that precalculates trigonometric functions in a table.

A.1.1 BASIC OPERATIONS

The addition of two fixed-point numbers is usually very straightforward (and subtraction is just a signed add):

```
#define add_fixed_fixed( a, b ) ((a)+(b))
```

We have to watch out, though; the operation may overflow. As opposed to floats, the overflow is totally silent, there is no warning about the result being wrong. Therefore, you should always insert a debugging code to your fixed-point math, the main idea being that the results before and after clamping from 64-bit integers to 32-bit integers have to agree.[1] Here is an example of how that can be done:

```
#if defined(DEBUG)
int add_fixed_fixed_chk( int a, int b )
{
  int64 bigresult = ((int64)a) + ((int64)b);
  int smallresult = a + b;
  assert(smallresult == bigresult);
  return smallresult;
}
#endif

#if defined(DEBUG)
#  define add_fixed_fixed( a, b ) add_fixed_fixed_chk( a, b )
#else
#  define add_fixed_fixed( a, b ) ((a)+(b))
#endif
```

---

1   Code examples are not directly portable. Minimally you have to select the correct platform 64-bit type. Examples: long long, __int64, int64

Another point to note is that these fixed-point routines should always be macros or inlined functions, not called through regular functions. The function calling overhead would take away most of the speed benefits of fixed-point programming. For the debug versions using regular functions is fine, though.

Multiplications are more complicated than additions. Let us analyze the case of multiplying two 16.16 numbers and storing the result into another 16.16 number. When we multiply two 16.16 numbers, the accurate result is a 32.32 number. We ignore the last 16 bits of the result simply by shifting right 16 steps, yielding a 32.16 number. If all the remaining bits are zero, either one or both of the operands were zero, or we underflowed, i.e., the magnitude of the result was too small to be represented in a 16.16 fixed-point number. Similarly, if the result is too large to fit in 16.16, we overflow. But if the result is representable as a 16.16 number, we can simply take the lowest 32 bits. Note that the intermediate result must be stored in a 64-bit integer, unless the magnitude of the result is known to be under 1.0 before multiplication. We are finally ready to define multiplication:

```
#define mul_fixed_fixed( a, b ) (int)(((int64)(a)*(int64)(b)) >> 16)
```

If one of the multiplicands is an int, then the inputs are 16.16 and 32.0, the result is 48.16, and we can omit the shift operation:

```
#define mul_fixed_int( a, b )    (int)((int64)(a) * (int64)(b))
```

Multiplications overflow even more easily than additions. The following example shows how you can check for overflows in debug builds:

```
#if defined(DEBUG)
int mul_fixed_fixed_chk( int a, int b )
{
  int64 bigresult = (((int64)a) * ((int64)b)) >> 16;

  /* high bits must be just sign bits (0's or 1's) */
  int64 sign     = (bigresult >> 32);
  assert( (sign == 0) || (sign == -1) );

  return (int)bigresult;
}
#endif
```

Note also that multiplications by power-of-two are typically faster when done with shifts instead of normal multiplication. For example:

```
assert((a << 4) == (a * 16));
```

Let us then see how division works. Dividing two 16.16 numbers gives you an integer, and loses precision in the process. However, as we want the result to be 16.16, we should shift the nominator left 16 steps and store it in an int64 before the division. This also avoids losing the fractional bits. Here are several versions of the division with different arguments (fixed or int), producing a 16.16 result:

```
#define div_fixed_fixed( a, b )  (int)(  (((int64)(a))<<16)  /  (b)  )
#define div_int_int( a, b )      (int)(  (((int64)(a))<<16)  /  (b)  )
#define div_int_fixed( a, b )    (int)(  (((int64)(a))<<32)  /  (b)  )
#define div_fixed_int( a, b )    ((a)  /  (b))
```

These simple versions do not check for overflows, nor do they trap the case $b = 0$. Division, however, is usually a much slower operation than multiplication. If the interval of operations is small enough, it may be possible to precalculate a table of reciprocals and perform multiplication. With a wider interval one can do a sparse table of reciprocals and interpolate the nearest results.

For slightly more precision, we can incorporate rounding into the fixed-point operations. Rounding works much the same way as when converting a float to a fixed-point number: add 0.5 before truncating to an integer. Since we use integer division in the operations, we just have to add 0.5 *before* the division. For multiplication this is easy and fairly cheap: since our divider is the fixed value of $1 << 16$, we add one half of that, $1 << 15$, before the shift:

```
#define mul_fixed_fixed_round( a, b ) \
    (int)( ((int64)(a) * (int64)(b) + (1<<15)) >> 16)
```

Similarly, for correct rounding in division of a by b, we should add $b/2$ to a before dividing by b.

A.1.2 SHARED EXPONENTS

Sometimes the range that is required for calculations is too great to fit into 32-bit registers. In some of those cases you can still avoid the use of full floating point. For example, you can create your own floating-point operations that do not deal with the trickiest parts of the IEEE standard, e.g., the handling of infinities, NaNs (Not-a-Numbers), or floating-point exceptions.

However, with vector operations, which are often needed in 3D graphics, another possibility is to store the meaningful bits, the mantissas, separately into integers, perform integer calculations using them, and to *share the exponent* across all terms. For example, if you need to calculate a dot product of a floating-point vector against a vector of integer or fixed-point numbers, you could normalize the floating-point vector to a common base exponent, perform the multiplications and additions in fixed point, and finally, if needed, adjust the base exponent depending on the result. Another name for this practice of shared exponents is *block floating point*.

Using a shared exponent may lead to underflow, truncating some of the terms to zero. In some cases such truncation may lead to a large error. Here is a bit contrived example of a worst-case error: $[1.0e40, 1.0e8, 1.0e8, 1.0e8] \cdot [0, 32768, 32768, 32768]$. With a shared exponent the first vector becomes $[1, 0, 0, 0] * 1e40$, which, when dotted with the second vector, produces a result that is very different from the true answer.

The resulting number sequence, mantissas together with the shared exponent, is really a vectorized floating-point number and needs to be treated as such in the subsequent calculations, until to the point where the exponent can be finally eliminated. It may seem that since the exponent must be normalized in the end in any case, we are not saving much. Keep in mind, though, that the most expensive operations are only performed once for the full dot product. It may even be possible that the required multiplication and addition operations can be done with efficient multiply-and-accumulate (MAC) operations in assembler if the processor supports such operations.

Conversion from floating point vectors into vectorized floating point is only useful in situations where the cost of conversion can be amortized somehow. For example, if you run 50 dot products where the floating-point vector stays the same and the fixed-point vectors vary, this method can save a lot of computation. An example where you might need this kind of functionality is in your physics library. A software implementation of vertex array transformation by modelview and projection matrices is another example where this approach could be attempted: multiplication of a homogeneous vertex with a 4×4 matrix can be done with four dot products.

Many processors support operations that can be used for normalizing the result. For example ARM processors with the ARMv5 instruction set or later support the CLZ instruction that counts the number of leading zero bits in an integer. Even when the processor supports these operations, they are only typically expressed either as compiler-specific intrinsic functions or through inline assembler. For example, a portable version of count-leading-zeros can be implemented as follows:

```
/* Table stores the CLZ value for a byte */
static unsigned char clz_table[256] = { 8, 7, 6, 6, ... };

INLINE int clz_unsigned( unsigned int num )
{
  int res = 24;

  if (num >> 16)
  {
    num >>= 16;
    res -= 16;
  }

  if (num > 255)
  {
    num >>= 8;
    res -= 8;
  }
```

```
    return clz_table[num] + res;
}
```

GCC compiler has a built-in command for CLZ that can be used like this:

```
INLINE int clz_unsigned( unsigned int num )
{
  return  __builtin_clz(num);
}
```

The built-in will get compiled to ARM CLZ opcode when compiled to ARM target.

The performance of this routine depends on the processor architecture, and for some processors it may be faster to calculate the result with arithmetic instructions instead of table lookups.

In comparison, the ARM assembly variant of the same thing is:

```
INLINE int clz_unsigned( unsigned int num )
{
  int result;
  __asm
  {
    clz    result, num
  }
  return result;
}
```

A.1.3 TRIGONOMETRIC OPERATIONS

The use of trigonometric functions such as *sin*, *cos*, or *arctan* can be expensive both in floating-point and fixed-point domains. But since these functions are repeating, symmetric, have a compact range $[-1,1]$, and can sometimes be expressed in terms of each other (e.g., $sin(\theta + 90°) = cos(\theta)$), you can precalculate them directly into tables and store the results in fixed point.

A case in point is *sin* (and from that *cos*), for which only a 90° segment needs to be tabulated, and the rest can be obtained through the symmetry and continuity properties of *sin*. Since the table needs to be indexed by an integer, the input parameter needs to be discretized as well. Quantizing 90° to 1024 steps usually gives a good trade-off between accuracy, table size, and ease of manipulation of angle values (since 1024 is a power of two). The following code precalculates such a table.

```
short sintable[1024];
int ang;

for( ang = 0; ang < 1024 ; ang++ )
```

```
{
  /* angle_in_radians = ang/1024 * pi/2 */
  double rad_angle = (ang * PI) / (1024.0 * 2.0);
  sintable[ang] = (short)(-sin(rad_angle) * 32768.0);
}
```

In the loop we first convert the table index into radians. Using that value we evaluate *sin* and scale the result to the chosen fixed-point range. The values of *sin* vary from 0.0 to 1.0 within the first quadrant. If we multiply value 1.0 of *sin* by 32768.0 and convert to short, the result overflows to zero. A solution is to negate the *sin* values in the table and negate those back after the value is read from the table.

Here is an example function of extracting values for *sin*. Note that the return value is *sin* scaled by 32768.0.

```
INLINE int fixed_sin( int angle )
{
  int phase  = angle & (1024 + 2048);
  int subang = angle & 1023;

  if      ( phase == 0    ) return  -(int)sintable[ subang ];
  else if ( phase == 1024 ) return  -(int)sintable[ 1023 - subang ];
  else if ( phase == 2048 ) return   (int)sintable[ subang ];
  else                      return   (int)sintable[ 1023 - subang ];
}
```

A.2 FIXED-POINT METHODS IN ASSEMBLY LANGUAGE

Typically all processors have instructions that are helpful for fixed-point computations. For example, most processors support multiplication of two 32-bit values into a 64-bit result. However, it may be difficult for the compiler to find the optimal instruction sequence for the C code; direct assembly code is sometimes the only way to achieve good performance. Depending on the compiler and the processor, improvements of more than 2× can be often achieved using optimized assembly code.

Let us take the fixed-point multiplication covered earlier as an example. If you multiply two 32-bit integers, the result will also be a 32-bit integer, which may overflow the results before you have a chance to shift the results back into a safe range. Even if the target processor supports the optimized multiplication, it may be impossible to get a compiler to generate such assembly instructions. To be safe, you have to promote at least one of the arguments to a 64-bit integer. There are two solutions to this dilemma. The first (easy) solution is to use a good optimizing compiler that detects the casts around the operands, and then performs a narrower and faster multiplication. You might even be able to study the machine code sequences that the compiler produces to learn how to express operations so that they lead to efficient machine code. The second solution is to use inlined assembly and explicitly use the narrowest multiply that you can get away with.

Here we show an example of how to do fixed-point operations using ARM assembler. ARM processor is a RISC-type processor with sixteen 32-bit registers (r0-r15), out of which r15 is restricted to program counter (PC) and r13 to stack pointer (SP), and r14 is typically used as a link register (LR); the rest are available for arbitrary use.

All ARM opcodes can be prefixed with a conditional check based on which the operation is either executed or ignored. All data opcodes have three-register forms where a constant shift operation can be applied to the rightmost register operand with no performance cost. For example, the following C-code

```
int INLINE foo( int a, int b )
{
  int t = a + (b >> 16);

  if(t < 0)     return −t;
  else          return t;
}
```

executes in just two cycles when converted to ARM:

```
adds  r0,r2,r3,asr #16  ; r0 = r2 + (r3 >> 16) and update flags
rsbmi r0,r0,#0          ; if result (r0) was negative, r0 = 0 − r0
                               (reverse subtract)
```

For more details about ARM assembler, see www.arm.com/documentation.

Note that the following examples are not optimized for any particular ARM implementation. The pipelining rules for different ARM variants, as well as different implementations of each variant, can be different.

The following example code multiplies a u0.32 fixed-point number with another u0.32 fixed-point number and stores the resulting high 32 bits to register r0.

```
; assuming:
; r2 = input value 0
; r3 = input value 1

umull  r1,r0,r2,r3       ; (high:low) r0:r1 = r2*r3

; result is directly in r0 register, low bits in r1
```

In the example above there is no need to actually shift the result by 32 as we can directly store the high bits of the result to the correct register. To fully utilize this increased control of operations and intermediate result ranges, you should combine primitive operations (add, sub, mul) into larger blocks. The following example shows how to multiply a normalized vec4 dot product with a vertex or a normal vector represented as 16.16 fixed point.

We want to make the code run as fast as possible and we have selected the fixed-point ranges accordingly. In the example we have chosen the range of the normalized vector of the transformation matrix to be 0.30, as we are going to accumulate the results of four multiplications together, and we need 2 bits of extra room for accumulation:

```
; input:
; r0   = pointer to the 16.16 vector data (will be looped over)
; r1-r4 = vec4 (assumed to be same over N input vectors) X,Y,Z,W
;
; in the code:
;     r8   = high 32 bits of the accumulated 64-bit number
;     r7   = low  32 bits -''-

ldr   r5,[r0],#4      ; r5 = *r0++;    (x)
ldr   r6,[r0],#4      ; r6 = *r0++;    (y)
smull r7,r8,r1,r5     ; multiply X*x: (low:high) r7:r8 =  r1 * r5
ldr   r5,[r0],#4      ; r5 = *r0++;    (z)
smlal r7,r8,r2,r6     ; multiply AND accumulate Y*y
ldr   r6,[r0],#4      ; r6 = *r0++;    (w)
smlal r7,r8,r3,r5     ; multiply AND accumulate Z*z
smlal r7,r8,r4,r6     ; multiply AND accumulate W*w

; 64-bit output is in r8:r7,
; we take the high 32 bits (r8 register) directly
```

As we implemented the whole operation as one vec4 · vec4 dot product instead of a collection of primitive fixed-point operations, we avoided intermediate shifts and thus improved the accuracy of the result. By using the 0.30 fixed-point format we reduced the accuracy of the input vector by 2 bits, but usually the effect is negligible: remember that even IEEE floats have only 24 significant bits. With careful selection of ranges, we avoided overflows altogether and eliminated a 64-bit shift operation which would require several cycles. By using ARM-specific multiply-and-accumulate instructions that operate directly in 64 bits, we avoided doing 64-bit accumulations that usually require 2 assembly opcodes: *ADD* and *ADC* (add with carry).

In the previous example the multiplication was done in fixed point. If the input values, e.g., vertex positions, are small, some accuracy is lost in the final output because of the fixed position of the decimal point. For more accuracy, the exponents should be tracked as well. In the following example the input matrix is stored in a format where each matrix column has a common exponent and the scalar parts are normalized to that exponent. The code shows how one row is multiplied. Note that this particular variant assumes availability of the ARMv5 instruction CLZ and will thus not run on ARMv4 devices.

```
; input:
; r0   = pointer to the 16.16 vector data
; r1   = pointer to the matrix (format: x0 y0 z0 w0 e0 x1...)
;
; in the code:
```

```
; r2-r6   = X,Y,Z,W,E (exponent)

ldmia  r1!,{r2-r6}    ; r2 = *r1++; r3 = *r1++; ... r6 = *r1++;
ldr    r7,[r0],#4     ; r7 = *r0++; (x)
smull  r8,r9,r2,r7    ; multiply X*x
ldr    r7,[r0],#4     ; r7 = *r0++; (y)
smlal  r8,r9,r3,r7    ; multiply and accumulate Y*y
ldr    r7,[r0],#4     ; r7 = *r0++; (z);
smlal  r8,r9,r4,r7    ; multiply and accumulate Z*z
ldr    r7,[r0],#4     ; r7 = *r0++; (w)
smlal  r8,r9,r5,r7    ; multiply and accumulate W*w

; Code below does not do tight normalization (e.g., if
; we have number 0x00000000 00000001, we don't return
; 0x40000000, but we subtract the exponent with 32 and return
; 0x00000001). This is because we do only highest-bit
; counting in the high 32 bits of the result. No accuracy
; is lost due to this at this stage.
;
; If tight normalization is required, it can be added with
; extra comparisons.

; The following opcode (eor) calculates the rough abs(r9)
; value. Positive values stay the same, but negative
; values are bit-inverted -> outcome of ~abs(-1) = 0 etc.
; This is enough for our range calculation. Note that we
; use arithmetic shift that extends the sign bits.
; It is used to get a mask of 111's for negative numbers
; and a mask of 000's for positive numbers.

eor    r7,r9,r9,asr #31 ; r7 = r9 ^ (r9 >> 31)

clz    r7,r7          ; Count Leading Zeros of abs(high) [0,32]
subs   r7,r7,#1       ; We don't shift if CLZ gives 1 (changes sign)

; note:  if (clz-1) resulted in -1, we just want to take the high
;        value of the result and not touch the exponent at all.
;        This is achieved by appending rest of the opcodes with
;        PL (plus) conditional.

; note2: ARM register shift with zero returns the original value
;        and register shift with 32 returns zero. The code below
;        works thus for any shift value from 0 to 32 that can come
;        from the CLZ instruction above.

subpl  r6,r6,r7       ; subtract from the base exponent
rsbpl  r3,r7,#32      ; calculate 32-shift value to r3
movpl  r9,r9,lsl r7   ; r9 = high bits << (leading zeros-1)
orrpl  r9,r9,r8,lsr r3 ; r9 = low  bits >> (32-(leading zeros-1))

; output in r9 (scalar) and r6 (exponent)
```

In these examples we showed the programs as a list of assembly instructions. It is not possible to compile them into a working program without some modifications. Here is an example of an inlined assembly routine that you can actually call from your C program (using an ARM GCC compiler):

```
INLINE int mul_fixed_fixed( int a, int b )
{
  int result, tmp;
  __asm__ (        "smull %0,%1,%2,%3       \n\t"
                   "mov   %0,%0,lsr #16     \n\t"
                   "orr   %0,%0,%1,lsl #16  \n\t"
                   : "=&r" (result),  "=&r" (tmp),
                   : "r"   (a),       "r"  (b)
                   : ""
          );
  return result;
}
```

Here the compiler allocates the registers and places the register of *result* to argument %0, *tmp* to %1, *a* to %2, and *b* to %3. For result and tmp = means that the register is going to be written to, and & indicates that this register cannot be used for anything else inside this __asm__statement. The first line performs a signed multiply of *a* and *b* and stores the low 32 bits to *result* and the high 32 bits to *tmp*.

The second line shifts the result right 16 times, the third line shifts *tmp* left 16 times, and combines *tmp* and *result* into *result* using a bitwise OR. The interested reader may want to consult a more in-depth exposition on GCC inline assembly [S03, Bat].

Another compiler that is used a lot for mobile development is the ARM RVCT compiler. It also handles the register allocation of the inline assembly. RVCT goes a step further though: there is no need to specify registers and their constraints as they are automatically handled by the compiler. Here is the previous example code in the inline assembler format used by RVCT:

```
INLINE int mul_fixed_fixed( int a, int b )
{
  int result, tmp;
  __asm
  {
    smull result, tmp, a, b
    mov   result, result, lsr #16
    orr   result, result, tmp, lsl #16
  }
  return result;
}
```

For a list of supported instructions, check ARM Instruction Set Quick Reference Card [Arm].

A.3 FIXED-POINT METHODS IN JAVA

Fixed-point routines in Java work almost exactly as in C, except that you do not have to struggle with the portability of 64-bit integers, because the `long` type in Java is always 64 bits. Also, since there is no `#define` nor an `inline` keyword in Java, you need to figure out alternative means to get your code inlined. This is crucially important because the method call overhead will eliminate any benefit that you get from faster arithmetic otherwise. One way to be sure is to inline your code manually, and that is what you probably end up doing anyway, as soon as you need to go beyond the basic 16.16 format. Note that the standard `javac` compiler does not do any inlining; see Appendix B for suggestions on other tools that may be able to do it.

The benefit of using fixed-point in Java depends greatly on the Java virtual machine. The benefit can be very large on VMs that leverage Jazelle (see Appendix B), or just-in-time (JIT) or ahead-of-time (AOT) compilation, but very modest on traditional interpreters. To give a ballpark estimate, a DOT4 done in fixed-point using 64-bit intermediate resolution might be ten times faster than a pure float routine on a compiling VM, five times faster on Jazelle, but only twice as fast on an interpreter.

On a traditional interpreter, `float` is relatively efficient because it requires only one bytecode for each addition, multiplication, or division. Fixed point, on the other hand, takes extra bytecodes due to the bit-shifting. The constant per-bytecode overhead is very large on a software interpreter.

On Jazelle, integer additions and multiplications get mapped to native machine instructions directly, whereas `float` operations require a function call. The extra bytecodes are still there, however, taking their toll. Finally, a JIT/AOT compiler is looking at longer sequences of bytecode and can probably combine the bit-shifts with other operations in the compiled code, as we did in the previous section.

To conclude, using fixed-point arithmetic generally does pay off in Java, and even more so with the increasing prevalence of Jazelle and JIT/AOT compilers. There is a caveat, though: if you need to do a lot of divides, or need to convert between fixed and float frequently, you may be better off just using floats and spending your optimization efforts elsewhere. Divides are very slow regardless of the number format and the VM, and will quickly dominate the execution time. Also, they are much slower in 64-bit integer than in 32-bit floating point!

JAVA PERFORMANCE TUNING

Although M3G offers a lot of high-level functionality implemented in efficient native code, it will not write your game for you. You need to create a lot of Java code yourself, and that code will ultimately make or break your game, so it had better be good.

The principles of writing efficient code on the Java ME platform are much like on any other platform. In order to choose the best data structures and algorithms, and to implement them in the most efficient way, you need to know the strengths and weaknesses of your target architecture, programming language, and compiler. The problem compared to native platforms is that there are more variables and unknowns: a multitude of different VMs, using different acceleration techniques, running on different operating systems and hardware. Hence, spending a lot of time optimizing your code on an emulator or just one or two devices can easily do you more harm than good.

In this appendix we briefly describe the main causes of performance problems in Java ME, and suggest some techniques to overcome them. This is not to be taken as final truth; your mileage may vary, and the only way to be sure is to profile your application on the devices that you are targeting. That said, we hope this will help you avoid the most obvious performance traps and also better understand some of the decisions that we made when designing M3G.

B.1 VIRTUAL MACHINES

The task of the Java Virtual Machine is to execute Java bytecode, just like a real, nonvirtual CPU executes its native assembly language. The instruction set of the Java VM is in stark contrast to that of any widely used embedded CPU, however.

To start with, bytecode instructions take their operands off the top of an internal *operand stack*, whereas native instructions pick theirs from a fixed set of typically sixteen *registers*. The arbitrary depth of the operand stack prevents it from being mapped to the registers in a straightforward manner. This increases the number of costly memory accesses compared to native code. The stack-based architecture is very generic, allowing implementations on almost any imaginable processor, but it is also hard to map efficiently onto a machine that is really based on registers.

Another complication is due to bytecode instructions having variable length, compared to the fixed-length codewords of a RISC processor. This makes bytecode very compact: most instructions require just one byte of memory, whereas native instructions are typically four bytes each. The downside is that instruction fetching and decoding becomes more complex.

Furthermore, the bytecode instruction set is a very mixed bag, having instructions at widely varying levels of abstraction. The bytecodes range from basic arithmetic and bitwise operations to things that are usually considered to be in the operating system's domain, such as memory allocation (`new`). Most of the bytecodes are easily mapped to native machine instructions, except for having to deal with the operand stack, but some of the high-level ones require complex subroutines and interfacing with the operating system. Adding into the equation the facts that all memory accesses are type-checked and bounds-checked, that memory must be garbage-collected, and so on, it becomes clear that designing an efficient Java VM, while maintaining security and robustness, is a formidable task.

There are three basic approaches that virtual machines are taking to execute bytecode: interpretation, just-in-time compilation, and ahead-of-time compilation. The predominant approach in mobile devices is *interpretation*: bytecodes are fetched, decoded, and translated into machine code one by one. Each bytecode instruction takes several machine instructions to translate, so this method is obviously much slower than executing native code. The slowdown used to be some two orders of magnitude in early implementations, but has since then been reduced to a factor of 5–10, thanks to assembly-level optimizations in the interpreter loops.

The second approach is to compile (parts of) the program into machine code at runtime. These *just-in-time* (JIT) compilers yield good results in long-running benchmarks, but perform poorly when only limited time and memory are available for the compiler and the compiled code. The memory problems are exacerbated by the fact that compiled code can easily take five times as much space as bytecode. Moreover, runtime compilation will necessarily delay, interrupt, or slow down the program execution. To minimize the disturbance, JIT compilers are restricted to very basic and localized optimizations. In theory, the availability of runtime profiling information should allow JIT compilers to produce smaller and faster code than any static C compiler, but that would require a drastic increase in the available memory, and the compilation time would still remain a problem for interactive applications. Today, we estimate well-written C code to outperform embedded JIT compilers by a factor of 3–5.

The third option is to compile the program into native code already before it is run, typically at installation time. This *ahead-of-time* (AOT) tactic allows the compiler to apply more aggressive optimizations than is feasible at runtime. On the other hand, the compiled code consumes significantly more memory than the original bytecode.

Any of these three approaches can be accelerated substantially with hardware support. The seemingly obvious solution is to build a CPU that uses Java bytecode as its machine language. This has been tried by numerous companies, including Nazomi, Zucotto, inSilicon, Octera, NanoAmp, and even Sun Microsystems themselves, but to our knowledge all such attempts have failed either technically or commercially, or both. The less radical approach of augmenting a conventional CPU design with Java acceleration seems to be working better.

The Jazelle extension to ARM processors [Por05a] runs the most common bytecodes directly on the CPU, and manages to pull that off at a negligible extra cost in terms of silicon area. Although many bytecodes are still emulated in software, this yields performance roughly equivalent to current embedded JIT compilers, but without the excessive memory usage and annoying interruptions. The main weakness of Jazelle is that it must execute each and every bytecode separately, whereas a compiler might be able to turn a sequence of bytecodes into just one machine instruction.

Taking a slightly different approach to hardware acceleration, Jazelle RCT (Runtime Compilation Target) [Por05b], augments the native ARM instruction set with additional instructions that can be used by JIT and AOT compilers to speed up array bounds checking and exception handling, for example. The extra instructions also help to reduce the size of the compiled machine code almost to the level of the original bytecode.

As an application developer, you will encounter all these different types of virtual machines. In terms of installed base, traditional interpreters still have the largest market share, but Jazelle, JIT, and AOT are quickly catching up. According to the JBenchmark ACE results database,[1] most newer devices appear to be using one of these acceleration techniques. Jazelle RCT has not yet been used in any mobile devices by the time of this writing, but we expect it to be widely deployed over the next few years.

B.2 BYTECODE OPTIMIZATION

As we pointed out before, Java bytecode is less than a perfect match for modern embedded RISC processors. Besides being stack-based and having instructions at wildly varying

---

1 www.jbenchmark.com/ace

levels of abstraction, it also lacks many features that native code can take advantage of, at least when using assembly language. For instance, there are no bytecodes corresponding to the kind of data-parallel (SIMD) instructions that are now commonplace also in embedded CPUs and can greatly speed up many types of processing. To take another example, there are no conditional (also known as predicated) instructions to provide a faster alternative to short forward branches.

Most of the bytecode limitations can be attributed to the admirable goal of platform independence, and are therefore acceptable. It is much harder to accept the notoriously poor quality of the code that the `javac` compiler produces. In fact, you are better off assuming that it does no optimization whatsoever. For instance, if you compute a constant expression like `16*a/4` in your inner loop, rest assured that the entire expression will be meticulously evaluated at every iteration—and of course using real multiplies and divides rather than bit-shifts (as in `a<<2`).

The lack of optimization in `javac` is presumably because it trusts the virtual machine to apply advanced optimization techniques at runtime. That may be a reasonable assumption in the server environment, but not on mobile devices, where resources are scarce and midlet start-up times must be minimized. Traditional interpreters and Jazelle take a serious performance hit from badly optimized bytecode, but just-in-time and ahead-of-time compilers are not immune, either. If the on-device compiler could trust `javac` to inline trivial methods, eliminate constant expressions and common subexpressions, convert power-of-two multiplications and divisions into bit-shifts, and so on, it could spend more time on things that cannot be done at the bytecode level, such as register allocation or eliminating array bounds checking.

Given the limitations of `javac`, your best bet is to use other off-line compilers, bytecode optimizers, and obfuscators such as GCJ,[2] mBooster,[3] DashO,[4] ProGuard,[5] Java Global Optimizer,[6] Bloat,[7] or Soot.[8] None of these tools is a superset of the others, so it might make sense to use more than one on the same application.

B.3 GARBAGE COLLECTION

All objects, including arrays, are allocated from the Java heap using the `new` operator. They are never explicitly deallocated; instead, the *garbage collector* (GC) automatically reclaims any objects that are no longer referenced by the executing program.

---

2 `gcc.gnu.org/java`
3 `www.innaworks.com`
4 `www.preemptive.com`
5 `proguard.sourceforge.net`
6 `www.garret.ru/Äknizhnik/javago/ReadMe.htm`
7 `www.cs.purdue.edu/s3/projects/bloat/`
8 `www.sable.mcgill.ca/soot/`

Automatic garbage collection eliminates masses of insidious bugs, but also bears significant overhead. Explicit memory management using `malloc` and `free` has been shown to be faster and require less physical memory. For example, in a study by Hertz and Berger [HB05], the best-performing garbage collector degraded application performance by 70% compared to an explicit memory manager, even when the application only used half of the available memory. Performance of the garbage collector declined rapidly as memory was running out. Thus, for best performance, you should leave some reasonable percentage of the Java heap unused. More importantly, you should not create any garbage while in the main loop, so as not to trigger the garbage collector in the first place.

> **Pitfall:** There is no reliable way to find out how much memory your midlet is consuming, or how much more it has available. The numbers you get from `Runtime.getRuntime().freeMemory()` are not to be trusted, because you may run out of native heap before you run out of Java heap, or vice versa, and because the Java heap may be dynamically resized behind your back.

A common technique to avoid generating garbage is to allocate a set of objects and arrays at the setup stage and then reuse them throughout your code. In other words, start off your application by allocating all the objects that you are ever going to need, and then hold on to them until you quit the midlet. Although this is not object-oriented and not very pretty, it goes a long way toward eliminating the GC overhead—not all the way, though. There are built-in methods that do not facilitate object reuse, forcing you to create a new instance when you really only wanted to change some attribute. Even worse, there are built-in APIs that allocate and release temporary objects internally without you ever knowing about it.

Strings are particularly easy to trip on, because they are immutable in Java. Thus, concatenating two strings creates a new `String` object simply because the existing ones cannot be changed. If you need to deal with strings on a per-frame basis, for example to update the player's score, you need to be extra careful to avoid creating any garbage. Perhaps the only way to be 100% sure is to revert to C-style coding and only use `char` arrays.

B.4 MEMORY ACCESSES

One of the most frequent complaints that C programmers have about Java is the lack of direct memory access. Indeed, there are no pointers in the Java programming language, and no bytecode instructions to read or write arbitrary memory locations. Instead, there are only references to strongly typed objects that reside in the garbage-collected heap. You do not know where in physical memory each particular object lies at any given time, nor how many bytes it occupies. Furthermore, all memory accesses are type-checked, and in case of arrays, also bounds-checked. These restrictions are an integral part of the Java security model, and one of the reasons the platform is so widely deployed, but they also rule out many optimizations that C programmers are used to.

As an example, consider a bitmap image stored in RGBA format at 32 bits per pixel. In C, you would use a byte array, but still access the pixels as integers where necessary, to speed up copying and some other operations. The lack of type-checking in C therefore allows you to coalesce four consecutive memory accesses into one. Java does not give you that flexibility: you need to choose either bytes or integers and stick to that. To take another example, efficient floating-point processing on FPU-less devices requires custom routines that operate directly on the integer bit patterns of `float` values, and that is something you cannot do in Java. To illustrate, the following piece of C code computes the absolute value of a `float` in just one machine instruction, but relies on pointer casting to do so:

```
float fabs(float a)
{
  int bits = *(int*)(&a);      // extract the bit pattern
  bits &= 0x7fffffff;          // clear the sign bit
  return *(float*)(&bits);     // cast back to float
}
```

Type-checking is not the only thing in Java that limits your choice of data structures and algorithms. For example, if you want to build an aggregate object (such as an array of structures) in C, you can either inline the component objects (the structures) or reference them with pointers; Java only gives you the latter option. Defining a cache-friendly data structure where objects are aligned at, say, 16-byte boundaries is another thing that you cannot do in Java. Moreover, you do not have the choice of quickly allocating local variables from the CPU stack. Finally, the lack of pointer arithmetic forces you to follow object references even when the target address could be computed without any memory accesses.

Unlike type checking, array bounds checking does not limit your choice of data structures. It does impose a performance penalty, though, and the more dimensions you have in the array, the higher the cost per access. Thus, you should always use a flat array, even if the data is inherently multidimensional; for instance, a 4 × 4 matrix should be allocated as a flat array of 16 elements. Advanced JIT/AOT compilers may be able to eliminate a range check if the array index can be proven to be within the correct range. The compiler is more likely to come up with the proof if you use `new int[100]` rather than `new int[getCount()]` to allocate an array, and `index<100` instead of `index<getCount()` to iterate over its elements. Do not let this complicate your code too much, however, as this sort of optimization may be beyond the capabilities of the current compilers.

To minimize memory accesses in general, it is a good idea to use the built-in primitive types such as `int` and `float` rather than objects. Also, the input parameters and local variables of a method are likely to be faster than class variables or instance variables. Finally, using `System.arraycopy` pays off almost universally: it amounts to a native `memcpy` with some extra type-checking and range-checking up front. The savings can be huge compared to doing the same checks for each element separately.

B.5 METHOD CALLS

Method invocations in Java are more expensive and more restricted than function calls in C or C++. The virtual machine must first look up the method from an internal symbol table, and then check the type of each argument against the method signature. A C/C++ function call, on the other hand, requires very few machine instructions.

In general, `private` methods are faster to call than `public` or `protected` ones, and stand a better chance of being inlined. Also, `static` methods are faster than instance methods, and `final` methods are faster than those that can be re-implemented in derived classes. `synchronized` methods are by far the slowest, and should be used only when necessary. Depending on the VM, native methods can also bear high overhead, particularly if large objects or arrays are passed to or from native code.

As a final note, code and data are strictly separated in Java. There is no way for a method to read or write its own bytecode or that of any other method. There is also no way to transfer program control to the data area, or in fact anywhere else than one of the predefined method entry points. These restrictions are absolutely mandatory from the security standpoint, but they have the unfortunate side-effect that any kind of runtime code generation is prevented. In other words, you could not implement a JIT compiler in Java!

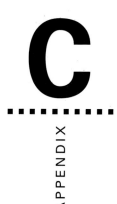

GLOSSARY

AABB Axis-Aligned Bounding Box

AOT Ahead-Of-Time compilation; particularly for Java

API Application Programming Interface

ARB OpenGL Architecture Review Board

ARM Advanced RISC Machines; a popular embedded processor family

ARM7 ARM processor family with ARMv4 instruction set

ARM9 ARM processor family with ARMv5 instruction set

ARM11 ARM processor family with ARMv6 instruction set

ARMv4 ARM processor instruction set version four

ARMv5 ARM processor instruction set version five

ARMv6 ARM processor instruction set version six

baseband The part of a mobile phone that handles radio communication

BRDF Bidirectional Reflectance Distribution Function

BREW Binary Runtime Environment for Wireless; an execution environment controlled by Qualcomm

BSP Binary Space Partitioning

BVH Bounding Volume Hierarchy

CDC Connected Device Configuration; the high-end configuration of mobile Java

CL Common Lite; the OpenGL ES profile with no floating-point support

CLDC Connected Limited Device Configuration; the mainstream configuration of mobile Java

CLZ Count Leading Zeros; machine instruction on ARMv5 processors and later

CM Common; the mainstream OpenGL ES profile

COLLADA COLLAborative Design Activity; an interchange format for digital content creation tools; a Khronos standard

CPU Central Processing Unit

DAG Directed Acyclic Graph

DCC Digital Content Creation; usually relates to tools for creating 3D content, such as 3ds Max or Maya

DCT Discrete Cosine Transform; used in, e.g., JPEG image compression

DLL Dynamic Link Library

DOM Document Object Model; relates to SVG and other W3C standards

DSP Digital Signal Processor

EG Expert Group

EGL OpenGL ES Native Platform Graphics Interface; a Khronos standard

FBO Frame Buffer Object

FIFO First-In-First-Out, a queue data structure

FPU Floating-Point Unit

GCC GNU C Compiler

GL Graphics Library (short for OpenGL)

GPS Global Positioning System

GPU Graphics Processing Unit; graphics hardware

GSM Global System for Mobile

IEEE Institute of Electrical and Electronics Engineers

IVA Imaging and Video Accelerator; particularly in mobile devices

Java ME Java Micro Edition; the most ubiquitous application platform for mobile devices

JAR Java Archive; the delivery format of Java applications

JCP Java Community Process; the Java standardization organization that produces JSRs

JIT Just-In-Time compilation; particularly for Java

JNI Java Native Interface

JPEG Joint Photographic Experts Group; a compressed image file format

JSR Java Specification Request

JSR 135 Mobile Media API (MMAPI)

JSR 184 Mobile 3D Graphics API (M3G)

JSR 226 Scalable Vector Graphics API

JSR 239 Java bindings for OpenGL ES

JSR 248 Mobile Service API for CLDC

JSR 287 Scalable Vector Graphics API 2.0

JSR 297 Mobile 3D Graphics API (M3G) 2.0

JVM Java Virtual Machine

JWT Java Wireless Toolkit by Sun Microsystems

LCD Liquid Crystal Display

LCDUI Limited Connected Device User Interface, in Java MIDP

LOD Level-Of-Detail; a technique for showing simpler models for far-away objects to speed up rendering

MAC Multiply-And-Accumulate; a machine instruction for multiplication followed by addition

M3G Mobile 3D Graphics API (JSR 184)

MHz Megahertz

midlet A Java application for mobile Java (Java MIDP); also known as MIDlet

MIDP Mobile Information Device Profile; the most widespread Java profile

MSA Mobile Service Architecture (JSR 248); combines multiple JSRs into a more unified platform

native code Machine code; compiled into the native instruction set of the CPU

NDC Normalized Device Coordinates

node Element in a scene graph

OBB Oriented Bounding Box

OpenGL Open Graphics Library

OpenGL ES OpenGL for Embedded Systems; a Khronos standard

OpenKODE A collection of Khronos multimedia APIs, plus a core API that abstracts operating system resources to minimize source code changes when porting games and applications

OpenMAX A Khronos API that provides streaming media codecs (for sound, video) and application portability

OpenML Open Multimedia Library; the first standard produced by Khronos (not aimed for embedded devices)

OpenSL ES Open Sound Library for Embedded Systems; a Khronos standard

OpenVG Open Vector Graphics; a Khronos standard

OS Operating System

PDA Personal Digital Assistant; a handheld data organizer

PNG Portable Network Graphics; a popular lossless image format

PVS Potentially Visible Set

RAM Random Access Memory

RISC Reduced Instruction Set CPU

ROM Read-Only Memory

QVGA Quarter-VGA resolution; 320×240 or 240×320 pixels

RGB Red-Green-Blue

RGBA Red-Green-Blue-Alpha

RVCT RealView Compiler Tools from ARM

S60 Symbian-based UI platform from Nokia, previously known as Series 60

SDK Software Development Kit

SVG Scalable Vector Graphics; a W3C standard

UI User Interface

URL Universal Resource Locator; a link to Internet content

VBO Vertex Buffer Object

VGA Video Graphics Array, a display resolution of 640×480 pixels

VM Virtual Machine; particularly for Java

WIPI Wireless Internet Platform for Interoperability; mobile platform used in South Korea

W3C World Wide Web Consortium

XML eXtensible Markup Language

XREF eXternal REFerence; particularly in the M3G file format

BIBLIOGRAPHY

[AB06]   Remi Arnaud and Mark C. Barnes. *COLLADA: Sailing the Gulf of 3D Digital Content Creation*. AK Peters, Ltd., 2006.

[Air90]   John Airey. *Increasing Update Rates in the Building Walk-through System with Automatic Model-Space Subdivision and Potentially Visible Set Calculations*. PhD thesis, UNC CH CS Department, 1990.

[AMH02]   Tomas Akenine-Möller and Eric Haines. *Real-Time Rendering, Second Edition*. AK Peters, Ltd., 2002.

[AS06]   Kurt Akeley and Jonathan Su. Minimum triangle separation for correct Z-buffer occlusion. In *Eurographics/SIGGRAPH Workshop on Graphics Hardware*, pages 27–30, 2006.

[BAC96]   Andrew C. Beers, Maneesh Agrawala, and Navin Chaddha. Rendering from compressed textures. In *Proceedings of the 23rd annual conference on Computer graphics and interactive techniques (SIGGRAPH)*, pages 373–378. ACM Press, 1996.

[Bat]   Batched. Arm gcc inline assembler paper. `http://www.milw0rm.com/papers/128`.

[Bly06]   David Blythe. The Direct3D 10 system. *ACM Transactions on Graphics*, 25(3):724–734, 2006.

[BN76]   James F. Blinn and Martin E. Newell. Texture and reflection in computer generated images. *Communications of the ACM*, 19(10):542–547, 1976.

[Boo01]   Carl De Boor. *A Practical Guide to Splines*. Springer, 2001.

[BSD+89]   A.C. Barkans, B.D. Schroeder, T.L. Durant, D. Gordon, and J. Lach. Guardband clipping method and apparatus for 3d graphics display system. U.S. Patent 4,88,712, 1989.

[BW95]   Armin Bruderlin and Lance Williams. Motion signal processing. In *Proceedings of the 22nd annual conference on Computer graphics and interactive techniques*, pages 97–104, 1995.

[Cat72]   Edwin Catmull. A system for computer generated movies. In *Proc. ACM Annual Conf.*, pages 422–431, August 1972.

[Cat74]   Edwin Earl Catmull. *A subdivision algorithm for computer display of curved surfaces*. PhD thesis, 1974.

[CR74]   E. Catmull and R. Rom. A class of local interpolating splines. In
            R. Barnhill and R. Riesenfeld, editors, *Computer Aided Geometric Design*,
            pages 317–326. Academic Press, 1974.

[Cro77]   Franklin C. Crow. Shadow algorithms for computer graphics. In
            *SIGGRAPH '77: Proceedings of the 4th annual conference on Computer
            graphics and interactive techniques*, pages 242–248. ACM Press, 1977.

[EK02]   C. Everitt and M. Kilgard. Practical and robust stenciled shadow volumes
            for hardware-accelerated rendering. Technical report, NVIDIA
            corporation, 2002.

[EMP+02]   David S. Ebert, F. Kenton Musgrave, Darwyn Peachey, Ken Perlin, and
            Steven Worley. *Texturing & Modeling: A Procedural Approach*. Morgan
            Kaufmann, third edition, 2002.

[Fen03]   Simon Fenney. Texture compression using low-frequency signal
            modulation. In *Proceedings of the ACM SIGGRAPH/EUROGRAPHICS
            conference on Graphics hardware*, pages 84–91. Eurographics
            Association, 2003.

[FvFH90]   James D. Foley, Andries van Dam, Steven K. Feiner, and John F. Hughes.
            Computer graphics: principles and practice (2nd ed.). Addison-Wesley
            Longman Publishing Co., Inc., 1990.

[Gou71]   Henri Gouraud. Computer display of curved surfaces. *IEEE Transactions
            on Computers*, 20(6):623–629, 1971.

[GW02]   Rafael Gonzales and Richard Woods. *Digital Image Processing, Second
            Edition*. Prentice Hall, 2002.

[Hö7]   Claus Höfele. *Mobile 3D Graphics: Learning 3D Graphics with the Java
            Micro Edition*. Thomson Course Technology, 2007.

[HB05]   Matthew Hertz and Emery D. Berger. Quantifying the performance of
            garbage collection vs. explicit memory management. In *OOPSLA '05:
            Proceedings of the 20th annual ACM SIGPLAN conference on Object
            oriented programming, systems, languages, and applications*, pages 313–326.
            ACM Press, 2005.

[Hei]   Tim Heidmann. Real shadows real time. *IRIS Universe*, (18):28–31.

[Hop99]   Hugues Hoppe. Optimization of mesh locality for transparent vertex
            caching. In *Computer Graphics (SIGGRAPH '99 Proceedings)*, Computer
            Graphics Proceedings, Annual Conference Series, pages 269–276. ACM,
            ACM Press/ACM SIGGRAPH, 1999.

[HS98]   Wolfgang Heidrich and Hans-Peter Seidel. View-independent
            environment maps. In *Eurographics/SIGGRAPH Workshop on Graphics
            Hardware*, pages 39–45, 1998.

[HS99]   Wolfgang Heidrich and Hans-Peter Seidel. Realistic, hardware-accelerated shading and lighting. In *SIGGRAPH '99: Proceedings of the 26th annual conference on Computer graphics and interactive techniques*, pages 171–178. ACM Press/Addison-Wesley Publishing Co, 1999.

[JCP03]   JCP. *Mobile 3D Graphics API (JSR-184)*. Java Community Process, 2003. `http://www.jcp.org/en/jsr/detail?id=184`.

[JCP05]   JCP. *Mobile 3D Graphics API (JSR-184) v1.1*. Java Community Process, 2005. `http://www.jcp.org/en/jsr/detail?id=184`.

[JCP06]   JCP. *Mobile Service Architecture (JSR-248)*. Java Community Process, 2006. `http://www.jcp.org/en/jsr/detail?id=248`.

[KB84]   Doris H.U. Kochanek and Richard H. Bartels. Interpolating splines with local tension, continuity, and bias control. In *Proceedings of the 11th annual conference on Computer graphics and interactive techniques (SIGGRAPH)*, pages 33–41. ACM Press, 1984.

[KG03]   Lucas Kovar and Michael Gleicher. Flexible automatic motion blending with registration curves. In *Proceedings of the 2003 ACM SIGGRAPH/ Eurographics symposium on Computer animation*, pages 214–224. Eurographics Association, 2003.

[KGP02]   Lucas Kovar, Michael Gleicher, and Frédéric Pighin. Motion graphs, 2002.

[Khr03]   Khronos. *OpenGL ES Native Platform Graphics Interface (Version 1.0)*. The Khronos Group, 2003.

[Lan98]   Jeff Lander. Skin them bones: Game programming for the web generation. *Game Developer Magazine*, pages 11–16, May 1998.

[Lan02]   H. Landis. *RenderMan in Production*. ACM SIGGRAPH course, 2002.

[Len04]   Eric Lengyel. *Mathematics for 3D game programming & computer graphics, second edition*. Charles River Media, 2004.

[LG95]   David Luebke and Chris Georges. Portals and mirrors: Simple, fast evaluation of potentially visible sets. In *Symposium of Interactive 3D Graphics*. ACM Press, 1995.

[LK05]   Sing Li and Jonathan Knudsen. *Beginning J2ME: From Novice to Professional, Third Edition*. Apress, Inc., 2005.

[Ltd]   ARM Ltd. Arm instruction set quick reference card. `http://www.arm.com/pdfs/QRC0001H_rvct_v2.1_arm.pdf`.

[MB05]   Tom McReynolds and David Blythe. *Advanced Graphics Programming Using OpenGL*. Morgan Kaufmann, 2005.

[Mil94]   Gavin Miller. Efficient algorithms for local and global accessibility shading. In *Proceedings of ACM SIGGRAPH 94*, pages 319–326, 1994.

[Moo65]   Gordon E. Moore. Cramming more components onto integrated circuits. *Electronics*, 38(8), 1965.

[OG97]   Marc Olano and Trey Greer. Triangle scan conversion using 2d homogeneous coordinates. In *Proceedings of ACM SIGGRAPH/ Eurographics Workshop on Graphics Hardware*, pages 89–95, 1997.

[PARV05]   Kari Pulli, Tomi Aarnio, Kimmo Roimela, and Jani Vaarala. Designing graphics programming interfaces for mobile devices. *IEEE Computer Graphics and Applications*, 25(8), 2005.

[PD84]   Thomas Porter and Tom Duff. Compositing digital images. In *Computer Graphics (SIGGRAPH '84 Proceedings)*, Computer Graphics Proceedings, Annual Conference Series, pages 253–259. ACM, ACM Press/ACM SIGGRAPH, 1984.

[Pho75]   Bui Tuong Phong. Illumination for computer generated pictures. *Communications of the ACM*, 18(6):311–317, 1975.

[PMTH01]   Kekoa Proudfoot, William R. Mark, Svetoslav Tzvetkov, and Pat Hanrahan. A real-time procedural shading system for programmable graphics hardware. In *SIGGRAPH '01: Proceedings of the 28th annual conference on Computer graphics and interactive techniques*, pages 159–170. ACM Press, 2001.

[POAU00]   Mark S. Peercy, Marc Olano, John Airey, and P. Jeffrey Ungar. Interactive multi-pass programmable shading. In *Proceedings of the 27th annual conference on Computer graphics and interactive techniques (SIGGRAPH)*, pages 425–432. ACM Press/Addison-Wesley Publishing Co., 2000.

[Por05a]   Chris Porthouse. *Jazelle DBX white paper*. ARM Limited, 2005. `http: //www.arm.com/pdfs/JazelleWhitePaper.pdf`.

[Por05b]   Chris Porthouse. *Jazelle RCT white paper*. ARM Limited, 2005. `http: //www.arm.com/pdfs/JazelleRCTWhitePaper_final1.0_.pdf`.

[PT96]   Les A. Piegl and Wayne Tiller. *The NURBS Book*. Springer, 1996.

[RH94]   John Rohlf and James Helman. Iris performer: a high performance multiprocessing toolkit for real-time 3d graphics. In *Proceedings of the 21st annual conference on Computer graphics and interactive techniques*, pages 381–394. ACM Press, 1994.

[Ros04]   Randi Rost. *OpenGL Shading Language*. Addison Wesley, 2004.

[S03]   S. Sandeep. Gcc-inline-assembly-howto. `http://www.ibiblio.org/ gferg/ldp/GCC-Inline-Assembly-HOWTO.html`, 2003.

[SAM05]   Jacob Ström and Tomas Akenine-Möller. ipackman: high-quality, low-complexity texture compression for mobile phones. In *HWWS '05: Proceedings of the ACM SIGGRAPH/EUROGRAPHICS conference on Graphics hardware*, pages 63–70. ACM Press, 2005.

[Sho85]   Ken Shoemake. Animating rotation with quaternion curves. In *Proceedings of the 12th annual conference on Computer graphics and interactive techniques (SIGGRAPH)*, pages 245–254. ACM Press, 1985.

[Sho87]   Ken Shoemake. Quaternion calculus and fast animation. In *SIGGRAPH Course Notes*, pages 101–121, 1987.

[SKv+92]   Mark Segal, Carl Korobkin, Rolf van Widenfelt, Jim Foran, and Paul Haeberli. Fast shadows and lighting effects using texture mapping. In *Proceedings of the 19th annual conference on Computer graphics and interactive techniques*, pages 249–252. ACM Press, 1992.

[Smi95]   Alvy Ray Smith. A pixel is not a little square, a pixel is not a little square, a pixel is not a little square! (and a voxel is not a little cube). Technical Report Technical Memo 6, Microsoft Research, 1995.

[Str03]   Gilbert Strang. *Introduction to Linear Algebra*. Wellesley-Cambridge Press, third edition, 2003.

[SWN05]   Dave Shreiner, Mason Woo, and Jackie Neider. *OpenGL Programming Guide: The Official Guide to Learning OpenGL, Version 2 (5th Edition)*. Addison-Wesley, 2005.

[Wil83]   Lance Williams. Pyramidal parametrics. *SIGGRAPH Comput. Graph.*, 17(3):1–11, 1983.

[WW92]   Alan Watt and Mark Watt. *Advanced animation and rendering techniques*. ACM Press/Addison-Wesley Publishing Co., 1992.

[ZSD+00]   Denis Zorin, Peter Schröder, Tony DeRose, Leif Kobbelt, Adi Levin, and Wim Sweldens. Subdivision for modeling and animation. SIGGRAPH 2000 Course Notes, ACM SIGGRAPH, http://mrl.nyu.edu/publications/subdiv-course2000/, 2000.

Index